Risk and Crisis Management Planning:

A Workbook for Organization and Program Administrators

Connie Coutellier

ISBN: 978-1-58518-097-4
Library of Congress Control Number: 2007943226
Cover design: Bean Creek Studio
Book layout: Bean Creek Studio
Cover photos: Amran Ahmad, Angela Downes, Suz Welch
Text photos: (camp) Amran Ahmad, Wayne Bebee, Connie Coutellier, Angela Downes, Suz Welch; (other) ©2008 Jupiterimages Corporation

Healthy Learning
P.O. Box 1828
Monterey, CA 93942
www.coacheschoice.com

Contents

Organizational Management Worksheets and Guidelines

Program Management Worksheets and Guidelines

5. IRS Sample Conflict-of-Interest Policy:

    a. Conflict-of-Interest Disclosure Statement

6. Sample Accident/Incident Report:

    a. Accident/Incident Report Instructions

7. Sample Waiver and/or Release Forms:

    a. Consent Form for a Trip Away From the Regular Program Site

    b. Acknowledgment of Disclosure of Risk and Permission to Participate in an Organization Activity

    c. Sample Hold-Harmless Clauses

    d. Sample Volunteer Release and Waiver of Liability

    e. Sample Volunteer Release and Waiver of Liability for Minors

8. Sample Code of Ethics

9. Sample Gift-Giving Policy—Camp Fire USA

10. Sample Records Management, Retention, and Destruction Policy:

    a. Sample Record-Retention Timetable

11. Sample Vehicle-Inspection Form

12. Sample Behavior-Management Policy

13. Sample Camp Discipline Code

14. Sample Code of Conduct—California 4-H

15. Sample Code of Conduct—Camp Fire USA (for Teens)

16. Sample Dismissal Clauses/Policies:

    a. Sample Camp Dismissal Policy

17. Sample Recommended Program Policies for Child Abuse Prevention (or Child Protection) in Camp Fire USA Programs

18. Sample Program Operational Plan for Activities Requiring Staff Members With Specialized Training or Certification

19. Sample Program Operational Plan for Activities Not Requiring Staff Members With Specialized Training or Certification

20. Sample Form for Dealing With Complaints

People lock their front doors, buckle their seat belts, leave a list for the babysitter, carry homeowner and auto insurance, warn their children about talking to strangers, install smoke alarms, keep emergency numbers by the phone, and discuss with their families what to do in case of a tornado or fire. These safety, or risk-management, plans are a part of their everyday routine, and they are almost automatic. They involve only an individual and his immediate family and friends. Therefore, in most cases, people haven't written them down.

At an organization's main office and at any program site, such as a resident or day camp, special event, childcare center, volunteer training weekend, or group meeting, the health and safety of everyone is in the hands of a team of people. A safety plan should be developed and written down so that everyone on the site—adults and participants alike— knows what to do at the proper time and can be sensitive to the situation. This book is all about preventing problems and emergencies, and then handling those that happen anyway.

Safety Planning

Most organizations believe that group experiences are an extraordinary opportunity to influence the lives of young people. Safety awareness and training have always been a part of most youth agencies' group experiences.

The current belief and conviction in safety awareness and training is reflected across the country, and in urban, rural, and suburban communities throughout the world. Programs take place at facilities owned and operated by organizations or at schools, churches, community centers, and homes. Most organizations have a set of policies or standards, have licensing requirements, and/or follow the standards set by accrediting bodies.

For example, Camp Fire USA councils, when receiving their charters to conduct programs under the name of Camp Fire USA, are required under the organization's bylaws to operate according to established policies and to maintain certain standards. These policies and standards address the quality of the program and the welfare of children, as well as the total operation of the council. Policies and standards are an integral part of the training and education of boards, staff, volunteers, and youth involved in the operation, as well as in program planning, delivery, and evaluation. Camp Fire USA refers to this risk-management manual as a national guideline to be used when developing council policies and procedures.

Other standards are referred to as the "standards of the field" and are accepted as the standards of a specific field or industry. In camping, they are the American Camp Association (ACA) standards. In childcare, they are the standards of the National Association for Education of Young Children or state licensing standards. In cases where no set of standards has been identified, an organization may be compared with the practices of similar organizations to determine the accepted standard of care.

Most organizations express a regard for the well-being of children in their safety practices. They are not only concerned with physical and mental health, safety, and sanitation, but also with creating an atmosphere that fosters concern for people. In such an environment, emotional and physical safety is inherent.

Most organizations express a regard for the well-being of children in their safety practices.

Quest for Adventure

Even in a world of high technology, in which computer games, movies, and television provide children with exciting virtual adventures, modern youth and adults still seek real adventure and an element of physical, mental, and emotional challenge in their lives. Organizations address this interest in many of their programs by providing exciting hands-on experiences that teach positive ways to seek adventure in life. These activities provide opportunities to cope with stress and pressure, make important decisions, and experience teamwork and personal achievement.

The objective, therefore, is not to eliminate challenge, but rather to manage it to acceptable levels. This objective is accomplished through risk-management plans that have the utmost forethought and prudence. The true nature of this type of risk is that it is more of a perceived risk than "the real thing," or an objective risk. Of course, all programs have both real and perceived risks. A good program administrator understands the difference, magnifies the perceived risk, and does everything to mitigate the objective risk. The goal is to maintain the thrill of adventure, the rush of adrenalin, and the benefits of such activities, while also making them safe, positive experiences. If such adventures are not available to youth, or are not affordable or assessable to the broader population, other less positive and perhaps unlawful behaviors will meet their need for adventure.

How to Use This Book

Because of vast differences in various parts of the country and the uniqueness of each organization, it is impossible to provide a safety or risk-management plan for every situation or activity. This book is a tool to help administrators create a plan that will fit the circumstances of managing their organizations and the sites and programs they provide. Such planning will not guarantee safety and should never be a substitute for legal advice. It will help alleviate the fear and feelings of powerlessness that administrators face when trying to protect their organization by reducing incidents, anticipating risks, and responding appropriately. With the increase in the number of lawsuits and new and more serious social issues such as child abuse, violence, terrorism, and health risks impacting programs, a risk-management plan is essential to help protect the future of any agency.

The worksheets included in the book and on the CD are divided into two main categories: those that address the overall crisis and risk management of the organization and those that address the crisis and risk management of each program. The organizational worksheets in Chapter 5, "Organizational Risk-Management Planning," are listed with a number preceded by the letter O. Chapter 6, "Program-Risk Management Planning," includes worksheets that are specific to a program or event and are identified with a number preceded by the letter P. When combined, the organizational section and a plan for each program become the overall risk-management plan for the organization. Some worksheets refer to other sections where policies for the organization (O) should be consistent with the ones for any program (P). These sections are cross-referenced or referred to in the rationale or guidelines. The first section of both the organizational worksheets and the program worksheets—labeled Crisis Management—refers to situations in which the information may be needed during a crisis. The organizational worksheets may be completed by the director, office manager, and/or a board task force.

The program worksheets should be completed by the program director or administrator, and be specific to the circumstances of that site or the program for which he is responsible. Some program worksheets may be the same for every program, which means that the program administrators may want to discuss them before beginning this task. The completed worksheets should be current, on the site to which they refer, and accessible to the director/administrator. Some programs, such as a camp or childcare program on a site owned by the organization, may require use of nearly all of the worksheets. Other programs, such as special events or short-term programs, may only use a few.

When the plan is completed, the organization needs to design a training program and provide that training to help staff and volunteers understand their responsibilities in risk management. The Organizational Risk-Management Plan includes providing employees and volunteers working in the main office with a safe working environment. Staff and volunteers using sites not owned or directly supervised by the organization may need to use or adapt some worksheets to their specific working environments or meeting places. Program staff or volunteers supervising a small group of children may not think of such things as fire drills in their meeting places, how to turn utilities off in case of emergency, the security of participants, transportation matters, etc.

The plan should be completed, or agreed upon, by an appropriate team of persons in the organization. The team might be called a Risk-Management Planning Task Force. In most nonprofit organizations, any related policy decisions will require approval by the board of directors. The task force creating or reviewing the plan might include such people as a lawyer, organization president, executive director and/or program administrator, public relations chairperson or staff member, member of a healthcare profession, site manager, local law enforcement authority, and others involved in matters related to health and safety. Figure 1-1, which is found at the end of Chapter 1, may help identify exposures and guide the overall risk-management plan. As the Risk-Management Planning Task Force begins its work, the members may want to divide the responsibilities by section, topic, and/or by program-delivery system.

The first step is to decide which worksheets are generic, or should be handled in the same manner for any operation, program, or site. Any material requiring a policy decision must have board action. Those worksheets that do not apply should be crossed out or noted DNA (does not apply). Any intervention points not covered in the worksheets should be written and added into the book.

Most organizations believe that group experiences are an extraordinary opportunity to influence the lives of young people.

Chapter 1 of this book will also help the task force understand more about the field of risk management and make the overall risk-management plan for the organization easier to create, including specific plans for each program or site. Chapter 2 will help the team identify possible emergency or crisis situations and the unique special plans needed. The relationship between adults and youth is very important to any human service agency. Chapter 3 covers planning for risk reduction, control, and analysis, which includes preventive intervention points, factors, and control procedures to reduce the extent of any loss. The issues of supervision, managing children's behavior, and child abuse are addressed in Chapter 4.

Chapter 5 focuses on crisis management and planning for the overall organization and provides worksheets to address crisis management and the information that administrators will need immediately. The planning section, which includes worksheets, will help the organization prevent or reduce exposures. Chapter 6 includes the crisis-management worksheets needed at each program site and the planning worksheets specific to that program. All worksheets have a section called "Guidelines and Information to Help Complete the Plan." The person responsible for completing each worksheet should be sure to read this section before doing so. Appendix 1 offers additional resources, samples, and forms that may be helpful in designing the plan.

For those organizations that operate camps, it may be helpful to know that many worksheets provide a resource to address the ACA standards in part or in total. Appendix 3 also has a cross-reference to the ACA standards.

Once a workbook has been completed, plans made and agreed upon, and training provided for each program or operation, the risk-management plan becomes operational. Such preparations help reduce risks through preventive measures or provide the systems to handle almost any crisis or emergency. Should an emergency situation occur, no fumbling for procedures or phone numbers should take place. Plans are specific, in the appropriate place, and ready for use. Once the first plan is completed and agreed upon, it will be easier to write other plans for other sites, program activities, or events.

RISK MANAGEMENT

Chapter One

Risk management is a structured process to protect an organization's assets, especially its human assets, from injury or loss. It is an integrated approach to identifying the nature and scope of a problem and deciding how to best deal with it. Risk management enables administrators to reduce or eliminate the uncertainty of loss and minimize the adverse effects. When an organization reduces future uncertainty, it tends to instill greater confidence. By actively pursuing safety programs, screening and training staff, and taking specific measures to avoid loss, the organization increases its own stability and enhances the public trust.

Some of the terms used in risk management may seem confusing and technical, and others are specific to the legal and insurance fields. It is important to have at least a basic understanding of these terms to communicate with persons in these fields and to help devise plans that provide protection from loss. This chapter begins with an explanation of some of these terms and concludes with forms that can be used to identify risks specific to a program or site. A glossary is also included in the Appendix.

Risk-Management Planning

A risk is an uncertainty or probability concerning the loss of resources. Risk-management plans are systems to identify, evaluate, reduce, prevent, or control loss of resources associated with the agency or the operation of a site or program. The purpose of a risk-management program is:

- To provide for the safety of participants and staff
- To protect the organization, including its officers, directors, staff, and volunteer resources
- To provide for the continued operation of the organization

Understanding Legal Liabilities

Good risk-management plans are designed to protect the organization and provide for a safe experience for participants and staff. Risk-management plans are also intended to reduce or prevent legal and public-relations problems. No agency, person, or organization, regardless of the plan, is exempt from litigation. Legal entanglements are both costly and time-consuming. Increased knowledge and awareness of legal ramifications of actions or nonactions, as well as a good risk-management plan, may save the organization both time and money. A good public-relations plan may also reduce the possibilities of legal entanglements. If parents believe that a program has qualified leadership, possesses medical insurance, and is the well-run, safe program announced in the program flyer or brochure, they may be less likely to challenge that perception.

It is necessary to obtain good legal advice to determine what an organization should include in a risk-management plan if it is to provide a safe experience and avoid unnecessary legal exposure. The law and government rules and regulations are highly complicated. The laws in the United States that affect nonprofit organizations are a complex network of federal, state, and local statutes (written laws), court decisions, and administrative regulations. These laws change as society and issues change, and they vary greatly from state to state. For that reason, it is futile to attempt to list or catalog all of the laws that affect a certain organization. However, a checklist of typical legal liabilities is included in Appendix 4.

In the legal and political climate that currently exists in the United States, virtually anybody can be sued for anything at any time. Obviously, this rule holds true for nonprofits. This lawsuit-happy environment has not, however, deterred most youth service organizations from continuing to provide challenging programs for children and youth.

Anyone can file a lawsuit, but only a small percentage of all suits filed ever reach trial, and of those that do, only a tiny percentage result in a verdict for the plaintiff (i.e., the person who filed the suit). Precautions can and should be taken, however, to minimize the likelihood that an adverse ruling (judgment) will result if an organization is in fact sued. Such planning and preparation is the major purpose of this book, along with providing high-quality, safe experiences for staff and participants.

The commentary and worksheets presented in this book will help the administrator evaluate whether an organization is unnecessarily at risk from claims. A lawyer familiar with the organization's operations and programs can also be a valuable asset in risk-management planning.

The law is generally classified into criminal law and civil law. Criminal law is based on the premise that the offenders must be punished. The law-enforcement system (i.e., the government) prosecutes the criminal on behalf of the public. The guilty defendant is punished by either incarceration in a jail or prison, a fine paid to the government, or, in exceptional cases, execution of the defendant. Crimes include both misdemeanors and felonies. Felonies are the more serious crimes such as murder, kidnapping, burglary, rape, arson, etc. Misdemeanors include crimes such as traffic offenses, indecent exposure, petty larceny, disorderly conduct, etc. In contrast, a defendant in civil litigation is never incarcerated and never executed. In general, a losing defendant in civil litigation only reimburses the plaintiff for losses caused by the defendant's behavior.

Civil law is a body of laws meant to regulate relations between individuals, or between individuals and corporations, concerning property rights, personal dignity and freedom, and personal injury. The injured party brings suit against the other party for breach of contract or negligence. The offender or organization (i.e., the defendant) may have to pay a large dollar amount to the victim. Although most legal concerns of organizations are in the category of civil law, criminal behavior is an increasing concern. When organizations are responsible for the safety of participants and/or a duty to provide a safe environment, but fail to do so, they may be held liable for negligence in a civil action. In some cases, such as allegations of child abuse, criminal action may be brought against the person alleged to have committed the act, as well as a civil action against the youth agency supervising the child when the incident occurred. Aspects of civil law that are of most frequent concern to agencies are those involving contracts, property, corporate structure, administrative rules and regulations, and torts, which are discussed later in this section.

Contracts are enforceable written or oral agreements. If the terms of a contract are not met or are violated and damage occurs, the law may provide a remedy in court. Contractual agreements also are a means of protecting an organization by transferring the risk to another party. Sometimes the other party will want to shift the risk away from their organization, them personally, or their business back to the original organization. When the party that enters into a contract with an organization undertakes some risk, such as transporting children, the organization must be sure that the party has adequate insurance coverage to handle the risk. The organization should ask for a "certificate of insurance" and carefully review it to see that the limits are sufficient, the expiration date is inclusive of the contract dates, the desired coverage is included, and, when appropriate, the organization is named as an additional insured.

If the risk is high, it may be helpful to seek legal advice on what should be transferred and what should be assumed. Examples of contractual liabilities are those that arise out of rental or lease agreements, collaborative efforts, joint use agreements, service contracts, special event agreements, contractual labor, hold-harmless agreements, permission and waiver forms, etc.

Contracts often include indemnification (hold-harmless) clauses or exculpatory clauses (waivers and releases). Indemnification provisions shift the responsibility for payment of damages to someone else by contract. Such a provision usually specifies which party has allocated the risk of liability to a third party (i.e., their insurance company). In other words, this provision is a written agreement as to who will assume the responsibility and carry the liability insurance. Such agreements may attempt to cover compensatory and punitive damages and even legal costs. Indemnification for claims against directors and officers is explained in the Legal Liabilities of Directors section later in this chapter.

Exculpatory clauses purport to waive the right of an injured party to recover damages due to negligence. Opinions differ regarding the legal validity of such agreements, but they may deter people from proceeding with damage claims.

Torts are civil wrongs or injuries to another person that are recognized as grounds for a lawsuit. These wrongs result in an injury or harm that constitutes the basis for a claim by the injured party. Under the law, compensation must be paid by the tortfeasor, or the offender/wrongdoer, to the injured person(s). While some torts are also crimes punishable with imprisonment, the primary aim of tort law is to provide relief for the damages incurred and deter others from committing the same harm. An organization and/or its employees can also, under some circumstances, be held liable for the acts of others. This situation could occur, for example, when an organization is not careful in checking the background of an employee or volunteer who causes injury to others. In such circumstances, the organization could be liable for the acts of that person. The responsibility of persons and organizations is imposed by law and applies to personal injury, bodily injury, and property loss or damage to a third party due to the negligence of the organization, its employees, or its volunteers.

Intentional torts are those acts or failures to act that intentionally or knowingly cause harm. Intentional torts are an area of increasing concern. For almost all intentional torts, the employee or volunteer is individually responsible and is not acting under the direction of the employer or organization. In many such cases, both civil charges that require that damages are to be paid and criminal charges can be brought. The act must be the proximate cause of injury; intent to do harm must exist, and actual injury must occur. Intentional torts include slander, invasion of privacy, restraining or confining someone against their will, and assault and battery.

Assault and battery is the combination of two violent crimes: assault (threat to do harm) and battery (physical harm). Corporal punishment and physical or sexual abuse can be criminal and/or civil assault and battery. In either case, action is brought against the offender. In civil assault and battery, action may also be taken in most circumstances against the person or organization that was responsible to protect the injured party from an unreasonable risk of harm. Where the defendant's conduct is found to be intentional, willful, wanton, or malicious (i.e., desire to cause harm), gross negligence (i.e., conscious indifference), or highly reckless, the courts may permit an award of punitive damages in addition to compensatory damages. Punitive damages are particularly important in torts involving dignitary harms (e.g., invasion of privacy) and civil rights, where the actual monetary injury to plaintiff(s) may be small. When a court orders punitive damages, it means that the defendant has to pay special and exceptional damages (called so because they make an exception to the rule that damages are to compensate, not to punish). Conduct would be labeled "malicious" if it is accompanied by ill will or spite, or if it is for the purpose of injuring another. Conduct would be seen as "reckless disregard of plaintiff's rights" if, under the circumstances, it reflects complete indifference to the safety and rights of others.

Torts that are not intentional are generally referred to as negligence. In negligence cases, damage can be awarded for an injury that was reasonably foreseeable. Among the types of damages that the injured party may recover are loss of earning capacity, pain and suffering, and reasonable medical expenses. They include both present and future expected losses. An individual or organization can purchase insurance that will pay damages and attorney fees for tort claims. Such insurance coverage is a standard part of homeowner's insurance policies, automobile insurance, and insurance for businesses. In contrast, it is not possible for a defendant to purchase insurance to pay for his criminal acts.

Negligence

Who is liable or responsible according to the law if evidence of negligence exists? The corporation is generally responsible for the actions of its officers, directors, employees, and others acting on its behalf, as long as they are acting within the scope of their duties. The corporate entity, individual board members, administrators and/or supervisors, service personnel, volunteers or paid program leaders, and even student trainees may be joined in a suit as potentially responsible. It is, then, the responsibility of the court to determine who is liable and to what extent. The doctrine of respondeat superior, which applies to both nonprofit and for-profit corporations, states that the corporate entity is accountable for the actions of employees or volunteers in service to the organization if they are acting within the scope of their responsibility and authority. These actions are separated into three basic levels:

- The corporate entity and individual board members
- Administrative and supervisory personnel
- Persons in direct leadership or service roles

Each level has different roles and responsibilities and, as such, different liabilities. Corporations are generally not responsible for intentional injury caused by a corporate representative acting outside of his regular scope of authority or responsibility.

In tort law, the standard of care is the degree of care a reasonable or prudent practitioner of the same specialty would utilize under similar conditions. The following conduct may be the basis for alleging negligence, or failure to provide the expected standard of care, and result in legal liability:

- Carelessness in hiring or recruiting practices, including failure to screen, select, verify skills, and/or supervise staff and volunteers in a manner consistent with the standards of the field. This practice is sometimes referred to as "negligent hiring."
- Failure to provide training in the supervision of children, in emergency procedures, and in procedures for any incident that was foreseeable
- Failure to provide appropriate supervision ratios and expectations for supervision in activities and at all other times that children are in the care of the program provider
- Failure to provide safe transportation by qualified drivers, operate a safe vehicle, and follow procedures for internal control and supervision while transporting and during loading and unloading
- Entrustment of equipment or animals to a person who is too young, or for other reasons is not equipped or trained to handle the condition

- Failure to have safety procedures, or failure to teach, instruct, or practice existing procedures

- Inadequate warning of hazards, or warnings not appropriate for the age or physical or mental capabilities of the participant

- Failure to take immediate action on hazardous conditions, or failure to perform routine maintenance such as testing water, alarms, and extinguishers or repairing, especially after notice, steps, rails, lights, equipment, etc.

- Failure to provide proper or adequate equipment that is in good condition and appropriate for the intended use

- Failure to prevent secondary injury through actions or non-actions, or through the treatment of an injured person. If the program provider assumes the duty to render aid, the law imposes a duty of competent and appropriate action.

Legal Liabilities of Directors

State laws require nonprofit boards or trustees to perform certain specific duties or standards of action that define their fiduciary responsibilities. They are as follows:

- The Duty of Obedience—assures that the agency functions according to the law

- The Duty of Care—shows "due care" in board operations

- The Duty of Loyalty—supports the agency and avoids conflicts of interest

Members of the organization, funders, and the community expect board members to do the following:

- See that the mission of the organization is fulfilled

- Conserve and protect the assets of the corporation

- Ensure the future viability of the organization

- Provide safe and healthy programs for children

- Ensure compliance with federal, state, and local fair employment laws and regulations

With the decline of charitable immunity (the legal doctrine that at one time protected charitable organizations from financial responsibility for causing harm), legal liability for most nonprofit organizations is the same as it is for other businesses. Generally, when legal actions against directors of nonprofit organizations occur, it is on the basis that the board or an individual failed to take action or that the action taken was inadequate or irresponsible. Even if the organization and its directors are absolved of any liability, legal fees can be substantial.

Since anyone acting on behalf of the organization is capable of creating legal liability, and thus jeopardizing the organization's existence, the board must take risk management seriously and not allow anyone to be excluded from the risk-management process. Legal action has been taken against boards and board members for actions such as:

- Negligent actions of employees
- Violations of Civil Rights Acts
- Conflicts of interest
- Mismanagement or nonmanagement
- Improper expenditures
- Waste of assets
- Poor investments
- Failure to exercise due care
- Violations of reporting laws or regulations

Directors are expected to function as "reasonably prudent persons" as they carry out their fiduciary responsibility to act for the organization's benefit. Although the specific laws in each state may differ, four major categories of violations of fiduciary responsibility exist. They are mismanagement, nonmanagement, self-dealing, and principles of good faith.

Mismanagement is a failure to follow fundamental management principles. Examples include actions or nonactions that result in a financial loss or legal action taken due to the following:

- Lack of provisions made to protect assets or to protect the health and safety of program participants
- Failure to review reports on problems that are instead just "rubber stamped" or accepted at face value
- Conclusions and decisions made when other available information clearly suggests a different direction
- Inadequate controls and reporting systems

Techniques to reduce, prevent, or control loss due to mismanagement include the following:

- Having informed decision-makers establish policies that are consistent with best practices or standards of the field
- Taking action that is consistent with established policies
- Monitoring what is happening in the organization
- Providing supervision, monitoring, and evaluation of the executive director.

Nonmanagement is a failure to use existing opportunities for good management. Examples include actions or nonactions that result in a financial loss or legal action taken due to the following:

- Failure to attend board and committee meetings
- Failure to review existing data that are relevant to a decision
- Failure to use existing control systems
- Failure to enforce bylaws, standards, and guidelines

Techniques to reduce, prevent, or control loss due to nonmanagement include the following:

- Acting on policy to remove board members who are not fulfilling their responsibilities
- Establishing policies and procedures to govern the authority and work of committees and individuals assigned to tasks by the board

Self-dealing occurs when a board member personally benefits or takes advantage of his position taking action, rather than focusing on the interests of the organization. Examples include actions or nonactions that result in a financial loss or legal action taken due to the following:

- Failure to disclose a potential conflict of interest
- Voting on or influencing decisions that benefit themselves

Techniques to reduce, prevent, or control loss due to self-dealing include the following:

- Following policies for voting and proceeding after disclosure of a conflict of interest
- Recording actions in the board minutes
- Securing competitive bids

Serving on a nonprofit board may offer opportunities for a board member to benefit from the decisions of the board. A board member may sell office supplies, be an insurance broker or lawyer, or have a member of his family or a business associate who may benefit from a decision of the board. All efforts must be made to disclose any potential conflicts of interest in keeping with board policy and procedures. A sample conflict of interest policy is included in Appendix 5.

Principles of good faith deal with the expectation that board members will exercise their powers and duties in good faith and in the best interest of the organization. Examples include actions or nonactions that result in a financial loss or legal action taken due to the following:

- Errors in judgment and not seeking professional advice on legal, auditing, insurance, and employee-relations issues
- Failure to provide for risk-management controls and risk financing
- Personal liability for breach of fiduciary duty
- Lack of an ethical fundraising program

Techniques to reduce, prevent, or control loss due to failure to adhere to principles of good faith include the following:

- Exercising care and diligence and acting in the best interest of the organization, and having knowledge of the mission, core values, bylaws, articles of incorporation, obligations, and policies
- Having knowledge of the organization's risk exposures and risk-management plan
- Having knowledge of laws that affect board responsibility and the operation of the organization, such as the Sarbanes Oxley Act (requires that publicly traded companies adhere to rules that increase board members' roles in overseeing financial transactions and auditing procedures) and the Volunteer Protection Act (limits the liability of volunteers serving in nonprofit organizations)
- Purchasing Directors and Officers Insurance
- Keeping accurate minutes and records of decisions and attendance
- Ensuring leadership continuity with an executive succession plan and knowledge of key records in case of an emergency transition

Board members can also be held responsible for decisions made in their absence. Individual board members cannot speak on behalf of the board. A board is a legally constituted entity that has the status of a person. As such, boards act only through consensus. They are obligated to serve as agents of the organization as a whole. Individual board members do not represent special interest groups and can only function in a duly constituted meeting of the whole.

Many nonprofit corporations agree to indemnify (or hold harmless) their directors and/or officers from any suits arising out of the performance of their duties as members of the board. Basically, the organization will reimburse a director or officer for expenses and judgments involved in personal liability suits. Many states permit indemnification only as provided for in an organization's charter or bylaws. Some general liability insurance policies cover some losses that directors and officers cause if their actions cause property damage or bodily injury. Harm caused by their decisions can and should be covered by directors and officers (D&O) insurance. The terms of the coverage depend on the particular policy, but it usually protects the board and covers expenses incurred in resolving a claim. In most policies, D&O insurance does not provide for the insurer to defend against a claim. The organization will usually need to pay the attorney fees and then seek reimbursement.

Legal Liabilities of Administrators and Supervisors

Organizations are generally liable for the negligent wrongdoings of both paid staff and volunteers, all of whom are subject to the same risks, such as accidental injury, health difficulties, etc. Administrators and supervisors can be held liable for the following five basic functions:

- Good supervision plans
- Reasonable safety rules
- Competent staff. Evidence of such competency may be found in background checks and references, certifications, previous experience, and/or the interviewing processes.
- The negligent acts of persons reporting to them
- The program services being conducted properly

An administrator may also be liable for not remedying dangerous conditions, repairing defective equipment, or handling maintenance after "notice," which means not taking action after being told about a hazardous condition or not making regular inspections of the site. If a violation of a policy or rule takes place and the administrator fails to take action, it may be construed as condoning the violation, and the administrator or the corporate entity could be held liable.

Legal Liabilities of Direct Program Leaders

Program leaders, both paid and volunteer, can be liable for any injury that is caused by any negligent action or nonaction taken by them. The negligence of the employee or volunteer may be imputed to the organization through the doctrine of respondent superior. If the employee commits an intentional tort, he generally "stands alone" and would usually have to rely on his own personal assets or insurance. Such cases involve actions such as ultra vires, or acting outside the scope of authority or responsibility of the individual, willful and wanton conduct, and use of excessive force.

The general approach in America's "suit-happy" society is to sue everyone connected with the incident (e.g., employer, employee, organization, supplier, manufacturer, board of directors). Even if an organization is insured, its resources could be tied up for a long period of time. The loss of time and the cost of the defense may be substantial, even if the organization is found to be without fault.

Proof of Negligence

To prove negligence, four elements must exist. To prove that negligence did not take place, only one of those four elements needs to be shown to be absent. First, duty must be owed by the person in charge to the participant or staff member. The duty is a relationship or obligation recognized by the law to exercise the standard of care against unreasonable risks. The duty owed by the organization is to protect the participants and staff from unreasonable risk of injury. The duty is both a legal and moral duty. However, only the legal duty is enforceable in court. The court or judge determines if duty was owed. The doctrine of in loco parentis (in place of the parent) means that the organization or an individual assumes the rights, duties, and responsibilities of the parents with regard to conduct and discipline of the child, particularly in resident situations.

Second, a breach of duty must exist to prevent an accident that was foreseeable. Conduct cannot be considered negligent if the risk could not be reasonably anticipated. If the event was not foreseeable, then the organization has no duty to provide protection. The reason for failure to see the risk or consequences of an act or event is irrelevant. The determination of negligence or breach of duty is made by a jury and is based on the standard of care required of administrators and program staff, which would establish that the accused did everything he could do based on the current body of knowledge. A person cannot take steps to prevent an accident that was not foreseeable, but administrators and program staff are responsible for foreseeing or being alert to those things that might cause injury.

Administrators are also responsible for knowing the current standard of care that is expected of a professional for the nature of the activity, type of participation, and the environmental conditions. Is another organization or authority setting the standard for the type of program or operation being implemented? For example, the ACA standards program is often considered the standard of care for operating a day or resident camp. State licensing may determine the standard of care in a childcare operation. The standard of care may also be determined by what other related agencies, camps, or programs are doing. The standard of care often changes over time or as a particular issue, such as child abuse, becomes more frequently tested in court. Degrees of negligence determine the degree of legal fault, from ordinary negligence to gross negligence. Gross negligence is more serious than failure to exercise ordinary care and may result in exemplary damages. Gross negligence also negates volunteer immunity statutes.

Third, the breach of duty or a substandard act must be directly related to the injury. The injured party must be able to show that what the leader did or did not do was the proximate cause of the injury, and that the harm would not have occurred if the negligent conduct had not happened.

Finally, actual damage or loss must be sustained as a result of the injury. The amount of damages is often determined by what compensatory monetary award would, as much as possible, restore the injured to his preinjury condition. The types of compensable awards include economic loss, physical pain and suffering, physical impairment, and emotional distress. Many states now have comparative negligence or fault, in which damages are awarded on the basis of comparing the fault of the defendant (sponsor) to the fault of the plaintiff (injured) claimant. Comparative negligence is a partial defense that reduces the amount of damages that a plaintiff can recover in a negligence-based claim, based upon the degree to which the plaintiff's own negligence contributed to the damages. A jury usually must decide the degree to which the plaintiff's negligence contributed to cause the damages, versus the combined negligence of all sued defendants. It is a modification of the doctrine of contributory negligence, which disallowed any recovery by a plaintiff whose negligence contributed, even minimally, to causing the damages.

Possible defenses for tort action or reduction in the award require proof of the following. However, these defenses may prove to be invalid because of the victim's age or a lack of capacity of the victim to make a judgment:

- The expected standard of care was being met.

- The claimant contributed to his own injury (contributory fault).

- The claimant knew about and assumed the risk (assumption of risk).

- The negligence was not the direct cause of the injury and releases or waiver agreements were signed.

The following steps might minimize the likelihood of a suit, assist in the defense, or help minimize the claim if a suit is filed. The organization's administrators and/or staff should:

- Inform participants, parents, and staff of procedures, making sure that everyone is knowledgeable of any risks they are assuming related to the activity

- Act quickly and effectively to render aid and/or secure medical help or other appropriate help. Follow emergency procedures, which include training staff in procedures and taking prompt, competent action when an emergency occurs.

- Notify a supervisor and/or lawyer and insurance carrier.

- Be concerned, helpful, and courteous, but stay within the facts and refer any questions of a legal nature to the attorney or insurance carrier. The natural feeling at the time of injury is to feel sorry that the incident happened or even feel at fault or guilty.

- Avoid making unnecessary remarks to the injured, witnesses, friends, or parents that might be later used against the individual or organization. Avoid making conclusions or statements against interest or admission of fault such as: "I'm sorry, it was my fault." "I should have..." "I knew that needed repaired." "This is the third time I've told that staff member to..." Promptly prepare written reports of each detail, including distances, locations, witnesses, and the sequence of events. It may be helpful to take pictures of the scene if they could help prove a fact and a lack of guilt.

- Gather any evidence or measurements that might be used as evidence in the individual's or organization's favor. Store and label reports and evidence to be destroyed after the statute of limitations has run out. (If the incident may be considered an issue of abuse, records should become a part of permanent storage, as there may be no statute of limitations).

- Avoid automatically assuming that changes in procedures will keep such a situation from reoccurring. Evaluate what has been learned and review this information with an objective outsider, such as an attorney, before making changes.

- Avoid giving a statement or agreeing to pay any bills or expenses without first consulting with an attorney.

- Remember that the legal system often takes years before a case comes to court. Be sure to avoid depending on an individual's memory of the situation or upon someone who is no longer employed.

Many of the problem areas that may result in tort actions are covered in the worksheet part of this manual. The most important questions for each employee to ask himself are as follows:

- "Could anyone get hurt?"

- "Did I do everything possible to prevent that from happening?"

- "If someone is hurt, did I do everything I could have done to lessen the injury?"

Governmental administrative rules and regulations are a fact of life. Considering them in all phases of planning is time-consuming, but it is essential. These regulations include everything from requiring a safe water supply to sex discrimination laws, and they vary from state to state. Most national organizations monitor and attempt to keep informed of pending and new federal legislation and/or regulations affecting the organization's operations and programs. Become involved in local organizations such as the American Camp Association Section, United Way, and other community groups to keep abreast of pending state and local regulations.

Risk Identification

Before a plan can be developed, the organization must identify what assets are exposed to risk. What does it have to lose? Are they tangible resources such as people, monies, or property, or are they intangibles such as markets, reputation, or communication? Losses of either type can affect the organization's ability to deliver future programs. It is important to identify all resources and/or assets, regardless of whether they are considered insurable.

To identify risk exposures and design risk-management plans, it is important to understand what the exposures are and the possible legal liabilities tied to those risks. Exposures can be grouped in a number of ways. A systematic approach might be according to areas of exposure, such as:

- Standard of care exposures
- Property exposures
- Operational and financial exposures
- Human resource exposures

Standard of care exposures involve the expected level of care provided to youth participants and adults that is imposed by law or assumed under contract. Property exposures includes the exposure of buildings, equipment, and other property to loss through fire, theft, vandalism, negligence, floods, explosion, utility shutdown, etc. Operational and financial exposures include loss of income and fidelity risks, which are exposures due to misuse, theft, destruction of money, or improper performance or nonperformance of accounting duties. Such risks can also jeopardize future funding. When a loss of human resources takes place, the loss may be of the valuable services of a staff member or volunteer and/or a loss in participation. Insurance claims history, financial statements, policies, history of legal entanglements, program records, maintenance records, physical inspections, checklists, questionnaires, interviews with staff, contracts, and the experiences of other nonprofits will provide some of the resources for identifying risk exposures.

Risk Evaluation

Once a risk is identified, the frequency and severity of the risk should be determined. The frequency is how often it happens or is likely to happen. The severity is how serious the financial repercussions of such an occurrence would be, including both the seriousness of an injury and the impact on the organization. An insurance company can probably provide a history of those losses for which claims were made. Some of the loss may not occur as an immediate financial loss, but rather as a loss of memberships, community relations issues, or diminishing support, all of which are ultimately financial losses.

Assessing liability potential is difficult. However, reviewing recent court cases, local claims history, settlements, jury awards, cost of defense, etc., involving other nonprofits should help an organization evaluate the potential loss.

Risk Treatment

After the risk, or exposure to loss, has been identified, it must be determined how much or how severe the loss from the exposure might be and what the chances are of actually losing it. This information will help determine the treatment or plan for handling the risk. An organization must analyze the alternatives available for dealing with the exposure. Risk exposures may be handled by choosing to transfer, retain, avoid, or reduce the risk. Transfer and retention are risk-financing techniques used to retain the loss and determine how to either finance it or transfer the cost to another party. Avoidance and reduction are risk-control techniques used to minimize the risk of loss. In a risk-management plan, the risks will be addressed by both financial and control techniques. Identifying and handling risks is the overall risk-management plan for providing a safer experience and lending stability and structure to an agency's operations. The plan also helps an organization prevent or minimize the effect of incidents that may result in a loss due to personal injury, property damage, or legal action.

The objective of risk management is to protect an organization against losses by reducing the frequency and severity of the loss and then by financing the loss through the most effective means. Two key risk-management adages are as follows:

- Never risk more than the organization can afford to lose.
- Never risk a lot for a little.

Risk-Financing Techniques

Risk transfer is a common means of handling risk. Risks with low frequency and high severity, such as loss of limb, other permanent injury, death, or extensive property loss, are most often transferred in the form of insurance. While other methods of risk transfer exist, insurance is the most important. It is one of the safest methods, it is efficient, and the cost can be identified. Services normally associated with insurance are loss-prevention services and guidance, claims adjustments, legal defense services, and risk-management guidance. Insurance does not prevent the incident or a lawsuit, but it does help with financial coverage to the extent of the limits spelled out in the policy. Careful consideration should be given to the deductible, ceiling, and exemptions in a policy.

However, insurance is only one of the devices used to meet losses, and it may not be the best device in a given situation. Some risks may not be insurable, and some risks simply should not be insured. Organizations must always compare the cost of insurance to the exposure to loss. For example, it may cost more to insure a small building than the building itself is worth. Also, organizations must look at the other methods of handling the exposure to make sure that the risk would not be better handled by avoidance, retention, or reduction. Reduction should always be considered, since proper reduction of the risk can make the risk exposure more acceptable to the transferee.

Other methods of transfer of risk include leases, sales contracts, purchase contracts, service contracts, indemnification or hold-harmless agreements, suretyship, and bailment. Suretyship means assuming an obligation to pay the debt or answer for the default of another. Bailment is the act of placing property in the custody and control of another, usually for safekeeping and later return of the property. One of these methods may be desirable if the other party is in a better position to control losses or can more readily absorb losses. Transfer of a risk to someone who cannot handle the exposure does not accomplish much, since the loss will then come back to the organization, in which case it may be completely unexpected and leave the organization with no plan to handle the loss. Transferring risks, like other methods for handling risk, requires careful planning.

Risk retention means that the organization keeps the risk exposure and accepts the responsibility for any consequences should that risk occur. The loss would have to be absorbed by the organization. Such losses might include those financial losses that are not desirable to insure, that cannot be transferred, such as deductibles, or that are in excess of the coverage in a policy. Risks that occur frequently, but are not severe, may also be retained. These situations might include risks involving personal injuries that do not require outside medical care or those involving small property damage, such as broken windows. Retention is also justified if it is the cheapest way to handle the risk, or if no other method is available for handling the risk and the organization can afford to cover the loss. Retention may be partial, as in the use of higher deductibles in insurance. Partial retention results in reducing costs.

Losses can be handled out of current income or by setting up a reserve fund with segregated assets that can be readily converted into cash. In any event, the retention must be based on reasonably predictable losses and a definite ability to pay losses when they occur.

Risk-Control Techniques

Risk avoidance is the strongest method of dealing with risk exposures, since it completely eliminates the risk. Of course, all activity cannot be stopped just to avoid risk. Other techniques are employed to handle risk if the risk is justified. It is essential that an organization answer the following questions about each of its programs, activities, and operations:

- Is the risk justified? If the activity has little or no value, it can be readily terminated. If the risk is great compared to the value of the activity, the activity may not be justified.

- Can the risk be properly handled by some method other than avoidance? If the risk cannot be transferred without great cost or loss of quality, perhaps it should be avoided.

- Can the risk be assumed by the organization or can it be partially assumed or partially transferred? If the loss potential is too great to be self-assumed, or if participation in the loss cannot be absorbed by the organization and/or others, perhaps the activity is not justified.

- Can the risk be reduced? If it cannot be reduced to the point where it can be transferred or self-assumed, the activity probably is not justified and should be avoided.

Risk reduction is a method for reducing the risk or controlling the loss. It's perhaps the most important method, because it is needed even when transfer or retention are used. Losses can be better controlled through risk reduction. Certain loss-control measures can reduce the possibility of loss and thus reduce frequency. Other approaches may help reduce the severity.

Identification of the cause of loss or injury can help determine what loss-control measures might work. Loss-control measures include planning and implementing intervention systems for preventive maintenance, injury control, information distribution, and record-keeping. Reduction of the risk may make one of the other methods of handling loss acceptable.

Monitoring Treatment

Risk-management plans are constantly evolving. Once the treatment or method for handling the risk is determined and loss-control measures are put into place, a system for monitoring effectiveness and updating plans should be scheduled. Periodic review of past decisions, new loss exposures, loss experience, insurance increases, or other changes in circumstances may dictate new decisions.

The risk-management exposure chart in Figure 1-1 will help identify an organization's exposures. The chart is related to the exposures and the frequency and severity of a loss. It should help an organization determine the best method or methods for handling the risk related to the organization's operations or a given program or site. Combining and comparing charts from each operation or program can provide consistency in the overall risk-management plan and will document decisions made to handle risk by transferring, retaining, reducing, or avoiding them. If risk reduction is one of the methods used, the last column of Figure 1-1 is used to make notes of the risk-reduction actions taken. A copy of the chart is also on the resource CD that is included with this book, so it can be reproduced, shared, and easily updated.

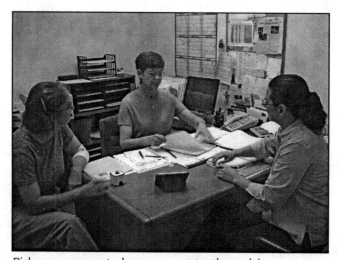

Risk-management plans are constantly evolving.

Board Exposures			
Legal Liabilities of Trustees/Directors (Check all that apply)	Examples or Types of Actions/Nonactions Resulting in Financial Loss and/or Legal Action	Sample Techniques to Reduce, Prevent, or Control Loss	Risk-Control Methods and Technique(s) and Steps Taken
☐ Mismanagement	No provisions made to protect assets or to protect the health and safety of participants; board reports not carefully reviewed before acceptance; conclusions/decisions made when other available information clearly suggests a different direction; inadequate controls and reporting systems	Informed decision-makers establish policies consistent with best practices or standards of the field; taking action consistent with established policies; monitoring what is happening in the organization; providing supervision and evaluation of the executive director	
☐ Nonmanagement	Failing to attend board and committee meetings; having data relevant to a decision and not using it; having control systems and not using them; lack of responsibility for decisions made in a member's absence	Acting on policy to remove board members not fulfilling responsibilities; establishing policies and procedures to govern the authority and work of committees and individuals assigned tasks by the board	
☐ Self-Dealing	Not disclosing a potential conflict of interest; voting on or influencing decisions that benefit themselves.	Following policies for voting and proceeding after disclosure of a conflict; recording action in minutes; Gathering competitive bids	

Figure 1-1. Risk-management exposure chart

	Examples or Types of Illness/ Injury, Financial Loss, and/or Legal Action Taken	Sample Techniques to Reduce, Prevent, or Control Loss	Risk-Control Methods and Technique(s) and Steps Taken
❑ Principles of Good Faith	Human judgment errors; not seeking professional advice on legal, auditing, insurance, and employee-relations issues; failing to provide for risk-management controls and risk financing; personal liability for breach of fiduciary duty that constitutes intentional and malicious acts against an employee Lack of an ethical fundraising program; failing to provide for leadership sustainability Exercising care and diligence and acting in the best interest of the organization; having knowledge of the mission, core values, council's bylaws, articles of incorporation, charter obligations, and policies	Having knowledge of the council's risk exposures and the strategic risk-management plan Having knowledge of laws affecting board responsibility and operations of the council, including the Sarbanes Oxley Act, Volunteer Protection Act, and D&O insurance Keeping accurate minutes and records of decisions and attendance Ensuring leadership continuity with an executive succession plan and having knowledge of key records in case of an emergency transition	
Personnel Exposures			
Employment Liabilities (Check all that apply) ❑ Employer/employee relationship Harassment, slander, discrimination, etc	Inappropriate actions, including criminal behavior by an employer or other staff member, wrongful dismissal, invasion of privacy, hostile work environment, discrimination based on age, race, religion, sex or disability, etc.	Establishing personnel policies, training processes, policies on search and seizure, etc.	

Figure 1-1. Risk-management exposure chart (cont.)

Standard of Care Liabilities (Check all that apply)	Examples of Types of Illness/Injury, Financial Loss, and/or Legal Action Taken	Sample Techniques to Reduce, Prevent, or Control Loss	Risk-Control Methods and Technique(s) and Steps Taken
❑ Hiring/firing	Wrong classification of exempt/nonexempt; discrimination claims; illegal pre-employment interview questions; wrongful action against "whistleblowers"; fines by government regulatory bodies	Having knowledge of employment laws, including Federal Equal Employment Opportunity (EEO) Laws, Fair Labor Standards Act (FLSA), Family Medical Leave Act (FMLA), workman's compensation, unemployment compensation, Bona Fide Occupational Qualification (BFOQ), Sarbanes Oxley Act Establishing hiring policies and personnel policies; writing letters of agreement with the staff to address at-will status; having a documented evaluation process reviewed by a lawyer	
❑ Vacation or Payroll Accrual	Allowing vacation or payroll to accrue beyond the ability to pay or replace staff in a timely manner; obligation or commitment to pay for time worked	Establishing personnel policies that specify the use of vacation time; having current knowledge of, and complying with, federal and state employment laws, etc.	
❑ Government Regulations and Tax Liabilities	Failure to meet government reporting criteria (tax requirements, fines by government regulatory bodies)	Undergoing OSHA compliance audits; having current knowledge and compliance with other regulations and requirements, etc	

Program Operation Injury Exposures

Standard of Care Liabilities (Check all that apply)	Examples of Types of Illness/Injury, Financial Loss, and/or Legal Action Taken	Sample Techniques to Reduce, Prevent, or Control Loss	Risk-Control Methods and Technique(s) and Steps Taken

Figure 1-1. Risk-management exposure chart (cont.)

Standard of Care Liabilities (Check all that apply)	Examples of Types of Illness/Injury, Financial Loss, and/or Legal Action Taken	Sample Techniques to Reduce, Prevent, or Control Loss	Risk-Control Methods and Technique(s) and Steps Taken
☐ Hiring/Firing	Wrong classification of exempt/nonexempt; discrimination claims; illegal pre-employment interview questions; wrongful action against "whistleblowers"; fines by government regulatory bodies	Having knowledge of employment laws, including Federal Equal Employment Opportunity (EEO) Laws, Fair Labor Standards Act (FLSA), Family Medical Leave Act (FMLA), workman's compensation, unemployment compensation, Bona Fide Occupational Qualification (BFOQ), Sarbanes Oxley Act Establishing hiring policies and personnel policies; writing letters of agreement with the staff to address at-will status; having a documented evaluation process reviewed by a lawyer	
☐ Vacation or Payroll Accrual	Allowing vacation or payroll to accrue beyond the ability to pay or replace staff in a timely manner; obligation or commitment to pay for time worked	Establishing personnel policies that specify the use of vacation time; having current knowledge of, and complying with, federal and state employment laws, etc.	
☐ Government Regulations and Tax Liabilities	Failure to meet government reporting criteria (tax requirements, fines by government regulatory bodies)	Undergoing OSHA compliance audits; having current knowledge and compliance with other regulations and requirements, etc	

Program Operation Injury Exposures

Standard of Care Liabilities (Check all that apply)	Examples of Types of Illness/Injury, Financial Loss, and/or Legal Action Taken	Sample Techniques to Reduce, Prevent, or Control Loss	Risk-Control Methods and Technique(s) and Steps Taken

Figure 1-1. Risk-management exposure chart (cont.)

☐ Staff Selection/Training (volunteer or paid)	Negligent hiring claims, including lack of screening or training, unqualified staff, etc.	Using screening procedures; developing training, including driver screening/training, training for late hires or those that miss all or part of the training, background checks, etc.
☐ Staff Supervision/Behavior (volunteer or paid)	Negligent hiring claims, failure to supervise staff, failure to enforce procedures, drunkenness or drug use by staff, etc.	Establishing supervision training, guidelines for appropriate and inappropriate staff behavior, on-duty procedures, plans for supervision of volunteers, supervisor observation of staff with children, etc.
☐ Health Services	Injury from failure to provide appropriate first aid or emergency care; failure to meet special medical needs or dispense medications properly; exposure to bloodborne pathogens, etc. Injury from inappropriate actions by healthcare staff, malpractice claim, etc.	Adhering to healthcare procedures; providing first aid training and/or assuring qualified healthcare staff; having knowledge of professional healthcare individuals' malpractice insurance or coverage with supplementary or general liability insurance; being licensed to practice in state where program is located, etc. Exposure Control Plan (OSHA)
☐ Personal Injury (abuse, assault, invasion of privacy, discrimination, search and seizure)	Inappropriate actions, including criminal behavior, by staff or other participants; lack of protection in public places or from intruders; participant recruitment practices, misuse of children's photos, etc. Injury or loss from selection or use of unsafe or poorly designed facilities	Writing safety regulations and personnel policies; implementing ADA requirements; establishing guidelines for release of personal information; designing facilities to reduce one-on-one situations; working with local police CPTED officer (Crime Prevention Through Environmental Design); planning for maximum visibility; adding

Figure 1-1. Risk-management exposure chart (cont.)

Category	Exposure	Management Strategies
❑ Maintenance	Injury from failure to report or maintain facilities and equipment; unsafe electrical or gas lines; in appropriate shower water temperatures, vehicle mechanical failure, etc.	bathroom door vents so requests for help can be heard; keeping windows uncluttered; developing a system for signing in guests and stopping intruders; Developing systems to report problems, maintenance plans, and identified cutoff points; training personnel; marking emergency exits, etc.
❑ Food Service	Injury from unsafe water, hazardous foods containing infectious or toxic microorganisms (e.g., e. coli, salmonella)	Adhering to procedures for storage, how to handle potentially hazardous foods, sanitation, controlled access, etc.
❑ Attractive Nuisances	Injury (participants, staff, or intruders) from failure to control access or unauthorized use of ropes course, lake, pool, firearms, etc.	Having fences, signs, security system, etc.
❑ Participant Supervision	Injury from failure to supervise adequately; not maintaining appropriate participant-to-staff ratio; participant-to-participant child abuse; release of participants to unauthorized people, etc.	Developing procedures for transporting persons; procedures for prevention of child abuse and adult/child contact; guidelines for discipline of children, training on appropriate participant-behavior techniques, regular analysis of incidents, required documentation, etc.
❑ Defective or Tampered Products	Illness or injury from defective merchandise or contaminated food, including a food product sale and other merchandise sold; defective program or safety equipment, etc.	Using a credible food and equipment source; controlling access, having a crisis-management plan, etc.

Figure 1-1. Risk-management exposure chart (cont.)

	Examples of Types of Illness/Injury, Financial Loss, and/or Legal Action Taken	Sample Techniques to Reduce, Prevent, or Control Loss	Risk-Control Methods and Technique(s) and Steps Taken
❏ Program Activities	Injury from inadequate safety regulations and emergency procedures; failure to provide qualified leadership or inform parents of risk, etc	Having safe and appropriate equipment, signed permissions for participation, supplementary insurance, certifications, etc. Review of all ACA specialized activity standards	
❏ Vehicle Operation	Injury from the number of passengers exceeding capacity of the vehicle; lack of seatbelts, unqualified driver; improper loading or unloading; poor selection of commercial provider, etc.	Having insurance, safety regulations, credible vehicle provider, safety checks, etc.	

General Administration Exposures

Operational Financial Liabilities (Check all that apply)	Examples of Types of Illness/Injury, Financial Loss, and/or Legal Action Taken	Sample Techniques to Reduce, Prevent, or Control Loss	
❏ Internal Controls	Claims by "whistleblowers", embezzlement, fines for not meeting legal obligations Poor or no procedures/policies for handling of petty cash, cash receipts/disbursements, reimbursements, inventory control, bank reconciliation, etc., to prevent: • Theft • Embezzlement • Inadequate records • Financial commitments beyond budget or ability to pay • Bankruptcy	Having knowledge of Sarbanes Oxley Act and procedures for handling employee complaints for inappropriate financial management Using generally accepted accountings principles. (GAAP) Having insurance policies/procedures and segregation of duties that specify who has authority to control access to funds and records, make purchases, pay and enter into contracts; using professional accounting services; having policies on staff reimbursement; undergoing	

Figure 1-1. Risk-management exposure chart (cont.)

Risk	Exposure	Risk-management strategies
		external audit or review; regularly training for persons responsible for finance; bonding employees who handle money
❑ False Advertising	Misleading or incomplete information on facilities, activities, or personnel, etc.	Developing brochures, videos, and written material that correctly describes facilities, staff, programs, etc.
❑ Sponsorship	Lending endorsement to an activity not in the organization's control; the image of co-sponsors	Having appropriate insurance and board review of endorsements/sponsorships
❑ Ethical Fundraising	Loss of reputation and future donations; not turning down donations that benefit the donor rather than the organization; use of fundraising consultants whose compensation is directly tied to the amount raised; prospective funders receive vague information on the council's financial status; money accepted from anyone—no questions asked.	Giving donors acknowledgment for their support and inform them of how the donation will be used; carefully guarding donors' privacy; ensuring that accurate reports are summated to funders on time; evaluating the council's expense-to-income income regularly—no more than 25% is spent on fundraising; honoring donors' restrictions
❑ Human Resources Loss (staff, participants, volunteers)	Personal injuries, such as an accident or illness, preventing participation or causing disability (long- or short-term), death, disease, or psychological impairment, that in turn cause: Loss of income if the activity cannot be offered Loss of public credibility	Having arrangements with crisis-intervention services and psychological support; having insurance for loss of income; establishing procedures for refunds and early staff release; acquiring legal support; utilizing public relations procedures; having back-up staff; adhering to procedures to

Figure 1-1. Risk-management exposure chart (cont.)

Contract Liabilities (Check all that apply)	Examples of Types of Illness/Injury, Financial Loss, and/or Legal Action Taken	Sample Techniques to Reduce, Prevent, or Control Loss	Risk-Control Methods and Technique(s) and Steps Taken
	Loss of participants and/or staff due to physical injury or stress due to incidents or the results of accidents; Closing a program due to epidemic or illness; Loss of key talent of volunteers or staff	deal with crises; appointing spokespersons; having a crisis communication plan; planning for contacting parents for unanticipated closures	
❏ Participant/User Group Registration	Loss of program fees, deposit, reputation, future income/participation	Having an agreement that specifies terms, waivers, releases, refund policy, permission to participate, permission to treat, etc.	
❏ Program Activity Contracts	Loss of control over quality of service; inability to receive or give future services(e.g., horse leasing or public stable use, rafting, community swim pool, permits for access)	Having an agreement that specifies terms, what to transfer or retain, and conditions of use—reviewed by a lawyer	
❏ Insurance	Loss from inappropriate coverage, limits, deductibles	Regularly reviewing coverage; planning for risk financing and appropriate resources	
❏ Sales or Purchase Orders	Responsibility for unauthorized purchases; obligation for payment; loss of credit	Having policy/controls on binding or committing the organization without the authority to do so. Limiting the authority to sign for the organization	
❏ Grants	Responsibility to fulfill grant obligations; loss of reputation; future grants, etc.	Regularly reviewing timelines and stipulations	

Figure 1-1. Risk-management exposure chart (cont.)

	Examples of Types of Illness/Injury, Financial Loss, and/or Legal Action Taken	Sample Techniques to Reduce, Prevent, or Control Loss	Risk-Control Methods and Technique(s) and Steps Taken
☐ Contracts for Service	Reputation, obligation for payment, quality of services delivered (e.g., food service, product sale materials and products, construction, specialist services such as fundraising)	Having agreements that specify the terms, what to transfer, and what to retain—reviewed by a lawyer	
☐ Lease/Rental	Inability to provide/receive services for groups/programs; guest/user groups; rental cancellations; loss of future business	Having agreements that specify the terms, what to transfer, and what to retain. Writing a refund policy that includes a force majeure clause ("greater force," such as an act of God)—reviewed by a lawyer	
☐ Notes, Mortgage, Loans	Reputation; loss of line of credit; future loans, etc.	Having policies/controls on binding or committing the organization without the authority to do so, and procedures that limit the authority to sign for the organization, etc.	

Property/Equipment Ownership Exposures

Property, Buildings, and Equipment Liabilities (Check all that apply)	Examples of Types of Illness/Injury, Financial Loss, and/or Legal Action Taken	Sample Techniques to Reduce, Prevent, or Control Loss	Risk-Control Methods and Technique(s) and Steps Taken
☐ Property of Others	Loss of equipment or personal items not owned by the camp	Establishing procedures for possession, use, and replacement	
☐ General Oversight and Maintenance	Fines from lack of knowledge of laws, codes, permits, regulations, etc., affecting operation	Purchasing insurance; determining acceptable deductibles, ceilings, and what is feasible to retain (without insurance)	
	Inadequate insurance due to cost and/or availability; insuring buildings not worth insuring;	Purchasing safety, rescue, or other equipment	

Figure 1-1. Risk-management exposure chart (cont.)

	inaccurate inventories and knowledge of value of items in buildings Not making repairs needed on aging property or equipment Fines from lack of knowledge on OSHA requirements for maintenance logs, lockout/tagout rule, material safety data sheets, records, and reporting, etc. Inadequate safety equipment on site due to cost and/or availability	Supervising the site when it is not in full use Keeping inventories of equipment and supplies Establishing long-term maintenance plans and annual safety examinations Having accessible descriptions of electrical lines and cutoff points Determining appropriate storage and handling of equipment, hazardous materials, and records—Hazard Communication Plan (OSHA)
Natural/Man-made Hazards/Disasters From: ☐ Fire/Smoke ☐ Land Movement/Earthquakes ☐ Collapse ☐ Blizzard, Ice, Hail ☐ Flood ☐ Wind, Tornado, Hurricane ☐ Lighting ☐ Explosion ☐ Terrorism ☐ Act of Violence in the Community	Loss of buildings and equipment, roads, natural features, etc. Loss of perishables or records and data from utility outages Loss of income for unusable property Loss of income from cancellation or emotional stress due to acts of terrorism, violence, or disasters affecting the community	Considerations affecting losses in this category: • Area of the country and known risks • Distance from emergency services • Seasons of site use • Availability of backup power • Backup systems for computerized records and documents Establishing a refund policy, including a force majeure clause; establishing emergency plans for natural disasters; training staff and participants of their roles in an emergency plan; posting emergency numbers; establishing relationships with local fire and law-enforcement officials

Figure 1-1. Risk-management exposure chart (cont.)

		Establishing action plans to help staff and participants when disaster affects their family or community
❑ Theft and/or Vandalism	Loss of equipment, buildings, natural features, etc. Loss of income resulting from damage. Loss from selection or use of unsafe or poorly designed facilities; easy targets for crime (e.g., child abuse, cash, technology)	Establishing relationships with local law-enforcement officials (CPTED officers); improving on-site security; keeping incident reports and photos; posting trespassing signs; maintaining insurance; monitoring easy targets such as vending machines and computers, etc.
❑ Collision or Breakdown of Vehicles or Machinery	Loss of income or needed services for unusable equipment; loss of, or damage to, equipment	Having a maintenance plan; training staff; keeping incident reports and photos; maintaining insurance
❑ Loss of Utilities	Loss of perishables or records and data on computers; loss of income	Having a cancellation policy, backup systems for refrigeration, computerized records, documents, and insurance
❑ Environmental Pollution, Sewer Backup or Contamination	Fines or loss of potential income due to sewage, toxic materials, leaks of underground tanks, insect/weed control, etc.	Monitoring garbage storage capacity; purchasing leakproof containers; developing an environmental impact plan, etc.

Figure 1-1. Risk-management exposure chart (cont.)

CRISIS AND EMERGENCY MANAGEMENT

Chapter Two

An emergency involves danger and the immediate potential for serious personal harm or property loss. When the danger is eliminated, the emergency is over. A crisis is defined as an unstable situation or crucial time or state of affairs that has reached a critical phase. A crisis may contain elements of danger or a dangerous condition, and needs to be addressed quickly. However, unless immediate action must be taken to stabilize the situation to prevent or reduce personal harm or property loss, it is not an emergency. In a crisis, time is available to consult the crisis-response team. Prior to the occurrence of any crisis, this team should be established, the crisis-management plan should be written, and strategies should be discussed. Depending on the size of the organization, the team should include the executive director, public relations director, board president, and legal counsel. The crisis-response team may or may not include the persons who deal with the emergency. Additional persons may be added depending on the nature of the crisis.

While it is important to have plans for dealing with emergencies and crisis situations, the need for immediate action is the critical element in an emergency. The purpose of creating, practicing, and adhering to the emergency plan is to first prevent the problem. Then, when necessary, emergency procedures help responsible persons to recognize the problem, take action to solve the problem, and minimize or eliminate the danger. In a crisis, time may be available for additional planning and discussion. In some emergencies, follow-up crisis-response tasks may be needed after the immediate danger is gone and the situation is no longer an emergency. However, either a crisis or an emergency may result in office or program disruption and distract from the purpose, goals, and strategic plans of the agency.

Dealing With Emergencies

Emergencies are always stressful. This stress is caused by fear, confusion, time, importance, and often conflict. The fear is of the unknown, of not knowing for sure what is going to happen. Confusion, which is the scattering of attention, or the opposite of concentration, comes from not knowing what to do. Time, or the ability to act quickly, plays tug-of-war with fear and confusion. The importance assigned the problem then enters in. How bad is the situation? What is most important to do first? Is the danger life-threatening? If conflict arises either in the solutions themselves or among the people handling the problem, the conflict compounds the stress.

Having competent leadership and a well-rehearsed and easily understood plan are the essential ingredients needed to reduce stress. As the fear and confusion are reduced, persons can begin to act quickly, knowing the sequence of important acts and the direction of the solution.

The director or person in charge must be willing and able to make decisions, make things happen quickly, and accept responsibility for the results.

Meaningful communication with others causes prompt, accurate action. The director should already have established a level of trust and competence before an emergency occurs. The director must know how to bring order to relieve stress. Everyone involved knows what to do, understands their responsibility for themselves and others, and has discussed and practiced the emergency procedures.

Remember to keep the crisis worksheets needed to handle emergencies on hand, along with any other materials that will be needed on short notice. Also, it is essential that everyone involved follows the emergency procedures, keeps calm, and continually assesses the situation.

Managing a Crisis

Once the emergency is over and the element of danger or potential for additional harm or loss has subsided, the situation may still require crisis response. The director or another member of the crisis-response team may take the lead as crisis manager and be charged with controlling the damage and returning the operation to normal as soon as possible. The agency's survival can depend on how well the emergency was handled and/or how well the crisis response was dealt with. Some crisis situations, such as a suspected act of embezzlement, may never have been an emergency, but could lead to an emergency if not dealt with promptly and appropriately.

Crisis management includes assessing the situation, notifying authorities, dealing with the press, and working with the team to notify legal counsel, board members, staff members, next of kin, participants, parents, and appropriate persons. The team also helps to confirm the facts, document data, locate witnesses, and analyze information. These steps are all necessary in controlling the damage, informing the media of progress, and returning the operation to normal. To document how a crisis was handled, the team should record facts, file a step-by-step report of the actions taken, provide supporting data, and be prepared to be an ongoing team until the incident is completely closed.

The following are examples of situations that may put the operation in crisis, but they are not emergencies:

- Staff arrest
- Walkout by staff
- Loss of funding
- Acts of terrorism or violence in the community
- Food poisoning or communicable disease outbreaks
- Threats
- Product tampering

- Theft
- Vandalism
- A major conflict on the site
- Death of someone in a staff member's or participant's family
- A major emergency or natural disaster off the site
- The site being cut off from the "outside world"

Types of Emergencies or Crisis Situations

It is important to try to assess every possible emergency or crisis before it happens and develop a response plan to deal with it. While it is impossible to list every possible emergency or crisis, the crisis-management worksheets in Chapters 4 and 5 contain information and detailed plans to help address most emergency procedures and crisis responses. Listing emergency or crisis situations can be depressing at the least. The following categories were considered in designing the worksheets and will make it easier for the crisis team to begin thinking about different types of emergencies or crisis situations, what makes them unique, and what kind of emergency action or crisis response is required.

Emergency or Crisis-Response Procedures Related to Natural or Man-Made Hazards

Natural hazards on certain areas of a site, such as cliffs, bodies of water, poisonous snakes, biting or attacking animals, or insects, might cause an emergency. In some areas, man-made hazards such as construction sites, vacant lots with glass and trash, drains or sewers, and traffic, may be present. The first step is to determine the types of hazards in the area. What is the real danger they pose, if any? Then design a plan to reduce the risk, prevent an emergency, or deal with any possible emergency resulting from the hazard.

Emergency or Crisis-Response Procedures Related to Natural or Man-Made Disasters

In the event of natural disasters, such as wind, lightning, avalanches, volcano eruptions, extreme heat or cold, tornadoes, earthquakes, hurricanes or floods, and fires, the emergency may be widespread. While no liability may exist when an act of God is the proximate cause, the organization does have a duty to provide appropriate protective action when such an act occurs. It is important to determine the natural disasters that occur in the geographic area, as well as their resulting impact. Find out as much as possible about conditions leading to these disasters and their warning signs.

Consideration must also be made to handle man-made and natural disasters, either in the immediate community or in the outside world, that can cause emotional stress or affect the families or friends of staff members or participants. Acts of terrorism, school shootings, tsunamis, hurricanes, and war can all increase anxiety. If any widespread disaster happens in the community where the office is located or where staff, board members, or participants live, the organization will need to decide what information is disseminated and how. It must be decided how to coordinate information between staff and families and among board members. Remember, if people are being evacuated, the phone system may not be an effective way to reach people. Establishing an emergency call-in location outside of the area or directions for using an established email address for emergency contact may be helpful. A system must also be designed to identify and refer people who need extra support. Resources from the following websites may be helpful:

- **The Emergency Email Network** (www.emergencyemail.org/) allows users to receive emergency notification of natural disasters or other emergencies in their area.

- **The Centers for Disease Control and Prevention** (www.bt.cde.gov\EmContact\index.asp) has information on what to do if someone believes that a biological or chemical threat has occurred.

- **The U.S. Department of Homeland Security** (www.fema.gov\areyouready) has a downloadable "Guide to Citizen Preparedness" that includes information about terrorism, bomb threats, suspicious parcels and letters, chemical and biological weapons, homeland security alerts, etc.

- **The American Academy of Pediatrics** (www.aap.org\terrorism) has information about disaster preparedness to meet children's needs.

To develop a crisis-response plan to handle any emergencies on the organization's site, it is essential to contact local agencies such as the weather bureau, fire department, National Guard, or Civil Defense to secure information and establish a working relationship. Make sure that all responsible parties are well-trained and knowledgeable in carrying out the disaster plans. Secure and maintain the appropriate equipment necessary to carry out the plans. Remember that the natural or man-made disaster will be affecting the surrounding communities and so the site may not get help as quickly as people would like. Certain emergency situations are related to program activities or to the operation of facilities or equipment.

Emergency or Crisis-Response Procedures Related to Program Activities

Activity-related emergencies can take place during any activity, but are more common in waterfront activities, horseback riding, field trips, climbing and rappelling, etc. Staff selection and supervision is a critical part of the preplanning to reduce risk in such activities. The orientation, testing, and training of participants are also critical, as is the use of appropriate equipment. Specific safety precautions for reducing the risk and dealing with possible emergencies are suggested in Chapter 6. Appendices 18 and 19 also have forms for designing an operational plan for each activity, including one form for activities that require certified or specially trained staff and another that is more general.

Emergency or Crisis-Response Procedures Related to the Operation of the Facility or Equipment

Operational emergencies include explosions, building collapses, electrocution, loss or contamination of water, and food or other poisoning. Such emergencies may be prevented, or risks reduced, through regular safety checks and maintenance of facilities and equipment. All facilities should be in compliance with current building, electrical, plumbing, and fire codes. Familiarity with the Occupations Safety and Health Administration (OSHA) requirements is essential.

Equipment must only be operated by those trained in its use. It is essential that the worksheets are used to survey a site for potential operational hazards and develop a plan to deal with them. Employees must know how to contact local utility companies, the health department, and the fire department in an emergency.

Emergency or Crisis-Response Procedures Related to the Behavior of People

Some emergencies may be caused by the behavior of people. Such emergencies include kidnapping, missing persons, running away or hiding, harassment, intrusion, fighting, child molestation or abuse, drug or alcohol overdose, or holding hostages. The crisis responses to any of these emergencies tend to be highly emotional. Therefore, it is even more important to develop a well-thought-out plan of action. The worksheets in Chapters 5 and 6 will help to outline the actions required to deal with these types of emergencies.

In developing the plan for behavior-related emergencies, it is important to include the establishment of relationships with police, social services departments, and other local authorities. Notifying and dealing with parents, dealing with media, and obtaining legal assistance must also be included.

Emergency or Crisis-Response Procedures Related to Pre-existing Medical Conditions

Some emergencies might occur because of a pre-existing medical condition (e.g., asthma, AIDS, allergies, diabetes, heart conditions, hemophilia, epilepsy, or handicapping conditions). The best prevention for these emergencies is to make certain that designated persons are aware of the conditions and that precautions are taken, such as using trained personnel, having adequate supervision, following safety rules, properly maintaining emergency equipment, and updating emergency help numbers. The Americans with Disabilities Act (ADA), which was passed in 1991, has important implications for hiring and serving persons with disabilities. Information about these implications is included in the Worksheets O-17 and P-27. Detailed plans for dealing with any medical emergency, including having all pertinent information on hand, having systems for carrying out the plan, having properly trained and informed staff to provide first aid, and maintaining proper health and medical equipment/supplies in appropriate places are on a number of worksheets in Chapters 5 and 6. Information about incident reports is on Worksheets O-35 and P-43 and a sample incident report form is found in Appendix 6.

Crisis Communication—
Prepare, Manage, and Respond

The crisis-response team must develop a crisis operational plan and a crisis-communication plan before a crisis occurs. The operational plan should include strategies to continue conducting business even as a crisis is ongoing. The communications plan should include notification of employees, participants, parents, the media, and other relevant audiences, including volunteers, board members, and other community organizations.

The organization must establish a central location where crisis-response team members will meet in the event of a crisis. It is important to keep a copy of all materials related to handling a crisis, including worksheets and manuals, in a central location, so that team members know where to find this information. The crisis-management plan must be reviewed annually. When a crisis occurs, people may have little time to think or react, which why it is so important to call the crisis-response team together and gather all of the facts available. The group must ask every potential question, and then find the answers. Were all safety guidelines and organization policies being followed? Consider the legal aspects of the crisis. Did the situation involve minors? While an attorney might advise "no comment" in many situations, consider that public opinion develops immediately. A carefully worded statement or key message points will offer clarity and reassurance to parents, other children, staff, volunteers, media, and the public (Figure 2-1). Making arrangements for ongoing communication with legal counsel and insurance agents is also very important. The emergency or incident that caused the crisis may be over in a matter of minutes, but the follow-up to a crisis can take days, weeks, or even months.

- Remain calm. Be honest and compassionate. Show concern for children and youth, their welfare, and their families.

- Designate one media spokesperson. Only one person should communicate with the media to ensure a consistent message.

- Designate one area for media interviews. This policy protects children, volunteers, and staff from media wandering through the facility asking difficult questions.

- Determine key message points. Keep answers brief. Answer the reporter's question and then stop talking. Television reporters in particular are looking for a short "sound bite." If an answer is too long or rambling, the speaker runs the risk of being edited out of context. Remember that a speaker gets to make only two or three key points. A good example of a beginning key message for a youth program is, "Ensuring that children have a safe and pleasant experience is our first priority."

- Avoid the use of jargon.

- Release only confirmed facts. Never speculate or answer hypothetical "what if" questions.

- Never lie or say "no comment." To the public, a "no comment" response often is the equivalent of "guilty" or "they're hiding something." If a speaker doesn't know the answer, he should say so, and then offer to track down the information for the reporter. If the information truly cannot be released because of a child's age or parent's request, say so.

- Do the homework. Know as much about the situation in advance as possible.

- Never place blame, but defuse negatives when possible.

- Be respectful of media deadlines. Ask the reporter what his deadline is. Be accessible and return phone calls within the hour.

- Request the general topic of an interview in advance; specific interview questions will not be available.

- Never ask to review a story before it airs or goes to press.

- Never speak "off the record."

Figure 2-1. Tips for dealing with the media in a crisis

RISK REDUCTION, CONTROL, AND ANALYSIS

Chapter Three

The risk-reduction plan is a major part of the overall risk-management plan. Risks cannot be avoided, but with good planning the severity and frequency of incidents can be reduced. To develop a risk-reduction plan, the organization needs to devise a prevention/intervention system that will reduce risks and help to handle emergencies and crisis situations.

Even if the decision is to handle a risk by transferring it to an insurance company or other party, or to retain it because it is not very frequent or severe, additional strategies can be implemented to save on insurance premiums or minimize the loss of reserves. In fact, by analyzing the transferred or retained risks, the organization may not only be able to reduce the cost of transferring or retaining risks, but also possibly avoid them altogether. For example, if a program site has a vandalism problem, hiring a part-time security guard or a caretaker to live on the site may save more money than paying the higher insurance premium and the accompanying deductible. Another way to receive a lower premium is by training staff in injury-control strategies.

The worksheets in this book are designed to help identify, evaluate, reduce, prevent, or control loss through prevention planning and implementation for the office and each program site. However, even with the best prevention plans, occasionally an emergency or crisis will happen. The crisis worksheets help identify those actions that must be taken immediately to intervene during or after an emergency or crisis, thus preventing or reducing further loss. These crisis worksheets often provide the basic information needed to provide staff members with the specific emergency procedures related to their jobs.

The risk-reduction plan is a major part of the overall risk-management plan.

Intervention Points

Several points that occur prior to, during, and after an incident—called intervention points—can be taken advantage of to help reduce the risk of loss. The risk of loss might be reduced by identifying intervention strategies for contributing factors, such as the human factor, the agent factor, or the environmental factor at these points.

Human Factors

Questions that may help identify intervention strategies that address human factors are divided into two categories. Those involving the participant, such as age, sex, skills, behavior, protective equipment, or experience, include the following:

- Can skill or experience levels improve?
- Can general or specific conditioning be improved?
- Are the problems and interventions linked to any known male and/or female physiological problems and/or differences?
- Is protective equipment needed or worn?
- Can protective equipment be made more easily usable, more attractive, or less costly?
- Can physical examinations be required before participation?
- Can certain disabled individuals or certain age groups be restricted from participation?
- Is a particular type of training or education needed?
- Can re-entry to activity after injury be restricted?
- Can behavior be modified?
- Can the injured person be stabilized, treated, and/or rehabilitated?

Those questions involving other persons, such as program leaders, specialists, supervisors, rescuers, peers, and administrators, are as follows:

- Can supervision be improved?
- Can a "peer pressure" be modified?
- Can an "image" problem be changed?
- Does maintaining the hazard offer a socio-cultural advantage? Can this issue be addressed?
- Can officiating and/or coaching change?
- Can legislation be introduced?
- Can rescue training be improved?
- Can improvements be made in the system of rescue treatment or rehabilitation?

- Can "game" rules be modified?
- Can some administrative action be taken?

Agent Factors

The agent factor of injury is energy. In effect, an injury results when an excessive or inappropriate energy exchange occurs between a person and the environment. If this energy is more than the body can withstand, injury occurs. Intervention with the "agent" includes factors such as choice of equipment, energy source or form, and the pathway of transmission. Safety equipment such as helmets and pads are often needed as preventive devices to help the body tolerate excessive energy. Questions that may help identify intervention strategies with agent factors are as follows:

- Can safety equipment prevent the hazard by making the body more tolerant of the hazard (e.g., arm guards for archery, helmets for riding and climbing)?
- Can the rate or spatial distribution of release of the hazard from its source be modified (e.g. break-away ski bindings)?
- Can the individual be protected from the hazard by a barrier (e.g., a fence around a pool)?

Environmental Factors

An injury may also result from interference with normal exchanges between the body and the environment, as would be the case in drowning. Using a waterfront activity as an example, the plan might include providing diving or safety instructions to the person and performing maintenance checks of the diving board or waterfront environment. An individual might intervene prior to any incident by being sure that only one person is on the board at a time or that all persons diving must demonstrate a certain diving skill level before being allowed on the board. Many programs have had to eliminate diving boards because of insurance requirements.

The plan may also include having lifeguards on hand to rescue the victim and having safety equipment, such as backboards, as well as medical services available to reduce further injury. Other environmental factors include hazards such as location, lighting, weather, maintenance, and size. Questions that may help identify intervention strategies with environmental factors are as follows:

- Can the creation of the hazard be prevented?
- Can the extent of the hazard be reduced?
- Can the release of the hazard be prevented?
- Can the individual be separated from the hazard by time or space (e.g., traffic limits and warning signs)?
- Can the relevant basic qualities of the hazard be modified (e.g., surface under adventure/challenge equipment, equipment design)?

Accident and Incident Analysis

Many of these questions can be answered with existing rules, training, maintenance routines, emergency procedures, etc., but a thorough analysis of accident or incident reports may show trends that require further study. Are certain activities or persons sustaining more injuries? What circumstances lead to the incident? Did the emergency procedures reduce or prevent compounding the injury or property the damage potential for loss? Such an analysis can be used to plan intervention strategies and reduce or prevent injuries and/or loss of resources. Figure 3-1 illustrates the risk-management program to reduce and control the extent of loss in money, personal injury, or property damage.

Risk-Management Planning

A **risk** is an uncertainty or probability concerning the loss of resources.

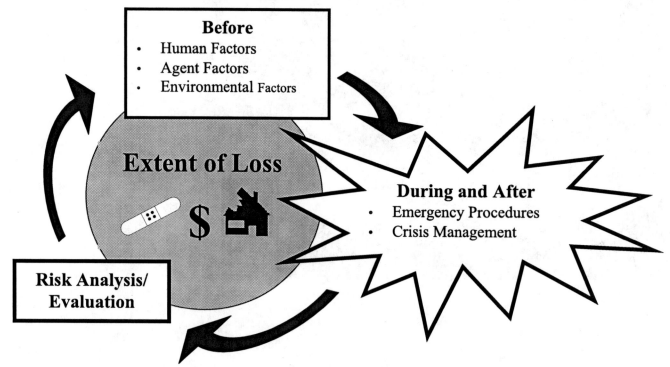

Risk-Management Plan
Systems to identify, evaluate, reduce, prevent or control the loss.

Risk-Identification
Exposure Categories
- Standard of Care
- Human resources
- Operational
- Financial
- Contracts
- Property

Risk-Treatment
Techniques
Risk-Financing Techniques
- Transfer
- Retain
Risk-Control Techniques
- Reduce
- Avoid

Intervention Points

Before
- Human Factors
- Agent Factors
- Environmental Factors

Extent of Loss

During and After
- Emergency Procedures
- Crisis Management

Risk Analysis/
Evaluation

Figure 3-1. Risk-management planning

It is important to look at all of the intervention points when designing the plan. It is also important to understand that some practical limitations exist with intervention strategies. These limitations usually involve the "human" factor. Consider what contributing factors entice or deter persons from taking the risk of embezzlement, breaking and entering, risking injury using broken equipment, overloading a car, or committing child abuse. How these and other incidents are prevented or handled when a crisis does occur will determine the extent of loss.

Youth and young adults often view safety rules or devices as interfering with the adventure and the thrill of risk-taking and rule-breaking, or they may just feel that "it will not happen to them" or that the rules are just too bothersome. For example, it is difficult to get people to wear life jackets and, in some cases, safety helmets. Youth need to be involved in designing the injury intervention strategies. Six basic steps should be considered when working with youth:

- Identify the injuries that have or could occur in each activity.

- Study what factor or factors contributed to the injury—the person, the agent, or the environment

- Assess intervention options that could be implemented to reduce or eliminate the contributing factors.

- Determine when intervention could most effectively be applied.

- Select and implement appropriate interventions.

- Evaluate impact.

Strategies should be consistent with the standards of the field and become the accepted way to participate in the activity. Then, the contributing factors leading to injury must be analyzed, along with limitations that might exist, to determine if such intervention will prevent loss or how much the frequency or severity of loss will be reduced.

Developing a risk-reduction plan, including injury-control strategies, should be the joint effort of many people. The worksheets in this book are designed to apply to many intervention points and emergency situations and become the risk-reduction and risk-control plan for preventing and handling almost any incident that may occur.

Risk Analysis

Risk management is an ongoing systematic process that requires planning, implementation, monitoring, and evaluation. The plans should be reviewed and/or revised periodically. This point is especially true at the opening and closing of the program season or any time the plan has been tested in actual crisis or emergency use. The ongoing risk-management monitoring is the responsibility of the organization's director and/or program administrator, and key volunteers related to a specific program.

- Ongoing monitoring includes six basic functions:

- Analyzing any new operations or activities proposed to identify potential exposures to loss

- Keeping abreast of trends, lawsuits, new laws, issues surrounding accidents, or incidents of other organizations and schools in the community and/or country

- Reviewing all incident/accident reports to identify trends or situations requiring preventative action

- Investigating any serious or fatal accidents or illnesses and developing any recommendations or changes needed to the risk-management plan and/or organization policies

- Developing or revising risk-management training plans and disseminating procedures or policies regarding safety and risk management

- Visiting program sites during operation and discussing the risk-management plan for the operation and activities with program administrators. Likewise, doing a specific review of the main office operations. Sometimes people overlook the things they see every day.

A year-to-year evaluative comparison may identify trends or problems that need to be addressed. A good risk manager is constantly alert to factors that need evaluation and welcomes input from other internal and external sources.

SUPERVISION, BEHAVIOR, AND CHILD-ABUSE PROTECTION

Chapter Four

Every organization that serves children has a legal duty to protect the children in its care. Therefore, the supervision of volunteer and paid staff and the adequacy of supervision for participants are key issues in any risk-management plan. The knowledge of, and the expectations for, appropriate behavior and the consequences of inappropriate behavior are important for both participants and staff. This chapter defines adequate or proper supervision of children and staff, describes positive behavior-management and disciplinary techniques, and provides guidelines for reducing the risk of child abuse.

Supervision of Children

In any activity sponsored by an organization serving youth, an inherent duty exists to supervise the participants. The responsibility for supervision involves selecting suitable and competent leadership and providing an environment that is relatively safe and free from harm, but not providing a guarantee or being an ensurer of safety. This responsibility also includes managing behavior, enforcing rules and procedures, providing emergency care, and being aware of, and responding to, dangerous conditions or interference from people outside the program.

Several types of supervision exist. Specific supervision is required for people in activities that need instruction and/or a person skilled and knowledgeable in the activity. That supervisor must be able to judge the participants' knowledge and skill levels, their appreciation for the potential risks or injuries, and their behavior-related or mental ability to participate in the activity. More specific supervision may be needed when the behavior of one or several participants may cause injury to themselves or others.

General supervision is based more on participant or group behavior in an activity or in an area. The supervisor needs to be aware of the behavior of individuals and of groups of people, the general area, and any dangerous conditions. A supervisor should always be within sight or sound of the children in his care. A change in the type of supervision may be needed when the skill and experience levels of a participant change. The supervisor still needs a level of skill in the activity to recognize dangerous behavior or conditions. The participant takes on some of the responsibility to perform as instructed and to abide by safety rules.

The question of who has the duty to provide supervision before or after an activity or program depends on the agreed upon responsibility for care between the parent and the program operator. For example, when children are on their way to a program after school, are dropped off at a bus stop after day camp, or take public transportation to a baseball game, who is responsible for supervision? If they are waiting on a snack or lunch to be served, moving from one activity to another, or finishing a swim and getting ready for dinner, who is responsible for supervision? What if two children get into a fight during this time? The answer may depend on how clear the responsibility for supervision was during that time and whether the supervision provided was adequate.

In addition to the type of supervision, it is important that an overall plan for supervision exists and that the expectations for being "on duty" are clearly understood. The competency of the person selected to supervise the situation, the location of the supervisor, the number of supervisors needed, the ratio of supervisors to participants, the age and/or experience of the participants, the type of activity, and the physical condition of the participants should all be taken into consideration in the supervision plan. These elements should be considered individually and in combination. A program may have enough supervisors, but they might not be in the right location, know what was expected of them, or know how to look for dangerous situations.

Two other key parts of a plan for supervision are the administration of the plan and the appropriateness of the plan itself. Are the rules and procedures appropriate for the situation? Are the deployment of staff and the supervision of that staff adequate and consistent with the plan? Have the rules been made known to the staff performing the duty and to the participants?

Supervision of Staff Members Who Directly Supervise Children

The staff supervising other staff members who have the direct responsibility for, and a relationship with, children play a key role in administering the supervision plan. The plan should include observation of the relationship between children and staff during both the planned activity times and the more informal free time or group living times. It should include circulation or observation at different times during the day and observation of any changes in how the children are responding to the staff or other participants.

Staff conferences should be held frequently and include both the performance of the job and feedback on the observed relationships. Are the staff members following the stated policies and disciplinary guidelines in the plan? Any identified problems should be discussed, documented, and followed up on.

Managing Children's Behavior

Managing behavior relevant to risk management involves several aspects. The first is the organization's philosophy and/or policies of behavior management and the management of group and individual behaviors of children. This aspect includes inappropriate discipline or abuse by persons such as volunteers, paid staff, or other participants involved in the program. The second aspect includes the intervening acts of third parties or people not directly involved or invited to participate in the program. This second concern, which includes intruders, such as those committing criminal acts, is addressed in Worksheets O-25 and P-8.

Effective behavior management begins with the program philosophy, is influenced by the environment, and is carried out with agreeable limits and boundaries. Discipline is a dynamic process of child guidance. The long-term goal is to encourage the development of self-control. Youth programs can have a major influence on a child's development. Paid and volunteer staff have a responsibility to help children learn to be self-directed and in control of their behavior. The basic principle concerning the appropriate type of discipline is that the organization has a responsibility to maintain control of participants, but the techniques used must not injure the child, emotionally or physically.

Behavior management should build on a child's need to develop a sense of self-worth. To promote this development, the program must be carefully planned to foster positive behavior. To accomplish this goal, many programs provide experiences in which:

- Children are involved in rule setting and help determine the consequences for misbehavior

- The site and activities are set up to promote positive interaction among children

- Staff members encourage children to learn how to solve problems and settle differences among themselves

The courts, however, when trying to establish whether appropriate supervision was in place, may look at the context or cause of the behavior and the responsibility of the supervisor to intervene. Was the injury caused because the participants were involved in "horseplay," just playing and had no intention of hurting anyone, being rowdy with intentions of interfering with someone, or committing an actual assault or attack on another person? Each of these terms attempts to classify the type of behavior that caused the injury and the level of supervision expected in each category. Was the incident foreseeable, had this behavior occurred before, or was something happening beforehand to provoke the behavior?

For example, when a child's behavior creates a risk for the emotional or physical health and safety of another child or the staff, the following procedures should be followed:

- The child is separated from the problem activity or situation.

- A staff member listens to the child and discusses the consequences of further misbehavior.

- Repeated misbehavior will be handled by a telephone conversation or conference with the parent (and may include the supervisor or director).

- The parent, child, and staff member (and supervisor or director) agree to a plan that will improve behavior or face the possibility of termination from the program.

The development of behavior-management policies should include more than consequences for misbehavior. To be effective, a variety of positive strategies should be employed.

Preventive strategies will keep conflict and stress to a minimum. For example:

- The environment is conducive to positive interaction.
- Adults model appropriate behavior and use their authority wisely.
- Staff members develop caring relationships with youth.
- Program activities are flexible in response to the changing interests of children.
- Activities are age appropriate, and relevant to the needs, interests, values, and capabilities of youth.
- Emotional expression is encouraged.

Interactive strategies will provide youth and adults the opportunity to deal constructively with stress and conflict. For example:

- Limits for behavior are fair, reasonable, and understood by youth.
- Youth understand the natural and logical consequences of exceeding limits.
- Adults help youth appropriately express negative feelings.
- Problem-solving and conflict-resolution opportunities are included in the program.
- A democratic decision-making process is used.
- Adults find opportunities to help youth see themselves as kind, cooperative persons who are capable of solving problems and resolving conflict.
- Praise and encouragement recognize actual effort and accomplishment (rather than "good character").
- Adults redirect aimless or inappropriate behavior into more constructive activities.

Crisis strategies will be necessary when youth and/or adults face occasional loss of control. For example:

- When adults lose control, they practice emergency coping techniques such as leaving the situation, deep breathing, etc.
- When youth lose control, staff members handle them in accordance with the program's policy. At no time should corporal punishment or

any other humiliating or frightening discipline techniques be used as a means of controlling behavior.

When a child's out-of-control behavior jeopardizes the physical or emotional health and safety of themselves, other children, or adults, the following actions are recommended:

- If the child threatens physical harm, staff members should physically restrain him with a minimum amount of force.

- Staff members must actively listen to the child's expression of hurt and anger.

- Staff members must communicate through verbal and nonverbal messages that they have faith in the child's ability to learn and practice self-control.

- Staff members should seek to understand the underlying causes of the crisis.

- When the child is calm, staff members should encourage him to explore possible problems and solutions related to the situation.

- Staff members should help the child rejoin the group when he is ready.

When out-of-control or destructive behavior becomes chronic or severe, the parent or guardian should be contacted by the program director. The parent, child, and the program director should discuss the situation in person or by phone, and develop an agreement for improvement. An agreement spelling out the behavior needed for improvement must be approved by the parent and signed by the child and the director. The program director monitors progress, provides encouragement to the child, and informs the parent of the results.

If a parent or child is unwilling to cooperate toward the improvement of the behavior, dismissal from the program may be necessary. Refer to Appendix 16a for dismissal policies. If the program frequently is dealing with out-of-control children, a closer look at the program's policies and practices is needed. A small minority of children should fall into this category.

Programs serving kids with special needs should develop an individualized behavior-management plan, if necessary. The parent and classroom teachers should be consulted in this process.

When a person intentionally does harm to another person, it may be considered assault and battery or "willful and wanton conduct." Particularly in sports such as football, soccer, and softball, an overt intention may exist to injure another player, but the utter disregard for the safety of others can bring liability for "reckless disregard" that infers intent to injure. Often this situation occurs after the "whistle has blown" to stop play or when a player has violated the rules and caused an injury. If the play is unduly rough and increases the likelihood of injury, and the supervisor did not intervene and enforce the rules, the supervisor can also be held negligent in failing to protect the children from this unreasonable risk of injury.

Bullying is a growing concern in schools and camps. According to the U.S. Department of Health and Human Services (USDHHS), bullying is defined as an aggressive behavior that is intentional, repeated over time, and involves an imbalance of power or strength. Bullying is a form of victimization and peer abuse. Bullies are often popular, and have power and social status. They usually have strong leadership skills and a small group of friends that encourage their behavior. It is important that staff recognize when these skills are used inappropriately and do not mistake them as positive traits or recognize them with favoritism.

> Studies show that between 15 and 25 percent of U.S. students are bullied with some frequency, while 15 to 20 percent report that they bully others with some frequency. Boys are more likely than girls to bully others. Girls frequently report being bullied by both boys and girls, but boys are most often bullied only by other boys (USDHHS).

Children who are being bullied may have a hard time defending themselves. Children who are being bullied may appear moody or depressed, have unexplained bruises or cuts, have torn or missing clothes or belongings, and be reluctant to go some places or participate in some activities. If a staff member suspects that a child is being excluded or bullied, he should remember that his attention is very powerful and is sought by each child. This attention will be noticed and show other children that he believes that the bullied child is worth spending time with. If he feels that he should talk with the child about the situation, he should begin by being supportive, telling the child that he is concerned about him, and asking questions. Sometimes youth are reluctant to talk about it. They may be ashamed or believe that an adult cannot or will not do anything about it. It is not helpful to tell them to work it out with the bully or to discuss it in a group with the bully present. However, staff members should take care to not build a dependency on the staff to always rescue them. Instead, staff members can help bullied children develop the skills to reduce the emotional reaction they exhibit and feel successful and included in the group. These children may need help in not blaming themselves and assistance from peers to help them to feel that they belong.

Staff members have a critical role to play in helping to stop bullying. It is their responsibility to be aware of the social interactions in the group and to take appropriate action to protect children from serious bullying. Staff members should discuss the situation and the consequences for bullying with their supervisor or director.

Reducing the Risk of Child Abuse

Studies provide information about the prevalence of child abuse to both boys and girls. Physical and sexual abuse each make up approximately one-third of reported child abuse, while neglect and emotional abuse account for the last third. It is estimated that one in three girls and one in seven boys will be sexually abused before their eighteenth birthdays. Children between the ages of five and 12 are at the greatest risk of sexual abuse. Some victims of serious bullying are verbally, sexually, or physically abused by other children.

- Child abuse can take many forms, including the following:

- Physical abuse includes shaking, beating, or causing other nonaccidental physical injuries such as bruises, broken bones, burns, or cuts.

- Sexual abuse includes intercourse, incest, rape, sodomy, or using children in pornography, prostitution, or other types of sexual activity.

- Emotional abuse includes verbal abuse and vulgarity and is evidenced by severe anxiety, depression, withdrawal, or improper aggressive behavior as diagnosed by a medical doctor or psychologist.

- Negligent treatment includes failure to provide warmth, affection, supervision, food, shelter, or attention. Allowing children to live in a very dirty house that could be a health hazard may also be considered neglect.

- Exploitation involves the use of a child by a parent, guardian, or custodian for material gain.

- Abandonment involves the failure of the parent to provide reasonable support or to maintain regular contact with the child, including providing normal supervision, when such failure is intentional and continues for an indefinite period.

Symptoms of Abuse

It is important to know that many children are afraid to tell anyone that they are being abused. They may, however, reveal this fact indirectly. It is shown in their drawings, through their stories, and through the way they respond when someone touches them. Most abused children show some of the following symptoms:

- Low self-esteem
- Anger
- Guilt
- Aggressive or disruptive behavior
- Withdrawal
- Delinquent behavior
- Poor school performance

Physical abuse, which is usually the easiest form of abuse to detect, occurs when someone inflicts bodily harm on another, resulting in physical injury. Most injuries are visible, such as burns, cuts, and bruises. However, broken bones, head injuries, and internal injuries may not be visible.

Abusers may try to avoid detection by causing injuries where they are covered with clothes or by devising stories to explain the injury. The victim may even agree with the story or make up another story to explain the injuries. Sometimes the victimized child is hesitant and the story may not substantiate the injuries sustained. Investigators will compare the injury with the story given to them by the child and the caretaker. Some indicators of physical abuse are as follows:

- Frequent unexplained injuries, bruises, or burns that are left untreated
- Fear of receiving medical help
- Bald spots (a sign of hair pulling)
- Abdominal swelling
- Avoidance of physical contact with others
- Wearing of clothing that covers the arms and legs, even in hot weather

Neglect is the failure to provide basic care for a child, including food, clothes, health care, shelter, and supervision. It usually involves a combination of several neglectful behaviors. Some indicators of neglect in children include the following:

- Being late or arriving early and staying late
- Being tired, listless, or exhausted
- Attempting suicide
- Begging or stealing food
- Being hungry
- Appearing dirty or inappropriately dressed
- Having unattended physical problems
- Being detached or overly dependent

Sexual abuse includes a variety of inappropriate behaviors, including those that are both direct and indirect mistreatment by an adult or another child. Indirect forms include pornography, voyeurism, or observation of a child while he is undressing, bathing, or urinating. Direct sexual abuse includes fondling private parts, observing masturbation, or making oral-genital contact or penetration. This event could be adult to child, child to adult, or child to child.

In most cases, the abuser is known or related to the child and may have an ongoing, trusting relationship built over time. The younger the child, the more likely he is to believe that the abuse is a show of affection. Children that are victims of sexual abuse often:

- Have unusual interest in, or knowledge of, sexual matters
- Are extremely moody
- Fear touching by others
- Have poor relationships with the opposite sex
- Are reluctant to be left alone with a particular person
- Exhibit overly aggressive behavior
- Cry easily
- Draw genitals or other related objects
- Receive unexplained gifts or money
- Run away from home often
- Have nightmares or insomnia
- Exhibit regressive behaviors, such as bed wetting
- Have itching or pain in genital areas

Children need to feel cared for and safe. Emotional abuse involves belittling, criticizing, and making a child feel worthless, unloved, and generally put down, most often verbally. This mistreatment may result in vicious emotional scars that impair psychological growth and development. These scars may include feelings of rejection, humiliation, intimidation, fear, and guilt.

While children are generally resilient, emotional abuse inflicted over a period of time, especially by a trusted adult, can shatter a child's self-image and undermine his sense of personal value. A child may not be able to interpret the meaning behind hurtful words and begin to believe them. Emotional abuse, like sexual abuse, may cause more harm to the child because the effects are hidden and deeper than the effects of physical abuse. A victimized child may have low self-esteem and be afraid to tell anyone.

Many cases of sexual abuse, physical abuse, or neglect also involve emotional abuse. Almost every state defines chronic, serious emotional abuse as a crime and thus a reportable offense. However, such cases are rarely prosecuted, because it is difficult to prove that such abuse has occurred and that the child has suffered severe psychological harm.

Adults that emotionally abuse children may do so for some of the same reasons that cause adults to physically abuse children. They may be under stress, unable to cope, have unreasonably high expectations of the child, or be patterning the behavior they experienced as a child. In contract to physical or sexual abuse, most people that emotionally abuse are unaware of their verbal assaults on a child. Some children are able to overcome such treatment, perhaps because some other adult in their life helps them understand that they are important and loved and that the hurtful words of one adult are not their fault or true. Children that are emotionally abused often:

- Show antisocial behaviors
- Are withdrawn
- Have some suicidal behaviors
- Act out their abuse by being abusive to other children

It is important that persons entrusted with children listen to what a child is saying, be sensitive to when pressures are building up, and take time to regain composure when a child acts out, instead of taking it out on the child. Times will arise when a staff member loses control and behaves in a way that can harm a child. Supervisors and coworkers can help by discussing the behavior in question with the program leader and reassuring the child that people do care about him. If the behavior continues, steps must be taken to remove the person from leadership. If a child is in a relationship where he is being seriously abused, the abuse must be reported to the authorities.

Risk-Reduction Strategies

It is safe to say that no one action will eliminate the risk of abuse. A combination of actions is the best approach to protecting children from abuse. The following guidelines may serve as risk-reduction strategies for organizations to use in formulating their own policies and procedures:

- Ensure that persons who are selected to work within the agency are not actual or suspected child abusers.
- Clarify expectations of staff behavior with children and ensure that staff members have the skills necessary to work with children.
- Establish policies that forbid contact between participants and paid or volunteer staff members outside the program without a signed statement from the parents acknowledging that they take full responsibility for overseeing the contact.
- Share part of the responsibility for identifying and eliminating abuse with parents.
- Teach children how to avoid abuse and get help in cases of real or threatened abuse.
- Handle allegations of abuse against personnel in a manner that protects all parties.

Because no single absolutely "right" thing exists to address each strategy, common sense and good judgment must be used. Management policies and procedures will vary based on local situations. Laws differ from state to state and are changing rapidly in response to federal legislation.

Implementing Screening and Relationship Procedures

The selection of the best qualified applicants and screening for possible child abusers or sex offenders are serious responsibilities. The organization should do criminal background checks, develop other procedures to screen out potential abusers, and ensure that any incidences of abuse are quickly identified and addressed. Remember that no profile for a "typical" child abuser or sex offender exists. They are as likely as any other applicant to appear pleasant and experienced in working with individual children and/or groups of children. Staff members should be informed that inappropriate behavior that threatens the health and safety of children will not be tolerated and that any criminal conduct will be reported to the authorities.

At least two adults should be present during program activities. The presence of two adults ensures backup coverage in case of emergency, prevents one person from having exclusive contact with a group of children, and helps protect adults from false allegations of child abuse.

The interaction of staff members and children sets the stage for achieving an organization's goals. Both successes and failures can be traced to the staff–child relationship. To promote positive and supportive relationships and to eliminate situations that may lend themselves to abuse, staff members should be trained in appropriate discipline and rewarding practices.

Program volunteers and paid staff members should never discipline children by use of physical punishment or isolation, or by failing to provide the necessities of life, such as food, shelter, and attention. They should not verbally or emotionally abuse or punish children. Staff members should also be taught appropriate techniques for showing affection, approval, sympathy, and support.

Staff members should be informed of the desirability of not being alone with a single child, unobserved by others without the knowledge of the program supervisor or another adult. When young children are taken on field trips or are otherwise away from their familiar program site, program leaders should have a simple means of identifying themselves (by name tag or clothing) so that children can locate them quickly. Children should be instructed to avoid any person not so identified.

Staff should respect the privacy of each child. Places must be provided for children and adults to change clothes, and two adults must be present when supervising showers. Boys and girls must have separate, private facilities for changing and showering.

Establish policies that forbid the exchange of contact information of any kind between participants and staff members, whether paid or volunteer, that may be used outside the program. Since children can often "find" a staff member on the Internet, encourage parents to be aware of their children's online activities and supervise them as they would any other aspect of life in their home.

Reporting Alleged Child Abuse

Suspected child abuse must be reported to the appropriate person or authority. Most states have mandatory reporting to authorities by some professions, though the appropriate authority may vary from state to state.

Any person who reasonably believes that a minor is, or has been, the victim of physical injury, abuse, child abuse, a reportable offense, or neglect that appears to have been inflicted on the minor by other than accidental means or that is not explained by the available medical history as being accidental in nature should immediately report or cause reports to be made of this information to a peace office or to Child Protective Services. This also includes anyone who reasonably believes that a denial or deprivation of necessary medical treatment or surgical care or nourishment has been made with the intent to cause or allow the death of an infant. The following persons are required by law to report any suspected abuse:

- Any physician, physician's assistant, optometrist, dentist, osteopath, chiropractor, podiatrist, behavioral health professional, nurse, psychologist, counselor, or social worker who develops the reasonable belief in the course of treating a patient

- Any peace officer, member of the clergy, priest, or Christian Science practitioner

- The parent, stepparent, or guardian of the minor

- School personnel or domestic violence victim advocates who develop the reasonable belief in the course of their employment

- Any other person who has responsibility for the care or treatment of the minor

A person making a report or providing information about a child is immune from civil or criminal liability unless such person has been charged with, or is suspected of, the abuse or neglect in question. A person acting with malice who knowingly or intentionally makes a false report of child abuse and neglect or who coerces another person to make a false report is guilty of a crime. A person who knowingly and intentionally falsely accuses another of maliciously making a false report of child abuse and neglect is also guilty of a crime.

In some cases, a child will disclose abuse to a trusted staff member. This report may stem from a situation at home or at some other place or program. Staff members should be instructed on what to do if a child discloses an abusive situation to them. They should take the child seriously and find a place that seems safe to the child. The place should be private and free from distractions, but within view of others. Staff members should assure privacy, but should not promise that they won't tell anyone or say something that may contradict the authorities. They should explain that the information will be confidential unless someone is hurting them. Staff members should adhere to the following guidelines:

- Be calm and show concern.
- Believe the child.
- Gather information but don't make judgments.
- Report to local child protective services.
- Leave the investigation to the authorities.
- Reassure the child that it's not his fault. Report again if the suspected abuse continues.

Sharing the Responsibility With Parents

An agency has a responsibility to inform and involve parents in efforts to eliminate abuse. Parents can play a key role in monitoring the behavior of paid and volunteer staff, as well as children. Parents should be informed about the program that their child is involved in, including a general description of activities, where they will take place, and the names of staff members responsible for the child's program.

Parents and guardians could sign a special activity permission slip for any activity scheduled at a time or place outside the regularly scheduled program. This action is different from a parent giving permission and taking full responsibility for contact between the child and a staff member outside the program. Parents should be encouraged to visit program sites and observe operation. Both announced and unannounced visits should be encouraged.

A check-in and check-out system should be maintained at program sites where children arrive and leave individually. Under no circumstances should children be released to anyone other than the parent, unless authorized in writing by the custodial parent or guardian. Children should not be released to adults under the influence of alcohol or other drugs. Finally, educational programs and/or materials on child abuse can be made available to parents through direct sponsorship of the organization or a collaborative effort with other agencies.

Teaching Children to Avoid Abuse

Many child-abuse-prevention programs aimed at children have been developed in recent years. In most comprehensive programs, children are taught that they own their bodies and have the right to decide who can touch them, as well as how and when they can be touched.

Children are taught to say "no" when touching is inappropriate and how to differentiate a good touch from a bad touch. They are taught to express their feelings regarding where touching is appropriate. Children are taught to differentiate appropriate and inappropriate secrets. And, most importantly, children are taught to tell a trusted person about any inappropriate behavior by adults. For prevention efforts to be effective, an ongoing effort must be made to provide children with frequent and regular access to the information they need to make good decisions.

Protecting All Parties

The organization should examine programs and identify situations that may provide a risk for child abuse and make program modifications to reduce the risk. Organizations should make contact with local child protective services before any allegations are made and find out how the organization can work with the services, what information they want, how they want it, and from whom.

When an allegation of abuse is made, it is essential that the interests of all parties affected or potentially affected by the allegations are protected. Thus, agencies often formulate policies and procedures to ensure protection of the child, the family, the accused person, and the agency.

For each program, the director or another person should be designated as the contact person for reporting suspected child abuse. In some states, the person the child disclosed the alleged abuse to is the mandated reporter. The contact person should follow the procedures established by the agency and the reporting procedure prescribed by the local child abuse investigative body. A written incident report should be completed on the same day the incident is reported. A decision needs to be made by the contact person, in consultation with the local investigative body, regarding how the child's parent or guardian will be notified of the report. Of course, parents always have the right to report any disclosure their child has made to them.

Any staff person, paid or volunteer, involved in a reported incident of child abuse should be suspended immediately from all activities involving the supervision of children. Employed staff may be suspended with pay until the appropriate level of investigation is conducted and appropriate action can be taken. Reinstatement of staff, paid or volunteer, to their duties occurs only after all allegations have been cleared to the satisfaction of the agency and/or the investigative body. Staff should maintain confidentiality in the handling of information in this area and are instructed to discuss matters pertaining to abuse or suspected abuse only with the contact person or investigating body.

Camp Fire USA is serious about the steps that must be taken to reduce the possibility of child abuse within its programs and about the kind of behavior management that will build a child's sense of self-worth. Camp Fire USA also is serious about its responsibility to protect all children by recognizing the symptoms of abuse and reporting suspected abuse. A sample of Recommended Program Policies for Child Abuse Prevention (or Child Protection) in Camp Fire USA Programs is in Appendix 17.

Several years ago, the National Assembly Child Sexual Abuse Task Force compiled a checklist of items that are being included in many youth agencies' strategies for the prevention of child sexual abuse (Figure 4-1). Since then, National Assembly Publications has identified a number of resources on child protection and screening volunteers. Visit www.nassembly.org/nassembly/ NAPublications.htm for more information.

❑   Staff volunteer screening procedures

❑   Administrative staff training

❑   Supervisor staff training

❑   Program leader training

❑   Youth leader training

❑   Parent education piece

❑   Procedures for handling accusations

❑   Youth education piece

❑   Youth training or program piece

❑   Procedures for reporting child abuse

❑   Legislative or advocacy action

❑   Procedures on records retention

❑   Procedures for witness requests

❑   Procedures for criminal-record checks

❑   Child sexual abuse insurance coverage

❑   Procedures for dealing with public and media

❑   Notification of parents of other participants

❑   Procedures for providing counseling for victims and staff

Figure 4-1. National Assembly Child Sexual Abuse Prevention Checklist

ORGANIZATIONAL RISK-MANAGEMENT PLANNING

Chapter Five

The following worksheets are tools to help administrators create a risk-management plan that will fit the circumstances of managing their organization and the site(s) and program(s) they provide. Such planning will not guarantee safety and should never substitute for legal advice. With the increase of lawsuits, new regulations, and emerging social issues, compiling this information will help alleviate the fear and feelings of powerlessness that administrators often face when trying to protect their organizations. A risk-management plan is essential to help protect the future of the agency by reducing the number of incidents, anticipating risks, and responding appropriately.

This chapter focuses on the organization's risk-management plan, crisis management, and planning for the organization's overall operations. The crisis management organizational worksheets (O-1 to O-10) address crisis-management planning and have the information that will be needed immediately. The organizational worksheets (O-11 to O-36) form the noncrisis planning section and include information to help the organization prevent or reduce exposures. Chapter 6 addresses program crisis management (Worksheets P-1 to P-20) and program risk-management planning (Worksheets P-21 to P-63) for each program and/or program site.

The worksheets could be divided by topic and the responsibility for completion assigned to a person skilled in each area. More information about writing the plan is provided in the Preface. Copies of the worksheets are in this book and on the enclosed Resource CD. Electronic worksheets are convenient for writing, making changes, emailing, and printing. The plan is in a table format and will expand as the lines are filled in. When a worksheet is completed and approved, it should be dated, printed, and put in a notebook. It is recommended that the office have an Organizational Risk-Management Plan notebook and a hard copy of each program site's risk-management plan in a master notebook. Each program site should have a copy of its plan. A hard copy and/or one on a disc should also be kept at a site convenient to the crisis response team. Remember, the office and a computer may not always be accessible, and the batteries in a laptop may not be charged and the electric power may be out during a crisis.

All worksheets have a section following the table called "Guidelines and Information to Help Complete the Plan." This section has critical information needed to complete the plan. Be sure to read this section before beginning each worksheet. As the Risk-Management Planning Task Force begins its work, members may want to divide the responsibilities by section, topic, and/or program delivery system.

Any material requiring a policy decision must have board action. Those worksheets that do not apply should be crossed out or noted "DNA," meaning "does not apply." Any intervention points not covered in the worksheets should be written and added to an existing worksheet or a new worksheet and placed into the book.

A few worksheets referred to as organizational worksheets (O) may be added to the program's plan or remain with the organizational plan (in the main office), depending on "need to know" or the assigned responsibility for that topic. For example, organizational policies on how to handle the media could be assigned to one organizational spokesperson, regardless of program or operation. The program site director only needs to have his contact number on the agency contact list. The list of insurance policies might be the same for all office and program sites and be managed by the main office. While the agency contacts may be the same for each site, it is important that each site has a copy in its book. An emergency number for the fire department may be 911 in most communities, but it might not be available at some sites.

#	Topic	Responsibility	Date completed
O-1	Who Is in Charge Where? Identification of person(s) and responsibilities in case of emergency at the office		
O-2	Emergency Phone Numbers Specific phone numbers for emergencies from the office		
O-3	Agency Emergency Contacts Identification of who should be called, where they can be reached, and in what situations		
O-4	Emergency Procedures for Hazards and/or Disasters—Office Identification of site hazards and action taken for the office(s)		
O-5	Emergency Procedures for Office Evacuation and Fires Plan for quickly organizing and evacuating the office		
O-6	Utilities—Office Type of utilities and location of emergency shutdowns for the office		
O-7	First Aid/CPR and Exposure to Bloodborne Pathogens—Office Who has first-aid training, minimum skills needed, where first-aid kits are located at the office, and what they contain		

Figure 5-1. Organizational worksheets

#	Topic	Responsibility	Date completed
O-8	Death of a Participant, Volunteer, Staff Member, or Family Member Procedures for handling fatal accidents or illnesses and for informing a visitor, participant, or staff member of a death in his or her family		
O-9	Emergency Media Plan Procedures for handling and informing the media in case of emergency		
O-10	Report of Alleged Child Abuse Procedures for handling a report of an alleged child-abuse incident, which may create a crisis and must be handled immediately		
O-11	Legal Liabilities of Trustees/Directors A board of trustees/directors can be held liable for failing to take action or taking an action that was inadequate or irresponsible		
O-12	Legal Counsel Selecting and working with legal counsel		
O-13	Office/Site Hazards Identification of natural and man-made hazards and action taken for the office(s), including plans for business interruption		
O-14	Office Operations, Maintenance, and Fire Prevention and Safety Office maintenance responsibilities and person(s) responsible		
O-15	Storage and Handling of Hazardous, Flammable, or Poisonous Materials Supervision and control of flammable, poisonous, and explosive materials		
O-16	Food Handling and Foodborne Illness Plan for handling and serving food in a safe manner to avoid salmonella or food poisoning		

Figure 5-1. Organizational worksheets (cont.)

#	Topic	Responsibility	Date completed
O-17	Serving Persons With Disabilities Information and plan for compliance with the Americans with Disabilities Act		
O-18	Insurance Coverage A listing of insurance, coverage, policy numbers, agents, and phone numbers		
O-19	Reevaluating Insurance Schedule and procedures for reevaluation, adjustments, etc.		
O-20	Insurance Safety Audit for Organization-Owned Sites Date of audit, recommendations made, and actions taken		
O-21	Record Retention and Destruction Establishing a system for retaining, storing, and destroying records		
O-22	Operational Financial Risks Procedures to protect the assets of the organization		
O-23	Business Use of Vehicles and Driver Authorization and Responsibility Identification of vehicles for business use and driver responsibility		
O-24	Fundraising and Special Events Plan to protect the organization's 501 (c) (3) status; establish fundraising policies and procedures that establish credibility and accountability		.
O-25	Security Plan for providing a secure working and service environment that allows business operation to continue in an uninterrupted and orderly fashion		
O-26	Technological Usage and Record Security Plan for staff, volunteer, and vendor access to personal information and computer, internet, telephone, and fax machines for business or personal use		

Figure 5-1. Organizational worksheets (cont.)

#	Topic	Responsibility	Date completed
O-27	Contracts for Services Transferring risk through contracts, and authority to negotiate contracts		
O-28	Screening of Staff and Volunteers Planning, implementing, and documenting the screening process		
O-29	Employment Practices Plan for keeping informed on state and federal laws and the reporting and record-keeping requirements		
O-30	Harassment—Sexual and Other Creating an environment where sexual harassment will not be tolerated		
O-31	Complaints Determining a process for handling complaints		
O-32	Supervision of Staff Supervising staff in the office		
O-33	Product Tampering Plan for dealing with complaints of product tampering		
O-34	Intellectual Property, Copyrights, and Royalties Protecting copyrighted materials and procedures for use of materials protected by copyrights and royalties		
O-35	Incident Report Procedures for maintaining in-depth, consistent information regarding an incident		
O-36	Risk-Reduction Analyses Identifying and evaluating risk-reduction steps		

Figure 5-1. Organizational worksheets (cont.)

ORGANIZATIONAL CRISIS WORKSHEET O-1

Who is in Charge Where?

Rationale

To avoid confusion and prevent misinformation from being given out, each person needs to be aware of his responsibilities and know who is in charge. In the event of a major emergency, the media scans police radios and will quickly arrive on the scene or call by phone. It is important to be prepared so that the media can do their job and the administrators can do theirs. The organization has a responsibility to provide accurate information to the public.

To avoid confusion and prevent misinformation from being given out, each person needs to be aware of his responsibilities and know who is in charge.

Plan

1. In case of emergency, who will be in charge:	Backup Person
At the main office?	
At the site of the emergency if not at a program site or the office?	
While staff are traveling or on a trip?	

2. What are the responsibilities of the person in charge at the site of the emergency?
3. How often will contact be made between the office and the site of emergency if not at the office (e.g., every hour, twice per day)?
4. If the office is not the emergency location, what are the additional responsibilities of the person in charge at the office?
5. Who determines if the office or emergency site will not be operational?
6. In case of emergency, who has the authority to develop brief factual statements, or "key messages," for media release?
7. Who has the authority to approve brief factual statements?
Phone #
8. Use the following as an outline for forming key messages in a brief statement.
The scenario facts [nature of the situation and who (by title or role) is involved]:

Indicate your cooperation with the authorities	
State concern for those involved	
Restate the facts of the scenario without editorializing	
Indicate openness for future updates and response	

The following people can approve a more detailed media release:
9. Who is the official spokesperson designated to respond to the media during an emergency?
10. In addition to the media, to whom should the brief factual statement be given?
11. When and how are other staff members informed and/or trained in their roles (or nonroles) in dealing with the media?

Guidelines and Information to Help Complete the Plan

❏ When clarifying in-town staff responsibilities, consider all of the procedures and all aspects of the operation. Worksheet P-1: Who Is in Charge Where? identifies the staff responsibilities for each program site. In addition to the office and active program sites, other in-town sites, such as a storage building or facility, may be closed or vacant when programs are not in operation. Refer to Worksheet O-5: Emergency Procedures for Office Evacuation and Fires. Organizational charts and staff training should provide the other staff members with information regarding who is in charge and the specific responsibilities of each staff member.

❏ Since the person handling a crisis is usually too busy to handle media inquiries, an official media spokesperson should be identified. A spokesperson should be chosen who has a general understanding of the media, possesses communications ability, and has experience interviewing and handling reporters. This person's responsibility will include speaking in an official capacity for the organization; therefore, he must have knowledge of, and sensitivity to, policies regarding what should or should not be disclosed, as well as some expertise and credibility. Refer to Worksheet O-9: Emergency Media Plan for more information on planning a response to the media.

❏ One person, perhaps the staff person in charge, should be authorized to develop and/or approve a brief factual statement for release to the media as soon as possible following an emergency. A "no comment" or a delay in releasing information may give the appearance of an attempted "cover-up" or result in reports based on rumor or inaccurate information. It is suggested that the brief statement includes the location, the type of incident, when it occurred, and whether it involved adults and/or children. The spokesperson must not give the specific names of persons involved until families have been notified.

❏ Copies of the brief statement should be distributed to all people who might receive inquiries. It should be stressed to staff and volunteers that they should release only the information included in the statement and not speculate about the incident to others. Questions that go beyond the information in the news release should be referred to the official spokesperson.

ORGANIZATIONAL CRISIS WORKSHEET O-2

Emergency Phone Numbers

Rationale

Information about available medical services will simplify and speed up the process of securing the needed treatment in the event of accident, injury, or illness. These emergency telephone numbers need to be posted in the office, along with what to report and the names of staff who can contact officials.

Plan

1. Information to give to an official or medical service:		
Give the name of the reporting party		
Office address		
Office phone #		
Directions to be given in case of emergency		
2. What are the emergency phone numbers and service information for:		
3. Local Officials	Name or Service Community	Number
Fire		
Police		
Sheriff		
Health department		
Animal control officers		
4. Medical Services		
Poison Control Center	Phone #	
Ambulance		
Name of service	Phone #	
What is the estimated response time?		
How many victims can the ambulance transport?		
Who goes with the injured?		
What forms are needed?		
Helicopter		
Name of service	Phone #	

When do you call for a rescue helicopter?	
What is the estimated response time?	
How many victims can the rescue helicopter transport?	
What forms are needed?	
Hospital	
What is the closest available hospital?	Phone #
Directions from the site to the hospital	
How long does it take to get there?	
What forms or pieces of information are needed for treatment?	
Insurance card	Other
When (if ever) is it necessary to call ahead for treatment?	
If needed, who notifies the family?	
What method of payment is required for treatment?	
Who should transport the injured party to the hospital?	
Alternates	
Alternate medical service	
Alternate services (e.g., urgent care service)	Phone #
Directions to the service from the site	
How long does it take to get there?	
Do you need an appointment or prior notification of arrival?	
What forms/information are needed for treatment?	
Insurance card	Other
If needed, who notifies the family?	
What method of a payment is required for treatment?	
Who should transport the ill or injured party to treatment?	
Alternates	
Specialty units (e.g., burn unit)	
What are the closest specialty units?	
Specialty	Phone #
Directions to the service from the site	
How long does it take to get there?	
Do you need an appointment or prior notification of arrival?	
What forms are needed for treatment?	
Insurance card	Other
What method of a payment is required for treatment?	

Guidelines and Information to Help Complete the Plan

❑ In many cities, calling 911 may be more appropriate than many of the emergency numbers listed in the plan. If these phone numbers are needed, they should be reviewed yearly and posted by phones where they are easily accessible. Each program site should have a similar list with numbers appropriate to the program site (refer to Worksheet P-2: Emergency Phone Numbers).

❑ It is also important to post information on what to say (e.g., name of reporting party, site address and phone number) to help alleviate anxiety, or in case a local official did not understand messages and needs to return a call for clarification.

❑ Designate a staff member to be responsible for transporting or traveling with a victim. Be sure that the victim has his identification and insurance card. Provide a map or make sure that the staff member is familiar with the directions from the office.

In many cities, calling 911 may be more appropriate than many of the emergency numbers listed in the plan.

ORGANIZATIONAL CRISIS WORKSHEET O-3

Agency Emergency Contacts

Rationale

It is important to know who needs to be contacted in case of a crisis or emergency, where they can be contacted, and of what types of emergencies they wish to be notified.

Plan

Determine who should be notified in what types of emergency situations and how quickly they should be told.

Title and Name	Office #	Home #	Cell #	Site Emergency	Image Issue	Serious Behavior Problem	Serious Injury	Natural Hazard or Disaster	Death	How soon? Immediately or within 24 to 48 hours?
CEO										
Board president										
Board	Attach list									
Staff	Attach list									
Legal counsel										
Insurance agent										
Media spokesperson										
Other										
National office										
National field staff										

Guidelines and Information to Help Complete the Plan

❑ This list should be the same for the office operation and each program (Worksheet P-3: Agency Emergency Contacts) and be located where those who need to contact other people will have access to it. It is important that the list be kept current and that any changes distributed on a regular basis.

❑ The board and staff list should include email addresses and emergency contact numbers. Email is often an alternate means of notification if the phones are inoperable or too busy to get a call in or out, as is often the case in widespread disasters or if the media has broadcast an incident.

❑ It may be helpful to establish a staff and board telephone tree to determine who calls others after the first person has been contacted. To help decide what information needs to be given, and to whom, use Worksheet O-4: Emergency Procedures for Hazards and/or Disasters—Office. The call should then include the information decided upon, along with the expected actions, if any, needed from the person receiving the call.

ORGANIZATIONAL CRISIS WORKSHEET O-4

Emergency Procedures for Hazards and/or Disasters—Office

Rationale

Emergency procedures for hazards, both natural and man-made, that are applicable to the office should be written and distributed or posted to help ensure a safer experience for both employees and visitors (refer to Worksheet O-5: Emergency Procedures for Office Evacuation and Fires).

Plan

1. Natural hazards

Types common in the office area	Warning signs	Safety precautions taken	Emergency action required

2. Natural and man-made disasters

Types common in the office area	Warning signs	Safety precautions taken	Emergency action required

3. Widespread disasters affecting the community where the office or staff live

How will facts be verified?	Who will be responsible?
How will staff at the office and/or away from the office be notified?	Who will be responsible?
In what circumstances would the office be closed?	Who will make the decision?
How will contact with the staff be maintained?	Who will be responsible?
How will contact with the board be maintained?	Who will be responsible?

4. Man-made hazards related to operation of the facility or equipment

Hazards identified but not eliminated	Warning signs	Safety precautions taken	Emergency action required

5. Man-made hazards related to the behavior of people

Hazards identified but not eliminated	Warning signs	Safety precautions taken	Emergency action required
Intruders (Worksheet O-25: Security) Personal safety in or around the building (Worksheet O-25: Security)			
Vandalism			
Drug and alcohol misuse			
Hostage			
Terrorism			
Other			

Guidelines and Information to Help Complete the Plan

❑ Being prepared with warning signs and the actions required when handling site hazards and widespread disasters specific to the area will help individuals remain calmer and know what to do. Worksheet O-13: Office/Site Hazards includes the identification of site hazards and plans for elimination, when possible. When elimination is not possible, Worksheet O-13 should include the organization's rationale, plans for protection, and procedures for avoiding the hazard. This worksheet can be used in staff training to address the prevention and any emergency action required if an incident does occur.

❑ Include warning signs and emergency actions required for natural disasters common to the area, such as tornados, earthquakes, floods, snow storms, lightning, forest fires, and mudslides, as well as man-made disasters, such as fires and acts of terrorism, that may be widespread and include the whole community. Local authorities may direct these operations.

❑ If any widespread disaster happens in the community where the office is located or where staff or board members live, the organization will need to determine what information is disseminated and how. Decide how to coordinate the information exchange between staff and families and among board members. Remember, the phone system may not be effective if people are being evacuated. It may be helpful to establish an emergency call-in location outside of the area or directions for using an established email address for emergency contact. A system must also be designed to identify and refer people who need extra support. Resources from the following websites may be helpful:

- The Emergency Email Network (www.emergencyemail.org) provides emergency notification of natural disasters or other emergencies in the area.

- The Centers for Disease Control and Prevention (www.cdc.gov) has information regarding what to do if someone believes that a biological or chemical threat exists in the area.

- The U.S. Department of Homeland Security has a downloadable guide to citizen preparedness on the FEMA website (www.fema.gov) that includes information about terrorism, bomb threats, suspicious parcels and letters, chemical and biological weapons, homeland security alerts, etc.

- The American Academy of Pediatrics (www.aap.org) provides information about "Disaster Preparedness to Meet Children's Needs."

❑ Emergency procedures for identified, but not eliminated, man-made hazards that are directly related to office and property should be considered, including exposed wires or pipes; broken furniture, shelves, equipment, or windows; nonfunctioning locks or alarms; and blocked exit doors.

❑ It is also important to consider natural and man-made hazards around office areas, such as difficult entry/exit from the road, dead trees, poisonous plants or animals, land irregularities, low-hanging wires, broken steps, abandoned roads and buildings, and poorly maintained sidewalks or parking areas.

❑ The plan should include man-made hazards related to the behavior of people, such as intruders, threats to personal safety outside the building, vandalism, kidnapping, harassment, drug or alcohol misuse, hostage situations, and child abuse. Specific worksheets have been included on staff (paid or volunteer) behavior expectations, sexual harassment, and preventing child abuse.

❑ Emergency action includes what to do and who to call for immediate help during a crisis, but does not include the follow-up reports or actions needed. Be sure that the phone numbers on Worksheet O-2: Emergency Phone Numbers are posted and included with the crisis information. Refer to Worksheet O-35: Incident Report to make a record of an incident.

❑ The Occupational Safety and Health Administration (OSHA) has a number of rules and reporting requirements when an employee gets hurt, such as the "confined space rule" that requires a written safety plan as well as staff training for spaces not designed for human occupation. The "lock out/tag out rule" on Worksheet O-6: Utilities—Office requires procedures to protect employees from accidental injury from any stored energy. Refer to Worksheet O-15: Storage and Handling of Hazardous, Flammable, or Poisonous Materials for rules for the use of chemicals or toxins often found in paint, cleaning supplies, yard equipment, and office machines. OSHA lists its requirements on its website (www.osha.gov), under a section entitled "OSHA Technical Manual."

ORGANIZATIONAL CRISIS WORKSHEET O-5

Emergency Procedures for Office Evacuation and Fires

Rationale

An evacuation plan enables the designated person in charge to quickly organize and move the occupants to a predetermined, safer location. With adequate warning, important papers may also be gathered or locked in safe storage. It is also important to have procedures in case of fire and have the appropriate type of firefighting equipment readily available at all times. Organizational Worksheets O-2: Emergency Phone Numbers and O-3: Agency Emergency Contacts include emergency contact numbers.

Plan

1.	Reasons the office might need to be evacuated
2.	Evacuation responsibilities
	Who determines the need for an evacuation?
	Who has written copies of the site evacuation plan?
	Who is in charge of evacuation?
	Backup?
	What valuable papers that cannot be replaced, such as deeds, historical documents, policies, etc., should be taken or locked in a safe place?
	Who determines safe return to the site?
3.	Primary and alternate routes out of the office
4.	Safe locations to go
5.	Method to account for persons on the site
	Staff
	Guests
6.	What are the procedures when a fire alarm is sounded or in case of fire?
7.	Where is the firefighting equipment for the office located?

Type of equipment	Location

Person(s) knowledgeable in their use
What are the fire control and firefighting procedures?
8. Who maintains the agency emergency contact information and is responsible for notification of those on the list?

Guidelines and Information to Help Complete the Plan

❑ When developing an evacuation plan, it is a good idea to consult with the building owner, Red Cross Disaster Services, Civil Defense, and the National Guard. If the site is being evacuated due to a threat of natural disaster, such as fire, flood, or hurricane, and time allows for the removal of valuable papers, it would be helpful to identify those to save or lock in a safe (waterproof/fireproof) place.

❑ Determine what the step-by-step procedures are in the event of a fire and who is responsible for what. The first concern should always be for the safety of people. Fire procedures should include evacuation and a system for checking to verify that everyone is clear of the fire. Establish methods for control through such actions as shutting doors to delay the fire's progress. Fireproof files or safes should be closed when not in use and be included in the evacuation procedures.

❑ Fighting the fire may sometimes be appropriate. Refer to Worksheet O-14: Office Operations, Maintenance, and Fire Prevention and Safety for the inventory of the firefighting equipment and alarms and safety checks.

❑ If the site is being evacuated in the event of a bomb threat, the presence of guns, or leakage of hazardous materials, staff members should follow the direction of authorities, remain as calm as possible, and provide support to those likely to panic.

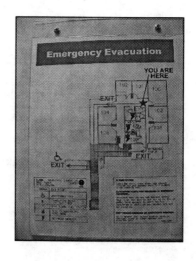

ORGANIZATIONAL CRISIS WORKSHEET O-6

Utilities—Office

Rationale

In case of an emergency, it may be important to shut down utility systems without delay.

Plan

1. Which staff members are knowledgeable of utility systems and have practiced shutting them down?			
Maintenance personnel			
Administrative personnel			
If the site is rented, what is the emergency contact number and where is it posted?			
2. Where are utility charts or physical descriptions of utility lines and shut-offs kept?			
3. Water and sewage			
Water service company			
Phone #			
Where are water shut-off valves located?	Are they clearly labeled?		Are tools to operate them kept nearby?
How is sewage disposed of?			
Who is responsible for problems?			
4. Electric			
Electric service company			
Phone #			
Where is the main electricity shut-off switch?			
What is the lock out/tag out procedure?			
What power sources are covered by this procedure?			
Who is responsible for training?			
Who is trained?			
Where are the breaker boxes and fuse boxes?			
Room	Location		Are all switches and fuses clearly labeled?

Who is responsible for conducting the annual electrical evaluation?			
Where is the written report kept?			
5. Gas			
Gas service company			
Phone #			
Where are gas shut-off valves?			
Room	Location		Are they clearly labeled?
6. Telephone			
Telephone service company			
Phone #			
Number of phones on site			
Where are the service boxes located?			

Guidelines and Information to Help Complete the Plan

❏ If the office location is rented, or if the organization has rented space out to other tenants, the responsibility for utilities needs to be established. Maintenance staff or other staff members that are responsible for some or all of the utilities should tour the office and practice operating the utility shut-off points.

❏ OSHA's "lock out/tag out rule" for electricity requires that responsible staff members have a written plan, an inventory of power sources, and training. OSHA lists its requirements on its website (www.osha.gov), under a section entitled "OSHA Technical Manual."

ORGANIZATIONAL CRISIS WORKSHEET O-7

First Aid/CPR and Exposure to Bloodborne Pathogens—Office

Rationale

Knowing who is currently certified in first aid and cardiopulmonary resuscitation (CPR) and having supplies accessible are important in the planning for first-aid coverage at the office. Bloodborne pathogens are pathogenic microorganisms that are present in human blood and can cause disease in humans. A list of bloodborne pathogens includes, but is not limited to, hepatitis B virus (HBV) and human immunodeficiency virus (HIV). OSHA requires employers to develop an "Exposure Control Plan" to eliminate or minimize employee exposure. This plan should be consistent with the program Worksheet P-17: Exposure to Bloodborne Pathogens.

Plan

First aid			
1. Who has current certification in first aid and/or CPR?			
Name	First-Aid Certification	CPR	Expiration Date
2. First aid supplies			
Where are they located?			
Who is responsible for restocking first-aid kits?			
How often?			
Suggested first-aid kits include:			
	Needles		Small roll of adhesive tape
	Scissors		Nonstick adhesive pads
	Tweezers		Band-Aids®
	Instant cold pack		Butterfly bandage
	Small bottle of alcohol or alcohol swabs		Triangle bandage
	Antibacterial soap		Other
	Nonlatex gloves		
Preventing exposure to bloodborne pathogens			
1. To determine exposure, list any staff positions that have potential exposure to others' blood by virtue of their job:			

2.	When/how do all staff members receive a copy of guidelines recommended by the CDC's "Universal Precautions"?
3.	Staff training includes appropriate response in case of emergency and:
	Where are records of training attendance, titles, and dates stored?
	Name and qualifications of person giving training
4.	Postexposure plan includes:
	Reporting exposure to the staff member in charge
	Contacting medical services to refer the employee for assessment
	Beginning a 15-second scrub of area with bacteriostatic soap, followed by application of disinfectant
	Arrangements for employees that have not been vaccinated to receive vaccination within 24 hours of exposure have been made with
	Begin psychosocial support process
	Complete workers' comp and incident-report forms with the employee
	Notify insurance
5.	Protective equipment, including resuscitation masks, gloves, and plastic seal-able bags for disposing contaminated materials are available in first aid kits in the following location
	The system for checking and/or replacing supplies and/or equipment is done by whom and when/how often?

Done by?	When?

6.	What are the procedures for disposing of contaminated equipment or waste?
7.	What is the exposure control plan for persons who have had exposure but are not employees?
8.	A log and the medical records for staff that have had some exposure as well as a copy of this plan are boxed and labeled as to identify the end of employment date plus 30 years for disposal date. These records are located
9.	Procedure for evaluating exposure incidents

Guidelines and Information to Help Complete the Plan

❑ First aid for adults at the office may be self-administered. If first aid is required as part of an employee's job, the organization is responsible for offering the employee hepatitis B vaccination shots.

❑ It may be helpful to seek medical advice on the content of first-aid kits. It is important to have a system to ensure that they are replenished periodically.

❑ If an employee is hurt on the job, refer to the OSHA requirements (www.osha.gov) and Worksheet O-35: Incident Report to record the incident.

❑ OSHA requires all employers that have employees with occupational exposure to have an exposure-control plan. It is unlikely that staff positions exist that include potential exposure as a part of the job in the office, but universal precaution training should be provided in the event of an accident. A sample of universal precautions is in Appendix 31.

❑ Exposure may be more likely for employees working at program sites. Refer to Worksheet P-17: Exposure to Bloodborne Pathogens for guidelines regarding the handling of exposures at program sites. Occupational exposure is reasonably anticipated contact with blood or other infectious materials that may result from the performance of an employee's duties. Again, it is important to review the OSHA requirements.

❑ All staff should receive training in appropriate response practices in case of emergency, including universal precautions. According to the concept of universal precautions, all human blood and certain human body fluids are treated as if known to be infectious for HIV, HBV, and other blood pathogens.

❑ Training usually includes the following appropriate response practices:

❑ Staff members are taught to approach care of minor injuries from a coaching perspective and specifically directed to refer injured people to healthcare services if self care is inappropriate or impossible.

❑ Staff members are instructed to use gloves when potential for contact with blood or blood tinged fluids exists. Gloves are in all first-aid kits.

❑ Staff members are instructed to respond in emergency situations to the level of their training, per the state's Good Samaritan regulations.

❑ Gloves may deteriorate faster when exposed to air. Putting gloves in film canisters or resealable bags may prolong their period of use. A regular system of checking and replacing supplies and equipment should include a time schedule (e.g., weekly, monthly). Hand-washing facilities should be readily available to employees; protective equipment should be made available; contaminated needles, equipment, or waste should be properly labeled and disposed of.

❑ Medical records that contain an employee's name, social security number, hepatitis B vaccination status, exposure incident reports, and follow-up procedures need to be kept confidential and maintained for the duration of employment, plus 30 years. The updated standard also requires employers to maintain a log of injuries from contaminated sharps.

❑ A postexposure plan should include immediate follow-up procedures. Follow-up is initiated by the employee, who must immediately (within 15 minutes) notify the staff member in charge, begin immediate cleansing, and acquire assistance with obtaining healthcare services. Postexposure procedures also include a confidential medical assessment, arrangement for vaccination, and other required steps recommended by a physician. Employees who have a blood-exposure incident are eligible for follow-up treatment.

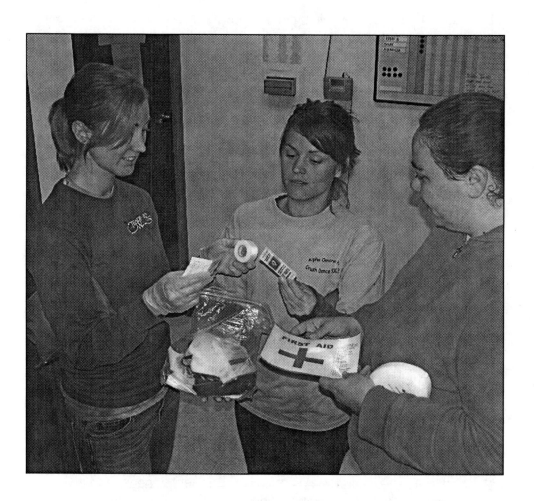

ORGANIZATIONAL CRISIS WORKSHEET O-8

Death of a Participant, Volunteer, Staff Member, or Family Member

Rationale

A fatal accident or the illness of a staff member or other guest at an office located in a metropolitan area is most likely handled by local authorities and medical personnel. Because of the difficulty and the emotional impact of such a tragedy, having a plan in place is essential. A procedure should also exist for informing staff members or guests of a death or serious injury of someone in their family or close to them. Once the victim has been pronounced dead by local authorities, the crisis is dealing with the emotional ramifications to kin, staff, and participants.

Plan

1. After the emergency and after steps have been taken for the care of the injured party, the first person to be notified is:	

2. Others to be notified (besides the next of kin) are:		
Name	Title	Phone

3. If local authorities do not assume responsibility, the person(s) responsible to notify the next of kin is:	
The procedures for notification of next of kin are:	
Additional procedures, if a staff member's death occurred while he is away from the office:	
4. Procedures for disposition of personal belongings:	
5. Decisions about support to the family on transportation of the body, funeral arrangements, or other support needed are made by:	
6. Support to other staff include:	
7. Procedure for informing a staff member or guest at the office of a death or serious injury in his family:	
8. Who reports employee deaths or hospitalizations to OSHA?	
9. Person responsible for completing incident report:	

Guidelines and Information to Help Complete the Plan

❑ The steps to be followed at the scene during an emergency are identified in the emergency procedures. After the emergency at the scene has ended and 911 or other authorities have been notified, the legal authorities or medical personnel will probably assume control. . Each agency will have a set of procedures that it is required to follow when such an incident occurs. These procedures usually include notification of next of kin.

❑ Since members of the press monitor police and emergency radio broadcasts, they will probably have knowledge of the incident as soon as the legal authorities have been notified. Refer to Organizational Worksheet O-9: Emergency Media Plan. It is critical that the next of kin is notified before any release is made.

❑ Once the emergency is over, agency contacts need to be made. If the executive director is not on the site, Worksheet O-3: Agency Emergency Contacts should give guidance regarding who in the organization should be notified. Worksheet O-35: Incident Report should be completed and the organization's national office notified. The executive director should notify the organization's president and lawyer as soon as possible.

❑ If notification of the next of kin is necessary, notification should be done in person and not by phone. If possible, legal counsel should be consulted before the executive director and/or the president visits the family in person.

❑ The executive director, president, or a religious leader familiar with the family may be of help in the notification, with the personal belongings, or when making funeral arrangements. The organization's contact persons should plan to attend the funeral, unless advised not to by legal counsel, and be ready for any future support needed by the family.

❑ OSHA also requires that serious accidents or the death of an employee are reported to them and that employers display a poster that explains the protection and obligations of employees. Refer to www.osha.gov for more information on OSHA regulations.

❑ Other staff members may need the support of a trained professional after the incident. It is normal for others on the scene to feel blame or think they should have done something differently. For liability reasons, they should be informed that they should not discuss the incident with the press or anyone else without first checking with the executive director.

❑ Determine by whom and how a staff member or guest should be informed of a death or serious injury in his family while at the office.

ORGANIZATIONAL CRISIS WORKSHEET O-9

Emergency Media Plan

Rationale

In a major emergency, the media scans police radios and will quickly arrive on the scene or call by phone. It is important to be prepared so that the media can do its job and the administrators can do theirs. The organization has a responsibility to provide accurate information to the public.

Plan

1. Approved media contacts	
The members of the media crisis-management team are:	
Who is the official spokesperson?	
	Phone #
Who is the backup spokesperson(s) if the official spokesperson is unavailable?	
	Phone #
2. In case of emergency, who has the authority to develop the brief factual statement or "key message" for media release?	
3. Who has the authority to approve brief factual statements?	
Phone #	
4. Use the following as an outline for forming key messages in a brief statement.	
The scenario facts [nature of situation and who (by title or role) is involved]:	

Indicate cooperation with the authorities	
State concern for those involved	
Restate the facts of the scenario without editorializing	
Indicate openness for future updates and responses	

5. The following people can approve a more detailed media release:

Person	Local	National

Executive director		
Board president		
Organization legal counsel		
Staff person in charge of the event		
Organization public relations specialist		
Other designated		
Other designated		
6. What kind of information is issued in the more detailed release?		
7. When and how are other staff members informed and/or trained in their roles (or nonroles) in dealing with the media?		
8. News media contacts established		
Name	Media	Phone #

Guidelines and Information to Help Complete the Plan

❑ Establishing a media crisis-management team to help design the plan and, if possible, be available in case of emergency will help the organization be prepared and present a more consistent and professional response to incidents. The team might consist of appropriate professional staff, board or committee members, legal counsel, local media representatives, or other public relations specialists.

❑ The emergency media plan should be used for incidents occurring in the office and all programs. The plan should include a system for referring inquiries to an official spokesperson. This person's responsibility will include speaking in an official capacity for the program and the organization.

❑ A spokesperson (or spokespeople) should be chosen who has a general understanding of the media, possesses communications ability, and has experience with interviews and reporters. This person need not be the program administrator, but must have knowledge of, and sensitivity to, policies about what should or should not be disclosed, as well as some expertise and credibility.

❑ The news media have a right to cover newsworthy events; however, the organization has a right to ask members of the media to wait until authorities arrive and facts have been gathered. Representatives of the media should receive the same courteous treatment as when the organization is asking for positive media coverage. Discuss the organization's legal rights with the legal counsel. Be sure the plan includes an absolute commitment to accuracy.

❑ One person, perhaps the staff person in charge, should be authorized to approve a brief factual statement for release to the media as soon as possible following an incident. A "no comment" or a delay in releasing information may give the appearance of an attempted "cover-up" or result in reports based on rumor or inaccurate information. The brief statements should include the location and type of incident, when it occurred, and whether it involved adults and/or children. Do not give specific names of persons involved until the authorities and the families have been notified. In case of serious injury or death, be sure that parents and/or next of kin are informed by personal contacts.

❑ Sample key messages should be developed prior to any emergency and incorporated into communications with the media and the public. Key messages should answer basic questions, be limited to three or four statements, express facts only, briefly describe the nature of the situation, list who is involved, indicate the organization's cooperation with the authorities, state concern for those involved, restate the facts for the scenario without editorializing, and indicate openness for future updates and responses.

The following is a sampling of general key messages from Camp Fire USA:

- Camp Fire USA always strives to provide safe, fun, and nurturing environments for children and youth.

- The health and safety of participants in our programs is our number-one concern.

- Camp Fire USA has policies for screening and training leaders to supervise children and provide age-appropriate programs.

- Camp Fire USA provides an inclusive environment that welcomes all children, youth, and adults regardless of race, religion, disability, sexual orientation, or other aspect of diversity.

❑ A longer, more detailed release may need the approval of more people, especially the executive director, the president, and legal counsel. Once again, it is important to release this information as soon as possible. The organization may want to contact the media with information before the media contacts the organization. Be sure the release is provided in writing.

❑ Copies of news releases should be distributed to anyone who might receive inquiries from the media, including staff members at the office. It should be stressed to staff and volunteers that they should release only the information included in the news releases and not speculate about the incident to others. Questions that go beyond the information in the news releases should be referred to the official spokesperson.

❏ Keep a brief biography of the executive director and program administrator, as well as a brief history of the organization. Security people may be needed to keep order or control access. Provide for a record of all calls received and contacts made during the crisis.

❏ Once the plan is developed, brief and train all staff members and key volunteers on the total plan, as well as on their specific duties and responsibilities.

❏ The media planning team should regularly reevaluate the emergency media plan.

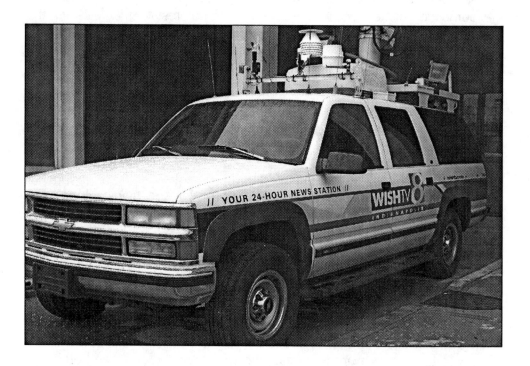

ORGANIZATIONAL CRISIS WORKSHEET O-10

Report of Alleged Child Abuse

Rationale

While an alleged child-abuse incident may not be an emergency, it may create a crisis and must be handled immediately. A report of an alleged child-abuse incident may happen during a program or long after the alleged incident happened. It could even be years later when the alleged victim is undergoing therapy. When receiving a report, it is important to take notes and have a plan for handling the information and perhaps the alleged victim. Refer to Worksheet P-60: Preventing Child Abuse for information regarding reporting requirements in each state.

Plan

1.	What is the basic information needed to report the alleged abuse to the child protection authorities and protect the child in the following situations?
	Reported by the victim and:
	• Involving someone outside the program
	• Involving an adult within the program
	• Involving another youth in the program
	Reported by another staff member and:
	• Involving someone outside the program
	• Involving an adult within the program
	• Involving another youth in the program
	Reported by a parent and:
	• Involving someone outside the program
	• Involving an adult within the program
	• Involving another youth in the program
	Reported by another child and:
	• Involving someone outside the program
	• Involving an adult within the program
	• Involving another youth in the program
2.	What are the essential guidelines to remember if speaking with the victim?

3. Who is the reporting authority in the state?		
Agency		
Contact	Phone	

4. The first person within the organization to be notified is:

5. Others to be notified are:

Name	Title	Phone
	Legal	
	Insurance agent	

6. What are the procedures for removal or suspension of an "accused" staff member until truth of allegation is determined?

7. Who is responsible for deciding on key messages for communication with staff or other campers as necessary?

8. What is the procedure for notifying other participants' parents, if necessary?

9. Who is responsible for preparation of a media statement?

10. Documentation required for organization records:

	Details of reported incident
	Victim name, address, phone, age, sex
	Time and place of the alleged incident
	Reporting party
	Others involved
	Witnesses
	Date, time, and person reporting to child protective authorities
	Response by child protective authorities
	Steps taken to prevent such an occurrence
	Final disposition

Guidelines and Information to Help Complete the Plan

❑ A youth services program administrator (or in some states a staff member) is a mandated reporter. When receiving a report of alleged abuse, this person's primary role is to gather the basic information related to the situation and report it to child protection authorities. Reporting alleged child abuse or neglect in good faith gives the reporting individual immunity from liability under civil law. In addition, this individual can be charged under criminal law for failure to report. It is not the organization's role to investigate before reporting.

❑ Another more sensitive and complex concern is the child's emotional and/or physical well-being and sense of personal safety. If the report has been made directly by the child, or if the child is still in the organization's care, someone may need to speak with the child. The organization only needs the basic information to report any suspicions. Whoever speaks to the child must be careful not to ask leading questions, instead only asking him to tell what happened. Professionals will question the child if the case is pursued. While it is okay to ask if the child can say who did it, the child should never be pressed to identify the abuser. Don't promise secrecy. Explain to the child what the organization plans to do and provide some sense of what will happen next.

❑ If the child names the abuser, that person must not be confronted, as doing so may jeopardize the case or cause the child more harm. If the child names a staff member or other participant, it is important to consult with child protective services before taking action to remove that person from the program or suspending a staff member with pay. Explain that suspension is not an accusation, but is necessary until the truth of the allegation is determined by the appropriate reporting authority.

❑ Worksheet O-9: Emergency Media Plan will help determine the key messages to the media and who the spokesperson will be. These statements may be different than the key messages necessary for communicating with other program staff or participants.

❑ It is important to complete the documentation while the incident is fresh, and then continue to log any additional information as the investigation continues. Refer to Worksheet P-43: Incident Report and Worksheet P-38: Record Retention and Destruction for Program for additional record-keeping information. Documentation should contain the facts only, not speculation. Steps taken to prevent such an occurrence should be a record of *what was done*, not "should haves," "if onlys," or what could be done in the future to prevent such an occurrence. Immediate changes in procedures should be done with care, as they could be construed as an admission of negligence. Changes should be part of the regular risk-reduction analyses process. Refer to Worksheet O-36: Risk-Reduction Analyses.

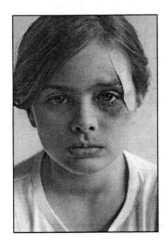

ORGANIZATIONAL WORKSHEET O-11

Legal Liabilities of Trustees/Directors

Rationale

A board of trustees/directors and/or individual trustees/directors can have legal action taken against them. Generally, legal action is taken on the basis that the board or an individual failed to take action or that the action taken was inadequate or irresponsible. A nonprofit board has specific legal duties or fiduciary responsibilities: the duty of loyalty, duty of care, and duty of obedience.

Plan

1.	How have board members received training and/or written information about the legal liabilities of trustees/directors?
	As a part of the recruiting process
	Included in board orientation
	Received written materials (board fact sheets)
	During board training
2.	Training includes information on their fiduciary responsibility:
	Duty of loyalty
	Duty of care
	Duty of obedience
3.	Training also includes the principle of good faith and the major categories of violations of their fiduciary responsibility
	Mismanagement
	Nonmanagement
	Self-dealing
4.	Training agendas, dates, attendance records are the responsibility of:
	Records are stored:
5.	Procedures for informing board members who miss training on their fiduciary responsibilities and legal liabilities:
6.	System for acknowledging receipt of written information if training was not provided or attended:
	Records are stored:
7.	Board member have copies of bylaws and policies
	The board maintains a current policies manual
	The board is familiar with any national charter requirements and the organization mission

	The board acts on policies to remove board member for not fulfilling responsibilities	
	The board has an established system for revision of bylaws and policies	
	Organization bylaws are approved by the national organization	
	Official board minutes are maintained by:	Location stored:
8.	The organization's conflict of interest policy:	
	Signed by board and staff members	Location where copies are stored:
	Includes procedures for voting on disclosures	
9.	Are board members informed about their directors and officers liability insurance?	

Guidelines and Information to Help Complete the Plan

❑ A board is a legally constituted entity that has the status of a person. Boards act only through consensus. They are obligated to serve as agents of the organization as a whole. Individual board members do not represent special interest groups and can only function in a duly constituted meeting of the whole.

> *Sample policy: No director shall, in his capacity as a director, claim the status of an agent of the organization unless specifically authorized to so do by the board. The President/CEO or Board Chairman is designated to act in the name of the organization for all normal and usual transactions.*

❑ Trustees/directors of nonprofit corporations are expected to perform their fiduciary responsibilities according to the principle of good faith, exercising care and diligence in making decisions in good faith for the best interests of the corporation. This responsibility requires that directors are reasonably informed, participate in discussions, and exercise judgment as a reasonably prudent person would in similar circumstances. While acting in this capacity, their legal duties are defined as follows:

- The duty of loyalty requires a trustee/board member to be motivated not by personal or private interests, but by what is good for the organization.

- The duty of care requires a trustee/board member to demonstrate "due care," be informed, and take appropriate action.

- The duty of obedience is the expectation of members to keep the organization on course, and act in accordance with the mission and all applicable laws and regulations.

❑ Three major categories of violations of fiduciary responsibility exist:

- Mismanagement includes failure to have provisions to protect assets or the health and safety of participants, reports not reviewed but just accepted at face value, decisions made when other information clearly suggests a different direction, or inadequate controls and reporting systems.

- Nonmanagement includes failing to attend board meetings and having information or control systems and not using them.

- Self-dealing is a form of disloyalty that involves using the organization to advance personal benefits when it is clear that personal gain outweighs the benefits to the organization.

❑ Board training should include information about the legal liabilities of trustees/directors. Chapter 1 includes more information about the legal liabilities of nonprofit boards and Appendix 4 presents a sample legal compliance checklist that may be helpful in preparing information for training. The checklist should be used as a starting point for good business practices for nonprofits and compared with state and federal reporting requirements and laws. Some applicable laws include:

- Corporate law (articles of incorporation, bylaws, policies, etc.)

- State laws (nonprofit corporation laws, charitable solicitation status, state tax exemptions, licensure, health and safety codes, charitable immunity status, etc.) The Nonprofit Risk Management Center has a resource on "State Liability Laws for Charitable Organizations and Volunteers" available for free download from their website: www.nonprofitrisk.org.

- Federal laws (IRS, FLSA, Employee Retirement Income Security Act, antidiscrimination laws, federal tax law, etc.)

❑ Since actions or nonactions that are not consistent with bylaws and policies can be considered mismanagement, a system for maintaining and updating policies and bylaws should be in place, and copies provided in a manual for all board members. A template for a conflict of interest policy is found in Appendix 5.

❑ The organization should have a directors and officers liability insurance policy. These policies are usually "manuscript policies" in the insurance business, which means that they are not standardized, and each company tends to make a lot of variations even within their own issued policies. Note: The Volunteer Protection Act—While extremely valuable, the intent of the act is to limit liability if a claim falls within the scope of the protection. However, the law does not prevent the volunteer from being sued. Furthermore, compensated individuals are not provided protection under the law. The law states that: "No volunteer of a nonprofit organization or governmental entity shall be liable for harm caused by an act or omission of the volunteer acting on behalf of the organization or entity."

Under this definition of coverage, protection is afforded to the volunteers unless one of the following events occurs:

- The volunteer does something that is outside of his job description.

- The volunteer does not have the required license or certificate for the job being performed.

- The volunteer's act that caused the injury was as a consequence of the operation of a motor vehicle.

- The volunteer caused the injury with willful, criminal, or reckless misconduct or gross negligence.

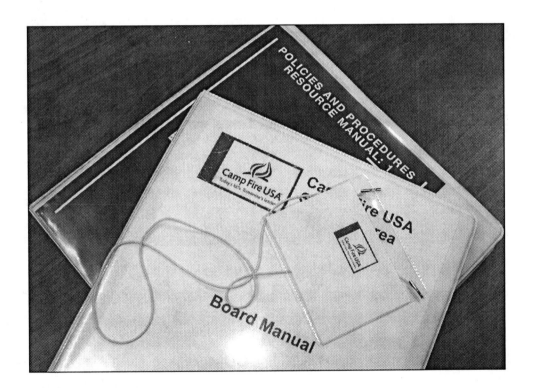

Legal Counsel

Rationale

Having a designated legal counsel or firm helps the organization be proactive with its handling of legal matters and prevent legal difficulties up front, rather than resolving them after they have arisen.

Plan

1. Name of the organization's attorney	Office phone number	Home phone number
Who may contact the attorney?		
Is the attorney familiar with program, facilities, operations, and staff?		
2. What documents have been reviewed by legal counsel?		

Guidelines and Information to Help Complete the Plan

❑ While the organization may have a lawyer on the board who can recommend a firm or an attorney, it would be a conflict of interest for board members or members of their firms to function in the official role of legal counsel.

❑ Provide the attorney with an orientation about the organization.

  • Set up a meeting with organization's attorney.

  • Familiarize her or him with program operation and personnel.

  • Arrange a tour of the facilities to familiarize the attorney with them.

  • Provide information on the organization's risk-management plan for review.

❑ Keep in periodic contact with the attorney to keep him apprised of the organization's operations and programs.

❑ In a lawsuit, legal counsel will often be provided by the insurance company and will ask for little, if any, input from the organization's attorney. To assure representation of the organization's interests, it is important to keep the organization's attorney apprised of the case.

ORGANIZATIONAL WORKSHEET O-13

Office/Site Hazards

Rationale

All hazards applicable to the office must be identified and then eliminated or reduced, and procedures must be written to help ensure a safer experience. Business-interruption procedures should also be in place in case it is necessary to temporarily or permanently close the office. For emergency procedures, refer to Worksheet O-4: Emergency Procedures for Hazards and/or Disasters—Office and Worksheet O-5: Emergency Procedures for Office Evacuation and Fires.

Plan

1. The office and the area around the office is surveyed for hazards before use and on a regular basis:	
Person(s) responsible	When?

2. The survey includes an appraisal of crime risk (crime prevention through environmental design, or CPTED)	
Person(s) responsible	When?

3. Office and area hazards identified to be eliminated are:			
Hazard Identified	How Eliminated	Date Completed	By whom?

4. Office and surrounding area hazards identified and not eliminated are:				
Hazard identified	Rationale for not eliminating	Protection from hazard (physical and/or human)	Rules or procedures regarding hazard	How and to whom disseminated

5. Business interruption procedures or policies include:	Person responsible
Alternate worksite if necessary	
Alternative way to deliver services	
Expanded check-writing authority	

	Ability to write checks and pay vendors	
	Method to notify participants/parents of closure	
	Backup of frequently used electronic documents	
	List of IT hardware and software to continue services	
	Contact numbers for agency partners and media	
	Office supplies	
	System for updating emergency services list	
	System for updating agency emergency contact list	
	System for updating staff and board phone tree and email list	
6. Is a safety orientation provided to staff members and user groups that includes the following?		
	Safety regulations and emergency procedures	
	Precautions for natural and man-made hazards on the site	

Guidelines and Information to Help Complete the Plan

❑ Touring the site with a small group of observant people and/or insurance company representatives can help identify risks. This group might also include a fire marshal and forester. Most local police departments have someone with the title of "crime prevention through environmental design" (CPTED) who will come to the office or program site and advise the organization on areas of risk in the facility. This process should include surveying the site for facility-design risks that reduce crime.

❑ The plan should include man-made hazards in the office such as exposed wires or pipes; broken windows, furniture, shelves, or equipment; nonfunctioning locks or alarms; improper storage of paper, supplies, or boxes; blocked exit doors; overflowing piles of trash; etc.

❑ For hazards around the exterior of the office, it is important to consider natural and man-made concerns such as dead trees, poisonous plants or animals, land irregularities, low-hanging wires, broken steps, trash, abandoned roads and buildings, poorly maintained sidewalks or parking areas, etc.

❑ Consider policies or procedures that may include rules about working late or alone, reporting hazards and broken equipment, etc. Refer to Worksheet O-25: Security.

❑ Protection from hazards may include fixing or removing items not in use, putting up fences or signs, training staff members in personal-security practices, installing alarms, removing large bushes where people could hide, establishing evacuation procedures, etc. Hazards that are eliminated should be identified on Worksheet O-4: Emergency Procedures for Hazards and/or Disasters—Office.

❑ Procedures or policies for business interruption should address situations in which the emergency is over, but the business operation cannot continue or reopen, either temporarily or permanently. Emergency procedures, insurance, evacuation, and record storage are handled in other worksheets. Also refer to Worksheet O-6: Utilities—Office and Worksheet O-4: Emergency Procedures for Hazards and/or Disasters—Office.

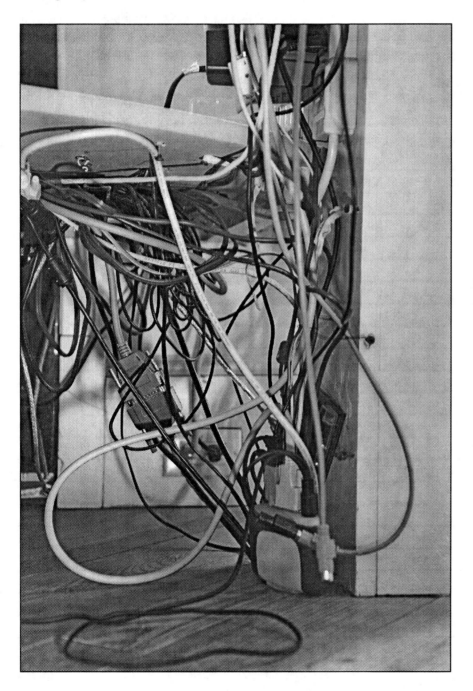

Office Operations, Maintenance, and Fire Prevention and Safety

Rationale

Analyzing maintenance needs, establishing a plan to maintain facilities in good repair and in a safe and clean condition, and having procedures for use of equipment may prevent accidents or illnesses from occurring.

Plan

1. List regular responsibilities for maintaining facilities and equipment in good repair and in a safe, clean, sanitary condition.

What are the responsibilities for:	Who?	How often?	By whom?
Kitchen or food areas			
Bathroom areas			
Maintenance facilities/storage			
Office areas			
Program areas			
Grounds			
Driveways and parking areas			

2. List hand tools, power tools, and other equipment used on site:

Equipment used on site	Persons approved to use	How safety checked	By whom?

3. Who is responsible for analyzing maintenance needs and how often are site maintenance surveys made?

4.	How are funds made available to carry out established maintenance plans?		

5. Operating and routine maintenance instructions are scheduled on the following mechanical equipment. Where are the specifications for parts or service kept?		
Equipment/brand	Maintenance scheduled	Specifications—parts + service

6. The routine safety check for fire prevention and safety includes:		
Inspection of:	How often is the safety check done?	By whom?
Firefighting equipment		
Electrical cords		
Circuits		
Shut-off devices		
Storage of combustibles		
Alarm systems		
Fire doors		
Exits		
Emergency lighting		
Appliances		
Fireplaces and chimneys		
Kitchen areas		

7.	Where are records of safety checks kept?		

8. Flammable materials are labeled and stored appropriately		
Office hazardous materials and location stored?	Who has access to them?	Who has been trained in their use?
Gas		
Liquid flammables		

9.	Where are floor plans for multi-room buildings kept?	

10. Smoke detectors and other detection devices in the office are inspected:	
By	How often?

Guidelines and Information to Help Complete the Plan

❑ A survey of maintenance needs and a plan of action with related costs should be made at least annually. An annual review and analysis of maintenance effectiveness should also be completed. Rodent control is an important part of all procedures for maintaining clean facilities, especially in buildings that have not been used or have been closed for the winter. Refer to hantavirus on Worksheet P-18: Insect- and Rodent-Transmitted Diseases. Also, visit the Centers for Disease Control and Prevention website for guidelines to "Seal up! Trap up! and Clean up!" (www.cdc.gov/ncidod/diseases/hanta/hps_stc/stc_spot.htm).

❑ A procedure should be established for reporting hazards, and a person should be designated to handle reports, assure that hazards are scheduled for correction immediately after notification, and follow-up documented to assure that the work has been completed. The person responsible for an area may be a staff member, volunteer, or contracted vendor. Work should be scheduled, if possible, to avoid interfering with the office operation or creating additional hazards.

❑ How frequently maintenance checks need to be completed may depend on usage and the age or condition of the facility or equipment. A file should be kept of all mechanical equipment that includes date and source of purchase, operating information, warranties, and the specifications for ordering parts and getting service.

❑ Persons using tools should be trained and experienced in their use. Manufacturers' instructions should be maintained on the site. Tools should be in good repair and have proper safety devices installed.

❑ A fire safety check by a qualified person should take place on a regular basis. If the office is in rented space that provides these services, find out how often they are done. Assign tasks that are not completed by the landlord to a staff member or volunteer. Battery-operated smoke detectors must be checked to see if batteries are functioning and have not been removed. A qualified person should complete an annual check of fireplaces and chimneys. Flammables should be stored in safe containers that are covered and labeled. Be sure that persons who have access to flammables are trained in their use. Records of safety checks must be kept in a safe, fireproof place and not in the building being checked.

❑ Obtain advice on appropriate firefighting equipment from the local or state fire marshal or fire department, the organization's insurance company, and/or the safety product and fire extinguisher companies. Have equipment checked and approved annually by the state or local fire marshal, fire department, or fire extinguisher company.

ORGANIZATIONAL WORKSHEET O-15

Storage and Handling of Hazardous, Flammable, or Poisonous Materials

Rationale

Hazardous, flammable, and poisonous materials may be mistaken for other substances, especially when not labeled and stored where usage can be supervised and/or controlled. OSHA's 1989 Hazardous Communication Standard requires a written plan and training on safe use and storage.

Plan

1. Storage and handling of hazardous, flammable liquids, or explosive materials for maintenance use are:				
Liquid	MDS	Used For	By	Stored
2. Storage and handling of hazardous, poisonous, or flammable liquids for program use are:				
Liquid	MDS	Used For	By	Stored
3. Storage and handling of hazardous or poisonous materials for maintenance, cleaning, and/or kitchen use are:				
Liquid or Material	MDS	Used For	By	Stored
4. Policies regarding training or verification of experience in the use of the above substances include:				
Policies and/or procedures have been reviewed by:				
Qualifications:				
5. Manufacturers' data sheets are kept:				

Guidelines and Information to Help Complete the Plan

❏ OSHA's Hazardous Communication Program requires that a written plan be in place that includes an inventory of all hazardous materials, a manufacturer's data sheet (MDS), which are available from the vendor when a product is purchased, and that persons using the materials have had training on how to read the MDS and use the materials (www.osha.gov). An exception to this rule would be hazardous material in a household container with a Consumer Product Safety Commission warning on the label. The cost of a violation may exceed $70,000. MDS should be kept where they are accessible to persons using hazardous materials

❏ Flammable liquids and/or explosive materials include gasoline, kerosene, paint thinner, and alcohol-based substances that may be used for maintenance. Poisons include bleach, cleaning agents, insecticides, weed killers, some craft supplies, and other substances labeled as poisonous that may be used in kitchens or maintenance areas.

❏ Policies and/or procedures should include where the materials can be safely stored, who can handle what substances, their appropriate use, the training or supervision required, and safe disposal. Local officials may have recommendations on these issues.

ORGANIZATIONAL WORKSHEET O-16

Food Handling and Foodborne Illness

Rationale

An office kitchen may have a variety of persons handling food, even if it is for their own personal consumption. A clean and sanitary workspace may prevent contamination or a foodborne illness. A foodborne illness outbreak can require the involvement of the local health department or other authorities. If it affects a large number of people, the incident will probably receive media coverage. If the kitchen is used for serving food at special events or meetings, or used by other groups, refer to Worksheet P-28: Foodborne Illness.

Plan

1. Food-handling procedures for kitchen and food service areas:
Procedures to assure good personal hygiene for persons handling any community food include:
Procedures for cleaning and sanitizing work surfaces and equipment include:
Procedures for sanitizing dishes and food-service utensils include:
Procedures for refrigerating foods and/or keeping food out of the "danger zone," which is between 40 and 120° F (4 and 38° C), include:
2. Food preparation and storage areas are protected from rodents and vermin by:
3. Local health department or authority

Name of contact	Phone number

Guidelines and Information to Help Complete the Plan

❑ This plan is for offices that have a kitchen for staff or volunteer use for personal consumption only. If the organization has a kitchen where food is prepared for others or allows other groups to use the kitchen, refer to Worksheet P-28: Foodborne Illness. Persons handling food served as snacks, hosting community potluck meals, or serving food from a local purveyor are among those who should adhere to the guidelines. Anyone can be a carrier of bacteria and other dangerous microorganisms.

❑ Foodborne illnesses, such as salmonella-B, E-coli, and novovirus, are bacterial infections and can be acquired from contaminated or inadequately processed foods, especially meat, eggs, poultry, and milk. By subscribing to www.emergencyemail.org, the organization will receive emergency alerts, including information about outbreaks of bacterial infections and foodborne illnesses.

❑ Human hands are a primary means of contaminating foods. Encouraging everyone to wash their hands, especially when leaving the bathroom, eating, or handling food, will help prevent the spread of dangerous bacteria and other microorganisms.

• The "danger zone" for food is 40 to 120° F (4 to 38° C), the temperature range in which dangerous bacteria multiply rapidly, which increases the possibility of foodborne illness. Safe food preparation is the result of both careful planning and good operating procedures. Cross-contamination requires the presence of a dangerous level of bacteria on one food product and the means of transporting it to another food product. The harmful organisms can be carried by utensils, equipment, cutting boards or surfaces, and human hands. Carefully cleaning and sanitizing work surfaces and equipment, washing hands between steps, using proper storage techniques, and separating work areas helps prevent cross-contamination. Cleaning and sanitizing work areas, surfaces, and equipment immediately after use prevents contamination. Harmful bacteria can lodge in the corners of work areas and equipment and be transferred to the next product that is prepared in the area. Water temperature for washing dishes and utensils should be at least 180° F (82° C) for rinsing, or an approved chemical sanitizer should be used. For more information, refer to the U.S. Department of Agriculture, Food Safety, and Inspection Service (www.foodsafety.gov).

❑ If several persons are showing symptoms of food poisoning, arrange for medical assistance and for cultures to be taken. Contact the local health department to take a survey of food service areas and drinking water. Follow the procedures of the health authorities and try to isolate what caused the problem. Be prepared to institute plans for dealing with the media and notifying the insurance carrier. Refer to Worksheet O-1: Who is in Charge Where?, Worksheet O-2: Emergency Phone Numbers, Worksheet O-4: Emergency Procedures for Hazards and/or Disasters—Office, and Worksheet O-9: Emergency Media Plan.

ORGANIZATIONAL WORKSHEET O-17

Serving Persons With Disabilities

Rationale

The Americans with Disabilities Act is a national mandate for the elimination of discrimination against persons with disabilities. In most youth services organizations, inclusiveness is a fundamental goal for all operations and services. The office should have accessible entrances and restrooms. The titles of most importance to youth services are Title I: Employment and Title III: Public Accommodations. This worksheet should be consistent with Worksheet P-27: Serving Persons With Disabilities.

Plan

1. The self-evaluation guidelines for Title I have been completed by:		
Required action has been determined and is assigned to be completed by:	Under the supervision of:	
2. The self-evaluation guidelines for Title III have been completed by:		
And reviewed by		
Required action has been determined and is assigned to be completed by:	Under the supervision of:	
3. The quick-look barriers checklist has been completed by:		
A list of action has been compiled by:		
List includes:		

Action Required	Cost of Action	Dates for Completion	Person(s) Responsible

4. Other plans to make operations and services more inclusive to persons with disabilities include:

Guidelines and Information to Help Complete the Plan

❑ The general rule on employment (July 26, 1994, employers with 15 or more employees) is to not discriminate with regard to job-applications procedures; the hiring, advancement, or discharge of employees; employee compensation; job training; and other terms, conditions, and privileges of employment. Refer to www.ada.gov for more information.

❑ Essential functions of the job are determined by the employer and are the key components or skills that must be performed. Applications may not ask if the applicant has a disability, but can ask if any reasons exist why the applicant would have difficulty in performing any of the essential functions of the job. Be sure that essential functions include any physical requirements, such as lifting, required mobility, communications skills, driving, etc.

❑ Reasonable accommodations include employee facilities that are readily accessible to, and usable by, individuals with disabilities; job restructuring; part-time or modified work schedules; acquisition or modification of equipment or devices; training materials or policies; the provision of qualified readers or interpreters; and other similar accommodations.

❑ Undue hardship means an action of significant difficulty or requiring significant expense when considered in light of several factors, such as the nature and cost of the accommodation, the overall financial resources, the type of operation, etc.

❑ Persons with disabilities need the opportunity to participate in integrated programs when such participation does not fundamentally alter the nature of the program being provided and when accommodations are reasonable and readily achievable.

❑ Readily achievable means easily accomplishable and able to be carried out without much difficulty or expense. Factors used to determine this aspect will include the nature and cost of the action required, the overall financial resources of the facility, and the type of operation.

❑ Participant applications may ask about disabilities. It is important to convey that this information is used to help determine appropriate supervision, support, and accommodations for the participant.

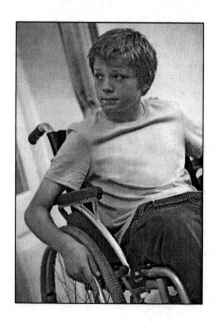

ORGANIZATIONAL WORKSHEET O-18

Insurance Coverage

Rationale

The insurance coverage for the organization is the responsibility of the board. The board and executive director need a working familiarity with the specific coverage available for the office, the board, participants, and program sites and business operations.

Plan

1. How is the insurance program managed?	
How is the insurance company and/or agent selected?	
Who may contact the insurance agent and in what circumstances?	
Who reviews policies when notification of a possible claim must be made?	
Where are insurance policies filed?	
Who has access?	
Who is responsible for notifying the insurance company if it is necessary to reserve a claim?	
Where are claim forms kept?	
What is the process for filing a claim?	
Who may file personal-injury or accidental claims?	
2. Which of the following types of insurance coverage does the organization have?	

Commercial General Liability

Company:	Policy #:	Date Expires:
Address:	Agent:	Phone #:

If not, why?

Fire and Extended Risk Coverage

Company:	Policy #:	Date Expires:
Address:	Agent:	Phone #:

If not, why?

Property and Equipment Damage

Company:	Policy #:	Date Expires:
Address:	Agent:	Phone #:

If not, why?

Vehicle Liability, Collision, etc.		
Company:	Policy #:	Date Expires:
Address:	Agent:	Phone #:
If not, why?		
Liability Coverage for Business Use of Non-Owned Vehicles		
Company:	Policy #:	Date Expires:
Address:	Agent:	Phone #:
If not, why?		
Umbrella or Catastrophe Liability		
Company:	Policy #:	Date Expires:
Address:	Agent:	Phone #:
If not, why?		
Sexual Misconduct		
Company:	Policy #:	Date Expires:
Address:	Agent:	Phone #:
If not, why?		
Employment Practices Liability		
Company:	Policy #:	Date Expires:
Address:	Agent:	Phone #:
If not, why?		
Hired or Leased Vehicles		
Company:	Policy #:	Date Expires:
Address:	Agent:	Phone #:
If not, why?		
Unemployment Compensation		
Company:	Policy #:	Date Expires:
Address:	Agent:	Phone #:
If not, why?		
Workers' Compensation		
Company:	Policy #:	Date Expires:
Address:	Agent:	Phone #:
If not, why?		
Participant Accident and Illness Insurance		
Company:	Policy #:	Date Expires:
Address:	Agent:	Phone #:
If not, why?		

Business Interruption or Loss of Income Insurance		
Company:	Policy #:	Date Expires:
Address:	Agent:	Phone #:
If not, why?		
Medical Malpractice		
Company:	Policy #:	Date Expires:
Address:	Agent:	Phone #:
If not, why?		
Officers and Directors Liability		
Company:	Policy #:	Date Expires:
Address:	Agent:	Phone #:
If not, why?		
False Advertising		
Company:	Policy #:	Date Expires:
Address:	Agent:	Phone #:
If not, why?		
Product Liability		
Company:	Policy #:	Date Expires:
Address:	Agent:	Phone #:
If not, why?		
Crime Insurance		
Company:	Policy #:	Date Expires:
Address:	Agent:	Phone #:
If not, why?		
Specialized Program Activities		
Company:	Policy #:	Date Expires:
Address:	Agent:	Phone #:
If not, why?		

Contract for Services

Contracts that specify additional insured on the contractor's liability policy include:

Contract with	For What	Insurance Carrier

Personal Effects of Participants and/or Staff		
Company:	Policy #:	Date Expires:
Address:	Agent:	Phone #:

If not, why?		
Use of an Organization-Owned Site by People Who Lease		
Company:	Policy #:	Date Expires:
Address:	Agent:	Phone #:
If not, why?		
Other		
Company:	Policy #:	Date Expires:
Address:	Agent:	Phone #:
If not, why?		
Other		
Company:	Policy #:	Date Expires:
Address:	Agent:	Phone #:
If not, why?		

Guidelines and Information to Help Complete the Plan

❑ Most insurance plans are the responsibility of the board, in conjunction with the executive director. Program administrators need to be able to understand and interpret the coverage that affects others on the site, initiate and follow up on appropriate claims, take steps to reduce potential claims, and manage resources.

❑ When choosing an insurance company or agent, be sure to investigate all options, look for experience in the specific type of operation, and understand the quality and scope of the coverage offered. Determine the appropriate staff and board members to meet with the insurance agent to discuss coverage, premiums, and interpretations. Compare limits of liability (deductibles and the maximum the policy will pay) and be sure to understand exclusions.

❑ It is important to maintain ongoing communications with the agent and have a current copy of the insurance policies at the site of activity. Find out when policies expire and when coverage is renegotiated. Be sure to have claim forms on site when appropriate and know filing deadlines.

❑ Determine who may contact the insurance agent. The policy will specify when the insurance company must be notified of a possible claim so that it can *reserve the claim*. Failure to do so may result in nonpayment. This allows the company to have money in reserve to complete the claim.

❑ The following list provides information on some of the types of insurance coverage listed in Worksheet O-18: Insurance Coverage. Coverage needs to be carefully evaluated and policies carefully reviewed. Some of the items may be covered in the liability or other type of policy. Each company operates different programs and not all coverage applies to every organization.

- A commercial general liability policy is designed to provide protection from lawsuits brought as a result of alleged negligence. Minimum limits are expected to be at least $1 million in general liability to $3 million in excess limits (generally called umbrella insurance). The policy should include, at the very minimum, coverage for products liability and personal injury and should include all employees, officers, and volunteers as additional insured(s). Be sure the policy provides coverage for sexual misconduct. Other coverage may be needed depending on the operations of the organization.

- It is important to have product liability insurance to cover organization-wide product sales, bake sales, and other sale or use of foods and goods. The organization should require the manufacturer of such products to add the organization as an additional insured so that their products liability insurance would interpose in the organization's behalf in case of a claim.

- When the organization contracts for other services, such as for bus transportation or horseback riding, the organization should see that it is an additional insured on the contractor's liability policy, as well as having its own coverage. Also refer to Worksheet O-27: Contracts for Service.

- Directors and officers liability (D&O insurance) is designed to directly protect the personal assets of directors, officers, and board members against wrongful action claims or to provide funds for an organization's indemnification of its board members. D&O insurance covers officers for errors and omissions, though the insurance coverages are not standardized. The organization's insurance agent should make every effort to customize coverage to meet the unique needs of the organization and its management structure. Read the policy carefully to determine who is covered and under what conditions coverage will be provided.

- When selecting umbrella, or catastrophic, liability, it is important to consider various risks and perils in terms of whether they are catastrophic in nature. Since the death or injury of one or more people in an accident may turn out to be an economic catastrophe, the organization should consider carrying umbrella liability for at least $1 million, in addition to the basic limits of the organization's comprehensive general liability and automobile liability coverage.

- Property insurance includes—at a minimum—insurance for fire, extended coverage, vandalism, and malicious mischief. It should be carried on buildings and contents owned by the organization and, ideally, for those for which the organization is responsible. "All-risk" coverage, including burglary and theft, should be seriously considered, as well as flood and earthquake insurance, if those exposures are present. Values should represent replacement cost of the property, or the actual cash value (replacement cost less depreciation), not the book value.

- Automobiles, station wagons, vans, trucks, and buses owned, leased, or used by the organization or its agents should be covered by automobile liability insurance with substantial limits. A minimum of $1 million combined single limit is recommended.

- All participants and guests in all programs should be covered by accident medical reimbursement insurance. Most of these policies do not have a deductible. In case of an accident, the agency policy would be used first to pay. This coverage helps those people with a deductible on their own insurance policies and shows the agency's concern for the well-being of all persons. Insurance to cover both accidents and illnesses should be purchased for resident camps and other extended-living programs.

- Employment practices liability insurance protects against the threats that employers face, such as allegations of sexual harassment, wrongful termination, and employment discrimination.

- Business interruption or loss of income insurance is coverage for when the normal operation of the organization is interrupted or suspended. It includes loss of business income, refunds, and added expenses incurred because of the interruption. An example is a forced evacuation because of a forest fire or flood, where the event or program cannot be continued or postponed. It does not include damage caused by the fire or water. Be sure to read any "triggers" in the policy that spell out when the policy does or does not take effect. For example, it may say that an official disaster organization or other authority must tell a camp when they are to evacuate. If the camp closes before receiving this notice, the policy will not cover them.

- Crime insurance (often includes bonding) should be purchased for all employees and officers of the organization. During product sales or other activities involving substantial sums of money, the fidelity coverage should be extended to cover volunteers who may collect money.

- Workers' compensation is a form of insurance that provides compensation for employees who are injured in the course of employment. State laws differ on coverage and premiums and what is covered. Most employers are required to carry workers' compensation insurance, and in most states heavy financial penalties may be imposed on an employer that does not.

ORGANIZATIONAL WORKSHEET O-19

Reevaluating Insurance

Rationale

Insurance policies should be flexible enough to reflect the constantly changing program or conditions. Adjustments in insurance coverage may be needed due to a change in a program or management, the purchase or disposal of facilities or equipment, a change in regulations, or new construction. A rider to a policy may be needed to cover special short-term conditions or programs.

Plan

1.	What is the schedule and procedure for reevaluating the insurance coverage?
	Who is involved in the evaluation?
	What data are used in the evaluation?
2.	How have buildings and equipment depreciated or been improved since the last audit?
3.	What is the procedure for adding or deleting equipment, facilities, or programs to or from the current policy?

Guidelines and Information to Help Complete the Plan

❑ All insurance coverage should be reviewed on a regular basis. Every year, basic coverage needs to be analyzed; every two or three years, the review should be more intensive.

> *Sample policy: All insurance coverage shall be reviewed at least annually by the finance committee. Premium payments are to be compared with policies. A schedule of insurance will be maintained that properly accounts for prepaid expenses.*

❑ The annual review should include an analysis of the coverage and limits of each policy, including what is not covered, and an assessment of changes in the value of buildings and other property being insured. A review of claims during the previous year should also be included. Collect data on insurance claims, including their severity and frequency. Doing so will help the committee reevaluate insurance coverage or be aware of, and reduce, loss in other ways.

❑ Be sure that the current appraised value of each listed facility or specified equipment is sufficient to realistically reflect the replacement or actual value. Inventory values should be checked against the sum insured to make certain that adequate coverage is actually in effect.

❑ A more in-depth review should include reappraisals of property and equipment, a competitive analysis of premiums being paid, and an evaluation of record-keeping procedures.

ORGANIZATIONAL WORKSHEET O-20

Insurance Safety Audit for Organization-Owned Sites

Rationale

Insurance companies will usually do a safety audit of an organization-owned site every two to five years, but an annual audit may be requested. This audit is a preventive program that can alert the staff and/or board to potential dangers. A safety-conscious auditor with little or no experience with the organization's operations can bring a different perspective to the site.

Plan

1. Organization-owned site			
Date of last safety audit:			
Person who conducted the audit:			
How often is the audit conducted?			
Next audit scheduled:			
Recommendations Made	Actions Taken or Insurance Policy Changes Made	Date Completed	Rationale for Noncompliance
2. Organization-owned site			
Date of last safety audit:			
Person who conducted the audit:			
How often is the audit conducted?			
Next audit scheduled:			
Recommendations Made	Actions Taken or Insurance Policy Changes Made	Date Completed	Rationale for Noncompliance

Guidelines and Information to Help Complete the Plan

❑ Be sure to respond to the safety audit report with specific actions taken, timelines, or rationale for noncompliance. Contact the agent to review previous reports and to schedule the next safety audit. Complete an audit for each site or facility that the organization owns.

ORGANIZATIONAL WORKSHEET O-21

Record Retention and Destruction

Rationale

A good record-retention and periodic-destruction policy and a retrieval system help the organization comply with legal requirements and may protect it in the event of litigation, audit, employee disputes, and other times when documents can be used to support or oppose a particular position. Information about retaining program-participant and program-administration records are in the program-management section. Refer to Worksheet P-38: Program Record Retention and Destruction for Program.

Plan

1. Does the record-retention policy include:	
The following categories?	Key person accountable:
Accounting and fiscal records	
Administrative records	
Communications records	
Contract-administration records	
Corporate records	
Insurance records	
Fund-development records	
Deeds and legal records	
Office supplies and printing records	
Participant records	
Personnel records	
Property/facilities records	
Public relations records	
Program records	
Product and other sales records	
Purchasing records	
Security records	
Tax records	
Other	

	Information on:
	Retention period
	Where stored
	How stored and the need for security
	Authority for disposal
	Method(s) of disposal
2.	Are both paper and computer files considered in the policy?
	Are computer records backed up? How frequently?
	How can backups be obtained?
	Who is authorized to retrieve them?
	Are copies of paper and computer records stored off-site?
3.	The state's statute of limitations is:

Guidelines and Information to Help Complete the Plan

❑ Records help the organization maintain a legal history, analyze decisions and incidents, and then plan and create a sense of accountability for actions taken. Record-retention and -destruction policies should address the following main categories:

- Legal documents such as deeds, bonds, articles of incorporation, bylaws, trademarks, surveys, etc., that should be considered permanent records

- Federal or local government records that must be retained and be available for a specific period before they can be confidentially destroyed

- Documents that should be kept to protect the organization, such as participation and medical records, training records, architects' plans, etc. These records are generally kept to protect and provide documentation on the organization's or an individual's actions, or to provide a historical record.

- A process for record storage and destruction that includes security and privacy issues

❑ Sample records for each of the suggested categories are as follows:

- Accounting and fiscal records—bank records, accounts payable, accounts receivable, financial statements, general ledgers, payroll registers, expense records, budgets, checks, petty cash, expense reports

- Administrative records—audit reports, correspondence, reports, directives from the board

- Communications records—postage records, email policy, bulletins, phone directories

- Contract-administration records—contracts with individuals and service providers, renters, grants, equipment manufacturers

- Corporate records—annual reports, articles of incorporation, bylaws, minutes of board meetings, charter agreements, licenses

- Insurance records—current and expired policies, audits, claims

- Fund-development records—United Way, donors, grants, events

- Legal records—claims and litigations, trademarks and copyrights, law records

- Office supplies and printing records—inventories, equipment records, shipping and receiving records

- Participant records—registration/participation information, waivers, permissions, photo releases, medical records, incident reports (refer to Worksheet O-26: Technological Usage and Record Security)

- Personnel records—application changes and termination records, accident reports, injury claims, attendance and training records, training manuals, job descriptions, performance evaluations, insurance records, benefit records (refer to Worksheet O-26: Technological Usage and Record Security)

- Property/facilities records—Depreciation schedules, inventories, maintenance and repair for buildings and equipment, property deeds, purchase or lease agreements, motor vehicle operations and maintenance

- Public relations records—exhibits, releases, handouts, internal publications, manuscripts, photos, public information activity

- Program records—brochures, program schedules, attendance records, volunteer and staff responsibilities and training records, evaluations

- Product and other sales records—vendor contracts and records, sales records, inventories, price lists, surveys, freight records

- Purchasing records—purchasing orders, quotes and bids, price lists

- Security records—classified materials violations, employee personnel files, safety and fire-prevention program records, visitor clearance, protective devices

- Tax records—employee withholding, IRS Form 990 reports, tax bills and statements

❑ It is helpful to identify a group of key people who will help design the policy and be involved in the implementation of the records-retention program.

❑ Several considerations must be made in determining how long to keep a document, when and how to store it, and how to dispose of the document.

- Does the law require retention of a particular document? Check federal, state, and local mandatory record-keeping requirements.

Samples of a retention table and a Record Management and Retention Policy appear in Appendix 10. It may be helpful to search the Internet for a records-retention timetable for a specific state.

- A number of state and federal laws involve the confidential handling of personal information regarding both customers/clients of the organization and other employees or volunteers. These laws may include, but not be limited to, Fair and Accurate Credit Transactions Act (FACTA), Health Insurance Portability and Accountability Act (HIPAA), The Economic Espionage Act, The Privacy Act, Gramm/Lech/Billey Act, Identity Theft Laws (where applicable), Trade Secrets Protections, and Implied Contract Breach. These issues should be considered when making decisions regarding the storage and destruction of these records.

- What is the purpose of the document and could it be of value to other purposes in the future? Would it be valuable to support or oppose a position in an investigation or litigation, or help explain a business decision?

- What would be the negative consequences if a document cannot be located in the future? Be sure not to destroy documents that could be needed in a pending dispute or litigation.

- Can a document be obtained from other sources? Do multiple copies exist?

- What are the internal and external risks to the security of personal data? Refer to Worksheet O-26: Technological Usage and Record Security.

❑ How long should a document be stored? Any record can be subpoenaed, so the decision about what records to keep is important. Decisions should be consistent from year to year and be evaluated carefully. Evaluate the applicable statues of limitation that govern the timeframe in which actions may be brought by or against the organization. Statutes of limitations vary from state to state. Even if a parent has not sued, the child, upon reaching 21, has until the statute of limitations runs out to sue on his own behalf. Records that may be related to an accusation of child abuse may have no statute of limitations. Refer to Worksheet P-38: Program Record Retention and Destruction for Program for information on participant records.

❑ Many accounting and fiscal records should be kept for three to seven years and be disposed of at the discretion of the administrator. Employment and payroll records must be kept according to the requirements of the Fair Labor Standards Act (FLSA), usually for two or three years. Refer to Worksheet O-29: Employment Practices regarding specific employee medical information.

❑ The policy should address both paper and electronic files. A policy about email can help reduce the inappropriate and potentially damaging use of email that is often found in employment and other disputes. The policy should prohibit the sending of email that would be in conflict with the organization's sexual harassment policy or ethics statement, or be racially or culturally derogatory. The length of time that email should be kept depends on its content and should be evaluated accordingly. Refer to Worksheet O-26: Technological Usage and Record Security. A sample policy is found in Appendix 26a.

❑ In determining the policy for how and where records will be stored and destroyed consider:

- Whether they will be kept in a paper copy or in some form of technology, such as microfilm or computer CD/DVD. Remember that the organization may not need them for years and technology changes at a rapid rate (e.g., computers do not even come with slots for floppy disks anymore). Storage in fire- and flood-proof places should also be considered.

- The security of personal information, including who has access to stored records and how those records are destroyed to protect staff and participant privacy

❑ FACTA is a federal law designed to minimize the risk of identity theft and consumer fraud by enforcing the proper destruction of consumer information. The Federal Trade Commission (FTC) of the United States' Disposal Rule was designed in November 2004 and became effective June 1, 2005 to further implement the policies set forth in FACTA. The Disposal Rule applies to businesses that utilize consumer information; however, it affects every person and business in the United States.

The FACTA Disposal Rule states that "any person who maintains or otherwise possesses consumer information for a business purpose" is required to dispose of discarded consumer information, whether in electronic or paper form. The Disposal Rule further clarifies the definition of compliance as "taking reasonable measures to protect against unauthorized access to or use of the information in connection with its disposal." These "reasonable measures" include:

- Burning, pulverizing, or shredding of physical documents
- Erasing or destroying of all electronic media
- Entering into a contract with a third party engaged in the business of information destruction

Operational Financial Risks

Rationale

To effectively manage and safeguard the organization's financial resources, it is important to assess and reduce the risk of financial loss by identifying the internal controls needed to achieve effective and efficient operations. Internal controls are systems to protect the assets, create reliable financial reporting, and promote compliance with laws and regulations.

Plan

1.	Is the trustee/board informed of its fiscal responsibility for safeguarding the resources of the organization, including the following?
	Conformity with the mission and the law
	Compensation and benefits liability
	Budgets, programs, and policies
	Use and receive reports from auditors and lawyers
	Capital campaigns and certain gifts
	Dissolution and reorganization plans
	Loans, debts, accumulations, and restricted accounts
	Investment advisors and endowments
	Sales, joint ventures, and businesses
	Establishment of bank accounts
2.	Who is responsible for oversight of the financial operations?
3.	Does the policy on internal controls include generally accepted accounting principles (GAAP) and address the following?
	Handling funds received and expended
	Preparing appropriate and timely financial reports to the board
	Conducting the annual audit
	Evaluating the staff and programs
	Maintaining inventory records
	Implementing personnel and conflict-of-interest policies
4.	Petty Cash
	What is the petty cash procedure regarding the amount of petty cash kept on hand?
	What is the maximum amount an individual may request?

	Who is responsible for maintaining petty cash?
	Who is responsible for reconciling petty cash?
	Who has access to petty cash?
	How is it secured?
	What is required for reimbursement from petty cash?
	Who authorizes payments?
	How is petty cash replenished?
5.	Cash Receipts
	How are checks received by mail handled?
	How often are deposits made?
	By whom?
	How are checks and cash given to individuals (staff, volunteers, etc.) handled?
	Who has access to checks and cash?
	How are they secured at the office?
	How are they secured outside of the office?
	What is the policy regarding acceptance of checks made out to others?
6.	Cash Disbursements
	What is the policy for cash disbursements?
	How are unused checks secured?
	If a facsimile signature is used, how is the stamp or plate secured?
	How are payments authorized?
	What is the refund policy?
	Who has the authority to purchase or commit agency funds?
	Who may enter in a contract on the organization's behalf?
	When are purchase orders issued?
	When is bidding required?
7.	Travel Reimbursement Policy
	When are travel expenses reimbursable?
	What is the mileage rate?
	What is the meal allowance per day?
	What is the policy on hotel allowances and airfare?
8.	Reconciliation and Analysis
	Are bank statements being reconciled monthly?
	By whom?
	Who is responsible for analyzing payroll and benefit accrual?
	Who is responsible for reviewing receivables?

	What is the policy for any write-offs of accounts receivable?
	Who is responsible for generating a monthly list of any outstanding unpaid invoices?
9.	Inventory Management and Control Responsibility and Procedures
	Who is responsible for securing the overall list of inventories and securing a copy off-site?
	Who is responsible for inventorying office furniture?
	Who is responsible for inventorying office equipment?
	Who is responsible for inventorying and managing office supplies?
	Who has access?
	How is it secured?
	Who is responsible for inventory in food service area?
	Who has access?
	How is it secured?
	In merchandise for sale?
	Who has access?
	How is it secured?
10.	Tax Liability
	Who is responsible for preparing and submitting the IRS 990?
	Who is responsible for employment-tax and wage-reporting compliance?
	Is sales tax being collected on goods sold?
	Who is responsible for collecting and remitting sales tax?

Guidelines and Information to Help Complete the Plan

❑ One of the primary roles of the trustee/board is fiscal responsibility for safeguarding the resources of the organization. Nonprofits agencies should refer to Worksheet O-11: Legal Liabilities of Trustees/Directors and Appendix 4 for a Legal Compliance Checklist for 501(c)(3) Nonprofits.

Sample policy: All investments of the organization will be in the name of the organization and shall be made for periods not to exceed one year. Investments may be made by the President/CEO with the approval of the Finance Committee. Investments shall be either: (1) direct obligation of, or obligations guaranteed by, the United States of America; or (2) certificates of deposit issued by a member of the Federal Deposit Insurance Corporation, not to exceed the maximum amount insured by the FDIC. Certificates of deposit may be renewed with approval of the President/CEO and the Finance Committee. When possible, interest is received by the organization on a monthly basis. A schedule of investments is presented regularly to the Finance Committee.

❏ Internal controls should include following generally accepted accounting principles (GAAP), which is the common set of accounting principles, standards, and procedures that companies use to compile their financial statements.

> *Sample policy: The accrual method of accounting will be used. Financial statements will be prepared monthly and presented to the Finance Committee and Board of Directors. Someone other than the preparer will approve journal entries. A chart of accounts conforming to United Way requirements will be maintained.*

> *Sample policy: An audit by an independent accountant will be performed annually and submitted for approval to the Finance Committee, Executive Committee, and Board of Directors and reported to funding and governing bodies as required. A form 990 will be prepared annually and submitted to the Internal Revenue Service and Camp Fire USA. The annual Camp Fire USA financial report will be prepared and submitted as requested.*

❏ Checks received by mail should be restrictively endorsed as soon as they are received, and then deposited in a timely manner. Restrictively endorsing involves stamping "for deposit only" with the organization's name immediately upon receipt to help limit the misuse of checks. Employees not involved in the actual receipt of cash should verify that all recorded collections were subsequently deposited. Procedures on how cash is to be handled (and by whom) should include a system of utilizing numbered receipts for any cash received. Copies should be reconciled with cash received.

❏ Provisions must be established for securing petty cash, cash receipts, and checks in the office, specifically when handling product sale money or other cash received outside the office (program fees, special events, camp stores, etc.). Provisions should include defining who has access to the money. Petty cash procedures must be provided to anyone who has access to petty cash.

❏ The procedures for cash disbursements should include the use of prenumbered checks, a system to secure and account for unused checks, the numbers and names or positions of those who are authorized to sign checks. It should also include the use of purchase orders and receiving documents required for payment and define exactly who may authorize payment. Check signers should not sign their own checks. One person should review all disbursements to ensure that duplicate payments are not being made. Paid invoices should be canceled after payment.

❏ A policy must be in place that outlines who has the authority to commit agency funds, make purchases, and enter into contracts on behalf of the organization, as well as any limits on authority.

Sample policy: The following individuals are authorized to sign checks: executive director/CEO, board chair, vice chair, and treasurer. All checks must be signed by two of the authorized signers.

Sample policy: All budgeted purchases of $_____ or less may be authorized by _____. Prior to approval of the purchase order, at least three competitive bids must be obtained. Final approval of the purchase will be made by the budget manager based on price, the quality of the item proposed by the bidder, delivery time, and other such factors deemed necessary and in consultation with the _____. Unbudgeted purchases of $100 or more must be approved by the _____ and _____, and appropriate measures must be taken to either cover the expense with additional income or reduce expenses in a like amount.

All purchases of more than $_____ must be approved by both the _____ and _____. Prior to approval of the purchase order, at least three written competitive bids must be obtained. Final approval of the purchase will be made by the budget manager, in consultation with the _____, based on price, the quality of the item proposed by the bidder, delivery time, and other such factors deemed necessary.

❑ The reimbursement procedures should list what expenses are reimbursable and at what rates. It may also include a maximum rate or provide guidance on the selection of hotels and the use of lowest available airfare rates.

❑ Oversight includes audits, preparation of financial statements, preparation and monitoring of the annual budget, cash flow projections, the monitoring of actual cash flow, etc.

❑ It is important to understand the tax liability applicable to the operation. The organization should determine responsibility for remitting payroll tax forms, filing 990s, paying into unemployment funds, and making provisions for any contingencies that might encumber the future operation of the organization.

❑ Form 990 is an annual reporting return that certain federally tax-exempt organizations must file with the IRS. It provides information on the filing organization's mission, programs, and finances. No one date exists on which all Forms 990 must be submitted to the IRS. Instead, a nonprofit's filing date is determined by the end of its fiscal year (the 12-month period for which the organization plans the use of its funds); each filing organization is required to file "by the fifteenth day of the fifth month after its fiscal year ends." Organizations can also receive up to two 90-day extensions.

❑ Appendix 22 has a list of basic requirements for a tax-exempt organization's compliance with employment tax and wage reporting. This information can also be found on the IRS website (www.irs.gov). In addition to the federal requirements, the state may have reporting requirements. Very strict penalties exist for failure to comply with these requirements. Refer to Worksheet O-29: Employment Practices for more information.

❑ Inventory management and control should include procedures for taking a periodic inventory, securing a copy off-site (for insurance and planning purposes), identifying who is in charge and who has access, and how the information is secured. Office equipment should include phones, computers, printers, video or camera equipment, etc. When a site is used for different purposes at different times or seasons, the inventory storage may change. For insurance purposes, it may be helpful to use a video camera to record the storage and office areas to accompany the actual inventory list.

> *Sample policy: All items with an original cost of $500 or more and a lifespan of at least five years are considered fixed assets. A schedule of fixed assets will be maintained with original cost, life expectancy, accumulated depreciation, and physical location. The purchase or disposal of all fixed assets is approved by the Board of Directors or Finance Committee. Fixed assets will be maintained in the Land, Building, and Equipment account. An inventory of all fixed assets will be reviewed and updated annually and compared with the schedule. Repairs to property or equipment that exceed $500 will not be considered as additions to fixed assets and will be expensed to the operating account. However, replacement of property or equipment will be expensed to the Land, Building, and Equipment account if the cost is $500 or more and the lifespan is at least five years.*
>
> *Annual depreciation will be expensed each year in December and calculated on the straight-line method. Fully depreciated assets shall be included on the schedule of fixed assets.*

❑ Is tax being collected and remitted on the selling of supplies? The state may allow exemptions on goods purchased, but not on goods sold.

❑ The New York State Attorney General's office has an excellent resource online on internal controls and financial accountability for nonprofits (http://www.oag.state.ny.us/charities/internal_controls.pdf). Although the Sarbanes-Oxley Act does not currently apply to nonprofits, www.independentsector.org/sarbanesoxley.html provides information that every organization should consider..

ORGANIZATIONAL WORKSHEET O-23

Business Use of Vehicles and Driver Authorization and Responsibility

Rationale

Organization-owned, leased, and/or privately owned vehicles used for any official business must meet the applicable requirements and be driven by someone with a current driver's license and a good driving record.

Plan

1. The policy on business use of owned or rented/leased vehicles is:			
2. What vehicles are owned or rented/leased by the organization?			
Vehicle	License #	OK for personal use?	
		Yes	No
3. What is the state law regarding driver's license classifications?			

4. Authorized drivers of organization-owned, rented, or leased vehicles

Driver	Driver License #	Type	Drivers have had training in:				
			Backing up and refueling	Loading and unloading passengers	Breakdowns, illness, and/or accident procedures	Safe operation of specific vehicle	Vehicle safety check

5. Who is responsible for maintenance of organization-owned, rented, or leased vehicles?
6. Are business-use drivers required to complete a driver information form?
7. Who is responsible for obtaining forms?
Where are they kept?
8. Where are copies of authorization and proof of insurance kept?
9. What assurance exists that vehicles are in safe operating condition?
10. A staff member using privately owned vehicles to transport staff or participants as a part of his or her job requires authorization and proof of insurance coverage for:

Liability	Minimum coverage limit?
Bodily injury	Minimum coverage limit?
Property damage	Minimum coverage limit?

Guidelines and Information to Help Complete the Plan

❑ Determine who will use organization-owned, rented, or leased vehicles, how they may be used, and who will be responsible for maintenance. Be sure that insurance coverage has been obtained for all uses and drivers.

❑ Drivers should have procedures for quarterly inspection of vehicles or within the three months prior to use. Vehicles should not be used if repairs affecting the safe operation of the vehicle have not been made. A sample vehicle inspection is presented in Appendix 11.

❑ It is helpful to require a vehicle safety inspection and a record of regular maintenance and insurance coverage for any vehicle (including commercial vehicles) being used for emergencies or in the implementation of the program.

❑ Drivers should understand that any traffic violation citation received is the responsibility of the driver. Staff members using their own private cars for transporting participants and/or staff members do so at their own risk, if they are not requested to transport persons as a part of their job.

Fundraising and Special Events

Rationale

For a nonprofit organization, it is important to protect the organization's 501(c)(3) status, establish fundraising policies and procedures that establish credibility and accountability, and abide by federal, state, and local laws and regulations.

Plan

1.	The organization plan for fundraising includes:
	A diverse funding source
	Annual financial statements available upon request
	Annual report available upon request
	Segregation of restricted funds
	An analysis of the cost and benefits of each fundraising activity is completed to ensure that the fundraising costs are reasonable in comparison to the dollars raised.
	A plan for regularly reconciling the organization's fundraising practices against the prevailing ethical practices of the National Association of Fundraising Executives or similar national body
2.	Who is responsible for written agreements with outside fundraising contractors or consultants?
3.	Organization websites that have opportunities for contributions include:
	A privacy policy
	Electronic access to IRS Form 990
	A statement of how the organization benefits from the sale of products, events, or other solicitation
4.	Legal and tax aspects
	IRS and state requirements are reviewed annually
	The state requirement for charitable registration/license is:
	Who is responsible for completing any charitable registration forms required by the state?
5.	Product sale
	The organization is insured for:
	Policies for any product sale include:
6.	Special events
	The organization's special events are insured for:
	Policies for special events include:

Guidelines and Information to Help Complete the Plan

❏ The organization's fundraising plan should include policies on unrestricted and restricted contributions.

> *Sample policy: Unrestricted Contributions, Other Than Real Property—Contributions up to and including $5000 that are not donor-restricted will be placed in the general operating fund. Placement of unrestricted contributions over $5000 will be determined by the Board of Directors upon Finance Committee recommendations.*

> *Sample policy: Restricted Contributions, Other Than Real Property—Restricted contributions up to $5000 may be accepted at the discretion of the Executive Director/CEO. Restricted contributions in excess of $5000 may be accepted by the Executive Director/CEO and the Board Chairman and/or Treasures. The Executive Director/CEO may authorize the use of all restricted contributions only in accordance with donor intent. Restricted funds will be managed in a separate account.*

❏ The annual report should include the organization's mission statement, a summary of the past year's service accomplishments, a roster of the officers and board of directors, and financial information.

❏ The same information should be on the organization's website, along with a privacy policy, electronic access to the most recent IRS Form 990, and, for contributors, a copy of the organization's IRS Determination Letter. Avoid implying any endorsement of corporate donors, or including any banners or links that may be considered an advertisement for a sponsor, evidence of lobbying, etc. Refer to Appendix 27 for sample privacy statement.

❏ It is important that the organization know the legal and tax aspects of giving, but not attempt to give tax or legal advice to a potential donor. This knowledge should guide the organization in:

- Making an effective appeal
- Avoiding problematic gifts and transfers
- Avoiding ethical charges of improper inducement of a donor
- In general, doing the right thing

The Better Business Bureau's Wise Giving Alliance (a merger of the National Charities Information Bureau and the Council of Better Business Bureaus' Foundation has a set of standards for charity accountability that may be helpful in designing this plan (www.give.org).

❑ The IRS and most states have laws governing solicitation. The IRS website includes an article on requirements for contributions (http://www.irs.gov/charities/contributors). The National Association of State Charity Officials provides a list of state offices that regulate charitable organizations and charitable solicitations (http://www.nasconet.org/agencies).

❑ Some types of income expose nonprofit agencies to taxes and may cause the IRS to revoke the nonprofit's exemption. Nonprofits are not taxed on donations or on dividends and interest earned on investments. Nonprofits, however, may be taxed on what the IRS calls "unrelated business income," which is income from a trade or business that is regularly carried on, but that is not substantially related to the nonprofit's exempt purpose. This federal tax is called Unrelated Business Income Tax (UBIT) and may be generated from activities such as selling unrelated products to raise money (unless doing so contributes to the purpose of the organization, for example, by teaching children sales skills and helping them learn to handle money). Receiving money for placing advertisements in brochures that are mailed with the nonprofit's postage permit may not only be considered unrelated business income but may also jeopardize the organization's further use of the permit. For more information on UBIT, refer to IRS Publication 598, available at www.irs.gov.

❑ Nonprofits are subject to restrictions on the use of charitable funds, including the following:

- A nonprofit must use funds derived from tax-exempt donations to accomplish the charitable purposes stated in the nonprofit's articles and bylaws.

- A nonprofit may not redirect the use of funds donated or raised for one purpose to a different purpose without permission from the donors.

- Lobbying and political activity are restricted. A 501(c)(3) nonprofit is prohibited from engaging in partisan political activity for or against a candidate. Although lobbying is not completely prohibited, a nonprofit cannot spend a substantial part of its time, money, and effort on lobbying.

- An employee or contractor may not receive a salary or payment that exceeds the value received by the nonprofit.

❑ State laws that regulate charitable organizations and charitable solicitations, including special events and product sales, should be reviewed yearly.

Sample policy: The fundraising activities of the organization shall be coordinated in accordance with the planning of the Financial Development Committee in support of the organization's budget and strategic plan. Projects to raise funds for the organization or any of its programs shall be approved by the Board of Directors. No fundraising projects shall conflict with the board-approved organization-wide fundraising activities. Fundraising projects shall be carried out in conformity with the applicable policies of the organization and federal, state, and local laws and regulations.

❑ For annual or one-time special events, organizations should consider additional special event insurance that covers such areas as:

- General liability
- Liquor liability
- Event cancellation
- Participant legal liability (sporting events only)
- Accidental death and dismemberment
- Spectator and participant medical
- Hired and non-owned automobile liability
- Hired and non-owned automobile physical damage
- Third-party property damage
- Rental equipment
- Unlimited certificates of insurance (including special certificates)

Refer to Worksheet O-18: Insurance Coverage for other insurance considerations.

❑ The organization should have a policy regarding serving alcohol on organization property and at special events.

Sample policy: Alcohol will not be offered or consumed in conjunction with the conduct of direct youth-service activities or duly-called business meetings of the organization at all levels. Alcohol will not be served at any functions held at facilities owned by the organization when the function has youth involvement or presence on the site. Functions that are adult-focused may serve alcohol with the approval of the Executive Committee. The Executive Committee may also restrict the type of alcohol served and the access. This policy also applies to community or user groups. If approval is given to a user group to serve alcohol, a hold-harmless agreement will be required. Alcohol may be served at organization adult-focused fundraising and social functions when serving alcohol is the social norm and when the focus of such functions is not on the consumption of alcohol. In all situations, applicable laws on the storage and use of alcohol will be observed. The misuse or abuse of alcohol or the behavior caused by such will not be tolerated.

ORGANIZATIONAL WORKSHEET O-25

Security

Rationale

Feeling personally secure is a state of mind based on knowing that reasonable precautions have been taken. The objective of security planning is to provide a relatively secure working and service environment that allows business operation to continue in an uninterrupted and orderly fashion.

Plan

1. What is your security plan regarding the following?		
	Plan	Rationale
Lighting		
Alarms		
Boundary barriers		
Brush and undergrowth around buildings		
Keys and locks		
Posting "no trespassing" signs		
Orientation of staff		
Personal belongings		
Visitors		
Parking area		
Money at the office		
Private files		
2. How are intruders dealt with?		
3. What kinds of follow-up are done when evidence of intrusion exists (e.g., vandalism, threatening notes)?		
4. What procedures are in place for handling visitors?		
5. How are staff members informed of security plans?		

Guidelines and Information to Help Complete the Plan

❑ Worksheet O-25: Security has a list of items that need to be considered when designing the security plan. Have a written rationale for every item implemented and for every item not implemented. A clear rationale helps interpret security measures and explain them to parents, board members, membership, the public at large, insurance companies, and various authorities.

- External lighting—Consider various types of lighting and how extensive the lighting should be. Lighting may not be in the control of the organization, in which case it will need to be negotiated with the landlord or public utility company. If the organization controls the exterior lighting, consider lights at doors, connecting walks or paths, and parking areas.

- Alarms—Consider which alarms would be best to use for security reasons.

- Boundary barriers—Plant or build structural barriers, such as fences or other constructions, that serve as a deterrent to unauthorized entry, but not as a hiding place for intruders. Most local police departments have someone with the title of "crime prevention through environmental design" (CPTED), who will come to the office or program site and give advice regarding areas of risk in the facility. This process should include surveying the site for facility-design risks that reduce crime.

- Keys and locks—Keys should be distributed according to need, as opposed to convenience. Keys should be collected or locks re-keyed when a staff position change occurs. Consideration should also be given to keys for locked files and petty cash and other money in the office.

- Orientation of staff—Impress upon staff the importance of safety without unduly alarming them. Discuss working late and safety leaving the building.

- Visitors—If visitors are permitted, they must be required to check in. Develop procedures for authorized and unauthorized visitors.

❏ Occasionally, what appears to be a prank or vandalism may be a sign of a more serious problem. Therefore, these incidents should always be investigated. Staff members should have a clear understanding of if and when to approach an intruder and what follow-up steps to take. Worksheet O-4: Emergency Procedures for Hazards and/or Disasters—Office includes emergency information about intruders.

ORGANIZATIONAL WORKSHEET O-26

Technological Usage and Record Security

Rationale

Policies and procedures are needed to address staff, volunteer, and vendor access to technology associated with the use of computers, the Internet, telephones, and fax machines for business or personal use. This policy should include protecting personal records and confidential business, marketing, and financial information used in the day–to-day business of the organization.

Plan

1.	List the organization's telephones and electronic communications systems/equipment, computers, and other business equipment and information systems that are used by the organization, but owned by individuals		
	Systems	# sole property of the organization	# owned by individuals for business use
	Telephone		
	Internet access		
	CD/radio systems		
	Equipment	# sole property of the organization	# owned by individuals for business use
	Computers (hardware)		
	Printers		
	Cameras		
	Fax machines		
	Telephones		
	Two-way radios		
	Pagers		
	Information sent, received, or stored	Security system that can be monitored	How stored
	Email		
	Voicemail		
	Electronic files		
	Computer software	Licensed for individual computers	Licensed for network use	# owned by individuals for business use
	Microsoft® Word			
	Microsoft Excel®			
	Other			

2.	What are the technology usage, rights, and security policies or procedures regarding the following?
	Computers
	Internet
	Internet security systems
	Organization or staff image on public domain
	Telephone
	Facsimiles (Faxes)
3.	The policy regarding official website postings of personal images or information:
	Meets the requirements of Children's Online Privacy Act
	does not permit identifying pictured children or adults
	only includes areas where personal matters may be discussed if they are in password protected areas and with the persons consent
	includes a Privacy Policy Statement posted that includes information collection, use and sharing
4.	The policy regarding volunteer-managed Web sites and listserves is:
	How are the policies are communicated to staff ?
	Is there an acknowledgement and release statement for staff?
	employees are expected to sign to sign the statement
5.	Volunteers in what roles are informed of these policies?
	How are the policies communicated to volunteers?
	Is there an acknowledgement and release statement for volunteers?
	volunteers are expected to sign the statement
6.	The security plan includes:
	A periodic review for compliance with state and federal laws.
	Who is designated to coordinate the security plan?
	Policies for volunteers and employees that have access to personal information of clients, other volunteers or staff including:
	receive training and copies of the organizations policies
	Have opportunities to ask questions about their rights and responsibilities as a full-time, part-time or temporary employee, volunteer, or member of organization and the consequences of noncompliance
	Have signed a statement acknowledging and agreeing to abide by the policies
	How often are the identification and evaluation of internal and external risks reviewed?
	A response to a breach of privacy or security or system failure that includes:

Guidelines and Information to Help Complete the Plan

❑ Security and technology-usage policies associated with day-to-day organization business should be provided to all staff members and volunteers upon acceptance to serve in an official organization role. Refer to Appendix 26a for a sample.

❑ The policy should cover sole ownership of the equipment or communications systems, as well as the information received, sent, transmitted, or stored in the systems/equipment. It should also cover the ownership and control of the organization's website, logo, and images.

❑ If the organization allows some private use of the organization's equipment/software (computers, telephones, faxes, cameras, LCDs, etc.) during breaks, or allows them to be borrowed with permission, these scenarios should be addressed in the policy.

❑ It is important that the organization ensures that all individuals associated with it, including youth participants and their parents, are assured of appropriate confidentiality and are treated with respect and professionalism at all times. It is also important that anything that is in the public domain about the organization reflects upon it positively. Accordingly, the following standards should be considered for all employees in connection with the use of the Internet and other electronic communications media:

- If an employee creates or maintains a website or blog about himself (e.g., MySpace, Facebook), he must exercise the highest degree of good judgment regarding the material placed on that site or blog. For example, such individuals should ask themselves: "What would prospective or current employees/participants/parents think about me and/or the organization if they accessed this site or blog?" If the answer is that the member might perceive something negative, then the material that may create a negative impression about the individual or the organization should not be placed on the site or blog.

- If an individual participates in a blog or other site, he may not identify himself as associated with the organization, either explicitly or implicitly, unless authorized in writing by the organization.

- Content placed on the Internet or transmitted via other media may not be potentially or actually defamatory, abusive, threatening, harassing, invasive of privacy, or injurious to any member or any other employee.

❑ If the organization maintains an official website, any picture, drawing, rendering, or other image requires the expressed written approval of all adults in the image and at least one parent or guardian of any youth under the age of 18 shown before being posted on the site. Specifically, if information is collected or disseminated, such as email addresses, birth dates, addresses, genders, or any other personal information from youth and children under the age of 13 from your website, it must meet the requirements of the Children's Online Privacy Protection Act (COPPA), which include the following:

- Obtaining verifiable parental consent before collecting, using, or disclosing information from a child (under the age of 13)

- Having and posting a privacy notice on the home page of the website and at each location where personal information of a child is being collected

- Understanding the responsibility to protect children's privacy and safety

❑ The organization should have an Internet privacy policy statement available on its website for anything that utilizes the web in securing personal information from users and participants. This policy should cover treatment of personally identifiable information that may be collected when a user is on the organization's website. A sample privacy policy statement is found in Appendix 27.

❑ Information about volunteer-managed websites is included in the sample usage policy found in Appendix 26.

❑ A number of state and federal laws involve the confidential handling of personal information regarding both customers and clients of the organization and other employees or volunteers. These laws include, but are not limited to, FACTA, HIPAA, The Economic Espionage Act, The Privacy Act, Gramm/Leach/Billey Act, identity theft laws (where applicable), trade secrets protections, and implied contract breach.

Employees and volunteers who have access to personal records must be informed of the organization's policies and agree to maintain the confidentially of all documents, credit cards, and personal information of any type and agree that such information may only be used for their intended business purpose

❑ The organization should provide volunteers and staff members with a statement to sign stating that they have received and agreed to comply with the usage and privacy policies. Refer to Appendix 26a for a sample. The consequences of a violation of the policy should be listed in the policy and stated in the agreement.

❑ The Fair and Accurate Credit Transactions Act (FACTA) includes regulations for handling personal information to prevent identity theft. Fines and penalties are in place if personal information isn't destroyed and gets out. The organization should designate a person to coordinate the security measures and create a plan to handle a breach in security or system failure that must be addressed immediately, including actions to repair the problem in the eyes of customers, government regulators, and management. Refer to Worksheet O-21: Record Retention and Destruction.

ORGANIZATIONAL WORKSHEET O-27

Contracts for Services

Rationale

A contract is an agreement between two parties that includes an offer and an acceptance. Contracts are also a method of transferring a risk to another party. It is important that the party assuming the risk can handle it or is able to cope with the financial ramifications of a breach of contract.

Plan

1. What contracts for services are needed?	Liability being:	
	Assumed	Transferred

2. Who has the authority to negotiate and sign contracts?	
Type of Contract	Who can negotiate?
Employment contracts	
Food service	
Maintenance	
Health services	
Program services	
Rental contracts	
Contracts for products	
Construction contracts	
Other(s)	

3. Certificates of insurance are required for contracts for:
4. Certificates of insurance are reviewed by:
5. Do contracts include the following as appropriate?
Terms, dates, and times
Costs, conditions for use, and minimum fees
Services provided
Cancellation and refund policies
Damage or loss fees
A "force majeure" provision

6.	Do user-group agreements specify responsibility for the following?
	First aid and emergency care and transportation
	Supervision and behavior of the group
	Supervision of recreational activities
	Providing safety orientation to participants
	Insurance coverage

Guidelines and Information to Help Complete the Plan

❑ A contract is a method of protection against loss that transfers the financial risk to another party or transfers or assumes certain liabilities. It is important to know if liability is being assumed or transferred under the contract and, if possible, the amount. If the organization is entering in to a contract and transferring the risk to another party, be sure that the other party has adequate insurance to handle the risk. Ask for and review a "certificate of insurance" to see if the limits are sufficient. When appropriate, the organization should be named as an additional insured.

❑ The board, in conjunction with the executive director, must establish who has the authority to sign contracts. The executive director may delegate some staff members to sign contracts for a limited amount.

❑ It is important to understand the difference between an independent contractor and an employee. Refer to www.dol.gov/esa/whd/flsa for guidelines on the classification and use of independent contractors. Employment contracts should only be for those services that meet the Fair Labor Standards Act criteria for an independent contractor. Most seasonal, part-time, and full time staff members receive a letter of agreement, not a contract.

❑ Waivers, releases, and exculpatory clauses, which are contracts that prevent a party from being held liable in case of injury caused by negligence, are covered in Worksheet P-37: Waivers, Permissions, and Agreements for Participation. Samples are found in Appendix 7.

❑ Contracts may include indemnification clauses or "hold-harmless" clauses that transfer the financial consequences of a loss or the responsibility for damages to another party. These transfers are most often done through insurance and are agreements between businesses, not individuals, as in a waiver or release.

❑ Some contracts, such as rental agreements for property or facilities for special events, may need to include a force majeure provision to address the conditions under which a party may terminate an agreement without liability, as in the case of major unforeseen events. Force majeure events typically include war, terrorism, major disasters, or when the event is affected by a cause beyond the control of the parties that makes it inadvisable, illegal, or commercially impractical to hold a successful event or provide the facility.

❑ Contracts for program services should include such things as who is responsible for providing and maintaining equipment, safety rules, participation requirements, emergency care, and/or other items included as the standard of care for the activity.

❑ The terms of the contracts should be specified in writing and reviewed by both parties to be sure that all aspects and considerations of the agreement are clearly understood. Be sure that the indemnification clause includes not only compensatory damages, but also both punitive damages and defense costs.

❑ Construction contracts usually include sections on the legal agreement, bonds and insurance, general conditions, special provisions, project specifications, and contract plans.

- The legal agreement is the standard agreement between the contractor and the organization or owner that binds them to the terms and conditions of the construction.

- Bonds and insurance must be included and provided by the contractor prior to the signing of the contract.

- The general conditions cover topics such as the standards and codes, resolution of disputes, guarantees, safety and protection on the site, unforeseen conditions, how any changes in work with are dealt with, tests and acceptance of work, payment, and suspension or termination of work.

- Special provisions are more specific to the project.

- Project specifications and contract plans detail exactly what work is required of the contractor, including cleaning up the worksite at the end of the project. Always plan a preconstruction meeting to discuss any issues that the organization or its staff may have or any disruption of the program or operation. Identify who the contractor will be dealing with during the construction. Approve the schedule and set up inspections and a procedure for final acceptance of the work before final payment is made.

ORGANIZATIONAL WORKSHEET O-28

Screening of Staff and Volunteers

Rationale

The screening process for paid staff and volunteers is probably one of the most important jobs an administrator does. It provides records of the screening process and helps control losses resulting from accusations of discrimination and negligent hiring. This process is instrumental to the quality of the program and the benefits of the program to a child. Note: The screening and hiring process for employees should be consistent with the organization's personnel and program screening policies (refer to Worksheet P-54: Screening of Staff and Volunteers).

Plan

1.	The documentation to support the screening process includes:
	Job descriptions for each position, shared with the applicant
	Application forms completed for each applicant
	A personal interview with each applicant
	Verification of previous work (including volunteer) history and two references
	Criminal background check (or voluntary disclosure statement for those under 18)
	Driving record for anyone regularly transporting children
	Documentation of skills required for the job
	Confirmation of volunteer status
2.	The interview process includes:
	A face-to-face or phone interview
	A set of consistent questions that will help determine skills specific to the job, or if appropriate, the suitability of staff to work with, or have access to, children
	An explanation of the job expectations, working environment, and the organizations' philosophy and/or goals for youth development that pertain to the job
3.	The procedure for reference checks includes:
4.	The criminal records background check procedures:
	The organization secured for doing criminal record background checks is:
	The person or position responsible is:

Types of positions	"Hits" or records that disqualify a person are:
Executive director	
Board members	
Staff or volunteers with direct access to children	
Staff or volunteers with direct access to children's personal information	
Drivers transporting children	
Staff or volunteers with access to money for financial records	

Procedures for handling situations in which the criminal record check recovered a "hit" or record are:		

5. The hiring process for employees and the forms were reviewed:

By	Qualification	Date

Guidelines and Information to Help Complete the Plan

❑ The hiring and screening process for employees and volunteers includes systems to ensure that applicants and employees receive fair and equal treatment. The process includes procedures for posting jobs, clear job descriptions, completed application forms, documented references, interviews, criminal background checks, and the documentation of each step.

❑ A lawsuit for negligent hiring is based on the theory that the employer is liable for the actions of an employee who was unfit or who created an unreasonable risk of harm. A negligent hiring lawsuit is an action wherein a parent sues the organization for injuries sustained by a participant that were caused by the careless actions of a staff member or of an unqualified staff member. This scenario also extends to volunteers. Parents have many expectations for the selection of staff members and volunteers that may have access to their child.

❑ A job description should be provided for each position that includes the essential functions of the job, any special knowledge or skills required, the level of responsibility required, and the line of accountability and supervision. Refer to Worksheet O-17: Serving Persons With Disabilities and Worksheet P-27: Serving Persons With Disabilities. Each position has a different set of issues to consider, but special considerations should be given for those working directly with children.

❑ Each new applicant for a paid or volunteer position should complete a personnel application form. The application should include a signed release for a background check. Verification includes checking work history for "gaps" and to see if the applicant has been employed as claimed. Applications or personnel files should be updated as a part of the evaluation process. Employers should not ask about any of the following, because to not hire a candidate because of any one of them is discriminatory:

- Race
- Color
- Sex
- Religion
- National origin
- Birthplace
- Age
- Disability
- Marital/family status

❏ A personal interview should be conducted with each applicant (either face-to-face or by phone). Although some applicants may not be working directly with children, if the organization serves youth they may have access to records or to information on children. Appendix 23 has a list of sample questions to ask potential staff members working directly with children, along with questions that should be avoided during the hiring process.

❏ Reference checks on all prospective staff members and volunteers will be conducted and documented prior to anyone assuming job responsibilities. References can be in the form of a letter, completed reference form, or documentation of a personal telephone discussion.

❏ Criminal background checks of adults who could have access to children or their personal information should be included in the screening process. Screening should be done upon entry as a staff member or volunteer and after any break in service. In addition to the more extensive criminal background check, the U.S Department of Justice National Sex Offender Public Registry provides a check of sexual offenders in the national data base as a free service (www.nsopr.gov).

> *Sample policy: All applicants (for paid or unpaid positions) who work directly with children or youth must complete an application form. The organization will complete at least two reference checks for each applicant. A criminal background check will be completed on all applicants who work directly with children and youth.*

❏ Procedures should be in place for decisions regarding a "hit" on criminal background checks. What types of "hits" would be disqualifying offenses?

For example, such hits might include felonies or misdemeanors classified as offenses against a person or against public order (e.g., prostitution, obscenity, child pornography), or a violation of a law for possession or distribution of a controlled substance. Does the decision vary with the job and or the conviction? Is a time limitation in place on some types of hits? Records obtained should be kept in restricted files. The Nonprofit Risk Management Center (http://www.nonprofitrisk.org) has additional information on criminal background checks and a list of state criminal history record repositories.

❑ "Voluntary disclosure statements" are signed statements attesting to the nonconviction of crimes against children. These may be used for staff members and volunteers, such as parents helping with a small group where they are supervised by another adult, those under 18 years of age, or international staff (in which case no available record exists). Volunteers should sign a Confirmation of Volunteer Status and Agreements to confirm that they are participating as volunteers. This statement may be added to the application form.

❑ A driving record should be obtained from those persons who regularly transport children. The organization should work with an insurance agent to obtain records and design a policy regarding what kinds of violations, such as driving under the influence (D.U.I.), speeding, and reckless operation, will prohibit someone from transporting participants in the program.

❑ The application and screening process should be reviewed by a legal or human resources professional at least every three years. Photographs should be taken of all staff members and volunteers working directly with children and then attached to their personnel records for identification at a later time if needed.

ORGANIZATIONAL WORKSHEET O-29

Employment Practices

Rationale

Employers are responsible for being informed on state and federal laws and the reporting and record-keeping requirements. Personnel policies and practices help assure consistency in administration and result in fewer misunderstandings. Personnel policies should be the same on Worksheet P-56: Employment Practices.

Plan

1. List positions by title	
Exempt:	Nonexempt:
2. Timesheets are required for nonexempt employees	If not, why not?
Any timesheets required for exempt employees are needed because:	
Timesheets are kept by:	
3. Who is the person responsible for OSHA records, including maintaining the log and the summary and record of each reportable occupational injury and/or illness?	
Location where OSHA records are kept:	
4. Labor law posters are posted at the following worksites:	Who is responsible for ensuring that posters are continually displayed?
5. Procedures for handling concerns/complaints about wages, benefits, hours, and working conditions are:	
6. The organization has personnel policies that include:	
Employment Policies/Practices	Date Last Reviewed
Employment at will	
Equal employment opportunity	
Problem-solving process	
Hiring	
Employment of relatives (nepotism)	
Employment categories	
Introductory period	

	Change in status	
	Position descriptions	
	Americans with Disabilities Act	
	Performance appraisal process	
	Safety	
	Personnel files	
	Employee Conduct and Business Practices	Date Last Reviewed
	Harassment	
	Consensual relationships	
	Attendance and punctuality	
	Professional appearance	
	Internal investigation/search	
	Conflicts of interest	
	Ethics	
	Technologies—computers/Internet	
	Outside work	
	Personal finances	
	Corrective action	
	Separation	
	Pay Practices	Date Last Reviewed
	Time records	
	Pay periods and paydays	
	Overtime	
	Leave Benefits	Date Last Reviewed
	Holidays	
	Vacation	
	Sick leave or personal leave	
	Medical leaves of absence	
	Funeral leave	
	Military leave	
	Jury duty leave	
	Benefit Information	Date Last Reviewed
	ERISA Rights	
	Brief summary of group insurance	
	Health continuation	
	Coverage—COBRA	

	HIPAA	
	Receipt of personnel policies acknowledgment	Date Last Reviewed
7.	Personnel policies reviewed by: (attorney)	Date Last Reviewed
8.	The organization has policies for dismissal of volunteers	Date Last Reviewed

Guidelines and Information to Help Complete the Plan

❑ The major federal employment laws currently affecting long-term care of employees include:

- Title VII of Civil Rights Act of 1964
- Age Discrimination in Employment Act (ADEA)
- Section 1981 of the Civil Rights Act of 1866
- Civil Rights Act of 1991
- National Labor Relations Act
- Fair Labor Standards Act
- Occupational Safety and Health Act
- Americans with Disabilities Act (ADA)
- Family and Medical Leave Act of 1993
- Veterans Protection/Preference Laws
- Pregnancy Discrimination Act of 1978
- Immigration Reform and Control Act of 1986
- Equal Pay Act

Refer to the Department of Labor (www.dol.gov) for more detailed information. Failure to post labor laws in a place of employment can result in fines of up to $7,500 per inspection. Search for labor law posters on the Internet and select those designed specifically for your state.

❑ The Fair Labor Standards Act addresses wage and hour requirements for "exempt" and "nonexempt" employees. The Department of Labor (www.dol.gov) provides more information on both federal laws and laws specific to each state.

❑ No statute of limitation exists for fraud. Severe financial ramifications may arise out of classifying a person incorrectly—exempt vs. nonexempt and employee vs. Independent contractor.

❑ In some states, summer camps may be considered seasonal and therefore exempt from federal minimum wage requirements. Refer to Worksheet P-56:

Employment Practices for information on seasonal exemptions and how to determine if a camp is considered seasonal.

❑ In most cases, a caretaker or site manager is considered a nonexempt employee and qualifies for minimum wage and overtime. The employee may receive a salary based on the hours he is expected to work each week. Overtime must be documented and paid at "time and a half" of the hourly salary for any hours beyond 40 in a week. Since in most situations the time needed in the summer is greater, it may be more economical to hire a seasonal assistant to handle the longer hours. The organization may also choose to pay the individual a flat rate per work week. Even though the work days and hours may vary per week during the year, the employer must meet the minimum wage and overtime requirements for hours in a week. Housing and food benefits may not be considered a part of the salary.

❑ The Occupational Safety and Health Act is designed to regulate employment conditions related to occupational safety and health and to achieve safer and more healthful workplaces. To help ensure that employees (often referred to as whistleblowers) are free to report safety and health concerns to OSHA, the Act prohibits any manner of discrimination against the employee. Visit www.osha.gov for more information on the whistleblower protection program.

❑ OSHA requires that employers with more than 10 full- or part-time employees at any one time in a calendar year keep injury and illness records on paid staff. They should be kept at the workplace for at least five years after the year to which they relate. Visit www.osha.gov for more on record-keeping requirements.

❑ In addition to the OSHA requirements, record-keeping requirements exist for the other laws covered in this section. Employment records relating to wages, hours (work time schedules), sex, occupation, condition of employment, etc., are required to be kept for two years. General employee information is required to be kept three years. Refer to Worksheet O-21: Record Retention and Destruction for more on this topic. States may have additional requirements.

❑ The National Labor Relations Act gives employees the right to unionize, or the right of collective bargaining for wages, working conditions, and benefits. Although unions are not common in 501(c)(3) organizations, this law also covers an employer's retaliation against two or more employees complaining about wages, hours, or working conditions.

❑ "At-will employment" is a doctrine that defines an employment relationship in which either party can terminate the relationship with no liability if no contract exists to govern the employment relationship. According to this legal doctrine, any hiring is presumed to be "at will"; that is, the employer is free to discharge individuals "for good cause, or bad cause, or no cause at all," and the employee is equally free to quit, strike, or otherwise cease work.

❑ In many states, an employee handbook with personnel policies and practices is viewed as a legal contract. Be careful about selecting words that can be misinterpreted or allow for no flexibility, such as permanent; will, should, and shall; probationary period; fair; is cause for termination; and shall be terminated.

❑ Persons being paid an hourly wage (nonexempt) cannot also be "volunteers" doing the same work for additional hours, but they may volunteer in a different area. Information on dismissal of volunteers is included in the Worksheet P-56: Employment Practices and in Appendix 30.

ORGANIZATIONAL WORKSHEET O-30

Harassment—Sexual and Other

Rationale

All employees and volunteers should have a right to work in an environment free of all forms of discrimination, including harassment. Sexual or other types of harassment, including inappropriate actions based on race, creed, color, gender, age, disability, religion, or national origin interferes with work performance and/or creates an intimidating, hostile, or offensive work environment. This policy should be consistent with Worksheet P-59: Harassment—Sexual and Other.

Plan

1. The policy that prohibits harassment is:
How are staff members and volunteers informed of the policy?
2. The consequences of such harassment results in:
Who is responsible for deciding on the consequences?
3. The complaint procedures are:
Who is responsible for investigating the complaint?
Where are complaints of harassment retained?
4. Who is responsible for determining and taking appropriate corrective action?

Guidelines and Information to Help Complete the Plan

❑ The policy should include the employee's right to work in an environment free from harassment and state that the organization will not tolerate sexual or other types of harassment of its employees or volunteers in any form. Abuse of the dignity of anyone through ethnic, racist, or sexist slurs, or through other derogatory or objectionable conduct, is offensive employee behavior and will be subject to corrective action.

❑ The policy should also forbid a supervisor from threatening an employee with suggestions that submission to, or rejection of, sexual advances will in any way influence any personnel decision regarding employment, evaluation, wages, advancement, assigned duties, shifts assignments, or any other condition of employment.

❑ Sexual harassment includes such actions as repeated offensive sexual flirtation, advances, or propositions; continual or repeated abuse of a sexual nature; graphic verbal commentary about an individual's body; sexually degrading words to describe an individual; and the display in the workplace of sexually suggestive objects or pictures. Sexual favoritism in the workplace that adversely affects the employment opportunities of third parties may take the form of implicit "quid pro quo" harassment and/or "hostile work environment" harassment.

❑ The procedures for making or dealing with a complaint should include the serious nature of such a charge and state that such a charge will be treated with the strictest confidence, not be shared with co-workers, and not be subject to fear of reprisal. Procedures should include the following steps:

- The employee/volunteer should clearly express displeasure to the harasser.

- The employee/volunteer should report the situation to his supervisor, unless the supervisor is the harasser, in which case the report should be made to that person's supervisor or a member of the administrative staff.

- A designated director, or in the case of the executive director, a member of the personnel committee, will investigate the complaint. The employee should not suffer retaliation for filing a complaint. The records should not be entered into the employee's file, but be retained in a separate confidential file.

- If the investigation confirms the allegations, appropriate corrective action must be taken.

Complaints

Rationale

Complaints often come into the office. At times, the receiver of the complaint encounters a person who displays anger and causes the receiver to become defensive. Sometimes the person receiving the complaint knows little or nothing about the situation and cuts the complainant short or argues back. Having a process to deal with complaints helps the listener hear the concern being expressed, and then handle it or refer it to the appropriate person. This plan should be consistent with Worksheet P-51: Complaints.

Plan

1. Staff positions that may deal with complaints from parents regarding:	
Registration/fees	
Program/activities	
Program administrator	
Program leader(s)	
Products/product sales	
Child abuse	
Supervision	
Facilities	
Transportation	
Other:	
2. Staff positions that may deal with complaints from vendors:	
3. Staff positions that may deal with complaints from funders:	
4. Staff positions that may deal with complaints from collaborations:	
5. Staff positions that may deal with complaints from youth:	
6. Staff training for handling complaints includes using a report form and:	
7. Type of complaints that require the person the taking complaint to inform a supervisor:	
8. Complaints and suggestions logged and reviewed by:	

Personnel	
Program	
Product sales	
Registration/fees	

Guidelines and Information to Help Complete the Plan

❑ People are more often interested in pursuing litigation when something irritates them. If they believe that they are being listened to and treated professionally or that a program has qualified leadership, medical insurance, and is the well-run, safe program announced in the flyer or brochure, they are less likely to challenge that record.

❑ Identify the appropriate staff person to handle various types of complaints, as well as a backup person or supervisor. Train other staff members that may receive calls in techniques to calmly refer the complaint to the designated staff person.

- Training should include how to:
- Ask the right questions
- Listen effectively
- Use positive nonverbal communication
- Identify the problem, not just the symptoms
- Establish comfort, rapport, and trust
- Disagree without becoming argumentative
- Understand another's point of view
- Remain firm when no change is possible
- Stay calm when the complainer is being abusive
- Defuse explosive situations and confront anger
- Convey respect and maintain a positive attitude

❑ A sample form for handling complaints appears in Appendix 20. It is important to log and periodically review complaints. Some complaints may need to be added to personnel files, while others may provide input to decisions about programs, staff structures, registration processes, or fees.

ORGANIZATIONAL WORKSHEET O-32

Supervision of Staff

Rationale

The supervision of staff is the responsibility of the executive director or his designee. Those staff members who work directly with children are included in the program management section on Worksheet P-58: Supervision of Staff.

Plan

1. List the positions that supervise staff members, including the executive director or his or her designee:	
Supervisors	People They Supervise
2. Have all staff members been provided a chart showing reporting lines and accountability?	
Job descriptions?	
Personnel policies?	
Orientation to the organization, their jobs, and other information?	
Information on safety issues and general office procedures?	
W-2 and other forms?	
4. What are the guidelines for acceptable and unacceptable staff behaviors?	
5. What problems might occur in terms of supervision?	
6. How have supervisors been instructed to handle these problems?	
7. What training in supervision and performance review have supervisors received?	
8. How and when do staff conferences and/or evaluations take place?	

Guidelines and Information to Help Complete the Plan

❑ In most cases, it is difficult for any one person to supervise more than seven or eight staff members at a time. Staff conferences and/or evaluations should happen on a regularly scheduled basis. However, major issues (coming from the supervisor or employee) that need to be addressed should not have to wait until a scheduled time.

❑ Training for supervisors should include an understanding of the job expectations and the plan for supervision. Clear guidelines for identifying and addressing both of these issues are included in the sample form in Appendix 29.

ORGANIZATIONAL WORKSHEET O-33

Product Tampering

Rationale

Although serious incidents during product sales are rare, the financial repercussions to the organization could be great if a problematic situation should develop and the organization does not have a well-implemented plan for dealing with it.

Plan

1. Who is the person designated as having primary responsibility for handling complaints?	
Name	Phone #
Persons to contact if the primary person is not available:	

2. After all information is gathered, who is consulted to resolve the disposition of the complaint?		
Person	Name	Phone #
President		
Product supplier		
National organization		
Attorney		
Insurance agent		
Food & Drug Administration		

3. When is it necessary to have tests of a product conducted by an independent testing lab?		
Who do you contact?		
Lab to Contact	Contact Name	Address
How long will testing take?		
Who receives the test results?		

4. Who is the official spokesperson to the media?
5. Who has the authority to approve a statement for media release?
6. What kind of information is issued in a brief statement?
7. Has the media statement been approved by the product supplier and the organization?
8. News media contacts established:

Name	Media	Phone #

Guidelines and Information to Help Complete the Plan

❑ The greatest potential risks for loss during a product sale originate from two similar, but in certain respects, different sources.

- A product may be contaminated during manufacturing or packaging. For example, the contamination may consist of some foreign material, such as glass chips, metal, or nut shells, found in candy. This loss should be covered by the supplier's product liability insurance.

- A product may be tampered with. Foreign material may be introduced into a product such as candy or the package after the product leaves the manufacturer's control. In this case, the manufacturer cannot be held responsible.

❑ In Camp Fire USA, all approved suppliers are required to meet Food and Drug Administration (FDA) standards and pass periodic inspections. All approved suppliers must furnish certificates of liability insurance with the organization as an additional insured party. Packaging must meet national specifications.

❑ The organization must be sure that each product is provided in shrink-wrapped, tamper-resistant packaging. Clearly define the system for handling food products from the point of delivery through the sale to the consumer. It is essential to check all packages as they flow through the distribution system. Suppliers will give credit for any package with a broken seal or that shows any evidence of mishandling. Sellers and consumers should be informed that the organization would cheerfully refund the money if any indication exists that the package is not satisfactory.

❑ In the event that the unthinkable happens, it is important to be prepared. Hold a meeting before the fundraising event begins with staff members, the product sale chairperson, and any other involved parties and establish a plan for what to do should an incident occur. Practice the plan using several hypothetical situations. For example, a customer reports to the police that glass has been found in a package of candy, but the police lab reports that the foreign material is crystallized sugar. A second example involves a customer reporting to a leader that metal was found in a package of popcorn. When finished, each person should be given a copy of the plan, and additional copies should be kept by the telephone, emailed so they can be saved for access from a home or office computer, and placed in an official file.

❑ When a complaint or report of an incident occurs, the following information must be gathered and recorded immediately:

- Date and time the report is received.
- Cause of complaint (e.g., type of candy)

- Date of the cause of complaint

- Name and address of the complainant

- Name of local, state, or federal regulatory agencies, if they are involved

- Name and phone number of person receiving the complaint

- What is the nature of the complaint? Does it appear to be an isolated case or could it have broader impact?

- Who verified the facts of the incident? Where are the actual packages alleged to be contaminated or tampered with? What is the process for obtaining the damaged product?

- If the product is sent for testing, the test results must be recorded and dated.

- In addition, initiate a daily log of the incident that includes recordings of all pertinent conversations. The log should also include all expenses incurred, copies of any newspaper articles, and a description of any impact a public announcement may have had on the fundraising event. (This information is important if a liability claim is filed.)

- It is important to discuss what needs to happen to avoid panicking or reacting before all of the facts are available.

- Refer to Worksheet O-31: Complaints for more information.

☐ Consult with the product supplier and the organization's national office before making any decisions to release information to the general public. This decision could affect fundraising events in progress all over the country.

☐ Be prepared—the organization could hear from the media before the incident is even reported to supervisors. It is essential that all employees avoid making any statements until all of the facts have been verified.

- The organization should not call a news conference unless it is a matter of life and death. If the public should be made aware of a situation, the organization should prepare and distribute news releases.

- The organization must not play favorites with the media. It must give the story to all media at the same time. If one paper or one station has an "exclusive," others will search for additional information or another angle to make stories of their own.

- The organization must be committed to accuracy—and never say, "No comment." It must also never hold back important information. On the other hand, it must not give out any information of which it is not absolutely sure. Don't speculate. Don't guess. Don't estimate.

- The organization must be as specific as possible in the lead or first sentence of the story. For example, don't mention "Camp Fire candy" if the problem is limited to "Camp Fire caramel clusters." Don't say "incidents" have been reported—if two incidents have occurred, the story should say "two incidents." The story should not say that the problem occurred in "Jackson County" if the reports were confined to southeast Kansas City.

❑ Refer to Worksheet O-9: Emergency Media Plan for additional information.

ORGANIZATIONAL WORKSHEET O-34

Intellectual Property, Copyrights, and Royalties

Rationale

It is important to copyright the materials that have been developed with agency resources for the exclusive use of the organization. Materials copyrighted by the organization are protected, though a significant degree of similarity must exist to establish infringement. Intellectual property infringements and copyright permission and violations related to a specific program are detailed on Worksheet P-39: Intellectual Property Infringements, Copyrights, and Royalties.

Plan

1. What copyrights have been registered by the organization with the Register of Copyrights at the Library of Congress?	
Name	Date

2. Who is responsible for securing copyrights?
3. Who is responsible for maintaining the graphic standards?
4. Who is responsible for obtaining permission from the copyright owner to use the name, service mark, and insignias on program merchandise?
5. Who is responsible for obtaining permission to reproduce any of the organization's copyrighted material that is not explicitly identified with permission to copy?
6. What is the procedure to request use of materials that are copyrighted by another person or organization?
Where are the records of permission to use copyrighted materials kept?
Who is responsible for these records?
7. Procedures for the use of original works of music, art, or film requiring royalties to be paid or permission to waive royalty fees secured include:

Guidelines and Information to Help Complete the Plan

❑ Intellectual property includes patents, trademarks, copyrights, and trade secrets. Intellectual property infringements are activities that infringe or misappropriate the intellectual property rights of others, including copyrights, trademarks, service marks, trade secrets, software piracy, and patents held by individuals, corporations, or other entities. For example, using a photograph of a child with a trademark, logo, or licensed artwork on their T-shirt on your website, in a brochure, or in a book may be an infringement.

❑ A copyright establishes the right of the owner to prevent the reproduction and use of its works by unauthorized competitors. A copyright can cover creative expression in the form of photographic, audio-visual, literary, graphic, and musical works in a tangible form. A person or agency cannot copyright an idea, procedure, system, concept, principle, etc.

❑ A trademark is a distinctive mark, symbol, word, or group of words used to distinguish the goods of a specific manufacturer and thus differentiate them from similar goods.

❑ The name, service mark, insignias, trademarks, and copyrighted materials are used and protected as specified by the organization. Any organization should guard against the unauthorized use of its name, insignias, and official uniforms and programs. Any infraction should be reported to the organization. Failure to protect the ownership of a copyright could lead to loss of the copyright, because the law may consider those materials to be in public domain.

❑ The owner of a copyright is entitled to seek an injunction restraining infringement, damages and profits, impoundment of the infringing article, and destruction of infringing copies and plates. The copyright law also provides for the recovery of full costs and attorney fees by successful parties.

❑ A royalty is a set amount that is paid to the owner of a copyright for either exclusive or nonexclusive rights by authorizing the manufacture, use, or sale of the product. Royalties are often paid for the use of music or songs, films, names, logos, etc.

❑ The performance or presentation of music, art, or films in situations where fees, registrations, or admissions are collected may be subject to royalty payments. For example, the performance or recorded use of copyrighted music—even with original lyrics—is subject to royalty, even if someone is simply adding music to the background of a slide show or videotape. Movies rented for home use cannot be shown in situations where a registration fee has been collected. Companies exist that rent movies for group showings and include the payment of royalties as a part of the rental fee.

ORGANIZATIONAL WORKSHEET O-35

Incident Report

Rationale

An incident report form will provide consistent information on office-related incidents. This information may be needed for follow-up or in case of legal action. *Note:* Worksheet P-43: Incident Report is a similar form found in the program section.

Plan

1.	The policy regarding incident reports answers the following questions:
	Who is responsible for completing incident reports?
	What incidents are reported on incident reports?
	How soon after the incident must the incident report be completed?
	Who is given copies of incident reports?
	Where are completed incident reports kept?
	Who is allowed access to completed incident reports?
2.	How are OSHA reports handled?
3.	Where are blank incident report forms kept?
4.	What statistical data are gathered from incident reports?

Guidelines and Information to Help Complete the Plan

❑ Incident reports should include any major accidents, illnesses, or inappropriate behavior that occurs at the office. A sample incident report form is found in Appendix 6. OSHA also requires that serious accidents or the death of an employee be reported to them and that employers display a poster that explains the protection and obligations of employees (www.osha.gov).

❑ Persons required to complete incident/accident report forms should be trained in their use. Incident report forms can be subpoenaed for legal evidence, so the information should relate only to the facts, not what should or could have been done or any statement placing blame on any party. A staff member or volunteer may fill in sections of the form that relate to their actions. Other sections may be completed by a designated on-site staff member.

❑ Information and statistical data on incident report forms should be regularly analyzed in an effort to reduce the risk of future incidents.

ORGANIZATIONAL WORKSHEET O-36

Risk-Reduction Analyses

Rationale

A system should be in place to identify, consider, and evaluate risk-reduction steps at least annually. This review should be completed for the incidents that occurred at the office, and then combined with the analyses for each program to form a comprehensive report.

Plan

1.	What types of reports are analyzed? (Information sorted by type of injury/behavior, activity, age, staff in charge, size of claim, trends, etc.)
	Office incident reports
	Program incident reports by program site
	Medical logs
	Insurance (exposures, cost, type of claim, size, etc.)
	Workman's compensation claims
	OSHA reports
	Financial trends
	Logs of the crisis-management team's work
	Media reports
	Site-maintenance reports
	Complaints (parent, vendor, staff, etc.)
	Legal action
	Other
2.	What are the categories of accidents, incidents, and/or injuries that are required to be reported?
3.	Who is required to complete reports and how soon should they be submitted?
4.	Who is to receive the reports?
5.	How often are reports analyzed and by whom?
6.	Who approves changes?
7.	What is the system for notification of any changes that result from analysis?

Guidelines and Information to Help Complete the Plan

❑ Reports may be categorized to help analyze and study different issues or trends. Categories might be determined in a variety of ways depending on the program or operation. They could include any injury requiring the filing of an insurance claim or workman's compensation claim form, injuries by type, activity, age, staff in charge, size of claim, type of behavior, etc. It may be helpful to go through the worksheets and identify areas that need to be tracked.

❑ Persons receiving reports should follow the procedures for the notification of appropriate people and the responsibility, if any, for addressing media inquiries. Refer to Worksheet O-35: Incident Report, Worksheet O-3: Agency Emergency Contacts, and Worksheet O-9: Emergency Media Plan. The process should also be evaluated as incidents are analyzed.

❑ Incidents should be analyzed on a regular basis (not right after an incident has taken place) to look for trends and any revisions needed in the risk-management plan. Although Appendix 32 has a sample risk-analysis health summary form to keep a running total of health and injury incidents by the health or program supervisor, a summary is probably not necessary for the office. Changes in either the reporting system or in procedures for handling situations and emergencies should be timely and communicated in writing whenever possible.

❑ A comprehensive report that includes all office operations and programs should be compiled and reviewed by the Risk-Management Task Force. As reports are compiled over several years, any trends that are identified and new recommendations should be made as needed.

PROGRAM RISK-MANAGEMENT PLANNING

Chapter Six

Each program should have a risk-management plan on site that is specific to that program and site. A program that operates on several different sites may only need to identify the site differences. The worksheets, which are also included on the Resource CD, could be divided by topic, and the responsibility for completion assigned to a person skilled in that area. Electronic worksheets are convenient when writing, making changes, and copying, but a hard copy is important in case the computers are not accessible. Each plan is in a table format and will expand as the lines are filled in. When a site-specific or common worksheet is completed and approved, it should be dated, printed, and put in each site's Risk-Management Plan notebook.

In addition to the one on site, each program site should have at least one duplicate hard copy of the plan in a notebook in the main office. Since the office or a computer is not always accessible, a disc or second hard copy should be stored in a different location. The batteries in a laptop may not be charged and, during a crisis, the electric power may be out.

Some worksheets, referred to as organizational worksheets (O), may be added to the program's plan or remain with the organizational plan (main office) depending on the "need to know" or the assigned responsibility for that topic. For example, organizational policies on how to handle the media could be assigned to one organizational spokesperson regardless of program or operation. The program site director only needs to have this person's contact

Each program should have a risk-management plan on site that is specific to that program and site.

number on the agency contact list. The list of insurance policies might be the same for all offices and program sites and be managed by the main office. While the agency contacts may be the same for each site, it is important that each site have a copy in its book. The emergency number for the fire department may be 911 in each site, or 911 may not be available at some sites.

This chapter includes the program crisis worksheets (P-1 to P-20) that are needed at each program site and the program risk-management planning worksheets (P-21 to P-63) specific to each program. All worksheets have a section called "Guidelines and Information to Help Complete the Plan." Be sure to read the guidelines section before getting started with each worksheet.

#	Topic	Responsibility	Date completed
P-1	Who is in Charge Where? Identification of person(s) and responsibilities in case of emergency		
P-2	Emergency Phone Numbers Specific phone numbers for emergencies		
P-3	Agency Emergency Contacts Identification of who should be called, where they can be reached, and in what situations		
P-4	Emergency Procedures for Hazards and/or Disasters Identification of site hazards and emergency actions taken for any site where a program is being held		
P-5	Utilities Type of utilities and the location of emergency shutdowns		
P-6	Firefighting and Other Emergency Equipment and Procedures Location and type of equipment and the access roads available		
P-7	Emergency Communication and Warning Systems Information on communications systems to reach persons on and off the site		

Figure 6-1. Program worksheets

#	Topic	Responsibility	Date completed
P-8	Security Plan for personal security, intruders, follow-up, and information provided		
P-9	Parent Contact How, when, and by who are parents informed in case of emergency		
P-10	Missing Persons Plan for responding to a person missing on or off the activity site		
P-11	Diversion Activities Plan for activities to occupy or distract youth away from the emergency situation		
P-12	Site Evacuation Plan for quickly organizing and evacuating a site		
P-13	Participant and Staff Whereabouts Information on where participant and staff lists are and the responsibility for maintaining them		
P-14	Emergency On-Site Transportation Procedures for providing emergency transportation on site		
P-15	Transportation Emergencies Plan to provide for passenger safety in case of a vehicular accident		
P-16	First Aid Who has first aid training, minimum skills needed, and where first-aid kits are located and what they contain		
P-17	Exposure to Bloodborne Pathogens Develop an exposure control plan and provide training in universal precautions to minimize exposure to bodily fluids		

Figure 6-1. Program worksheets (cont.)

#	Topic	Responsibility	Date completed
P-18	Insect- and Rodent-Transmitted Diseases Procedures for dealing with insect bites that can cause serious health problems		
P-19	Youth Suicide and Self-Mutilation Plan for training staff in identifying warning signs and handling suicide threats and self-mutilation		
P-20	Death of a Participant, Volunteer, Staff Member, or Family Member Procedures for handling fatal accidents or illnesses and for informing a participant or staff member of a death in his family		
P-21	Site Hazards—Natural and Man-Made Identification of site hazards and actions taken for the office(s)		
P-22	Site Operations and Maintenance Site maintenance responsibilities and person(s) responsible		
P-23	Property Use and Liability Procedures for using non-owned property or use of organization-owned property by other groups		
P-24	Safe Water Supply Requirements and responsibilities related to water for cooking, drinking, bathing, and swimming		
P-25	Notification of Operation Date and suggestions for informing fire and law-enforcement officials of the program		
P-26	Fire Prevention and Safety Fire-prevention safety check and identification of hazards		

Figure 6-1. Program worksheets (cont.)

#	Topic	Responsibility	Date completed
P-27	Serving Persons With Disabilities Information and plan for compliance with the Americans With Disabilities Act		
P-28	Foodborne Illness Plan for handling and serving food in a safe manner to avoid salmonella or food poisoning		
P-29	Storage and Handling of Flammable/Poison Materials Supervision and control of flammable, poisonous, and explosive materials		
P-30	Transporting Participants and Staff Who may transport participants and staff, when, and under what circumstances		
P-31	Health Services and Supervision Procedures for on-site health supervision		
P-32	Health Screening and Records Procedures for health screening and recordkeeping		
P-33	Personal Medications Procedures for handling and dispensing personal medications		
P-34	Insurance Safety Audit for Organization-Owned Sites Date of audit, recommendations made, and actions taken		
P-35	Federal, State, and Local Laws A listing of regulatory agencies and laws that pertain to the operation of the program		
P-36	Interstate and International Laws Laws pertaining to operating a program in another state or country		

Figure 6-1. Program worksheets (cont.)

#	Topic	Responsibility	Date completed
P-37	Waivers, Permissions, and Agreements for Participation Identification of risks that a participant or agency is assuming, and a list of where forms are kept and who has access to them		
P-38	Program Record Retention and Destruction Establishing a system for retaining, storing, and destroying records		
P-39	Intellectual Property Infringements, Copyrights, and Royalties Protecting copyrighted materials, and procedures for use of materials protected by copyrights and payment of royalties when required		
P-40	Contracts for Services Transferring risk through contracts, and establishing the authority to negotiate contracts		
P-41	Operational Financial Risks Procedures to protect the assets of the organization		
P-42	Participant Risk-Reduction Analyses A process to identify and evaluate risk-reduction steps		
P-43	Incident Report Procedures for maintaining in-depth, consistent information regarding an incident		
P-44	Emergency Drills Identification of types of drills needed and procedures for emergency drills		
P-45	Registration—Check-In and Check-Out Procedures for assuming the responsibility of a youth, including who may or may not pick up a child		

Figure 6-1. Program worksheets (cont.)

#	Topic	Responsibility	Date completed
P-46	Drop-In Programs Determining when the organization assumes the responsibility for supervision of a child		
P-47	Guests On-Site Procedures for ensuring the safety of approved guests on the site		
P-48	Parent Notification of Changes Plan for notification of parents if a problem, injury, or change impacts the communicated plans		
P-49	Weapons and Firearms Procedures for dealing with firearms used in the program and personal weapons on program sites		
P-50	Business Use of Vehicles/Driver Authorization Identification of vehicles for business use and driver responsibilities		
P-51	Complaints Determining a process for handling complaints		
P-52	Participant Supervision Plan Responsibilities and plans for general and specific supervision of participants		
P-53	Conduct of Participants and Staff Plan for communicating appropriate conduct and behavior expectations of participants and staff		
P-54	Screening of Staff and Volunteers Planning, implementing, and documenting the screening process		

Figure 6-1. Program worksheets (cont.)

#	Topic	Responsibility	Date completed
P-55	Staff Selection and Training for Emergencies Assessing the ability to recognize and handle emergencies and providing training in first aid and emergency procedures		
P-56	Employment Practices Plan for keeping informed on state and federal laws and the reporting and recordkeeping requirements		
P-57	Staff Training Determining content, implementation, and documentation of training for volunteer and paid staff		
P-58	Supervision of Staff Supervising volunteer and paid staff members that work directly with children		
P-59	Harassment—Sexual and Other Creating an environment in which harassment will not be tolerated		
P-60	Preventing Child Abuse Designing a comprehensive plan to reduce the risk of child abuse and reporting disclosures		
P-61	Activities Requiring Staff With Specialized Training or Certification List those activities requiring staff with specialized training or certification		
P-62	Weather and/or Environmental Health Effects on the Program When and how to change programs because of weather or environmental conditions		
P-63	Participants in Off-Site Field Trips or Excursions Procedures for program activities that take place off the regular site		

Figure 6-1. Program worksheets (cont.)

PROGRAM CRISIS WORKSHEET P-1

Who is in Charge Where?

Rationale

To avoid confusion and prevent misinformation from being given out, each person needs to be aware of his responsibilities and know who is in charge. In the event of a major emergency, the media scans police radios and will quickly arrive on the scene or call by phone. It is important to be prepared so that the media can do its job and the administrators can do theirs. Note that the information about media relations should be consistent with the organizational media plan in Worksheet O-9: Emergency Media Plan.

Plan

1. In case of emergency, who will be in charge:		Backup Person
At the site of the emergency?		
At the organization or main office (or other in-town location)?		
While participants are on a hike, trip, or excursion?		
2. What are the responsibilities of the person in charge at the site of emergency?		
3. How often will contact be made between the emergency site and the main office or in-town location (e.g., every hour, twice per day)?		
4. What are the responsibilities of the person in charge at the office or in-town location?		
5. What are the responsibilities of the person in charge if an emergency happens off-site?		
6. In case of emergency, who has the authority to develop brief factual statements or "key messages" for media release?		
7. Who has the authority to approve brief factual statements?		
Phone #		
8. Use the following as an outline for forming key messages in a brief statement.		
The scenario facts [nature of the situation and who (by title or role) is involved]:		
Indicate your cooperation with the authorities		
State concern for those involved		
Restate the facts of the scenario without editorializing		

Indicate openness for future updates and response	
The following people can approve a more detailed media release:	
9. Who is the official spokesperson designated to respond to the media during an emergency?	
10. In addition to the media, who should the brief factual statement be given to?	
11. When and how are other staff members informed and/or trained in their roles (or non-roles) in dealing with the media?	

Guidelines and Information to Help Complete the Plan

❑ When clarifying staff responsibilities during an emergency at a program site, be sure to consider all of the procedures and aspects of the operation, including those that must be handled at an in-town location or the main office away from the program site.

❑ Once responsibilities are clear, be sure that training takes place to inform the staff of who is in charge and of the specific responsibilities of each staff member.

❑ An official media spokesperson should be identified in case of emergency. A spokesperson should be chosen who has a general understanding of the media, possesses communications abilities, and has experience with interviews and reporters. Often the person handling the emergency is too busy to function in this role. This person's responsibility will include speaking in an official capacity for the program and the organization. Therefore, he must have knowledge of, and sensitivity to, the organization's policies about what should or should not be disclosed, as well as some expertise and credibility.

❑ One person, perhaps the staff person in charge, should be authorized to develop and/or approve a brief factual statement for release to the media as soon as possible following an emergency. A "no comment" or a delay in releasing information may give the appearance of an attempted "cover-up" or result in reports based on rumor or inaccurate information. The brief statements should include the location and type if incident, when it occurred, and whether it involved adults and/or children. The organization must not give specific names of persons involved until families have been notified.

❑ Sample key messages should be developed prior to program operation. Key messages should answer basic questions, express facts only, briefly describe the nature of the situation, list who is involved, and be limited to three or four statements that indicate the organization's cooperation with the authorities, state concern for those involved, restate the facts for the scenario without editorializing, and indicate openness for future updates and response.

❑ Copies of the brief statement should be distributed to all those who might receive inquiries. It should be stressed to staff members and volunteers that they should release only the information included in the statement and not speculate about the incident to others. Questions that go beyond the information in the news releases should be referred to the official spokesperson.

❑ Information gathered regarding participants and youth staff should be handled in an appropriate and confidential manner. Refer to Worksheet P-45: Participant Information, Registration—Check-In and Check-Out and Worksheet P-32: Health Screening and Records for information regarding the release of camper and staff information.

PROGRAM CRISIS WORKSHEET P-2

Emergency Phone Numbers

Rationale

These emergency telephone numbers need to be posted along with what to report and the names of staff who can contact officials. Information about available medical services will simplify and speed the securing of needed treatment in the event of accident, injury, or illness.

Plan

1. Information to give to an official or medical service:		
The name of the reporting party:		
The site address:		
The site phone #:		
Directions to be given in case of emergency:		
2. What are the emergency phone numbers and service information for:		
Local Officials	Name or Service Community	Number
Fire		
Police		
Sheriff		
Health department		
Veterinarian (small and/or large animal)		
Animal control officers		

3. Medical Services	
Poison Control Center	Phone #
Ambulance	
Name of service:	Phone #
When do you call for an ambulance?	
What is estimated response time?	
How many victims can the ambulance transport?	
Who goes with the injured?	
Can anyone else ride in the ambulance?	

What forms are needed?	
Helicopter:	
Name of service:	Phone #
When do you call for a rescue helicopter?	
What is estimated response time?	
How many victims can the rescue helicopter transport?	
Who goes with the injured?	
Can anyone else ride in the rescue helicopter?	
What forms are needed?	
Hospital	
What is the closest available hospital?	Phone #
Directions from the site to the hospital	
How long does it take to get there?	
What forms/information are needed for treatment?	

	Needed?	Where located?
Health history		
Physical exam form		
Parent permission		
Insurance forms		
Other		

When (if ever) is it necessary to call ahead for treatment?	
Do parents need to be reached before treatment will be given?	
What method of payment is required for treatment?	
In case of animal bite, does the hospital require you to bring the animal?	
Who should transport injured to hospital?	
Alternates	
Doctor	
Who is the closest available doctor?	Phone #
Directions from the site to the doctor	
How long does it take to get there?	
Do you need an appointment?	
Dentist	
Who is the closest available dentist?	Phone #

Directions from the site to the dentist		
How long does it take to get there?		
Do you need an appointment?		
Alternate Medical Service		
Alternate Services (e.g., emergency rescue service)		Phone #
Directions to the service from the site		
How long does it take to get there?		
Do you need an appointment or prior notification of arrival?		
What forms are needed for treatment?	Needed?	Where located?
Health history		
Physical exam form		
Parent permission		
Insurance form		
Other		
Do parents need to be reached before treatment is given?		
What method of a payment is required for treatment?		
Who should transport ill or injured individuals to the doctor?		
Alternates		
Specialty Units (e.g., burn unit)		
What are the closest specialty units?		
Specialty:		Phone #
Directions to the service from the site		
How long does it take to get there?		
Do you need an appointment or prior notification of arrival?		
What forms are needed for treatment?	Needed?	Where located?
Health history		
Physical exam form		
Parent permission		
Insurance form		
Other		
Do parents need to be reached before treatment is given?		
What method of a payment is required for treatment?		

❏ These phone numbers should be reviewed yearly and posted by phones where problems can be reported.

❏ The organization should also post information on what to say (e.g., the name of reporting party, site address, and phone number), to help alleviate anxiety or in case the local official did not understand messages and needs to return a call for clarification.

❏ Make preliminary visits to the medical facilities and doctors' or dentists' offices with health supervisors and key administrative personnel to secure information. Provide the ambulance with a map to the site.

❏ Designate staff members who are to be responsible for transporting or traveling with a victim.

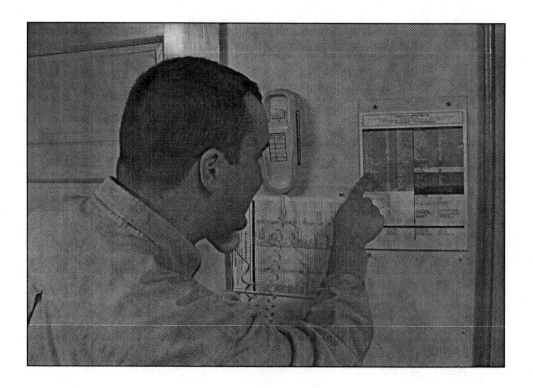

PROGRAM CRISIS WORKSHEET P-3

Agency Emergency Contacts

Rationale

It is important to know who needs to be contacted in case of an emergency, where they can be contacted, and for what emergencies they wish to be notified. Note: This worksheet should be the same as Worksheet O- 3: Agency Emergency Contacts and be repeated for each program site.

Plan

Determine who should be notified in what types of emergency situations and how quickly they should be told.										
Title and Name	Office #	Home #	Cell #	Site Emergency	Image Issue	Serious Behavior Problem	Serious Injury	Natural Hazard or Disaster	Death	How Soon? Immediately or within 24 to 48 hours?
Executive director										
Board president										
Board	Attach list with email									
Staff	Attach list with email									
Legal counsel										
Insurance agent										
Media spokesperson										
Other										

Organization's national office							
Field staff office/cell							

Guidelines and Information to Help Complete the Plan

❏ This list should be the same for office operation and program services and be located where persons needing access to the list have easy access.

❏ The board and staff list should include email addresses and an emergency contact number. Email is often an alternate means of notification if the phones are inoperable or too busy to get a call in or out.

❏ It may be helpful to determine who calls others after the first person has been contacted. Use the Worksheet P-4: Emergency Procedures for Hazards and/or Disasters to help decide what information needs to be given or shared with whom. The call should then include the information decided upon and the expected actions, if any, needed from the person receiving the call.

PROGRAM CRISIS WORKSHEET P-4

Emergency Procedures for Hazards and/or Disasters

Rationale

Emergency procedures for hazards or disasters, both natural and man-made, for each program site must be written and distributed or posted to help ensure a safer experience for participants, staff members, and user groups. See Worksheet P-6: Firefighting and Other Emergency Equipment Procedures and Worksheet P-12: Site Evacuation.

Plan

1. Natural Hazards			
Type Common to Program Area	Warning Signs	Safety Precautions Taken	Emergency Action Required
2. Natural and Man-Made Disasters			
Type Possible to Program Area	Warning Signs	Safety Precautions Taken	Emergency Action Required

3. Widespread Disasters Affecting the Community Where Participants Live	
How will facts be verified?	Who will be responsible?
What kinds of information will be shared with staff members?	Who will prepare statements?
What kinds of information will be shared with participants?	Who will prepare statements?
What factors will affect whether the program closes?	Who will make the decision?
Are there currently any serious contagious illnesses that could affect the program?	Who should be contacted if an outbreak occurs?

4. Man-Made Hazards Related to Operation of the Facility or Equipment			
Hazards Identified but not Eliminated	Warning Signs	Safety Precautions Taken	Emergency Action Required

5.	Contaminated Food or Water			
	Procedure for handling foodborne illness			
	Procedure for handling illness from contaminated water			
6.	Man-Made Hazards Related to the Behavior of People			
	Type Included for This Program	Warning Signs	Safety Precautions Taken	Emergency Action Required
	Intruders (see P-8: Security)			
	Vandalism			
	Kidnapping			
	Harassment (see P-59: Harassment—Sexual and Other)			
	Drug and alcohol misuse			
	Hostage			
	Terrorism			
	Other:			
7.	Is a safety orientation provided to participants, staff members, and user groups that includes:			
	Safety regulations and emergency procedures			
	Boundaries for where they can go			
	Expectations for behavior			
	Precautions for natural and man-made hazards on the site			

Guidelines and Information to Help Complete the Plan

❑ Worksheet P-21: Site Hazard Identification—Natural and Man-Made includes the identification of site hazards and plans for elimination when possible. When not possible, Worksheet P-21 includes rationale, plans for protection, and procedures for avoiding hazards. This worksheet addresses the prevention of incidents and any emergency action required if an incident does occur.

❑ Include warning signs and emergency actions required for natural disasters common to the area, such as tornados, earthquakes, floods, snow, lightning, forest fires, mudslides, etc., and such man-made disasters as fire, terrorism, epidemics, etc., that may be widespread and include the whole community. Local authorities may direct the operations.

❑ If any kind of disaster happens in the community where the participants and staff live while the program is in session, the organization will need to decide what information is disseminated and how, as well as how to coordinate information between staff members and families and between participants and their parents. A system must be designed to identify and refer people who need extra support. Refer to the Centers for Disease Control (www.cdc.gov) for information on any flu or virus that might affect the whole community or the program operation, such as the avian flu or norovirus. Worksheet P-2: Emergency Phone Numbers includes the number of the local health department.

❑ Emergency procedures for identified, but not eliminated, hazards related to the operation of the facility or equipment include both injuries caused by the operation of equipment and illnesses caused by contaminated food or water brought to the site, improper food-handling procedures, or faulty equipment. Procedures include handling multiple participants and staff members who are ill, working with the health department to determine the cause, and being prepared to answer questions from the media. See Worksheet P-28: Food Handling and Foodborne Illness for safety procedures and Worksheet P-2: Emergency Phone Numbers for health department and other emergency phone numbers. See Worksheet P-12: Site Evacuation for reasons for evacuation.

❑ OSHA has reporting requirements when an employee gets hurt, and rules such as the Confined Space Rule that requires a written safety plan as well as staff training for spaces not designed for human occupation. The Lock-out/Tag-out Rule on Worksheet P-5: Utilities requires procedures to protect employees from accidental injury from any stored energy. Rules are also in place regarding the use of chemicals or toxins often found in paint, cleaning supplies, yard equipment, and office machines (www.osha.gov).

❑ The plan should include man-made hazards related to the behavior of people, such as intruders, vandalism, kidnapping, harassment, drug or alcohol misuse, acts of terrorism, hostage situations, child abuse, etc., and include the other worksheets on security or conduct of participants and staff (paid or volunteer), sexual harassment, and the prevention of child abuse.

❑ Emergency action includes what to do and who to call for immediate help during a crisis, but not the follow-up reports or actions needed. Be sure that phone numbers are listed on Worksheet P-2: Emergency Phone Numbers and are posted and included along with crisis information. Refer to Appendix 6 for a sample Incident Report.

PROGRAM CRISIS WORKSHEET P-5

Utilities

Rationale

In case of an emergency, it may be important have the following information in a convenient location to enable the shut-down of utility systems without delay.

Plan

1.	Which staff members are knowledgeable of utility systems and have practiced shutting them down?		
	Maintenance personnel		
	Administrative personnel		
	If a site is rented what is the emergency contact number and where is it posted?		
2.	Where are utility charts kept?		
3.	Water and Sewage		
	Water service company		
	Phone #		
	Where are water shut-off valves located?	Are they clearly labeled?	Are tools to operate them kept nearby?
	How is sewage disposed of?		
	Who is responsible for problems?		
4.	Electric		
	Electric service company		
	Phone #		
	Where is the main electricity shut-off switch?		
	What is the Lock-out/Tag-out procedure?		
	What power sources are covered?		
	Who is responsible for training?		
	Who is trained?		
	Where are the breaker boxes and fuse boxes?		
	Room	Location	Are all switches and fuses clearly labeled?

Who is responsible for conducting the annual electrical evaluation?			
Where are the written reports stored?			
5. Gas			
Gas service company			
Phone #			
Where are gas shut-off valves?			
Room	Location		Are they clearly labeled?
6. Telephone			
Telephone service company			
Phone #			
Number and location of phones on site			
Where are service boxes located?			

Guidelines and Information to Help Complete the Plan

❏ The site manager and on-site director should review the utility charts, tour the site prior to the opening of the program, and practice operating the utility shut-off points.

❏ Several other staff members should also be familiar with utility operation. For example, cooks need to know where the main kitchen electrical, water, and gas cut-offs are located.

❏ OSHA's Lock-out/Tag-out Rule requires a written plan, an inventory of power sources, and a training record (www.osha.gov).

PROGRAM CRISIS WORKSHEET P-6

Firefighting and Other Emergency Equipment and Procedures

Rationale

It is important to take action to prevent fires and have the appropriate type of firefighting equipment readily available at all times. Being prepared for other emergencies requires having appropriate equipment available, in good condition, and ready for use, as well as having personnel trained in the use of that equipment.

Plan

1.	Preparation: What are the safety procedures in the event of a fire?
	How often are the procedures reviewed with the staff?
2.	Where is equipment in each building and who are the people in each building, facility, etc., knowledgeable in the use of the firefighting equipment?

Building	Type of Equipment	Location in Building	Person Knowledgeable in its Use

Where are fire access roads?

What are the fire control and firefighting procedures?

3. On Site

What safety and emergency equipment is kept on the site?	Where is it kept?	Who is responsible for checking and maintaining it?	When and how often is it checked?	Who is trained and authorized to use the equipment?

4. Off Site

What safety and emergency equipment is taken off site on trips?	Where is it dispensed from?	Who is responsible for checking and maintaining it off site?	When and how often is it checked?	Who is trained and/or authorized to use the equipment?

5. What other special emergency equipment has been secured or is needed for specialized activities?	
Activity	Equipment

6. Whose advice have you sought regarding the appropriateness of safety and emergency equipment?

Guidelines and Information to Help Complete the Plan

❑ Keep an inventory of the firefighting equipment in each building, facility, and program area. See Worksheet P-26: Fire Prevention and Safety for the inventory of the firefighting equipment and alarms and safety checks. See Worksheet P-12: Site Evacuation for evacuation procedures.

❑ Determine what the step-by-step procedures are in the event of a fire and who is responsible for what. The first concern should always be for the safety of people. Fire procedures should include methods of control by such actions as shutting doors to delay the fire's progress. Fireproof files or safes should be closed when not in use and be included in the evacuation procedures.

❑ Seek advice on other emergency equipment from a local doctor, Red Cross chapter, fire department, medical emergency professional, and safety product supply company.

❑ Check with those knowledgeable in specialized activities for appropriate safety equipment. Personnel responsible for using equipment should train on the specific equipment and understand the uniqueness of the site.

PROGRAM CRISIS WORKSHEET P-7

Emergency Communication and Warning Systems

Rationale

In a disaster situation, such as severe weather conditions, the primary communication system (e.g., telephone) is often inoperable. Some alternative means of communication is necessary to call for help or inform authorities. Some areas may need emergency communication systems within the site. Warning systems create an efficient method to quickly communicate to the entire site population. Everyone on the site should know what the various alarms mean and the actions they are to take.

Plan

1. Communication to or from off-site services:		
What kinds of emergency communications are available at the site?		
What is the back-up system in case the telephone is not working?		
Who has cell phones that can be used in an emergency?		
Name	Location	Number
Have they been tested in the area?		
Who is responsible for keeping them charged?		
Is there a pay phone in the area?		
2. Communications between buildings or program areas on-site:		
Is there an on-site communications system?	Type	
Is there a non-electric warning system? How is it practiced?		
What are the emergency warning signals for different situations?		
Warning signal	Situation or action to be taken	
Who can initiate the different warning systems?		
Is the communications system(s) periodically checked and practiced?		

When?	
By whom?	
Is a back-up battery or generator available in case of electrical failure?	
Can the above cell phones be used in emergencies for on-site communication?	

Guidelines and Information to Help Complete the Plan

❑ Explore possible types of systems with the police department, communication-systems specialists, or others knowledgeable in this field. Include mobile cell phones, CB systems, two-way radios, etc. Some staff members may have personal cell phones, but some cell phones do not work in remote areas. Non-electric warning systems include air horns, car horns, bells, or even sending runners. Signals should be established and practiced. For example, a steady horn means evacuate the site now, continual beeping means gather at a central designated place, etc.

❑ In addition to posting the warning system rules in strategic places, distribution may include the following:

- Staff members
- Office workers
- Local law enforcement officials
- Fire officials
- Civil defense offices
- School, church, or user groups

❑ Communications systems related to specialized activities or trips may need to be specific to each activity or trip and are included on the specialized activity form in Appendix 18.

PROGRAM CRISIS WORKSHEET P-8

Security

Rationale

Feeling personally secure is a state of mind based on knowing that reasonable precautions have been taken. The development of an active prevention program can provide a relatively secure working and service environment. The objective of security planning is to provide an environment that allows activities to continue in an uninterrupted and orderly fashion.

Plan

1. Preparation: What is your security plan regarding the following?

Subjects	Plan	Rationale
Lighting		
Paths		
Identification signs		
Alarms		
Boundary barriers		
Brush and undergrowth around cabins or buildings		
Keys and locks		
Posting "no trespassing" signs		
Off-season security		
Appeal of camp to outsiders		
Bed checks		
Buddy system for traveling on site		
Staff supervision		
Orientation of campers		
Orientation of staff		
Visitors		
Security patrols		
Entrance gate closed at night		

2. How are participants and staff members informed of security plans?
3. What information is given or withheld from parents/general public for security reasons?
4. How are intruders dealt with?
Follow-up: What kind of follow-up is done when evidence of intrusion exists (e.g., vandalism, threatening notes)?

Guidelines and Information to Help Complete the Plan

☐ Each of the items listed needs to be considered when designing the security plan. Have a written rationale for every item implemented and for every item not implemented. A clear rationale helps interpret security to parents, board members, participants, the public at large, insurance companies, and various authorities.

- External lighting—Consider types and how extensive. The plan may include lights at sanitary facilities, infirmary, living or program areas, connecting walks or paths, and parking areas.

- Paths—Consider paths leading out of camp, the isolation of connecting paths, and the brush near paths.

- Signs—Camps and program sites become more vulnerable if they utilize highway directional and entrance signs. Consider hanging signs on arrival or departure days only or using maps for parents driving to the site.

- Alarms—Consider which ones would be best to use for security reasons.

- Boundary barriers—Plant dense growth of hedgerows or brambles, or build structural barriers such as fences or other construction that serves as a deterrent to unauthorized entry. Contact a local forester for suggestions on natural barriers.

- Brush and undergrowth near buildings—The area immediately around a building or tent should be free of brush whenever possible.

- Keys and locks—Keys should be distributed according to need instead of convenience. Keys should be collected or locks rekeyed when a staff position change takes place. What buildings are locked and why?

- Posting "no trespassing" signs—Check on local requirements to make signs valid.

- Off-season security—Base the plan on needs and use.

- Appeal of the program site—Assess the attractiveness of a site to outsiders. Possibly appealing things include young girls or boys, horses, and waterfront equipment. Steps can be taken to reduce this appeal through a show of protection, a discussion of appropriate behavior of participants toward outsiders, less public exposure, etc.

- Bed checks— When participants are on the site overnight, routine checks on the correct number of participants provide safety and keep staff more alert.

- Buddy system—Traveling in pairs is always a good idea. Encourage night travel in groups. Encourage staff members to travel in pairs if at all possible.

- Staff supervision—Program staff should be scheduled or placed to provide maximum supervision at all times. Arrange staff so they will be sleeping in participant cabins, at least in the cabins of younger participants. In units housing older participants, staff members should either be in same sleeping facility or very close by (within sight or sound). Make arrangements for supervision between activities.

- Orientation of participants—Impress upon youth the importance of safety without unduly alarming them. Discuss rules such as traveling in groups, informing a leader or counselor whenever leaving the group, and using a flashlight after dark.

- Orientation of staff—Constantly impress upon staff members their role in helping to ensure the safety of everyone. Training should include a thorough discussion of all facets of the security and emergency procedures.

- Visitors—If visitors are permitted, require that they check in and wear identification while on the site. Be sure they check out and return their ID pass. Develop procedures for authorized and unauthorized visitors.

- Security patrols—Possibilities for consideration are a security service, staff patrols, and police patrol.

- Entrance gate closed at night—The entrance gate should be closed at night. Whether it is locked will depend on the location and situation. Be sure to allow for emergency access.

❑ Participants, staff members, program administrators, and site maintenance personnel should have a clear understanding of when and if to approach an intruder and what follow-up steps to take. Occasionally, what appears to be a prank or vandalism may be a sign of a more serious problem, so such situations should always be investigated.

❑ Information on where the program site is located should be given to parents, but not necessarily to the general public. Other information, including staff time off, when a facility is locked or unlocked, and participant or staff personal information, should be carefully evaluated before being given to anyone.

PROGRAM CRISIS WORKSHEET P-9

Parent Contact

Rationale

The parents are entrusting the organization with their most precious possessions—their children. It is the organization's responsibility to keep the parents informed of the well-being of their children and to provide as much support as possible.

Plan

1.	What is the policy about notifying parents of a participant's illness, injury, or involvement in another incident?
2.	In the case of a serious accident, how will the parent contact be made?
	Who does the contacting?
	Backup person?
	When should contact be made?
3.	In an emergency not involving death or a serious accident, how will the parent contact be made?
	Who does the contacting?
	Backup person?
	When should contact be made?
4.	What is done if the parents or guardian cannot be reached or do not have a phone?
5.	In the event of a serious accident, what type of follow-up support is provided for parents and/or legal guardians?
6.	In the event of a major emergency or disaster, what is the plan to contact the parents of all participants to relieve their anxiety and inform them about what their children are facing?
7.	Where is the list of alternative contact(s) to reach parents if a disaster has disrupted communications in the area?
8.	How do parents receive a phone number at the program site to call in case of family emergency?

Guidelines and Information to Help Complete the Plan

❑ The program should have a written policy made known to the parents that identifies when they will be notified in case of illness, injury, or involvement in an incident. The parent or guardian should be contacted whenever emergency treatment is necessary. The parent or guardian should be contacted as soon as possible following the incident to meet the participant at the hospital, pick the participant up at the site, or carry out whatever action is necessary.

❑ A home phone number, a number where a parent and/or guardian can be reached in case of emergency, and the number of a relative or friend of the family who can serve as an emergency contact should be listed on registration cards and health forms. The organization should contact local authorities for assistance if emergency contacts cannot be reached.

❑ The administrative and medical personnel of the program should discuss ahead of time who is responsible for calling parents, under which circumstances, and who will be the backup person if the designee is not on site.

❑ Care should be taken whenever contacting a parent so that undue alarm is not caused. However, all facts pertaining to the situation should be given. The caller should explain what the child has witnessed or experienced and how he is handling it. Information given to the parent should coincide with the information contained on the incident report form (refer to Appendix 6).

❑ In the event of death, great sensitivity and support will be needed. See Worksheet P-20: Death of a Participant, Volunteer, Staff Member, or Family Member. In most cases, the authorities will contact next of kin.

❑ In the event of a major emergency or disaster:

• All parents or guardians should be contacted immediately and informed of their children's welfare

• Parents should then be informed of any evacuation procedures that are necessary

• The organization's office can act as the phone calling station if the situation involves many participants. In a disaster with a widely affected area, telephone lines may be down. The organization should contact local authorities for assistance if emergency contacts cannot be reached. The national office or another agency may be able to help contact parents.

❑ Information gathered regarding campers and youth staff members should be handled in an appropriate and confidential manner. Refer to Worksheet P-45: Participant Information, Registration, Check-In, and Check-Out and Worksheet P-32: Health Screening and Records for information about releasing camper and staff information.

PROGRAM CRISIS WORKSHEET P-10

Missing Persons

Rationale

It is essential to have a well-developed plan to respond quickly to a person missing on the site or in an off-site activity.

Plan

1.	Preparation and training:
	Who has written copies of the plan?
	When are staff members trained in the procedure?
	How is the plan practiced?
	How often is a head count made?
	Who is responsible for making a head count?
2.	Immediate or first steps to take when someone is thought to be missing:
3.	Method or plan for search:
	Name of designated persons for internal search of the site:
	Names or position of designated persons for a water search for a lost person:
	What signal is used to identify that the person has been found?
	At what point would notification of law enforcement officials take place?
	At what point would notification of the executive director take place?
	At what point would notification of parents take place?
	Who from the organization is responsible to work with law enforcement and the media in case an Amber Alert is issued?

Guidelines and Information to Help Complete the Plan

❑ First steps to use when a child or staff member is thought to be missing might be:

- Question those who saw the person last. Was the person angry, depressed, or particularly excited about something? Did the person speak of any plans to go somewhere or have a favorite spot, friend, or counselor? Ask for the time and location where the person was last seen. Record all of this information.

- Check the area where the person was last seen.

- Check the sign-out book to see if the person left the site and, if so, with whom.

- If the person is not found, notify the designated person in charge of missing persons to continue the search procedures.

❑ Be specific with the internal search procedures so that all staff members are aware of their responsibilities. Write down the times of the search and notification on an incident report as they happen. Know who is included in the search and who is to stay with the rest of the youth. Other participants may be involved in diversion activities that are planned ahead of time (refer to Worksheet P-11: Diversion Activities). Being sensitive to the moods of participants and conversations that take place can often prevent problems.

❑ When it is determined that the help of a law-enforcement agency is needed, the organization must work cooperatively with them and follow their directions. It is their responsibility to determine whether an Amber Alert is issued.

Note: According to the National Center for Missing and Exploited Children, The Amber Alert Plan is a voluntary partnership between law-enforcement agencies and broadcasters to activate an urgent bulletin in the most serious child-abduction cases. Once law enforcement officials have been notified about an abducted child, they must first determine if the case meets the Amber Alert Plan's criteria for triggering an alert. Guidance on Criteria for Issuing Amber Alerts can be found on www.missingkids.com. Recognizing the importance of local determination of Amber Alert criteria, while acknowledging the importance of consistency across the country to help ensure a smooth Amber Alert system, the U.S. Department of Justice recommends the following criteria for Amber Alert programs nationwide:

- Law enforcement holds a reasonable belief that an abduction has occurred

- The abduction is of a child age 17 years or younger

- The law-enforcement agency believes that the child is in imminent danger of serious bodily injury or death

- Enough descriptive information exists about the victim and the abduction for law enforcement to issue an Amber Alert to assist in the recovery of the child

- The child's name and other critical data elements, including the Child Abduction flag, have been entered into the National Crime Information Center (NCIC)

PROGRAM CRISIS WORKSHEET P-11

Diversion Activities

Rationale

During an emergency situation, it is often necessary to occupy and/or distract the participants.

Plan

What are the diversion activities or techniques for the following situations?	Who is in charge?
When confined to cabins	
When the entire group is confined in one large building	
When the entire group is confined in a small area	
When the group has been confined in darkness	
During an emergency involving a bus or van breakdown or accident	
When the group must be excluded from an activity or living area	
When the group needs to be outdoors in adverse weather	
While an emergency involves an injured participant or staff member	
During a missing person search	

Guidelines and Information to Help Complete the Plan

❑ It is helpful to preassign several staff members to be in charge of diversion activities. Consideration should be given to dividing staff members between diversion activities and response to the emergency. A variety of songs, games, and other activities should be planned during staff training for use during possible emergencies. The list should consider the size of the group, the size of the space, and the probable length of time.

❑ During specialized activities, diversion activities should be specific to the situation or program area (e.g., the waterfront). These activities should be listed on the form for participation in specialized activities found in Appendix 18.

PROGRAM CRISIS WORKSHEET P-12

Site Evacuation

Rationale

An evacuation plan enables the site director to quickly organize and remove part or all of the population to a predetermined, safer location. With adequate warning, important papers may also be gathered.

Plan

1.	Reasons the site might need to be evacuated:
2.	Who has copies of the written site evacuation plan?
	Safe locations to go to:
	Alternate routes out of the site:
3.	Evacuation responsibilities:
	Who determines the need for an evacuation?
	Who is in charge of evacuation?
	Backup:
	Who is responsible for bringing personal medications?
	Who is responsible for bringing the first-aid kit?
	Who will stay behind if necessary?
	Who decides if the reason for evacuation is shared with the participants?
4.	Mode of transportation (refer to Worksheet P-14: Emergency On-Site Transportation):
	Alternate:
5.	Take the following (based on the emergency, possible return, and time of day):
	Participant and staff list with home phone numbers
	Participant and staff health forms
	Jackets
	Shoes
	Water/snacks
6.	What valuable papers that cannot be replaced, such as deeds, historical documents, policies, etc., should be taken?
7.	Method to account for persons on the site:
	Participants :
	Staff:

Guests:		
8. Notification of the office:		
Who makes the call?	Who needs to be notified?	What is the phone number?
9. Notification of authorities:		
Who makes the call?	Who needs to be notified?	What is the phone number?

10. What are the procedures for contacting parents?
11. What are the procedures for evacuating animals?
12. What is the plan to continue communications?
With site :
With organization officials:
With authorities:
With parents:
13. Who notifies neighbors if they are threatened by the emergency?
Neighbors' Names   Phone Numbers
14. Who determines safe return to the site?
15. What is the plan to provide follow-up information to parents?

Guidelines and Information to Help Complete the Plan

❑ Consult Red Cross Disaster Services, Forest Service, Civil Defense, and the National Guard for help in developing a plan. In some emergencies, someone may need to stay behind to help authorities guard the site, etc. It would be helpful to know in advance who will stay and in what circumstances.

❑ If the site is being evacuated due to threat of natural disaster, such as fire, flood, or hurricane, and time allows for removal of valuable papers, it would be helpful to identify those to save and/or have fireproof containers.

❑ If the site is being evacuated in the event of a bomb threat, use of guns, a dangerous intruder, or leakage of hazardous materials, staff members should take care to avoid panic, remain calm, and carefully decide whether or not to share the reason for evacuation. Neighbors should be notified if the site is being evacuated, especially if they are threatened by the emergency.

❑ If the program site is being closed and participants and staff members are being evacuated for health reasons, such as water contamination, a contagious disease (West Nile Virus, meningitis), insect- or rodent-transmitted diseases, or foodborne illness (novovirus, e-coli, hepatitis A), it is important to work with the department of public health. Parents should be notified, a letter prepared explaining the situation, and arrangements made for transportation home. A written statement should be prepared and a spokesperson identified for handling media calls (refer to Worksheet O-9: Emergency Media Plan.

❑ Follow-up for any evacuation should include a written incident report detailing information about when and if the program will resume.

PROGRAM CRISIS WORKSHEET P-13

Participant and Staff Whereabouts

Rationale

In the event of an emergency, everyone on the site must be accounted for. If a personal emergency should occur, staff members should be able to locate a particular participant or staff member quickly.

Plan

1.	What method do you have for knowing the whereabouts of each participant and staff member at all times?
	Does the organization have a list of participants and staff members by location, such as group or unit/cabin?
	Where is the check-in/check-out list for guests on the site?
	Who makes the lists?
	Who keeps the information on the whereabouts of each person?
2.	Where are the lists kept?
	Who has access to the lists?

Guidelines and Information to Help Complete the Plan

❑ A complete list or card file should include the name, age, address, home and business phone numbers, emergency contact phone numbers of both participants and staff members, and groups to which they are assigned. While this list should be accessible in case of emergency, care must be taken that information on participants and staff members remains confidential.

❑ The person in charge of each group can compile group or housing lists. These lists should be posted in a central location, such as the program office or infirmary. Staff members should also have a list of participants for whom they are responsible. Staff off-site sign-out sheets should be in a central location for staff to fill out as they leave and return to the site.

❑ Program planning sheets should be posted in each unit or meeting place to help locate individuals or groups. Copies could be kept in the program office. A total participant and staff list— with home phone numbers—should also be at the organization's main office. This information should be listed according to the dates that participants are on the site and corrected when changes are made.

PROGRAM CRISIS WORKSHEET P-14

Emergency On-Site Transportation

Rationale

When the situation calls for the use of transportation available on a program site, it is important to have immediate access to the vehicle and a driver. This worksheet may be used in conjunction with Worksheet P-12: Site Evacuation. Note: Worksheet P-2: Emergency Phone Numbers should be used if emergency medical services are needed from off the site.

Plan

1. In what situations would this vehicle be used instead of outside help such as an ambulance service?		
Are emergency vehicles checked for safety and reliability?		
Who is responsible for seeing that emergency vehicles have enough gas?		
Where is the nearest source for gas?		
2. List of available vehicles:		
Vehicle	Where is it parked?	Where are the keys kept?
Location of backup vehicle(s) and keys:		
3. Who are the designated emergency drivers?		
Does someone else ride along?		
If so, who?		
4. What emergency equipment is kept in the emergency vehicles?		

Guidelines and Information to Help Complete the Plan

❑ Designate on-site emergency vehicles and be sure that drivers and vehicles are insured for such use. Be sure the vehicle has gas or that the emergency driver has access to a fuel supply.

❑ On-site emergency vehicles should always be parked in the same place. Supply all emergency drivers with keys or put keys in a predetermined convenient location. If a vehicle is also used for another purpose, design a plan for a backup vehicle.

❑ When transporting a very frightened child or a vomiting or bleeding patient, it is advisable to have another person along to assist the patient.

PROGRAM CRISIS WORKSHEET P-15

Transportation Emergencies

Rationale

When the organization is providing transportation for participants, it is important to provide for their safety while loading and unloading, when traveling, and in case of a vehicular accident. Accidents can result in expenses for medical deductibles, legal fees, replacement of persons and/or equipment, loss of a program, etc. (refer to Worksheet P-43: Incident Report).

Plan

1. How often are mechanical evaluations required for vehicles transporting children?
2. What is the frequency and process for safety checks?
3. Who are the persons trained in vehicular accident procedures?   When?   By whom?
4. What are the step-by-step procedures to be used in the event of a vehicle accident?
5. Who notifies parents when an accident has occurred?

Guidelines and Information to Help Complete the Plan

❑ In the event of an accident in which the driver or another adult is able to function, trained adults will handle the emergency and take responsibility for first aid and the safety of passengers, providing care for the injured and supervising the uninjured.

❑ Accident procedures should also include notification of police and/or ambulance, the program or executive director, and parents, and the identification of any witnesses.

❑ The vehicle(s) involved should not be moved until police have authorized its movement. An incident/accident report should be completed and given to the director. It may be helpful to have a disposable camera in the glove compartment to take pictures of the accident scene.

PROGRAM CRISIS WORKSHEET P-16

First Aid/CPR

Rationale

The minimum qualifications of the certified or licensed person on the program site to provide emergency first aid and CPR at all times may depend on access to a higher level emergency medical system. Knowing who the current certified first-aid providers are and having supplies accessible are important steps in the planning for first-aid coverage on site, at specific activities, and on trips.

Plan

1. Who is the first line of care for emergency first aid?	
Where is he usually located?	
2. How long would it take for a person to access an emergency medical system?	
3. List staff members that have current certification in first aid, cardiopulmonary resuscitation (CPR), etc.	

Name	Unit or Location	Certification			Expiration Date
		FA	2nd level FA	CPR	

What are the minimum first aid expectations of all staff members?	
4. What activities or off-site trips must have a certified first-aid provider present?	
5. Who is responsible for restocking first-aid kits?	
How often are they restocked?	
6. First-aid kits are stocked and available at the following activity areas (check those applicable to the site):	

Activity Area	First-aid kit is located:
Lake and/or pool	
Archery	
Stables	
Crafts	
Units	
Dining area	
Sports area	
Vehicle	
School premises	
Other	

7. First-aid kits include:	

Needle for splinters	Small roll of adhesive tape	Tube of zinc oxide
Scissors	Small butterfly bandage	Elastic bandage
Tweezers	Large butterfly bandage	Moleskin
Safety pins	Tin of Band-Aids®	Insect sting kit
Small bottle of alcohol	Gauze pads	Nonlatex gloves
Alcohol swabs	Nonstick adhesive pads	Note pad or medical log form
Instant cold pack	Triangle bandage	Other:
Green soap or a small bar of antibacterial soap	Individual box or package (beltless) of sanitary napkins	Other:

8. User groups have been notified that first-aid services are the responsibility of:

Guidelines and Information to Help Complete the Plan

❑ Some programs, such as resident and day camps, assume responsibility for health services, while others, such as in-school programs, may only be responsible for notifying the school. If first aid is required as a part of an employee's job, the organization may be responsible for offering hepatitis B vaccination shots (refer to Worksheet P-17: Exposure to Bloodborne Pathogens). Employee application forms should identify each applicant's current certification, the certifying agency, and the expiration date.

❑ The American Camp Association standards specify that when access to the emergency medical systems (EMS) takes 20 minutes or less, a person with training in first aid and CPR should be on the site at all times. If EMS takes 20 to 60 minutes, the certification should be training in second-level first aid and CPR. If more than one hour is needed, training should be in wilderness first aid and CPR.

❑ It is essential to have first-aid kits available at all activity areas and on trips, and to have a system to ensure that they are replenished after each use. It may be helpful to seek medical advice on the content of first-aid kits. Because children may be allergic, over-the-counter medications should not be included in a first-aid kit unless recommended by a medical professional.

❑ Determine what the minimum first-aid skills should be for all staff members and design a system to provide in-service training. Refer to Worksheet P-57: Staff Training for information on what should be included in the training. Whenever possible, have the injured person take care of his own injury under the supervision of a staff member. It is recommended that volunteers have first-aid training. At the very least, minimum skills and precautions should be addressed in training. The organization should offer first-aid training as part of staff training or promote first-aid training events offered by other groups in the community prior to the program.

❑ Clearly explain the responsibility of first-aid providers to report any treatment to the designated health supervisor. Design a system or form to make the reporting consistent, complete, and included in the health log maintained by the health supervisor.

❑ Have a system for informing the person(s) responsible for first aid of any health-history information on staff members or participants that is important to their participation. Be sure that each first-aid provider has consent-for-treatment forms if the program is away from the activity site.

❑ In a drop-in activity center where children come and go, it is assumed that the parent or responsible adult is responsible for the children's health and safety. If possible, information cards should be filled out the first time a child attends. In the event of injury or illness, the parent or responsible adult should be called to deal with the problem. Simple first aid provided on site should be limited to cleaning and bandaging abrasions. In drop-in activity centers, staff members are not to transport a child to seek emergency care. If immediate care is needed and the parent or responsible adult cannot be located, the community's emergency medical system should be used (usually by calling 911).

❑ The organization should analyze the site and identify potential emergency-care needs for groups renting the site, including emergency procedures, contact information, allergies, supplies, and transportation needs. The organization should provide, or advise the user group to provide, adults with current CPR and first-aid certification. If minors are on the site without parents, the user group should also gather permission to provide emergency treatment.

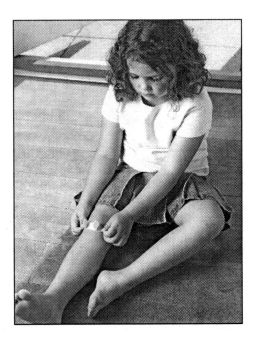

PROGRAM CRISIS WORKSHEET P-17

Exposure to Bloodborne Pathogens

Rationale

Bloodborne pathogens are pathogenic microorganisms that are present in human blood and can cause disease in humans. Such pathogens include, but are not limited to, hepatitis B virus (HBV) and human immunodeficiency virus (HIV). OSHA requires employers to develop an exposure control plan to eliminate or minimize employee exposure. This plan should be consistent with Worksheet O-7: First Aid/CPR and Exposure to Bloodborne Pathogens—Office.

Plan

1. To determine exposure, list all staff members who, by virtue of their job descriptions:		
...incur the risk of exposure to blood and other body fluids.	Date the staff member received education about the nature of the risk (attach training content)	Status of hepatitis B vaccination
...provide first-aid care as an ancillary task rather than a primary task.	Date the staff member received education about the nature of the risk (attach training content)	Informed about procedure to follow if exposure occurs?

2. When and how do all staff members receive a copy of the "Universal Precautions" recommended by the Centers of Disease Control and Prevention?	
3. Additional training for staff not expected to provide first aid includes:	
	Information regarding to whom staff and participants in need of health care should be referred
	Appropriate response practices in case of emergency
	Where are records of attendance at training, job titles, and dates stored?
	Name and qualifications of the person providing the training:
4. Procedures for disposing of contaminated equipment or waste:	
5. What is the postexposure plan for employees who have a suspected exposure?	

	Reporting exposure to the staff member in charge
	Contacting medical services and referring the employee for assessment
	Beginning a 15-second scrub of the area with bacteriostatic soap, followed by an application of disinfectant
	Arranging for employees who have not been vaccinated to receive vaccination within
	24 hours of exposure
	Beginning psychosocial support process
	Completing workers' comp and incident report forms with the employee
	Notifying insurance
6.	What is the exposure control plan for persons who have a suspected exposure, but are not employees?
7.	A log and the medical records for participants or staff members who have had some exposure, as well as a copy of this plan, are boxed and dated for disposal with the end of participation and/or employment plus 30 years. These records are located:
8.	Procedure for evaluating exposure incidents:

Guidelines and Information to Help Complete the Plan

❑ OSHA requires all employers that have employees with occupational exposure to have an exposure-control plan. A sample exposure-control plan is included in Appendix 31b, and a camp-specific plan is found in Appendix 31c. Occupational exposure is defined as reasonably anticipated contact with blood or other infectious materials that may result from the performance of an employee's duties. A sample exposure-control plan can be found on the CDC website (www.cdc.gov).

❑ Some staff positions, by virtue of their job descriptions, incur the risk of exposure to blood and other body fluids. Such positions include registered nurses (RN), licensed practical nurses (LPN), and physicians. Employers must make the hepatitis B vaccine and vaccination series available to all employees who have occupational exposures, in addition to providing postexposure evaluations and follow-ups for all employees who have had an exposure incident. Most healthcare workers will have had vaccinations as part of previous work. Training should include:

- Identification of risk areas: Contact with bloodborne pathogens (e.g., hepatitis, HIV), airborne pathogens (e.g., common cold, tuberculosis), and surface-borne pathogens (e.g., staph infections)

- Education about the nature of the risk: Methods of transmission, virulence of pathogens, resistance factors related to potential hosts, symptoms and information sources that provide clues to potential risk areas

- Work practices designed to minimize exposure

- Behavior expected from employees to minimize risk

❑ Individuals holding staff positions that provide first-aid care as an ancillary task rather than a primary task should receive information about the nature of the risk and what to do if an exposure occurs. If first aid is an ancillary task, then the vaccination may be offered to those persons upon exposure. The vaccination can be given within the first 24 hours of any exposure involving blood or other potentially infectious materials. In addition to offering the vaccine, incidents must be reported to the employer and include information on persons, circumstances, dates and times, and an "exposure incident" as defined by OSHA standards. Reports must be available to employees and OSHA.

❑ All staff members should receive training in appropriate response practices in case of emergency, including the "Universal Precautions," a sample of which is found in Appendix 31. According to the concept of Universal Precautions, all human blood and certain human body fluids are treated as if known to be infectious for HIV, HBV, and other blood pathogens. It is the responsibility of the program to train staff and provide appropriate protective equipment to implement this mandate. For more facts on HIV transmission, refer to the CDC website. In a resident or day camp, training usually includes the following appropriate response practices:

- Staff members are instructed to use a CPR mask for CPR and artificial respiration. Masks are kept at the waterfront and health center.

- Staff members are instructed to use gloves when the potential for contact with blood or blood-tinged fluids exists. Gloves are included in all first-aid kits. Staff members who want to carry a pair on their person may obtain them from the health center.

- Staff members are instructed to respond in emergency situations to the level of their training per state Good Samaritan regulations.

- Staff members are instructed to initiate the program's emergency response system immediately.

- Staff members participate in a discussion of emergencies to establish the defining attributes of their response.

- Staff members are educated to approach care of minor injuries from a coaching perspective and specifically directed to refer injured people to the healthcare team if selfcare is inappropriate or impossible.

❑ Employers must provide training to employees who have no previous experience in handling human pathogens. Training records must include dates, content, the qualifications of the person providing the training, and the names and job titles of persons attending. Training records must be kept for three years from the date of the training.

❑ Gloves may deteriorate faster when exposed to air. Putting gloves in film canisters or resealable bags may prolong their period of use. It is important to note that some people are allergic to latex gloves. A regular system of checking and replacing supplies and equipment should include a time schedule (e.g., weekly, monthly). Hand-washing facilities should be readily available to employees, protective equipment should be made available, and contaminated needles, equipment, or waste should be properly labeled and disposed of.

❑ Medical records that contain an employee's name, social security number, hepatitis B vaccination status, exposure reports, and follow-up procedures need to be kept confidential and maintained for the duration of employment, plus 30 years. The updated standard also requires employers to maintain a log of injuries from contaminated sharps. The organization must establish and follow a postexposure evaluation and follow-up procedure that includes a confidential medical exam and other required steps.

❑ A postexposure plan should include immediate follow-up procedures. Follow-up is initiated by the employee, who must immediately (within 15 minutes) notify a staff member or healthcare supervisor, undergo immediate cleansing, and receive assistance with emergency healthcare services. Postexposure procedures also include a confidential medical assessment, arrangement for vaccination, and other steps recommended by a physician. Employees who have a blood-exposure incident are eligible for follow-up treatment.

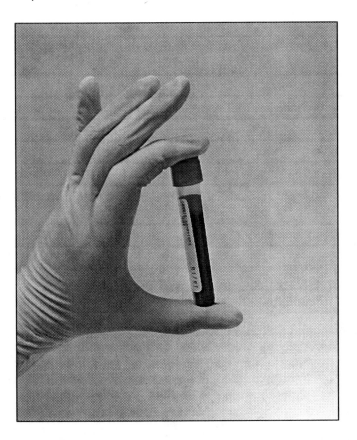

PROGRAM CRISIS WORKSHEET P-18

Insect- and Rodent-Transmitted Diseases

Rationale

Some insect bites can cause serious health problems and, in some instances, arboviral (i.e., insect-borne) diseases can cause an epidemic or death. To help identify those bites that need immediate medical attention and help reduce the risk of spreading a virus, it is important to identify high-risk areas, incidents in the area, symptoms, prevention techniques, and treatments. Contact with urine, droppings, or saliva from rodents carrying hantavirus may transmit the disease.

Plan

	Check for potentially dangerous insects or infected rodents in the area and document any evidence of infectious virus:
❑	Mosquitoes
1.	Encephalitis
	Evidence of mosquitoes carrying encephalitis:
	Prevention techniques:
	Symptoms verified by a doctor include, after seven to 10 days: high fever, headache, vomiting, drowsiness, stiff neck and/or back, severe irritability. Other:
	Recommended action, including notification of parents:
	Staff training includes:
2.	Dengue Fever
	Evidence of mosquitoes carrying dengue fever:
	Prevention techniques:
	Symptoms verified by a doctor include: flu-like reactions, sudden high fever, severe headache, measles-like rash, joint and muscle pain. Other:
	Recommended action, including notification of parents:
	Staff training includes:
3.	West Nile Virus
	Evidence of mosquitoes carrying the West Nile virus:
	Prevention techniques:
	Symptoms verified by a doctor include: fever, headache, tiredness, and body aches, occasionally with a skin rash (on the trunk of the body) and swollen lymph glands. While the illness can be as short as a few days, even healthy people have reported being sick for several weeks. The symptoms of severe disease (also called neuroinvasive disease, such as West Nile encephalitis or meningitis or West Nile poliomyelitis) include headache, high fever, neck stiffness, stupor, disorientation, coma, tremors, convulsions, muscle weakness, and paralysis. Other:

Recommended action, including notification of parents:
Staff training includes:
❏   Ticks
4.   Rocky Mountain Spotted Fever
Evidence of ticks carrying Rocky Mountain spotted fever:
Prevention techniques:
Symptoms verified by a doctor include, after seven to14 days: a mild or extremely high fever; blotchy rash on the ankles, wrists, palms, or soles of the feet; and headaches. Possibly muscle aches, persistent cough, or severe weakness. Other:
Recommended action, including notification of parents:
Staff training includes:
5.   Lyme Disease
Evidence of ticks carrying Lyme disease:
Prevention techniques:
Symptoms verified by doctor include, after two to 14 days: flu-like reactions, fatigue, headaches, joint aches, and minor stomach upsets. Approximately two-thirds of patients have a bull's-eye-like rash at the bite and some have a stiff neck. Other:
Recommended action, including notification of parents:
Staff training includes:
6.   Babesiosis
Evidence of ticks carrying Babesiosis fever:
Prevention techniques:
Symptoms verified by a doctor include: fever, headaches, chills, and fatigue. Other:
Recommended action, including notification of parents:
Staff training includes:
❏   Stinging Insects (honeybees, yellow jackets, hornets, wasps, and fire ants)
Evidence of stinging insects in the area:
Prevention techniques:
Symptoms verified by a doctor include: pain, swelling, redness, and itching (allergy to an insect may cause swelling of the mouth, tongue, or throat and/or breathing difficulties). Other:
Recommended action, including notification of parents:
Staff training includes:
❏   Lethal Spiders
Evidence of black widow or brown recluse spiders in the area:
Prevention techniques:
Symptoms verified by a doctor include: Within a few hours, a black widow bite can cause pain, slight swelling, faint red marks, severe muscular and abdominal pain, stiffness, chills, fever, and nausea. Within eight hours, a brown recluse may produce only a red bump or blister that turns into a deep ulcer. Mild fever, rash, nausea, and lethargy may also occur. Other:

Recommended action, including notification of parents:
Staff training includes:
Procedures for any serious bite or sting from insects identified above:
❏   Infected Rodents
7.   Hantavirus pulmonary syndrome (HPS)
Evidence of infected deer mice in the area:
Prevention though rodent-control techniques:
Symptoms verified by a doctor include: early symptoms one to five weeks after exposure include fever, chills, and muscle aches, especially in large muscle groups; headaches; dizziness and nausea; and abdominal pain and diarrhea, followed in four to 10 days after initial phase by an abrupt onset of respiratory distress and shortness of breath. Other:
Recommended action, including notification of parents:
Staff training includes:

Guidelines and Information to Help Complete the Plan

❏ A doctor or health department official should verify symptoms in the area. Recommended action should include the treatment recommended by a doctor and any required notification to the health officials.

❏ Because some of the signs will not show while the child is in the program, a procedure should be in place to handle inquiries from parents after the child has left the program. A person should be designated to inform the parents if the child has had a bite that showed some of the symptoms, especially if problems have been seen in the area. Staff members should be aware of symptoms and instructed in the immediate action needed, if applicable.

❏ The Centers for Disease Control and Prevention (www.cdc.gov) maintains up-to-date information about insect- and rodent-transmitted diseases. Visit the website for prevention techniques and current maps of areas where disease can be found.

• Insects, ticks, and spiders

• High-risk areas for mosquitoes carrying encephalitis include the southern and central states; the north central states; the eastern seaboard from Florida to the Mid-Atlantic states, and the western states.

• High-risk areas for Dengue fever are along the Texas-Mexico border.

• High-risk areas for Rocky Mountain Spotted Fever are the southeastern seaboard, the south Atlantic states, and the south central states.

• Stinging insects are found throughout the United States. Africanized honeybees (commonly referred to as killer bees) are confined to Texas as of the publication of this book, but they are expected to invade the south central and southern states by 2012.

- High-risk areas for lethal spiders are mostly in the southern states.

- Deer ticks, which carry Lyme disease, are considerably smaller than wood or dog ticks. Nearly every state has reported cases of Lyme disease. Check with the health department in the area to see if occurrences are common.

- Head lice are parasitic insects found on the heads of people. Anyone who comes in close contact (especially head-to-head contact) with someone who already has head lice is at greatest risk. Treatment to rid the person of lice is important to keep him from infesting others. However, lice do not carry or spread disease. For more information on the treatment of infestations, see the CDC website (www.cdc.gov).

❑ Infected rodents

- Rodent control in and around the area is the primary strategy for preventing hantavirus infection. Refer to Worksheet P-22: Site Operations and Maintenance for guidelines.

- Opening or cleaning cabins, sheds, and buildings that have been closed during the winter is a potential risk. Infested trail shelters or areas used periodically may be infested.

- Infected rodents shed the virus through urine, droppings, and saliva. HPS is transmitted to humans through a process called aerosolization, which occurs when dried materials contaminated by rodent excreta or saliva are disbudded and inhaled by humans.

- Although HPS is rather rare, 30 states (mostly western states) have reported HPS, although some cases have been reported in the East. More than half of the reported cases have been in the Four Corners area (Arizona, Colorado, New Mexico, and Utah).

- Since the signs will not show while the child is in the program, a procedure should be in place to handle inquiries from parents after the child has left the program. A person should be designated to inform parents if a child is diagnosed or if other cases have been reported in the area.

- Staff training should include facts about hantavirus symptoms and transmission, including avoidance of handling dead rodents.

PROGRAM CRISIS WORKSHEET P-19

Youth Suicide and Self-Mutilation

Rationale

Suicide has teetered between being the second- and third-leading cause of death among youth. Every year, a half-million young people attempt suicide. A young person's attempt may be based on a combination of long-standing problems coupled with a triggering event. "Cutting" and other forms of self-mutilation may also be a sign of emotional pain. The young person in crisis may reach out to, or confide in, a trusted program leader.

Plan

1.	Preparation: Procedure for dealing with suicide threats, attempts, or warning signs:
2.	Staff training includes:
	Warning signs
	Suicide-awareness skills
	Procedures for dealing with threats
3.	Suicide threats should be reported to:
4.	Person(s) authorized to discuss suicide threats, attempts, or warning signs with parents:
5.	Procedure to dealing with self-mutilation threats, attempts, or experiences:
6.	Staff training includes:
7.	Self-mutilation experiences should be reported to:
8.	Person(s) authorized to discuss a self-mutilation attempt or experience with parents:
9.	Physician or professional resource to provide expertise or services to a troubled youth or staff member:
10.	Procedures for dealing with other staff or youth after a threat, attempt, or actual suicide or self mutilation experience has happened:

Guidelines and Information to Help Complete the Plan

❏ Youth suicide

- Threats should be treated seriously. People who threaten suicide do, in fact, commit suicide—and may try again if the attempt was not successful. Procedures for dealing with threats, attempts, or warning signs should be communicated with staff and include identification of the person(s) in whom the troubled person has confided and developed a trusting relationship. Procedures should also include identifying when the situation merits discussing the situation with a professional resource and/or the parents.

- Warning signs are important, especially if more than one sign is present and persists over a period of time. The National Mental Health Association (or their local affiliate) is a good resource and has identified the following as warning signs:

   √   Decreased appetite

   √   Interrupted or changed sleep patterns

   √   Avoidance of friends and normal social activities

   √   Angry outbursts, tearfulness, or increased touchiness

   √   Withdrawal, uncommunicative

   √   Marked personality change from outgoing to isolated, or from quiet to extremely active

   √   Frequent physical complaints or fatigue

   √   Use of drugs, alcohol, or self-abusive behavior (including intentional reckless driving)

   √   Preoccupation with death

   √   Obsessive fear of nuclear war

   √   Irrational, bizarre behavior

   √   Overwhelming sense of guilt or shame

   √   Feelings of sadness, hopelessness, or despair

   √   Previous suicide attempt

   √   Giving away treasured belongings or writing a "will"

   √   An apparently normal or unusually calm period following a very troubled period

   √   A good resource for teen suicide is Children at Risk in the Camp Community by Gerard W. Kaye.

❑ Cutting and self-mutilation

- According to the Mayo Clinic, self-injury may occur in many forms, including cutting the skin or burning the skin with a cigarette. It's often an attempt to get temporary relief from increasing emotional pain. The intent behind the injury isn't suicide, but people who repeatedly injure themselves are at greater risk of suicide.

- Self-injury can be associated with mental illnesses such as:

   √   Borderline personality disorder

   √   Antisocial personality disorder

√   Post-traumatic stress syndrome

√   Eating disorders, such as bulimia

√   Substance-abuse disorders

- Self-mutilation can also become an overwhelming preoccupation. An affected person may want to stop the behavior, but find that he is unable to do so. In these cases, doctors consider self-injury to be an impulse-control disorder. Cutting isn't always a mental disorder. Some may do it for attention or as a result of drug use or peer influence.

PROGRAM CRISIS WORKSHEET P-20

Death of a Participant, Volunteer, Staff Member, or Family Member

Rationale

The most difficult incident to address is that of a fatal accident or illness of a participant or staff member. Because of this difficulty and the emotional impact of such a tragedy, having a plan in place is essential. An incident report form should be completed and the national organization's risk-management coordinator should be notified. A procedure should be in place for informing a staff member or participant of a death or serious injury of someone in his family or close to him.

Note: Use the emergency phone numbers to notify local authorities or medical personnel. Once the victim has been pronounced dead by legal authorities, the crisis shifts to dealing with the emotional ramifications to kin, staff members, and participants.

Plan

1. After the emergency, and after steps have been taken to care for the injured, the first person to be notified is:	
2. Others to be notified (besides the next of kin) are:	

Name	Title	Phone

3. If legal authorities do not notify the next of kin, the person(s) to take this responsibility is:	
The procedures for notification of next of kin are:	
Additional procedures if the death occurred on a trip away from the program site:	
4. Procedures for taking the parent or guardian to the deceased:	
5. Procedures for the disposition of personal belongings:	
6. Decisions about support to the family on transportation of the body, funeral arrangements, or other support needed are made by:	
7. Support to other participants and staff members includes:	
8. Procedure for informing a staff member or participant of a death or serious injury in his family:	
9. Who reports employee deaths or hospitalizations to OSHA?	
10. Person responsible for completing incident report:	

Guidelines and Information to Help Complete the Plan

❑ The legal authorities, medical personnel, and staff members on the scene will be the first to have knowledge of the death. After the emergency procedures have been followed at the scene, the legal authorities or medical personnel will probably assume control, including notification of next of kin.

❑ As soon as the legal authorities have been notified, the press will have knowledge of the incident (see Worksheet O-9: Emergency Media Plan). It is critical that the next of kin is notified before any release is made. The parents of other participants will also be concerned if the incident is reported by the news.

❑ Steps to be followed at the scene are identified in the emergency procedures and reported on an incident report form. If the program director and/or the executive director are not at the scene, Worksheet P-3: Agency Emergency Numbers should give guidance regarding who in the organization should be notified. Worksheet P-43: Incident Report should be completed and the national office notified. The executive director should notify the president and the organization's lawyer as soon as possible.

❑ OSHA also requires that serious accidents or the death of an employee be reported to them and that employers display a poster that explains the protection and obligations of employees (www.osha.gov).

❑ The legal authorities will probably assume the responsibility of notifying next of kin. If not, or in addition to the authorities doing so, the executive director, program administrator, and/or president should notify the family in person—never by phone. If possible, legal counsel should be consulted before the executive director and/or president visits the family in person.

❑ The program leader, religious leader, or other people familiar with the family may be of help in notifying the next of kin, making arrangements to take the family to where the deceased is, handling the deceased's personal belongings, or making funeral arrangements. If the incident occurred while on a trip, the authorities and/or the executive director should help with arrangements for sending the body home.

❑ Organizational contact persons need to be briefed on the accident so that they can be supportive, but must not discuss any responsibility for the incident with the family. It is important to provide support to the family throughout the process and until the shock wears off. Organizational contact persons should plan to attend the funeral, unless advised not to by legal counsel, and be ready for any future support needed by the family.

❑ Other parties involved, such as staff members and other participants, may need the support of a trained professional after the incident. It is normal for other participants or staff members to feel blame or to feel that they should have done something differently. For liability reasons, they should be informed that they should not discuss the incident with the press or anyone without first checking with the executive director.

❑ The plan should also include how, and by whom, a participant or staff member should be informed of a death or serious injury in his family while he is in the program.

PROGRAM WORKSHEET P-21

Program Site Hazard Identification— Natural and Man-Made

Rationale

All hazards, both natural and man-made, on each site must be identified and then eliminated or reduced, and procedures must be written to help ensure a safer experience. Business-interruption procedures should also be in place in case it is necessary to temporarily or permanently close the office or program site (refer to Worksheet P-4: Emergency Procedures for Hazards and/or Disasters).

Plan

1. The site is surveyed for hazards before participants arrive and on a regular basis thereafter:			
When		Person(s) responsible	

2. The survey includes appraisal of crime risk (CPTED)			
When		Person(s) responsible	

3. Site hazards identified to be eliminated are:

Hazard Identified	How Eliminated	Date Completed	By Whom

4. Site hazards identified and not eliminated are:

Hazard Identified	Rationale for not Eliminating	Protection from the Hazard (Physical and/or Human)	Rules or Procedures Regarding the Hazard	How and to Whom Disseminated

5. Business-interruption procedures or policies include:	Person responsible
Alternate worksite, if necessary	
Alternative way to deliver program services	
Expanded check-writing authority	
Ability to write checks and pay vendors	
Method to notify participants/parents of closure	

Backup of frequently used electronic documents	
List of IT hardware and software to continue services	
Contact numbers for agency partners and media	
Office supplies	
System for updating emergency services list	
System for updating agency emergency contact list	
Phone tree established/email list serve	

Guidelines and Information to Help Complete the Plan

❑ Touring the site with a small group of observant people and/or insurance company representatives can help identify risks. This group might include a fire marshal, forester, or others. Most local police departments have someone with the title of "crime prevention through environmental design" (CPTED), who will come to the office or program site and advise the organization on areas of risk in the facility. This process should include surveying the site for facility design features that may either increase or help prevent opportunities for child abuse, abduction, or another crime to occur.

❑ The plan should include man-made hazards such as low-hanging wires, dumps, abandoned roads and buildings, exposed pipes, broken steps, broken playground equipment, piles of trash, discarded needles, unfenced swimming pools, livestock medication, and other hazards in program areas. It should also include natural hazards such as dead trees, poisonous plants or animals, land irregularities, etc.

❑ Protection from hazards may include such things as putting up a fence or sign, training staff members in personal security practices, teaching staff members to identify snakes, making a display of poisonous plants to watch for, installing alarms, removing large bushes where people could hide, establishing evacuation procedures, etc.

❑ Safety policies or procedures may include such things as a rule that persons must walk on designated paths, designating a steep eroding area as "off limits" to staff and participants, reporting hazardous trees, etc.

❑ The upper bunk of a bunk bed may be considered a man-made hazard if it is used by children under 16 years of age. Beds should be equipped with guardrails. The Consumer Product Safety Commission recommends that the bottom of the guardrail be no more than three-and-a-half inches from the top of the bed frame and that the top should extend five inches above the mattress.

❑ Business-interruption procedures and policies address situations in which the emergency is over, but the business cannot reopen either temporarily or permanently. Additional information on business-interruption procedures include Worksheet P-34: Insurance Safety Audit for Organization Owned Sites, Worksheet P-12: Site Evacuation, and Worksheet P-38: Program Record Retention and Destruction.

❑ For other worksheets that will help with program site hazard identification, refer to Worksheet P-5: Utilities, Worksheet P-4: Emergency Procedures for Hazards and/or Disasters, Worksheet P-23: Property Use and Liability, and Worksheet P-8: Security.

PROGRAM WORKSHEET P-22

Program Site Operations and Maintenance

Rationale

Analyzing maintenance needs, establishing a plan to keep facilities in good repair and in a safe and clean condition, and having procedures for proper use of equipment may prevent accidents or illnesses from occurring.

Plan

1. List regular responsibilities for keeping facilities, grounds, and equipment in good repair and in a safe and clean condition.

What are responsibilities for the:	Who?	How Often?	Checked By:
Food service area			
Dining area			
Bathroom area			
Maintenance facilities			
Office facilities			
Program areas			
Living areas			
Grounds			
Playgrounds			

2. List hand tools, power tools, and other equipment used on the site:

Equipment Used On Site	Persons Approved to Use	How Equipment Is Safety-Checked	By Whom

3. Who is responsible for analyzing maintenance needs and how often are site-maintenance surveys and/or safety checks made?			
How are funds made available to carry out established maintenance plans?			
4. Operating and routine maintenance instructions are scheduled on the following mechanical equipment. Where are the specifications for parts or service kept?			
Equipment/Brand	When Scheduled		Specifications—Parts + Service

Guidelines and Information to Help Complete the Plan

❑ A survey of maintenance needs and a plan of action with related costs should be made at least annually. In addition, an annual review and analysis should be made of maintenance effectiveness. Rodent control is an important part of all procedures for maintaining clean facilities (refer to hantavirus on Worksheet P-18: Insect- and Rodent-Transmitted Diseases), especially in buildings that have not been used or have been closed for the winter. Refer to the Centers for Disease Control and Prevention for guidelines to "Seal up, Trap up, and Clean up" (www.cdc.gov).

❑ The responsibilities for the food service area should include maintaining temporary storage of garbage and rubbish in containers that are leakproof and securely covered or tied when not in use.

❑ A procedure should be established for reporting hazards, and a person must be designated to handle reports, assure that hazards are scheduled for correction immediately after notification, and follow up to assure that the work has been completed. Persons responsible for an area may be a staff person, volunteer, or contracted vendor. Work should be scheduled, if possible, to not interfere with the office or create additional hazards.

❑ How often periodic maintenance checks need to be done may depend on the usage, age, and/or condition of the facility or equipment. A file should be maintained of all mechanical equipment that includes date and source of purchase, operating information, warranties, and specifications for ordering parts and getting service.

❑ Persons using tools should be trained and experienced in their use. Manufacturers' instructions should be maintained on the site. Tools should be in good repair and have proper safety devices installed.

❑ A fire safety check by a qualified person should take place on a regular basis. If the office is in rented space that provides these services, find out how often they are done. Assign tasks that are not completed by the landlord to a staff member or volunteer. Battery-operated smoke detectors must be checked to see if batteries are functioning and have not been removed. A qualified person should complete an annual check of fireplaces and chimneys. Flammables should be stored in safe containers that are covered and labeled. Be sure that persons who have access to flammables are trained in their use. Records of safety checks must be kept in a safe, fireproof place and not in the building being checked.

❑ The organization should obtain advice on appropriate firefighting equipment from the local or state fire marshal or fire department, insurance company, and the company product safety division and/or fire extinguisher company. Have equipment checked and approved annually by the state or local fire marshal, fire department, or fire extinguisher company.

❑ OSHA has reporting requirements in place for when an employee gets hurt, as well as rules such as the Confined Space Rule, which requires that a written safety plan and staff training policy must be in place regarding spaces not designed for human occupation. The Lock-out/Tag-out Rule on Worksheet P-5: Utilities requires procedures to protect employees from accidental injury from any stored energy. OSHA has also established rules on the use of chemicals or toxins often found in paint, cleaning supplies, yard equipment, and office machines (www.osha.gov).

PROGRAM WORKSHEET P-23

Property Use and Liability

Rationale

Using other people's or organizations' property for programs, such as schools, churches, or farms, or having other persons or groups utilize property owned by the organization may be cause for certain liabilities.

Plan

1. Use of Non-Owned Property			
Permission was secured by:		To use property owned by:	
In ease of emergency, the owner can be reached at:			
During the day:		At night:	
Hazards identified by the owner are:			
Areas or equipment on site that are not available for use:			
Site was inspected by:		On (date):	
Precautions given to participants:			
2. Organization-Owned Property			
Hazards Identified		Notice Given By How Given	

Site inspected for maintenance problems before use by:			
Equipment or Areas not Available for Use	Notice Given By	How Given	How Enforced

Do procedures for rentals include requests for:	
Certificate of insurance	Who verifies?
Evidence of being named as additional insured	Who verifies?
If copies of the above are not provided with the agreement, what are the follow-up procedures?	

Guidelines and Information to Help Complete the Plan

❑ Three classifications have been established of persons on lands not owned by the person on the land. Invitees are those who pay to come or come on invitation without a fee. Trespassers enter illegally without permission. Licensees enter with a limited permission, such as to attend a closing camp ceremony or hunt on the property. Many states have added a fourth category: recreational user statutes that encourage landowners to permit the public to use of their property for outdoor recreation by limiting their liability for injuries. The landowner owes all four categories a "duty for notice" of hazardous situations, such as a dangerous hole, vicious dog, rifle range, etc.

❑ Licensees become trespassers if they go beyond the limits of their permission, such as when a hunter decides to swim in the pool. Trespassers become licensees when they are ignored or allowed to remain on the property. More protective duty may be required.

❑ A property owner who leases or permits persons to use the property retains liability for injury related to the premises. It is, therefore, important to maintain the property in good condition, make it clear what can or cannot be used, and identify hazards. Proper maintenance includes replacing light bulbs that may cause hazards in the dark, as well as replacing broken boards, protruding nails, or broken equipment.

❑ Be sure that persons using organization-owned property can reach someone in case of emergency before their arrival and during their stay. Office staff may not be available after hours. Agreements for use of organization-owned property should include a hold-harmless clause indicating they will indemnify or hold the organization harmless against claims and legal expenses arising from the use of the property.

❑ A certificate of insurance showing that a renting group carries liability insurance to cover activities should back agreements for use of organization-owned property. The organization should request to be named as an additional insured under the group policy and be sure the group insurance is primary.

PROGRAM WORKSHEET P-24

Safe Water Supply

Rationale

Because many diseases are transmitted through water, a safe, ample supply of water is imperative for cooking, drinking, bathing, and swimming. In many states, water for swimming as well as drinking must be approved. Young children may not be able to regulate hot water by hand.

Plan

1. Water supply
What are state and local requirements for assuring that drinking water and water used for swimming is safe?
Who is responsible for collecting water samples for testing?
Where are they tested?
What is the procedure for getting the samples there?
How often is the water tested?
Who receives reports on water condition?
Who is responsible for responding to unsatisfactory reports?
What local resources are available to help with providing safe water?
2. Facilities for hand-washing and bathing
Hand-washing facilities with soap or waterless, hand-sanitizing products are available adjacent to all toilet facilities.
Hand-washing facilities with soap or waterless, hand-sanitizing products are available adjacent to all areas where food is prepared or served.
3. Water temperature
A system other than individual hand adjustment to prevent scalding at taps of bathing, showering, and hand-washing facilities is in place.
Who is responsible for testing?

Guidelines and Information to Help Complete the Plan

❑   Contact the local or state health department for information on safe water for drinking and swimming. If the organization is using a water source that is not a part of a community water supply, the water needs to be tested within 30 days of first use by participants or staff members, or quarterly if in continual use.

❑ A system to regulate water temperature, other than adjusting by hand at the tap, is important to prevent scalding when the water source is used by children. Systems include thermostatically controlled temperature valves, mixing valves, and water heater thermostats. Recommended safe water temperature is usually not higher than 110° F (43° C). Hand-washing facilities help prevent the spread of disease.

PROGRAM WORKSHEET P-25

Notification of Operation

Rationale

A relationship should be established with local emergency officials, including an annual notification of program operation to verify appropriate response information.

Plan

A notification of site operation or a program event was made to the following local emergency officials:	
Law enforcement	Date
Fire services	
Civil Defense or Homeland Security	
Forest Service/National Park	

Guidelines and Information to Help Complete the Plan

❑ If at all possible, have both the fire and law-enforcement officials visit the site. At that time, a letter can be presented to them. If that is not possible, a letter should be delivered in person or mailed six to eight weeks prior to the program opening (refer to Worksheet P-2: Emergency Phone Numbers).

❑ Even when a program is covered by municipal emergency services, annual contact helps to establish an ongoing relationship and provide updated information for emergency services.

PROGRAM WORKSHEET P-26

Fire Prevention and Safety

Rationale

It is important to have a fire-prevention safety evaluation done on a regular basis and to have systems in place that will reduce the possibility of a fire and provide for adequate ventilation, temperature control, and space.

Plan

1. The routine safety evaluation includes:		
Inspection of:	How often is the safety check done?	By whom?
Firefighting equipment		
Electrical cords		
Circuits		
Shut-off devices		
Storage of combustibles		
Alarm systems		
Fire doors		
Exits		
Emergency lighting		
Appliances		
Fireplaces and chimneys		
Open fire areas		
Cooking areas		

2. Where are records of safety checks kept?

3. Flammable materials are labeled and stored appropriately

Where are on-site hazardous materials stored?	Who has access to them?	Who has been trained in their use?
Gas		
Liquid flammables		
Explosives		

4. All sleeping quarters in buildings have one emergency exit in addition to the main door, and all sleeping floors have a direct emergency exit to the outside.

Types of Sleeping Quarters	Emergency Exit

5. Where are floor plans for multi-room buildings kept?	
6. Smoke detectors, carbon monoxide detectors, and other detection devices in all permanent sleeping quarters and other enclosed buildings used by participants or staff members are inspected:	
By:	How often?

7. What is the means for ventilation and temperature control in permanent sleeping quarters?
8. Are beds arranged to provide at least 30 inches between sides and freedom of movement within the space?
9. Do upper bunks used by children have guardrails?

Guidelines and Information to Help Complete the Plan

❑ Enclosed buildings and buildings used for sleeping should have smoke detectors, and those with fuel-burning equipment should be constructed or equipped with carbon monoxide (CO) detection equipment. An electrical check should be made annually.

❑ A fire safety check by a qualified person should take place on a regular basis (at least annually). After a change in participants and/or staff, fire extinguishers and battery-operated smoke detectors must be checked to ensure that extinguishers have not been discharged and that batteries are functioning and have not been removed. A qualified person should complete an annual check of fireplaces and chimneys. Flammables should be stored in safe containers that are covered and labeled. Be sure that persons who have access to flammables are trained in their use.

❑ Permanent sleeping quarters include buildings, cabins, platform tents, yurts, and RVs that remain in a fixed location. Upper bunks used by children must have guardrails. Moveable beds should be checked periodically to be sure that space between beds has not been changed and that freedom of movement and access to exits is intact. Records of all safety checks must be kept in a safe, fireproof place and not in the building being checked.

PROGRAM WORKSHEET P-27

Serving Persons With Disabilities

Rationale

The Americans with Disabilities Act (ADA) is a national mandate for the elimination of discrimination against persons with disabilities. In most youth service organizations, inclusiveness is a fundamental goal for all operations and services. The titles of most importance to youth services are Title I: Employment and Title III: Public Accommodations. This information should be consistent with Worksheet O–17: Serving Persons With Disabilities.

Plan

1. The self-evaluation guidelines for Title I have been completed by:	
Required action has been determined and is assigned to be completed by:	Under the supervision of:
2. The self-evaluation guidelines for Title III:	
Have been completed by:	And reviewed by:
Required action has been determined and is assigned to be completed by:	Under the supervision of:
3. The quick-look barriers Checklist has been completed by:	
A list of actions has been compiled by:	
The list includes:	

Action Required	Cost of Action	Dates for Completion	Person(s) Responsible

4. Other plans to make the organization's operations and services more inclusive to persons with disabilities include:
5. Programs/activities/services that would fundamentally alter the nature of the program or where adaptation for certain disabilities would not be readily achievable include:

Guidelines and Information to Help Complete the Plan

❑ For current information on the Americans with Disabilities Act, refer to www.ada.gov. If the organization is a "public accommodation" under the definitions of the Americans With Disabilities Act, it may not deny enrollment or employment to persons protected by that act. Persons with AIDS and persons who test positive for the HIV virus are protected under the ADA.

❏ The ADA's general rule on employment required for employers with 15 or more employees is to not discriminate in regard to job application procedures, the hiring and advancement or discharge of employees, employee compensation, job training, and other terms, conditions, and privileges of employment.

❏ *Essential functions of the job* are determined by the employer and are the key components or skills that must be performed. Applications may not ask if the applicant has a disability, but can ask if any reasons exist why the applicant would have difficulty performing any of the essential functions of the job. Be sure that essential functions include any physical requirements such as lifting, required mobility, driving, etc., as well as any communication skills.

❏ *Reasonable accommodations* means making facilities used by employees readily accessible to, and usable by, individuals with disabilities, and /or involve job restructuring by providing part-time or modified work schedules; acquisition or modification of equipment or devices, training materials, or policies; the provision of qualified readers or interpreters; and other similar accommodations.

❏ *Undue hardship* is defined as an action requiring significant difficulty or expense when considered in light of several factors, such as the nature and cost of the accommodation, the overall financial resources, the type of operation, etc.

❏ Programs must also be accessible. The intent of the law is that persons with disabilities have the opportunity to participate in activities with their nondisabled peers. All buildings, vehicles, and program activities do not need to be accessible, but the benefits of participation should be the same and not separate. For example, housing individuals with disabilities in a separate area or having a special session and requiring persons with disabilities to *only* participate in that session is unacceptable.

❏ Persons with disabilities need the opportunity to participate in integrated programs when such participation does not *fundamentally alter the nature of the program* being provided and when accommodations are *reasonable and readily achievable*.

❏ *Readily achievable* means that something is easily accomplishable and able to be carried out without much difficulty or expense. Factors used to determine this include the nature and cost of the action needed, the overall financial resources of the facility, and the type of operation.

❏ Applications for participants may ask about disabilities. It is important to convey that this information is used to help determine appropriate supervision, support, and accommodations for the participant.

PROGRAM WORKSHEET P-28

Food Handling and Foodborne Illness

Note: Most of the information in this worksheet is from the U.S. Department of Agriculture, Food Safety and Inspection Service (www.foodsafety.gov).

Rationale

Persons handling food include not only food-service personnel, but also other staff members and even participants who may be serving snacks, cooking out, having a sack lunch, or picnicking. A foodborne-illness outbreak can involve the local health department or other authorities, and, if it affects a number of people, the incident will probably receive media coverage. It is important to select food purveyors who have a good record of providing "safe" food.

Plan

1. Person in charge of food service:	Experience or training required:
2. Who selects food purveyors?	Title:
3. Who is responsible for checking references or records for safety in providing food?	
4. Persons/positions who will be handling food:	
5. Food-handling procedures include:	
Procedures to ensure good personal hygiene for persons handling food:	
Requirements for washing or sanitizing hands:	
Procedures for cleaning and sanitizing work surfaces and equipment:	
Procedures for sanitizing of dishes and food-service utensils:	
Procedures for safe thawing of meats and poultry:	
Procedures for refrigerating foods and/or keeping food out of the "danger zone," which is between 40 and 120° F (4–49° C):	
Procedures for cooking and holding temperatures above the "danger zone," or above 140° F (49° C):	
Procedures for safe cooling:	
Procedures for safe reheating:	
Food preparation and storage areas are protected from rodents and vermin by:	
6. How are user groups informed of procedures for use of kitchen facilities owned by the organization?	
7. Local health department or authority:	

Name of contact:	Phone number:

8. Discussed procedures to handle this type of medical emergency with doctor:
Special instructions (refer to Worksheet P-2: Emergency Phone Numbers):
9. Person(s) to notify the health-insurance carrier (refer to Worksheet P-3: Agency Emergency Contacts):

Guidelines and Information to Help Complete the Plan

❑ The person in charge of the food service should have training in food-service management that includes sanitation, food preparation and protection, hygiene, personnel supervision, and recordkeeping. If a contracted food service is used, the written agreement should include a requirement for appropriate licenses and credentials.

❑ Salmonella-B is one of the most common bacterial infections and can be acquired from contaminated or inadequately processed foods, especially meat, eggs, poultry, and milk. Salmonella usually results in gastroenteritis, symptoms of which include diarrhea, abdominal cramps, vomiting, and fever occurring six to 72 hours after ingestion of contaminated food. The very young and the very old are particularly vulnerable.

❑ Other foodborne illness, such as novovirus, e-coli, and hepatitis A, are explained on the U.S. Food and Drug Administration website (www.fda.gov).

❑ Persons handling food include not only food-service personnel, but also other staff members and even participants who may be serving snacks, cooking out, having a sack lunch, or picnicking. In some cases, maintenance staff members lift, stack, or move heavy food-service equipment or crates and packages. Persons purchasing food supplies need to know basic information about contamination.

❑ Food-service workers can be carriers of bacteria and other dangerous microorganisms. Smoking can cause ashes to fall into the food. In addition, handling a cigarette may carry microorganisms from the worker's mouth, to his fingers, and then into the food. Without proper hair covering, bacteria, as well as hair, fall from the scalp into the food. Human hands are a primary means of contaminating foods. Encouraging everyone to wash their hands, especially when leaving the bathroom, eating, and handling food will help prevent the spread of dangerous bacteria and other microorganisms.

❑ Cleaning and sanitizing work areas, surfaces, and equipment immediately after use prevents contamination. Harmful bacteria can lodge in the corners of work areas and equipment and be transferred to the next product that is prepared in the area. Water temperature for washing dishes and utensils should be at least 180∞ F (88° C) for rinsing, or an approved chemical sanitizer should be used.

❏ The "danger zone" is 40 to 120° F (4–49° C), the range of temperature in which dangerous bacteria multiply rapidly, thereby increasing the possibility of foodborne illness. Safe food preparation is the result of both careful planning and good operating procedures. Forecasting the number of portions, using standard recipes, and preparing the right amount will help eliminate leftovers and last-minute substitutions.

❏ Thawing meats and poultry in a refrigerator prevents the product temperature from reaching the danger zone. Thawing on the counter is dangerous, because the temperature of the outside parts rises faster than the core. If a product must be thawed rapidly, place it in a watertight plastic bag in a sink with constantly running water.

❏ Harmful bacteria and microorganisms are everywhere in the kitchen and in the food itself. Most harmful bacteria cannot survive temperatures above 140° F (60° C) for very long. The food must be heated and maintained above that temperature or the growth will resume.

❏ Cross-contamination requires both the presence of a dangerous level of bacteria on one food product and the means of transporting it to another food product. The harmful organisms can be carried by utensils, equipment, cutting boards or surfaces, and human hands. Careful cleaning and sanitizing of work surfaces and equipment, washing hands between steps, using proper storage techniques, and separating work areas help prevent cross-contamination.

❏ Improper cooling has been shown to be the primary cause of food poisoning. The quicker the product cools or is reheated, the less opportunity bacteria will have to multiply. When food is left out for long periods before refrigerating or when it is refrigerated in large, deep containers, cooling occurs slowly [e.g., a large 8-pound roast may take more than five hours to fall from 135° F (57° C) to 70° F (21° C) and up to 17 hours to dip to 45° F (7° C)]. Food will cool more rapidly in a shallow pan than in a stockpot, and slices and smaller portions will cool more quickly.

❏ Reheating foods to an internal temperature of 165° F (74° C) is important in preventing the spread of foodborne illness. Bringing foods up to the serving temperature of 110 to 125° F (43 to 52° C) will only bring the food into the danger zone, where harmful bacteria can resume their growth. Use a chef's thermometer to check the internal temperature before serving.

❏ If several persons are showing symptoms of food poisoning, arrange for medical assistance and cultures to be taken. Contact the local health department to take a survey of food-service areas, drinking water, and water used for swimming. Follow the procedures of the health authorities and try to isolate what caused the problem.

❑ If moving those who are ill is not recommended by the health authorities, the organization must set up an area with beds, toilets, and sinks to provide care. Watch for signs of dehydration and monitor the overall medical status of the individuals. Provide a liquid such as Gatorade®, as well as extra linens, soap, toothbrushes, thermometers, and any medications recommended by a physician.

❑ The organization must be prepared to institute plans for dealing with the media and notifying the insurance carrier and parents, and then responding to parent inquiries (refer to Worksheet O-9: Emergency Media Plan, Worksheet P-3: Agency Emergency Contacts, and Worksheet P-9: Parent Contact).

PROGRAM WORKSHEET P-29

Storage and Handling of Hazardous, Flammable, or Poisonous Materials

Rationale

Hazardous, flammable, poisonous, and explosive materials may be mistaken for other substances, especially when not labeled or when stored where usage cannot be supervised and/or controlled. OSHA's 1989 Hazardous Communication Standard requires a written plan and training on safe use and storage.

Plan

1. Storage and handling of hazardous, flammable liquids or explosive materials for maintenance use include:				
Liquid	MDS	Used For	By	Stored

2. Storage and handling of hazardous or flammable liquids for program use include:				
Liquid	MDS	Used For	By	Stored

3. Storage and handling of hazardous or poisonous materials for maintenance, cleaning, and/or kitchen use are:				
Liquid or Material	MDS	Used For	By	Stored

4. Storage and handling of hazardous or poisonous materials for program use include:				
Liquid or Material	MDS	Used For	By	Stored

5. Policies regarding training or verification of experience in the use of the these substances include:
Policies and/or procedures have been reviewed by:
Qualifications:
6. Manufacturers Data Sheets are kept:

Guidelines and Information to Help Complete the Plan

❑ Policies and/or procedures should include where the materials can be safely stored, who can handle what substances, their appropriate use, the training or supervision required, and safe disposal. Flammable liquids and/or explosive materials include gasoline, kerosene, paint thinner, and alcohol-based substances that may be used for maintenance or in program activities. Poisons include bleach, cleaning agents, insecticides, weed killers, livestock medications, and some craft supplies, and may be used in program areas, kitchens, maintenance areas, or health facilities. Local officials may have additional recommendations.

❑ The OSHA's Hazardous Communication Program requires that a written plan be in place that includes an inventory of all hazardous materials, a Manufacturers Data Sheet (MDS), which are available from the vendor when the product is purchased, and that persons using the materials have had training on how to read the MDS and use the materials. An exception to this rule would be hazardous material in a household container with a Consumer Product Safety Commission Warning on the label. The cost of a violation may exceed $70,000. MDS should be kept where they are accessible to persons using hazardous materials.

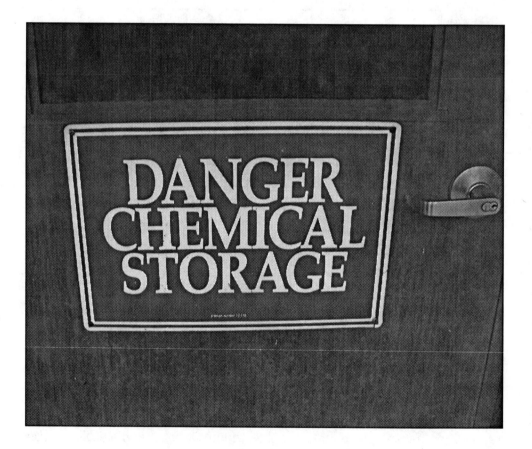

PROGRAM WORKSHEET P-30

Transporting Participants and Staff Members

Rationale

When the organization is providing transportation for participants, it is important to provide for their safety by determining who may transport participants and staff members, when, and under what circumstances; what safety precautions will be taken; and how accidents should be handled. Note: Plans for handling accidents appear in Worksheet P-15: Transportation Emergencies.

Plan

1. Who regularly transports participants?	
What drivers are required to complete a driver's information form?	
Whose responsibility is it to obtain these forms?	
Who verifies driving records?	
How often are driving records verified?	
Does a state or insurance-company requirement exist specifying a minimum age for drivers who are transporting children? If yes, what is the age?	
Who verifies that the driver's license is appropriate for the vehicle driven?	

2. In what circumstances and in what vehicles are participants and/or staff members regularly transported?		
Circumstances/Vehicle	Capacity	Supervision Required

3. What information is provided to parents when the organization is providing transportation?	
4. What is the organization's policy about transporting children in 15-passenger vans?	
5. What is the supervision ratio for vehicles that carry 15 or more passengers?	
What training is required for drivers?	
What training is provided to the second adult?	

6. Training for drivers is done by:	Qualifications:

7. Training is required for the following positions:

8. Is behind-the-wheel training and practice required when a vehicle is of a different size or capacity than the driver's regularly driven vehicle?			
All Approved Drivers	Those Who Received Behind-the-Wheel Training	When	By Whom

9.	Training on written safety procedures includes:

	Use of seatbelts
	Defensive driving
	Responsibilities for controlling passengers
	Evidence of skill with the vehicle to be used
	Backing up
	Loading and unloading passengers
	Location of passengers during refueling
	Dealing with breakdowns
	And, when appropriate, such topics as:
	Safe driving tactics for gravel roads
	Avoidance of people, animals, and other vehicles
	Mountain driving
	Driving in adverse weather conditions (e.g., fog, snow, rain, heavy wind)
	Information on the area (e.g., deer crossings, dangerous intersections, high-water areas)
	Other:

10.	The safety procedures for vehicles transporting participants and staff members include:

	Safety education for riding		When relief drivers are needed
	Safety education in case of an accident		Highway stops
	Use of seat belts		Permission for treatment slips in each vehicle
	Adequate supervision and minimum required		Health forms required for each participant
	Other:		Types of vehicles that can and cannot be used to transport youth

	Who is responsible for determining that procedures are being followed?
	When and how are participants and staff members trained in these procedures?
11.	Vehicles used for transporting participants and/or staff members are equipped with:

	First-aid kits
	Flares/reflectors
	Seatbelts for each passenger
	Fire extinguishers
	Jacks, spare tires
	Communications systems

12.	What are the arrival/departure procedures to control traffic and provide personal safety?
13.	If travel is more than one hour, what kinds of programming will occur during transit?
	Who is responsible?

Guidelines and Information to Help Complete the Plan

❏ Determine who may, on a regular basis, transport participants and/or staff members before the program begins. Many states and insurance policies specify age requirements for drivers that transport children. All drivers transporting participants or staff should be at least 18 years of age and have a current driver's license. In situations where participants drive to and from a program and/or during program operation, it is recommended that the driver carry written consent from each passenger's parents to ride with a licensed driver under 18. Parents should also be notified that the organization is not responsible for transportation.

❏ When transporting youth, it is recommended that two adults be present in the vehicle. In the event that two adults cannot be present, the alternative is one adult and two or more youth. An adult should not be alone with a youth (other than his own child) without the advance written permission of the youth's parents.

❏ Safety procedures should include safety education for rider conduct, safe seating, use of seatbelts, backing up, loading and unloading, highway stops, relief drivers, adequate supervision, keeping permission for treatment forms in each vehicle, types and ownership of vehicles used or not used, what to do in the event of an accident, etc. Buses should also have procedures for evacuation.

❏ Safety procedures for participant and/or staff-member transportation should include the type and capacity of vehicle(s) in which persons may be transported. Only vehicles designed to transport persons should be used. Capacity should be monitored according to the manufacturer's instructions. Vehicles being towed on public highways or roads should not carry passengers. Hay wagons should have side rails, maintain a predetermined slow speed, and be driven only on private property. Participants should know and understand these safety rules.

❏ Participants and staff members should be trained in safe loading and unloading of passengers and have designated areas for waiting. Staff members should supervise the area. When children are traveling longer than an hour, quiet, safe programming should occur during transit and be led by a staff member other than the driver.

❏ There is growing concern regarding the crash involvement and safety of 15-passenger vans and the resulting injuries and fatalities.

   • On July 15, 2003, the National Transportation Safety Board (NTSB) stated that "…the safe operation of 15-passenger vans requires a knowledge and skill level different and above that for passenger cars, particularly when the vans are fully loaded or drivers experience an emergency situation." The NTSB also recommended that all 50 states and the District of Columbia establish a driver's license endorsement for 15-passenger vans that requires drivers to complete a training program on the operation of these vehicles and pass a written and skills test.

- On August 10, 2005, the **Safe, Accountable, Flexible, Efficient Transportation Equity Act: A Legacy for Users** (SAFETEA-LU) was signed in to law. The bill is a funding bill for federal-aid highways, highway safety programs, and transit programs. Encompassed within the bill are a number of sections related to transportation of school children by schools. In addition, a section is included regarding 15-passenger van safety. While the bill specifically refers to 15-passenger van use and schools, the youth service industry needs to be informed of the issues related to schools, as they might indicate future changes for the use of 15-passenger vans for any industry.

❑ According to a consumer alert, nearly three-quarters of all 15-passenger vans have improperly inflated tires, leading to an increased chance of a rollover crash. The National Highway Traffic Safety Administration website has information on the effects of tire pressure and van loading, and the results of a survey of state laws on 12- and 15-passenger vans used for school transportation (www.nhtsa.gov).

PROGRAM WORKSHEET P-31

Health Services and Supervision

Rationale

Determining the scope of health services needed, developing procedures that are reviewed by a licensed physician, and designating a health supervisor will help provide consistent health services on a program site (refer to Worksheet P-32: Health Screening and Records, Worksheet P-2: Emergency Phone Numbers, and Worksheet P-16: First Aid/CPR).

Plan

1.	What are the policies specifying the scope and limits of healthcare services provided?	
2.	Have the parents been notified about the scope and philosophy of healthcare before enrollment?	
3.	What is the system for evaluating the program's ability to meet the special medical needs of participants before enrollment?	
4.	Does the program site include access to an automated external defibrillator (AED), if needed?	
5.	Who is the person in charge of health services on site?	What are the qualifications of each person?
	Health supervisor	
	Backup supervisor	
	What is the person's authority and responsibly?	
6.	Health screening procedures (refer to Worksheet 32: Health Screening and Records)	
7.	What are the procedures for health services on site?	
	Management of the healthcare center	
	Provision of equipment and supplies	
	Provisions for isolation, quiet, and privacy	
	Securing medications	(refer to Worksheet P-33: Personal Medications)
	Protection from elements	
	Available water and toilet(s)	
	Continuous supervision of each person in the healthcare center.	
8.	General sanitation at program site	
	Food service area	
	Staff training	
9.	Who is the physician secured to be on call and to provide medical advice?	
	Name:	Phone #:

Has the physician provided standing orders or treatment procedures?	Date:
What was included in the physician's review of the health-services plan?	Date of last review:

Guidelines and Information to Help Complete the Plan

❑ The scope and limits of healthcare should be specified and the organization should define what services and personnel are and are not provided. For example, some programs or sites may provide more extensive services when participants are without their parents, have special needs, are staying for a longer period of time, or when access to medical care is not readily accessible. Refer to Worksheet P-27: Serving Persons With Disabilities to help determine accessibility.

❑ The health supervisor should be a physician, registered nurse, nurse practitioner, emergency medical technician (EMT), or paramedic who is licensed in the state in which the program operates. A person who has been certified by American Red Cross for Standard First Aid, Emergency Response, or Medic First Aid and CPR is also qualified.

❑ The site should evaluate the need for an automated external defibrillator (AED) and where it should be located. The evaluation includes the advice of medical and legal authorities, the age of participants and staff members, the nature of the activities, the location of the site in relation to medical services, storing the AED, training in the use of the AED, and any state or local regulations. Use of AEDs has become more common on program sites in the past few years.

❑ The health-services plan should be reviewed at least once every three years. It should include the following:

- Seasonal and long-term recordkeeping
- Screening
- General guidelines for routine care such as dispensing of medications
- Monitoring sanitation on the program site
- First aid
- Preparing and restocking first-aid kits
- Implementing standing orders or treatment procedures if a physician is not on site
- Obtaining emergency healthcare assistance
- Managing the infirmary or first-aid area

- Medication management (securing and handling medications)
- Training the staff on health and first-aid procedures

❑ It is helpful to secure one physician to be on call, provide treatment procedures and medical advice, and review medical and emergency procedures.

❑ Contracts with user groups should clearly state who is responsible for health supervision on the program site.

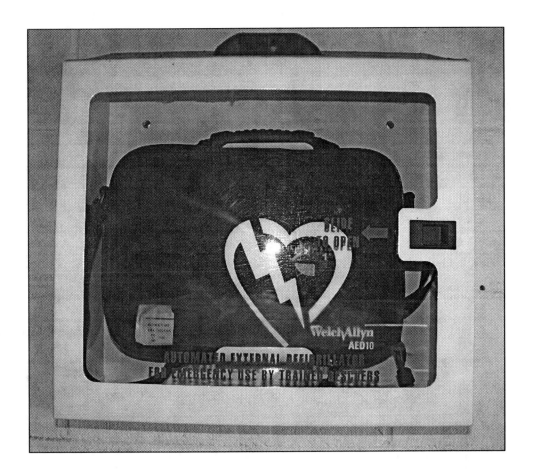

PROGRAM WORKSHEET P-32

Health Screening and Records

Rationale

It is important to have a system to check the health concerns of each participant upon arrival or before participants have been in any extensive contact with each other. Programs such as a resident camp may also require a review of health histories and a screening of participants and staff members. The confidentiality of certain medical conditions of both participants and staff members is an important right. Knowing who needs what information to ensure the health and safety of the participant is essential.

Plan

1. How extensive of a health screening is needed for this program?		If none is required, what is the rationale?	
2. Health screening is required for participants:		For staff members?	
Where?			
When?			
By whom?			
3. What is the name of the physician who has approved the health-screening procedures?			
4. Who is approved to do the health screening?			
5. What are the approved health-screening procedures?			
6. Health screening includes:			

Review of health history prior to arrival		Restrictions or concerns		Allergies and diet restrictions	
Check of health history or, for signature of either participant if minor, a parent or guardian		Current medication collected and treatment reviewed		Immunizations and tetanus	
Changes in health status, medications, or history since the form was completed		Written documentation of the results of the screening		Exposure to communicable diseases	

7. Observation of evidence of injury, disability, illness, or communicable disease by checking:

Temperature		Throat		Hair	
Eyes		Teeth		Hands	
Nose		Skin		Other:	
Ears		Feet			

8. Evidence of illness and/or communicable disease is referred to:

Who?	When?	Action Required

9. Evidence of possible child abuse is referred to:

Who?	When?	Action Required

10. Who is mandated by law to report possible child abuse?

11. Other concerns noted during the screening are referred to:

Who?	When?	Action Required

12. Does this program require participants to have a heath exam within the past 24 months?
    Yes   No   If yes, is the exam signed, dated, and include:

Information on any physical restrictions
Information on any current or ongoing treatment or medications

13. Where are participants' health examinations and/or health-history forms kept?

14. Where are staff members' health forms kept?

15. In the event of emergency treatment:

In addition to the health form, what other form(s) has a parent/guardian signed with permission to treat?	Who has the authority to approve such treatment?

16. Health form:

What information is shared?	
With whom?	
When?	
How?	

17. Who has access to:

The participant medical log, a running record of on-site medical treatment, or notes?
The insurance forms?
The staff medical log?

18. Health histories are current or updated prior to participation, signed, and include:

Name, address, and phone number	Description of current physical- or mental-health conditions
Age	Immunizations
Past medical treatment	Last tetanus
Name, address, and business phone numbers of adult(s) responsible for minor	Record of allergies or dietary restrictions
Name, address, and phone number of the child's physician or healthcare facility	Medications treatment required

Emergency contact number while the child is in program		Other restrictions or considerations while in the program
19. Who has the authority to contact parents or physicians for clarification of health history and/or physical examination in case of emergency?		
Name:	Title:	
20. How long are health records, histories, logs, and screening notes required to be kept in the state where the program is operating?		
Where are they kept?		

Guidelines and Information to Help Complete the Plan

❏ The nature of the program should be considered when planning the screening or review of the health histories of participants and staff members. Sports programs may require medical exams assuring fitness for participation, while drop-in centers may only have a system for observing children for obvious signs of illness, injuries, and communicable diseases as they enter. Some programs may require a written health history identifying allergies, past medical treatments, immunizations, medications, and any activities from which individuals should be exempted for health reasons.

❏ The person doing a health screening should be following the directions of a physician and be skilled in the identification of health concerns. Screening should happen prior to, or upon, arrival at the program site.

❏ Health forms should be kept in the health center. In programs with no health center, medical forms should be easily accessible to persons administering aid and should be maintained in workable systems familiar to all people needing access. The "privacy rule" (Standards for Privacy of Individually Identifiable Health Information) came about because of the Health Insurance Portability and Accountability Act of 1996 (HIPAA). An excellent resource on how this legislation affects camps can be found on the American Camp Association website (www.acacamps.org).

❏ The American Academy of Pediatrics (AAP) does not recommend universal testing/screening for HIV, even for healthcare workers. Their rationale is that most children (with the exception of those in foster care) are not at high risk for HIV. Additionally, the law requires the use of universal precautions at all times. It is the responsibility of the program to train staff and provide appropriate protective equipment to implement this mandate. For more facts on HIV transmission, refer to the Centers for Disease Control and Prevention website (www.cdc.gov).

❏ A bound medical log or other recordkeeping system should be maintained, including the screening and any medical attention or medications given while a participant was on site. Persons giving treatment should initial each entry. According to OSHA, the staff health log should be separate from the participant log. Appendix 32 includes a risk analysis health summary form used for logging a running total of health incidents by type, age, and seriousness.

❏ A plan for action is needed in case a possible communicable condition is spotted during screening or during program activities. Communicable conditions include chicken pox, measles, lice, impetigo, and meningitis. If evacuation of the site is necessary, refer to Worksheet P-12: Site Evacuation.

❏ The designated health supervisor should read each health history and note pertinent information that should be shared with administrative staff and any staff members who deal directly with participants. Consideration should be given to other staff members who may need to be made aware of certain conditions, such as diabetes, allergies, epileptic or other seizures, hemophilia, asthma, heart trouble, and physical or mental handicaps that may need special accommodations for participation.

❏ Procedures should include who should be notified and how and when they will receive notification of any special needs of participants in their care. Procedures should also include making health information about participants available to staff on all off-site activities.

❏ Medical records should be kept at least for the period of statutory limits in the particular state. If records for the year are kept until the youngest participant is past the statutory limit, then the entire years' records can be destroyed at the same time and can be marked accordingly. The statutory limits in many states are three years beyond the age of majority, but some states require records to be kept for a longer period of time. Records of exposures to bloodborne pathogens are required to be kept from the time of employment plus 30 years.

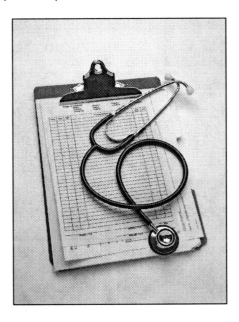

PROGRAM WORKSHEET P-33

Personal Medications

Rationale

In most situations, medications are collected for the safety of all participants. Circumstances may arise in which participants and/or staff members will need immediate access to emergency medication. Such situations include existing medical conditions such as allergic reactions to bee stings, heart conditions, etc. Situations in which the participants may take the responsibility of handling their own medications may also occur.

Plan

1. All medications are collected from:		
	When?	By whom?
Participants		
Staff members		

2. It is appropriate to allow participants/staff members to manage and control any use of their own prescriptive medication in the following circumstances:

When?	Rationale

3. Location where medications are kept:

4. If medications are not kept locked, explain the reason why.

5. What procedures have been made for safe storage of medications requiring refrigeration?

6. What is the policy for dispensing nonprescriptive medications?

7. List persons who have a key or the combination to the lock	Sample: Joe						
Who is responsible for checking that each medication is in its original container, that the dosage is indicated, and that the medication is prescribed for the person receiving it?							
Who has the authority to contact parents or physicians for clarification of medications, special conditions, or restrictions related to medications?							

Who can dispense daily medications?								
Who can dispense emergency medications?								

8. On organization-owned sites being used by short-term groups or rented to user groups, what provisions have been made for the following:

First aid and emergency care
Storage of supplies
Medication
Training or providing information to the group

Guidelines and Information to Help Complete the Plan

❑ The organization should establish procedures to assure that children who have medications receive them as prescribed and that the medication is not given to other participants. In camps and residential programs, medications (prescription and nonprescription) should be collected upon arrival and redistributed when the participants depart. On departure, medication should be given to the parent or guardian if the participant is a minor.

❑ Occasionally, participants and/or staff members will bring medication prescribed for other family members. The staff person in charge should reject any prescription medication not in a container showing it was prescribed to the participant. Nonprescription medications should only be dispensed according to the program's treatment procedures, or with the written and signed instructions of a parent or guardian or the participant's physician.

❑ A backup system should be established for accessing and dispensing emergency medications. If medications are left in the hands of the participant, a signed agreement that states that the participant will take responsibility for the medication should be on file.

❑ If at all possible, medications should be locked in a permanent cupboard—not placed in a case or box that can be carried away. If no permanent facility exists and it is not too hot, medications could be locked in a car that will remain on the site. Some medications require refrigeration (e.g., insulin).

❑ Contracts with groups or renters using organization-owned property should include written procedures detailing the responsibility for healthcare, care of first-aid supplies and medications, transportation, procedures for emergency care, and any reporting requirements.

PROGRAM WORKSHEET P-34

Insurance Safety Audit for Organization-Owned Sites

Rationale

Insurance companies will usually do a safety audit of an organization-owned site every two to five years, but an annual audit may be requested. This preventive program can alert the staff and/or board to potential dangers. The safety-conscious, non-camping-, and non-program-related auditor brings a different perspective to the site.

Plan

1. Insurance safety audit conducted by (company):			
Person who conducted audit:		Date of last audit:	
How often is the audit conducted?			
Next audit scheduled:			
2. Recommendations Made	Actions Taken or Insurance Policy Changes Made	Date Completed	Rationale for Noncompliance

Guidelines and Information to Help Complete the Plan

❑ Be sure to respond to the safety audit report with specific actions taken, timelines, or a rationale for noncompliance. Contact the organization's insurance agent to review previous reports and to schedule the next safety audit.

PROGRAM WORKSHEET P-35

Federal, State, and Local Laws, Ordinances, Codes, and Regulations

Rationale

All states have various laws and ordinances with which every organization, agency, or program must comply. Some states have identified specific programs that require a license or certified personnel to operate. By ensuring that these laws are followed, the organization is making a commitment to the safety of its members. These regulations also serve as a guide to protect both the children and the organization.

Plan

List the regulatory agencies that have laws, ordinances, codes, regulations, etc., that apply to this program.	List federal, state, and local laws, ordinances, codes, and/or regulations found at these agencies.	A copy can be obtained at:	Place where the copy is filed:

Guidelines and Information to Help Complete the Plan

❑ The following are suggested resources:

- Local government
  - √ Health department
  - √ Building department
  - √ Fire department
  - √ Law enforcement
- State government
- Health department
- Transportation department
- Social Services department
- Attorney
- American Camp Association section or national office
- Organization's national office

- Other local agencies working with youth
- Organization's local office

❑ The following are some of the areas of law and regulations that might apply to the operation:

- Building codes
- Food service
- Fire safety
- Child abuse/neglect
- Program activities (e.g., waterfront, horseback riding, shooting sports)
- Health regulations
- Security
- Environmental protection
- Employment regulations
- Accessibility
- Staff qualifications
- Staff training
- Fundraising

❑ The Nonprofit Risk Management Center has a resource on State Liability Laws for Charitable Organizations and Volunteers available for free download free from their website (www.nonprofitrisk.org).

PROGRAM WORKSHEET P-36

Interstate and International Laws

Rationale

An organization needs to be aware of local, state, and/or international laws when operating a program that is across a state or national border from the organization's legal address. Laws may vary from state to state and country to country. Staff members or participants from other states or countries may need to have special permission or papers to participate in the program.

Plan

1. Does all or any part of this program occur in a state or country different than the location of the organization's main office?
2. Laws, ordinances, codes, and regulations that pertain to these programs can be obtained from:
3. List programs that involve staff members or participants from other states or countries.
4. List the laws and regulations that pertain to international visitors.

Guidelines and Information to Help Complete the Plan

❏ The following areas must be considered:

- Parental permission may be needed to take minors across state borders
- Legal age of majority in state
- Whether medical personnel applying from other states or countries are licensed to practice in the state where the program is being offered
- Insurance coverage for serious injury or illness that might require medical service to continue after a program is over
- Transportation costs and/or supervision of staff members or participants from other countries or states if required to return home at other than arranged times
- Applicability of insurance or additional insurance that may be needed
- Security of legal documents while international staff or participants are in the program

PROGRAM WORKSHEET P-37

Waivers, Permissions, and Agreements for Participation

Rationale

Requiring the participant and his parent or guardian to sign forms prior to participation in an activity helps make the participant and/or parent aware of, and assume, some of the responsibility inherent in the activity. Such forms do not transfer responsibility for defective equipment or construction, poor instruction or supervision, or dangerous conditions from the organization to the participant. In drop-in activity centers where children come and go, the responsibility for health and safety, except in emergencies, is the responsibility of the parents.

Plan

1. What inherent risks are parents/legal guardians or participants assuming in a signed agreement?	
2. What permissions have or have not provided for in the agreement?	
3. What has the organization agreed to assume responsibility for?	
4. What else has the participant and/or his parents agreed to assume responsibility for?	
5. Where are agreement forms kept?	For how long?
Who has access to the forms?	

Guidelines and Information to Help Complete the Plan

❑ Exculpatory clauses are waivers and releases that are contracts that endeavor to limit or extinguish liability for injury. Organizations cannot contract away their duty to exercise ordinary care. As contracts, they must meet the criteria for a contract, which includes being of majority age. A parent cannot contract away the rights of a minor, since a minor can disallow such a contract upon reaching the age of majority. Waivers, however, are valid when properly written for persons of majority age. Parents can also waive their own rights. A waiver is often suggested for minors in the belief that it will deter people from proceeding with damage claims. The validity of these clauses varies from state to state and they are often interpreted very narrowly by the courts to exempt defendants from liability for ordinary negligence only; where gross negligence is alleged, the exculpatory clause will not exempt the defendant from liability.

❑ Permissions may involve photo releases, use of material written by participants, permission for routine healthcare, administration of medications and the seeking of emergency medical treatment, permission to release campers to persons other than legal parent or guardian, etc. If parents refuse to sign a permission to treat form for religious or other reasons, they should submit a signed form specifying the action to be taken and a release from liability if the child requires emergency treatment and the parents cannot be reached.

❑ It is recommended that an agreement to participate be used. It will show that the employee, the family, and/or the participant received notice of the risks involved. It is important to thoroughly explain the activity, supervision procedures, and expectations of participants, and detail exactly for what the agency will and will not be responsible. When a participant agrees to assume some responsibility for risk, he must "understand and appreciate" the risk and the reason for his actions or nonactions. In other words, a child and the parents must not only know the rules, but also why they exist or what happens if the participant breaks the rules. It also should include participant responsibilities, such as being responsible for conduct, agreeing to obey rules, taking responsibility for belongings, not willfully harming another person or person's property, etc.

❑ Agreements to participate should be signed by both the participant and his parents or legal guardian. The agreement should include such items as who is going to be responsible for any unusual or additional transportation, medical expenses, damages that may occur, etc.

❑ A sample of a participant agreement is found in Appendix 7. The organization may want to seek legal advice in creating such forms. Permission to participate should be signed by parents or legal guardians if the participant is a minor. Agreement forms may be included as a part of a registration form.

❑ Policies such as refund policies may or may not be included in the agreement. Printing something in a flyer and then noting in the agreement that the participant has read the flyer may be just as effective.

PROGRAM WORKSHEET P-38

Program Record Retention and Destruction

Rationale

A good recordkeeping system may help protect the organization if a legal problem occurs, as well as provide information to analyze incidents and create a sense of accountability for actions taken. Refer to Worksheet O-21: Record Retention and Destruction for information about policies and other records.

Plan

1.	The statute of limitations in the state is:	
2.	Records that should be dated with the year and kept until the youngest participant is 18 or 21 (circle one), plus the statute of limitations:	
	Type of Records	Where and How Stored
	Participant registration, including permission to participate and to give emergency medical care and photo releases	
	Health histories and physical exams	
	Medical logs	
	Incident reports and related medical records	
	Staff list with positions	
	Staff training records and content	
	Staff applications, qualifications, certifications, criminal-record checks, interview notes, and references (or policies showing staffing procedures)	
	Brochure and marketing tools	
	Parent information letters	
3.	Yearly program-administration records that should be kept permanently:	
	Type of Record	Where and How Stored
	Accreditation records	
	Incident reports of child abuse (at home or in the program—especially if criminal charges were made)	
	Organizational standards or policies	
	Insurance records	
	Risk-management plan	
4.	How is the security of personal information protected in storage and in the destruction process?	
	Storage	
	Destruction	

Guidelines and Information to Help Complete the Plan

❏ Any record can be subpoenaed, so the decision about what records to keep or destroy is important. Decisions should be consistent from year to year, but evaluated carefully. Statutes of limitations vary from state to state. Even if a parent has not sued, the child, upon reaching 21, usually has two years or until the statute of limitations runs out to sue on his own behalf.

❏ Some records should be considered for permanent retention or until superseded by a newer version (refer to Appendix 10).

❏ Many accounting and fiscal records should be kept for three to five years and be disposed of at the discretion of the administrator. Employment and payroll records must be kept according to the requirements of the Fair Labor Standards Act (FLSA), usually for two or three years. Refer to Worksheet O-21: Record Retention and Destruction for information on other administrative records.

❏ Records that may be related to an accusation of child abuse may have no statute of limitations. The burden of proof lies with the person making the charges, but keeping these records may show that the program administrators were providing an expected level of care.

❏ When determining how and where records will be stored and methods for destruction, it is important to consider:

- Whether they will be kept as a paper copy or in some form of technology, such as microfilm or computer CD/DVD. Remember that the organization may not need them for years and technology changes at a rapid rate (e.g., computers do not even come with slots for floppy disks anymore.) Storage in fire- and flood-proof places should also be considered.

- The security and destruction of personal information, including who has access to stored records and how records are destroyed to protect staff and participant privacy.

❏ The Fair and Accurate Credit Transactions Act (FACTA) is a federal law designed to minimize the risk of identity theft and consumer fraud by enforcing the proper destruction of consumer information. The Federal Trade Commission of the United States (FTC) developed the Disposal Rule to further implement the policies set forth in FACTA. The Disposal Rule applies to businesses that utilize consumer information; however, it affects every person and business in the United States.

The FACTA Disposal Rule states that "any person who maintains or otherwise possesses consumer information for a business purpose" is required to dispose of discarded consumer information, whether in electronic or paper form. The Disposal Rule further clarifies the definition of compliance as "taking reasonable measures to protect against unauthorized access to or use of the information in connection with its disposal." These "reasonable measures" include:

- Burning, pulverizing, or shredding of physical documents
- Erasure or destruction of all electronic media
- Entering into a contract with a third party engaged in the business of information destruction

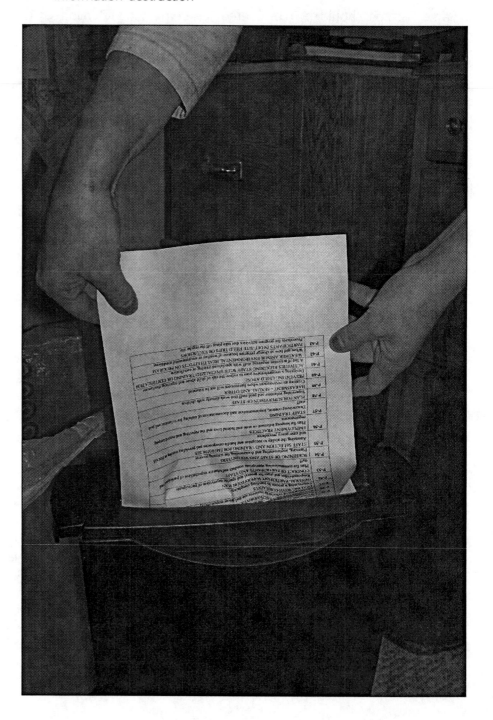

PROGRAM WORKSHEET P-39

Intellectual Property Infringements, Copyrights, and Royalties

Rationale

It is important to copyright or protect the materials that have been developed with agency resources for exclusive use of the organization and its authorized programs. Copyrighted materials are protected, though a significant degree of similarity must exist to establish infringement. Copyrights and royalties covered in the program section have to do with permissions and violations. Information on registered copyrights is included in Worksheet O-34: Intellectual Property, Copyrights and Royalties.

Plan

1. Who is responsible for obtaining permission from the national organization to use names, service marks, and insignias on locally developed merchandise for this program?
2. Who is responsible for obtaining permission to reproduce any copyrighted material or other intellectual property that is not explicitly identified for this program?
3. What is the procedure to request the use of materials that are copyrighted by another person or organization?
Where are records of permission to use copyrighted materials kept?
Who is responsible for these records?
4. Procedures for the use of original works of music, art, or film requiring royalties to be paid, or permission secured to waive these royalty fees, include:
5. Who is responsible for screening photos used in marketing materials for appropriateness and for intellectual property infringements on T-shirts, tattoos, or in other parts of a photograph?

Guidelines and Information to Help Complete the Plan

❑ Copyright is a form of protection provided by the laws of the United States (Title 17, U.S. Code) to the authors of "original works of authorship," including literary, dramatic, musical, artistic, and certain other intellectual works. A person or organization cannot copyright an idea, procedure, system, concept, principle, etc. A trademark is a distinctive mark, symbol, word, or words used to distinguish the goods of a specific manufacturer and thus differentiate them from similar goods.

❑ The name, service mark, insignias, trademarks, and copyrighted materials are used and protected as specified by the organization owning the copyright. Any program of the organization should guard against the unauthorized use of the name, insignias, official uniforms, and programs. Failure to protect the ownership of a copyright could lead to loss of the copyright, because the law may consider those materials to be in the public domain. Refer to Worksheet O-34: Intellectual Property, Copyrights, and Royalties for more information.

❑ The owner of a copyright is entitled to seek an injunction restraining infringement, damages, and profits, impounding of the infringing article, and the destruction of infringing copies and plates. The copyright law also provides for the recovery of full costs and attorney fees by successful parties.

❑ A royalty is a set amount that is paid to the owner for either exclusive or nonexclusive rights after authorizing the manufacture, use, or sale of the product. Royalties are often paid for the use of songs, films, names, logos, etc.

❑ Performing or presenting music, art, or films in situations where fees, registrations, or admissions are collected may be subject to royalty payments. For example, performance or recorded use of copyrighted music—even with original lyrics—is subject to royalty payments. This rule includes adding music to the background of a slide show or videotape. Movies rented for home use cannot be shown in situations where a registration fee has been collected. Companies exist that rent movies for showing to groups that include the payment of royalties as a part of the rental fee.

PROGRAM WORKSHEET P-40

Contracts for Services

Rationale

A contract is an agreement between two parties and includes an offer and an acceptance. Contracts are also a method of transferring a risk to another party. It is important that the party assuming the risk can handle the risk or any financial ramifications of a breach of contract.

Plan

1. What contracts for services are needed?	Amount of liability being:	
	Assumed	Transferred

2. Who has the authority to negotiate contracts?	
Type of Contract	Who Can Negotiate
Employment contracts	
Food service	
Maintenance	
Health services	
Horseback riding	
Swimming/boating	
Adventure/challenge activities	
Contracts for products	
Other(s)	

3. Who is responsible for reviewing/drafting contracts to include specific requirements for meeting any standards of the field?
What standards are appropriate for comparison?
4. Certificates of insurance are required for contracts for:
Certificate of insurance are reviewed by:
5. Dates of coverage and the limits of liability should be at least:
6. Do contracts include the following as appropriate?
Terms, dates, and times:
Costs, conditions for use, and minimum fees:
Services provided:

Cancellation and refund policies:
Damage or loss fees:
A force majeure provision:
7. Do agreements specify responsibility for the following?
First aid and emergency care and transportation:
Supervision and behavior of the group:
Supervision of recreational activities:
Providing safety orientation to participants:
Insurance coverage:

Guidelines and Information to Help Complete the Plan

❑ Contracts are a method of protection against loss by transferring the financial risk to another party or transferring or assuming certain liabilities to the organization. It is important to know the amount of liability being assumed under the contract.

❑ Waivers, releases, and exculpatory clauses are covered in Worksheet 37: Waivers, Permissions, and Agreements for Participation.

❑ Contracts may include indemnification clauses or "hold-harmless" clauses that transfer the financial consequences of a loss, or the responsibility for damages, to another party. These clauses are most often included in insurance contracts and are agreements between businesses, not individuals.

❑ Some contracts, such as rental agreements for property or facilities for special events, may need to include a force majeure provision to address the conditions under which a party may terminate an agreement without liability in case of major unforeseen events. Force majeure events typically include war, terrorism, or major disasters, or when the event is affected by a cause beyond the control of the parties making it inadvisable, illegal, or commercially impractical to hold a successful event or provide the facility.

❑ Contracts for program services should include such things as who is responsible for providing and maintaining equipment, safety rules, participation requirements, emergency care, and/or other items included as the standard of care for the activity. Refer to Worksheet P-31: Health Services and Supervision for information on healthcare that should be included in a user group contract.

❑ The terms of the contracts should be specified in writing and reviewed by both parties to ensure that all aspects and considerations of the agreement are clearly understood. Be sure the indemnification clause includes not only compensatory damages, but also both punitive damages and defense costs.

❑ Contracts for products include purchase order agreements with vendors, whether written or verbal. If the organization is transferring the risk to another party, it is important be sure that the other party has adequate insurance to handle the risk. Ask for and review a "certificate of insurance" to see if the limits are sufficient. When appropriate, the organization should be named as an additional insured.

❑ It is important to understand the difference between an independent contractor and an employee. Refer to the U.S. Department of Labor website (www.dol.gov) for guidelines on the classification and use of independent contractors. Employment contracts should only be used for those services that meet the Fair Labor Standards Act criteria for an independent contractor. Most seasonal, part-time, and full-time staff members receive a letter of agreement, not a contract.

PROGRAM WORKSHEET P-41

Operational Financial Risks

Rationale

To effectively manage and safeguard the organization's financial resources, it is important to assess and reduce the risk of financial loss by identifying the financial controls needed and determining if the controls merit the expense involved in implementing them. These risks pertain to this program and should be consistent with Worksheet O-22: Operational Financial Risks.

Plan

1.	Who is responsible for oversight of the financial operations of this program?
2.	Petty Cash
	What is the policy regarding the amount of petty cash kept on hand?
	What is the maximum amount an individual may request?
	Who is responsible for maintaining petty cash?
	Who is responsible for reconciling petty cash?
	Who has access to petty cash?
	How is it secured?
	What is required for reimbursement from petty cash?
	Who authorizes payments?
	How is petty cash replenished?
3.	Cash Receipts
	How are checks received by mail handled?
	How often are deposits made?
	By whom?
	How are checks and cash given to individuals (staff, volunteers, etc.) handled?
	Who has access to checks and cash?
	How are they secured at the office?
	How are they secured outside of the office?
	What is the policy regarding acceptance of checks made out to others?
4.	Cash Disbursements
	What is the policy for cash disbursements?
	How are unused checks secured?

	If a facsimile signature is used, how is the stamp or plate secured?
	How are payments authorized?
	What is the refund policy?
	Who has the authority to purchase or commit agency funds?
	Who may enter in a contract on the organization's behalf?
	When are purchase orders issued?
	When is bidding required?
5.	Travel Reimbursement Policy
	When are travel expenses reimbursable?
	What is the mileage rate?
	What is the meal allowance per day?
	What is the policy on hotel allowances and airfare?
6.	Inventory Management and Control Responsibilities and Procedures
	Who is responsible for securing the overall list of inventories and securing a copy off-site?
	Who is responsible for inventory in the program office?
	When and how is inventory taken?
	Who has access?
	How is it secured?
	Who is responsible for inventory in the program areas?
	When and how is inventory taken?
	Who has access?
	How is it secured?
	Who is responsible for inventory in the food service area?
	When and how is inventory taken?
	Who has access?
	How is it secured?
	Who is responsible for inventory in the merchandise for sale?
	When and how is inventory taken?
	Who has access?
	How is it secured?
	Who is responsible for inventory in the maintenance areas?
	When and how is inventory taken?
	Who has access?
	How is it secured?
7.	Tax Liability
	Is sales tax being collected on goods sold?
	Who is responsible for collecting and remitting sales tax?

Guidelines and Information to Help Complete the Plan

❑ Oversight for the program includes preparing and monitoring the annual budget, making cash flow projections, monitoring actual cash flow, etc.

❑ The petty cash policy should include:

- The amount of petty cash available
- The maximum amount any one person may request at one time
- How it is maintained
- Who has access to it
- What kinds of receipts or documentation is required
- Who is authorized to sign for reimbursements

❑ Checks received by mail should be restrictively endorsed as soon as they are received and then deposited in a timely manner. A policy on how cash is to be handled and by whom should include a system of utilizing numbered receipts for any cash received and copies that are reconciled with cash received. Reconciliation and analysis is probably handled by the main office (refer to Worksheet O-22: Operational Financial Risks).

Procedures must be established for securing petty cash, cash receipts, and checks in the office and for handling product sale money or other cash received outside the office (program fees, special events, camp stores, etc.). Procedures should specify who has access to the money.

❑ The policy for cash disbursements should include the use of prenumbered checks, a system to secure and account for unused checks, and the number and names or positions of those who are authorized to sign checks. It should also include the use of purchase orders and receiving documents required for payment and indentify who may authorize payment. Check signers should not sign their own checks. All disbursements should be reviewed by one person to assure that duplicate payments are not being made. Paid invoices should be canceled after payment.

❑ A policy should be in place that includes who has the authority to commit agency funds, make purchases, and enter into contracts on behalf of the organization. Procedures for purchase orders and any limits on authority should also be included.

❑ The travel reimbursement policy should detail what expenses are reimbursable and at what rates. It may also include a maximum rate or provide guidance on selecting hotels and finding the lowest available airfare rates.

❑ Inventory management and control should include procedures for taking a periodic inventory, securing a copy off-site in the main office (for insurance and planning purposes), identifying who is in charge and who has access, and detailing how the inventory is secured. When a program site is used for different programs at different times or seasons, the inventory storage may change. For insurance purposes, it may be helpful to use a video camera to record storage areas and leave the video to accompany the actual inventory list.

❑ It is important to understand the tax liability applicable to the operation. Is tax being collected and remitted on the selling of supplies? The state may allow exemptions on goods purchased, but not on goods sold. The organization should determine responsibility for remitting payroll tax forms, filing 990s, paying into unemployment funds, and making provisions for any contingencies that might encumber the future operation of the organization.

PROGRAM WORKSHEET P-42

Participant Risk-Reduction Analyses

Rationale

A system should be developed to identify, consider, and evaluate risk-reduction steps on at least an annual basis.

Plan

1. What are the categories of accidents, incidents, and/or injuries that are required to be reported?
2. Who is required to complete reports and how soon should they be submitted?
3. Who is to receive reports?
4. When are reports categorized and analyzed, and by whom?
5. Who is responsible for analyzing medical logs and how often are they reviewed?
6. What is the system for notification of any changes that result from the analysis?

Guidelines and Information to Help Complete the Plan

❑ Reports may be categorized to help analyze and study different issues or trends. Categories might be determined in a variety of ways depending on the program or operation. They could include any injury requiring the filing of an insurance or workman's compensation claim form, or include injuries by type, activity, age, staff in charge, size of claim, type of behavior, etc. Persons required to complete an incident/accident report form should be trained in their use.

❑ Persons receiving reports should follow the procedures for notification of appropriate people and responsibility, if any, for addressing media inquiries. Refer to Worksheet P-43: Incident Report, Worksheet P-3: Agency Emergency Contacts, and Worksheet O-9: Emergency Media Plan. The reporting process should also be evaluated as incidents are analyzed.

❑ Incidents should be analyzed on a regular basis (not right after an incident has taken place) to look for trends and any revisions needed in the risk-management plan. Refer to Appendix 32 for a sample risk-analysis health summary form that is used by the health or program supervisor to keep a running total of health and injury incidents. Changes in either the reporting system or in the procedures for handling situations and emergencies should be timely and communicated in writing whenever possible.

❑ A final report, including all office operations and programs, should be compiled and reviewed by the Risk Management Task Force.

PROGRAM WORKSHEET P-43

Incident Report

Rationale

An incident report form will provide consistent information on incidents that occur. Such information may be needed for follow-up or in case of legal action. Refer to Worksheet O-35: Incident Report to establish consistency with organizational and office policies.

Plan

1. The organization's policy regarding incident reports includes:
Who is responsible for completing incident reports?
What incidents are reported on incident reports?
How soon after the incident must the incident report be completed?
Who is given copies of incident reports?
Where are completed incident reports kept?
Who is allowed access to completed incident reports?
2. How are OSHA reports handled?
3. Where are blank incident report forms kept?
4. What statistical data are gathered from incident reports?

Guidelines and Information to Help Complete the Plan

❑ Incident reports should include any major accidents, illnesses, or inappropriate behaviors that occur on-site or during a program event. A sample incident report form is found in Appendix 6. OSHA also requires that serious accidents or the death of an employee be reported to them and that employers display a poster that explains the protection and obligations of employees (www.osha.gov).

❑ A leader, activity director, or counselor may fill in sections of the form that relate to their actions. Other sections may be completed by the on-site health supervisor or the program administrator.

❑ Persons required to complete an incident/accident report form should be trained in their use. Incident reports can be subpoenaed for legal evidence, so information should relate only to the facts, not what should or could have been done, and no statement should place blame on any party. Information and statistical data on incident reports should be regularly analyzed to make an effort to reduce the risk of future incidents.

PROGRAM WORKSHEET P-44

Emergency Drills

Rationale

Repeated emergency drills familiarize participants and staff members with emergency procedures and help to prevent panic.

Plan

		Warning System	Assembly Locations(s) and/or Action Required
1. What kinds of emergency drills are needed?			
	Fire		
	Tornado		
	Flood		
	Evacuation		
	Intruder		
	Earthquake		
	Missing persons		
	Other		
2. How often are emergency drills conducted with participants and staff members?			
3. Who initiates an emergency drill?			
4. Who is responsible for the list of all participants and staff members?			
5. How are staff members and participants given procedures on drills?			
6. How fast can participants and staff members complete the drill?			

Guidelines and Information to Help Complete the Plan

❑ Drill procedures may be posted in strategic places and be distributed to:

- Staff members
- Office workers
- Local law enforcement officials
- Fire officials
- The civil defense office
- School, church, or rented property owners

❑ The type of drills will depend on the type of emergencies possible in the area. Drills may include fire, flood, tornado, intruder, evacuation of the building and/or site, specific activity emergencies, etc.

❑ Drills for emergencies common to the area should be conducted with each new group within 24 hours of arrival on the site. Drills should include an accounting of every person on the site. Some drills, such as intruder and missing persons, may only need to be conducted with staff members.

❑ Fire drills should include the use of stairways instead of elevators as exits from floors above ground level. Drills should also include the use of alternative exits in case primary exits are blocked. Drills should periodically be conducted in cooperation with local authorities. Try to increase efficiency and time on each drill.

PROGRAM WORKSHEET P-45

Participation Information, Registration, Check-In, and Check-Out

Rationale

The program administrator or site manager assumes the responsibility for the health and welfare of the child when a minor participates in a program without being accompanied by a parent or designated guardian. The administrator or a designated program leader is responsible for ensuring that the child is returned to a parent who has legal custody or to the parent's designee.

Plan

1.	Procedures for registration include securing and maintaining the following information on each participant:
	Name
	Age
	Home address, telephone, and cell phone
	Who to contact in case of emergency
	Who is authorized to pick up the participant?
	Relationship Telephone
	Is anyone *not* authorized to pick up the participant? Relationship
2.	Where is this information kept?
3.	Who has access to the information?
4.	What written information is provided to parents regarding pick-up and drop-off times, and what are the safety procedures that parents should know about or pick-up and drop-off points?
5.	Who is responsible for care of participants before pick-up and after drop-off?
6.	What are the procedures regarding assuming responsibility for a participant during check-in?
7.	What are the procedures regarding relinquishing responsibility for a participant during check-out?
8.	What are the procedures for verifying absentees or "no-shows"?
9.	What are the procedures if someone wishes to check a child out early?
10.	When and how are parents notified if someone who is not authorized to do so requests to take a child from the organization's custody?
11.	When is the law-enforcement office called if an unauthorized person requests to take a child from the organization's custody?
	Who makes that call?
12.	What are the procedures for handling situations when a child has not been picked up at the end of a program?
	Who is responsible for implementation?
13.	What are the procedures for notifying parents of changes in pick-up or drop-off times or locations?

Guidelines and Information to Help Complete the Plan

❑ Every participant should have a completed registration or information form on file at the site. The form includes information on the name of the parent or responsible adult and a telephone number where he or she can be reached during the program hours. In addition, an emergency contact must be included. Registration information should also include a place for parents to indicate who will be authorized (or not authorized) to pick up the participant at the program site. A participant in a drop-in center should fill out a card the first time he comes. If feasible, the form should be signed by the adult.

❑ To protect the privacy of the participant, procedures should be established for where this information is stored and who has access to it (refer to Worksheet P-32: Health Screening and Records).

❑ Since many transportation plans are not complete at the time of registration, information on the registration card should be verified at check-in.

❑ During check-out, the person supervising the participants should know who is authorized to pick up each participant and what to do if someone comes who is not authorized.

❑ The child's ability to identify a person picking him up does not indicate authorization. Many children would willingly go with a relative or neighbor who says their mother said to pick them up, or with a divorced parent who does not have custody.

❑ A system to actually sign the child over to the person picking him up is the best assurance that the child has been turned over to the parent or another person authorized by the parent. File the names and relationships of persons who are authorized to pick up a participant. Also note any persons who are not authorized to pick up the participant (e.g., noncustodial parents).

❑ Check-out is also an opportunity to tell the parent how much the participant enjoyed the experience and how well he did, and begin the recruiting process for another year or program. When parents understand the rationale for such procedures, they are likely to cooperate and appreciate the concern and responsibility shown for the children in the organization's care.

❑ Procedures for notification of parents in case of emergency, delays, or weather conditions that may call for a change in travel times or locations should be communicated prior to the program experience.

❑ Additional guidelines for drop-in activity centers are covered in Worksheet P-46: Drop-In Programs.

PROGRAM WORKSHEET P-46

Drop-In Programs

Rationale

Some programs are designed to provide activities on a drop-in basis, such as a drop-in activity center or day camp. These programs are often in neighborhoods where children are left at home alone or where parents do not have the resources to pay for childcare. It is very important that it is clear when the organization is assuming responsibility and supervision of the child.

Plan

1.	Guidelines for ages being served include:
	Procedures for dealing with youth that arrive at the program that do not meet those guidelines are:
2.	Information on each child includes:
	Full name of child
	Name of parent or responsible adult
	Home address
	Telephone number
	Any special information the program leaders should know
	If possible, the signature of a parent
3.	A welcome note is sent home with a request for the above information and includes the following:
	Information about the program
	The sign-in/sign-out procedures
	The staff
	The responsibility for injury/illness
4.	Brochures, flyers, signs, and other recruitment or informational literature includes a brief statement on the:
	Program
	Sign-in/sing-out requirement
	Responsibility for injury/illness
5.	Procedures in case of injury or illness:

Guidelines and Information to Help Complete the Plan

❑ The issue of responsibility is a liability concern. In a drop-in program, children come and go (often several times during the program) and it is sometimes unclear who has the responsibility for their health and safety, especially from the time they leave the program and are in the direct care of their parent or guardian.

❑ Establish clear enrollment guidelines about the ages being served and have a plan for dealing with children who arrive but are not eligible to attend. Often youth that enroll in drop-in programs are not only home alone, but also have responsibilities for younger siblings. Some older youth may be good aides and role models for younger children.

❑ Each child attending should fill out an information card the first time he attends. The card should contain the name of the parent or responsible adult, a telephone number where he can be reached during the program hours, and, if possible, the signature of the parent or responsible adult.

❑ When a child fills out an information card, a welcome note should be sent home for the parent or responsible adult. The note should include some information about the program, explain the expectations that children sign in and out, and include a statement that the organization cannot be responsible for injury and will not treat injury or illness.

❑ In the event of injury or illness, the parent or responsible adult should be called and should be expected to deal with the problem. Helping a child clean a scrape or providing him with a bandage is acceptable, but staff members should not transport a child to seek treatment or emergency care. If immediate care is needed and the parent or responsible adult cannot be located, the community's emergency services system should be used (usually 911). Any injury or illness should be documented and an incident report should be completed.

PROGRAM WORKSHEET P-47

Guests On-Site

Rationale

To avoid confusion and provide for the safety of visitors, participants, and staff members, procedures for handling guests should be established and clearly understood by all parties.

Plan

1. What procedures are guests on the site required to follow?	How are they informed of these procedures?
For general visitation	
In case of emergency	
2. Are visitors permitted to use equipment or program facilities?	
If yes, under what conditions?	

Guidelines and Information to Help Complete the Plan

❑ The director needs to determine if and when visitors are appropriate on the site. Visitors may include people such as health inspectors, contracted plumbers, telephone repairpersons, parents, friends of staff, etc. Parents should always be allowed to visit the program.

❑ The director needs to determine—in advance—a system for knowing when visitors are on the site, who is responsible for the safety of visitors, and what action to take if an emergency occurs. Some program sites require that visitors wear nametags with their name and "guest" or "visitor" on them.

❑ A policy should be adopted and made clear to visitors that states if, when, and under what conditions visitors should be permitted to use program equipment and/or facilities.

PROGRAM WORKSHEET P-48

Parent Notification of Changes

Rationale

When parents entrust an organization with their children, they not only expect the child to be in a safe environment, but they also expect to be notified if a problem, injury, or a change in the communicated plans takes place.

Plan

Parents are notified the following takes place:	By whom?
A change in the program location	
A change in the pick-up or drop-off time	
An emergency related to the inappropriate conduct of other participants (such as):	
An emergency related to a natural or man-made disaster	
An emergency related to the inappropriate conduct of staff or volunteers (such as:	
An emergency related to an injury or illness (such as:	
Other:	

Guidelines and Information to Help Complete the Plan

❑ Permission slips should be worded to cover most situations and/or activities that will occur during the program. Parents should be notified if changes are made to these plans, or to the pick-up or drop-off time or location.

❑ Participants' emergency phone numbers should be on file to assist in the notification of parents in case of emergency. If it is a widespread natural or man-made disaster, notification may be difficult or delayed. A call-in phone number for parents to use or an email address may help if a widespread disaster occurs.

PROGRAM WORKSHEET P-49

Weapons and Firearms

Rationale

Shooting-sports equipment used in program activities and personal weapons brought on the site by staff must be made known to the administrator and locked up where they are not assessable to participants and other staff members. Policies and clear consequences about participants and staff members bringing weapons onto the program site should be made known and enforced.

Plan

1. Type and amount of shooting-sports equipment on the site:		
Type:	Amount:	Where and how are they stored and locked?
Is ammunition stored separately?		
Who has access to the key?		
What is the procedure for security?		
2. What is the policy regarding shooting-sports equipment or weapons owned by staff and stored in:		
Private residences?		
Trucks or cars?		
3. What is the policy regarding sharp-edged implements, such as knives, used for the program?		
Who has access?		
4. What is the policy regarding shooting-sports equipment, sharp-edged implements, and weapons brought onto the program site by participants and staff members?		
What is the procedure for search and seizure?		

Guidelines and Information to Help Complete the Plan

❑ Shooting-sports equipment include the following:

- Archery equipment
- BB guns
- Air guns (pellet guns)
- Firearms (cartridge guns of all types)
- Muzzle loaders (black powder guns of all types

❏ Sharp-edged implements include the following:

- Knives

- Hatchets or axes

- Any other sharp-edged implement

❏ Shooting-sports activities, including archery and riflery, require specialized knowledge and/or skills and therefore require a plan regarding the qualifications of the leader, operating procedures, controlled access, specialized care of equipment, and safety signals and commands (refer to Worksheet P-61: Activities Requiring Staff Members With Specialized Training or Certification). Shooting-sports equipment must be kept under lock, stored separate from ammunition, and have controlled access.

❏ Private residences of staff members living on the program site should not be accessible to participants or other staff members. Vehicles with gun racks or staff cars with firearms or weapons should be locked at all times.

❏ Staff members and participants should sign a statement as a part of their registration forms acknowledging and agreeing to abide by the program rules or policies, including those regarding firearms and other weapons on the site. Samples of discipline and dismissal policies are included in Appendix 16.

PROGRAM WORKSHEET P-50

Business Use of Vehicles and Driver Authorization and Responsibility

Rationale

Organization-owned, leased, and privately owned vehicles used for business purposes must meet the applicable requirements and be driven by someone with a current driver's license and good driving record. This plan should be consistent with the policy outlined in Worksheet O-22: Operational Financial Risks.

Plan

1. What vehicles are owned or rented/leased for this program?			
Vehicle	License #	Okay for personal use?	
		Yes	No

2. What is the state law regarding driver's license classifications?

3. Authorized drivers of organization-owned, -rented, or -leased vehicles:							
Driver	Driver's License #	Type	Drivers have had training in:				
			Backing up and refueling	Loading and unloading passengers	Breakdowns, illness, and/or accident procedures	Safe operation of specific vehicle	Vehicle safety check

4. Who is responsible for maintenance of organization-owned, -rented, or -leased vehicles?
5. Are business-use drivers required to complete a driver-information form?
Who is responsible for obtaining the forms?
Where are they kept?
6. Where are copies of authorization and proof of insurance kept?
7. What assurance exists that vehicles are in safe operating condition?
8. Use of privately owned vehicles requires authorization and proof of insurance coverage for:

Liability	Minimum coverage limit?
Bodily injury	Minimum coverage limit?
Property damage	Minimum coverage limit?

Guidelines and Information to Help Complete the Plan

❑ The plan should specify who will use organization-owned, -rented, or -leased vehicles, how they may be used, and who will be responsible for maintenance. Be sure that insurance coverage has been obtained for all uses and drivers. Drivers should understand that any traffic violation citation received is the responsibility of the driver.

❑ Drivers should have procedures for quarterly inspection of vehicles or inspection within the three months prior to use. Vehicles should not be used if repairs affecting the safe operation of the vehicle have not been made. Refer to the vehicle inspection information included in Appendix 11.

❑ It is helpful to require a vehicle safety inspection and a record of regular maintenance and insurance coverage for any vehicle (including commercial vehicles) being used for emergencies or in the implementation of the program.

❑ Staff members should understand that using their own private cars for transporting participants and/or staff members is done at their own risk if they are not requested to transport persons as a part of their job.

PROGRAM WORKSHEET P-51

Complaints

Rationale

Health, safety, and the satisfaction of participants and staff members are of the utmost importance. Sometimes staff members encounter a person who complains or displays anger and causes that staff member to become defensive. People receiving complaints often cut the complaint short or argue back. Having a process to deal with complaints helps the listener hear the entire concern being expressed. This plan should be consistent with Worksheet O-31: Complaints.

Plan

1. Staff positions that may deal with complaints from parents regarding:	
Registration/fees	
Program/activities	
Program administrator	
Program leader(s)	
Products/product sale	
Child abuse	
Supervision	
Facilities	
Transportation	
Other:	
2. Staff positions that may deal with complaints from vendors:	
3. Staff positions that may deal with complaints from funders:	
4. Staff positions that may deal with complaints from collaborations:	
5. Staff positions that may deal with complaints from youth:	
6. Staff training for handling complaints includes using a report form and:	
7. Type of complaints that require the person taking complaint to inform his supervisor:	
8. Complaints and suggestions logged and reviewed by:	
Personnel	
Program	
Product sales	
Registration/fees	

Guidelines and Information to Help Complete the Plan

❑ People are more often interested in bringing a suit when something irritates them. If they believe the program has qualified leadership, medical insurance, and is the well-run, safe program announced in the flyer or brochure, they are less likely to challenge that record.

❑ It is important to identify the appropriate staff person to handle various types of complaints, as well as the backup person or supervisor. Train other staff members who may receive calls in techniques they can use to calmly refer the complaint to the designated staff person.

❑ Training should include how to:

- Ask the right questions
- Listen effectively
- Use positive nonverbal communications
- Identify the problem, not just the symptoms
- Establish comfort, rapport, and trust
- Disagree without becoming argumentative
- Understand another's point of view
- Remain firm when no change is possible
- Stay calm when the complainer is being abusive
- Defuse explosive situations and confront anger
- Convey respect and maintain a positive attitude

A sample form for handling complaints is included in Appendix 20.

❑ Log and periodically review complaints. Some may need to be a part of personnel files, while others will provide input regarding decisions about programs, staff structures, registration processes, or fees.

PROGRAM WORKSHEET P-52

Participant Supervision Plan

Rationale

Just being "on duty" is not supervising. A plan should be in place for both general and specific supervision. General supervision is supervision by staff members of the play and general group living activities of children. Specific supervision is related to a specific activity, particularly specialized activities that need skilled instruction. Specific supervision plans should be covered in specialized activity sheets found in Appendix 18 and 19.

Plan

1. List those positions that have direct responsibility for general participant supervision:		

2. What ratio of staff members to participants has been established for general supervision?		
Participant Ages	# of Staff	# of Participants
4–5		
6–8		
9–14		
15–18		

3. Activities, locations, or situations (if any) where only one staff member is allowed to be present and procedures for child protection:

4. Provisions made to increase the ratio to serve children with special medical needs, including children that need:		
Participant Needs	# of Staff	# of Participants
Constant or individual assistance		
Close but not constant assistance		
Occasional assistance		
Minimal assistance		

5. A list of program participants and their leaders/counselors is completed by:

Lists are maintained by:

Lists are provided to:

6. What are the policies and procedures for supervision of participants in the following types of activities?

Roles and responsibilities when supervising structured times of the program

Roles and responsibilities when supervising "unstructured" times of the program

Roles and responsibilities for bathing and nighttime supervision, when applicable

Roles and responsibilities when participants are in public places or in contact with the public.

7.	How do supervisors know where leaders/counselors and participates are while a program is running?
8.	When were program leaders/counselors instructed on how to supervise the participants in their charge?
	What are the resources given to leaders/counselors on supervising participants?
	Where can they be found?

Guidelines and Information to Help Complete the Plan

❑ The policies and procedures for supervision should include not only the recommended ratio, but also the responsibilities of those staff members on duty. The recommended ratios may be different for some program activities or times of the day depending on the nature of the program, the special needs of children, the accessibility of supervisors, or the availability of additional staff on the program site. A minimum of two volunteer or paid staff members should always be on the program site, but if the group is within sight or sound of another adult, a small group may have only one adult supervising them (Figure 6-2).

Participant Age	Day Camp*	Resident Camp	Club	Child Care	Instructional Courses
4–5 1:6	1:5	2:10	2:15	2:15	
6–8 1:8	1:6	2:12	2:20–24†	2:30	
9–14	1:10	1:8	2:20	2:20–30†	2:30
15–18	1:12	1:10	2:24	N/A	2:40

*The minimum number of adults on any program site is two. In outdoor programs, groups are often in large outdoor spaces and not confined by buildings or walls, but other staff are on the site. Therefore, in a day or resident camp, two adults should be with each group unless they are within sight or sound of another group with an adult. In a resident camp, if the housing is such that a child calling for help could easily be heard from another cabin or tent, one adult may be housed with a group in the cabin or tent. Often a specialist staff member serves as a second adult in a cabin or tent at night if participants are either too far away to be heard or in a soundproof facility.

† In child care programs, the varying ratio is determined by license requirements, overall size of group, other staff on site, and variable daily attendance figures. Refer to Worksheet P-60: Preventing Child Abuse for procedures addressing one-on-one situations.

Figure 6-2. Recommended ratios of staff members to participants

Understanding that a minimum of two adults should always be on a program site, the recommended ratios for children with special needs are:

- Constant and individualized assistance: 1 to 1
- Close but not constant: 1 to 2
- Occasional assistance: 1 to 4
- Minimal assistance: 1 to 5

❑ The instructions on how to supervise should include the location of the supervisor, a pattern for circulating among participants, and backup supervision. Structured times include meals, organized activities, evening programs, etc. Unstructured times may be before and after meals or between organized activities, during free time, etc. Data shows that more incidents happen during unstructured and nighttime periods. Policies for situations when participants are mingled with the public should include roles and responsibilities, ratios, safety guidelines for participants, and emergency procedures in case someone is separated from the group.

❑ Training might include identification of things for which to look or listen. Children might act or say things that would alert staff to possible problems. For example, a child might tell another child: "I'm going to get you!" "You dummy, you stubbed your toe on that root again!" "Suzy has bruises on her back." A child might cry, show anger or depression, or otherwise exhibit an unusual behavior. Additional training opportunities should be made available during the time of employment after having some experience with children.

❑ Staff members should have written procedures for behavior management and be instructed on how to control a group of children. See Appendix 12 for a sample policy and procedures. Examples include giving clear instructions and asking questions to determine understanding, establishing limits, speaking in understandable tones, and acting immediately. Injuries that occur from spontaneous acts are usually not negligence. However, failure to stop undue rowdiness that may cause injury may be negligence. Participant supervisors are expected to know emergency and first-aid procedures that might be needed for the activities they are supervising.

PROGRAM WORKSHEET P-53

Conduct of Participants and Staff Members

Rationale

The appropriate conduct and behavior expectations of participants and paid or volunteer staff members are important and should be clearly communicated to provide a safe, comfortable environment for all.

Plan

1.	To provide a safe, secure environment, both participants and staff members must discuss and/or receive information/training on how to:		
	Focus attention on participant needs and interests		Create a supportive environment
	Show respect when speaking with all children		Guide group behavior in a developmentally appropriate manner
	Respond appropriately to socially sensitive issues		Emphasize that bullying, including cyberbullying, will not be tolerated
2.	The program's policy on bullying is:		
3.	Staff members also receives training in:	What resource was used or distributed?	
	Physical, social, emotional, and intellectual age characteristics		
	Prevention and intervention techniques for inappropriate behaviors		
	Appropriate discipline methods		
	The consequence of inappropriate behavior of participants or staff		
4.	To provide a comfortable level of privacy for both adults and children, procedures for group living in areas such as those used for sleeping, dressing, showering, and bathing include:		
5.	Staff, participants, and user groups are advised in writing of the policies for possession of personal property including:		
	Alcohol and drugs		Personal equipment (sports and electronic)
	Vehicles		Weapons (refer to Worksheet P-49: Weapons and Firearms)
	Animals		Cigarettes, cigars, pipes, etc.

Guidelines and Information to Help Complete the Plan

❑ "Willful and wanton conduct" is considered an intentional injury and is often associated with conduct that is recklessly disregardful of the interests or safety of others. Assault and battery, while terms that are most often used together, have different meanings. Assault is the threat to use force, while battery is the actual use of force. False imprisonment includes confinement or restraint of a person against his will.

❑ The consequence for intentional injuries referred to as "willful and wanton conduct," false imprisonment, or assault and battery should include immediate dismissal from the program. The situation must be referred to local law enforcement or child protection agency. Refer to Worksheet P-60: Preventing Child Abuse.

❑ Privacy is important to the dignity of participants and staff members, and methods to provide that privacy may be especially important to children and staff members who have not had previous group living experiences. To reduce the risk of accusations and for the protection of both staff members and participants, it is better to avoid one-to-one contact that is out of the sight of others.

❑ Staff members working directly with youth may have different values and/or approaches to dealing with the behavior of youth. Establishing policies and training staff members in consistent methods of positive behavior management and appropriate methods of discipline is a critical part of establishing a positive relationship. Research shows that children who are involved in setting rules have a marked decrease in bullying behavior. Refer to the sample discipline and dismissal policy in Appendix 16a.

❑ Bullying includes:

- Physical bullying—A child uses physical force to hurt another child or takes or breaks another child's belongings.

- Verbal bullying—A child uses words to threaten or hurt another child. Verbal bullying includes teasing, name calling, graffiti, put-downs, and ridicule.

- Relational bullying—A child disrupts another child's peer relationships by leaving him out, gossiping, making hostile gestures, or ostracizing him. Cyberbullying involves using cell phones, websites, and the Internet to bully others.

- Sexual bullying—A child makes unwanted sexual comments or gender-demeaning remarks and jokes, circulates pornography, touches the private parts of another child, or in extreme cases, commits molestation, assault, or rape.

The following is a sample policy from Camp Fire USA on bullying:

Camp Fire USA has a no-tolerance policy on all types of bullying. All incidents of bullying will be taken seriously. Children are respected and valued as individuals and building their self-confidence and self-esteem are important outcomes of all programs. A climate of openness, consultation, and participation, in which participant's views are sought, listened to, and respected, will do much to build the kind of sound working relationships in which hostile behavior is no longer an issue and bullying is not tolerated either by staff or participants.

❑ It is important that the organization ensures that all individuals associated with it, including youth participants and their parents, are assured of appropriate confidentiality and are treated with respect and professionalism at all times. It is also important that anything that is in the public domain about the organization reflects positively on the organization. Accordingly, the following standards should be considered for all employees in connection with the use of the Internet and other electronic communications media:

❑ If an employee creates or maintains a website or blog about himself (e.g., MySpace, Facebook), he must exercise the highest degree of good judgment regarding the material placed on that site or blog. For example, such individuals should ask themselves: "What would prospective or current employees/participants/parents think about me and/or the organization if they access this site or blog?" If the answer is that a visitor might perceive something negative, then the material that may create a negative impression about the individual or the organization should not be placed on the site or blog.

❑ If an individual participates in a blog or other site, he may not identify himself as associated with the organization, either explicitly or implicitly, unless authorized to do so in writing by the organization.

❑ Content placed on the Internet or transmitted via other media may not be potentially or actually defamatory, abusive, threatening, harassing, invasive of privacy, or injurious to any member or any other employee.

❑ Refer to worksheet O-26: Technological Usage and Record Security for information about use of the Internet. A sample policy and signature form for staff members is found in Appendix 26.

❑ Staff members should receive training in appropriate and inappropriate behavior between participants, between participants and staff, and between staff in the presence of participants.

❏ Training for staff includes both a discussion and written information about dealing with inappropriate physical and sexual behavior and the identification of signs of abuse.

❏ To support positive and supportive relationships, staff members do not discipline children by use of physical punishment or isolation, or by failing to provide food, clothing, shelter, or attention. They do not verbally or emotionally abuse or punish children. Staff members are taught appropriate techniques of showing affection, approval, and support.

❏ The following is a sample from an employment manual and personnel policy. A sample code of conduct for participants and staff is found in Appendices 13, 14, and 15.

> *Sample drug and alcohol policy: The use of illegal drugs by any participant or staff member while involved in any activity on Camp Fire property or engaged in any activity in which they are representing Camp Fire is prohibited.*

> *Alcohol will not be offered or consumed in conjunction with the conduct of direct service youth activities or duly called business meetings of Camp Fire at all levels. Alcohol will not be served at any functions held at organization-owned camp facilities. The misuse or abuse of alcohol or the behavior caused by such will not be tolerated.*

PROGRAM WORKSHEET P-54

Screening of Staff Members and Volunteers

Rationale

The screening process for paid staff and volunteers is probably one of the most important jobs an administrator does. It provides records of the screening process and helps control losses resulting from accusations of discrimination and negligent hiring. It is also instrumental to the quality of the program and the physical and emotional safety of program participants. Note: The screening and hiring process for employees should be consistent with the organization's personnel policies and Worksheet O-28: Screening of Staff and Volunteers.

Plan

1.	The documentation to support the screening process includes:
	Job descriptions for each position shared with the applicant
	Application forms completed for each applicant
	A personal interview with each applicant
	Verification of previous work (including volunteer) history and two references
	Criminal background check (or voluntary disclosure statement for those under 18)
	Signature agreeing to drug testing. ❑pre-employment, ❑random, and/or ❑regular
	Driving record for anyone regularly transporting children
	Documentation of skills required for the job
	Any minimum-age requirements for supervising children
	Confirmation of volunteer status
2.	The interview process includes:
	A face-to-face or phone interview
	A set of consistent questions that will help determine skills specific to the job, or if appropriate, the suitability of staff to work with, or have access to, children.
	Explanation of the job expectations, working environment, the organizations' philosophy, and/or goals for youth development that pertain to the job.
3. The procedure for reference checks includes:	
4. The criminal records background check procedures:	
	The organization secured for doing criminal record background checks is:

Types of Positions	"Hits," or Records That Disqualify a Person
☐ Program administrator	
☐ Staff or volunteers with direct access to children	
☐ Staff or volunteers with direct access to children's personal information	
☐ Drivers transporting children	
☐ Staff or volunteers with access to money for financial records	
☐	

Procedures for handling situations in which the criminal record check recovered a "hit" are:		
5. The hiring process for employees and the forms were reviewed:		
By	Qualification	Date

Guidelines and Information to Help Complete the Plan

☐ The hiring and screening process for employees and volunteers includes systems to ensure that applicants and employees receive fair and equal treatment. The process includes procedures for posting jobs, clear job descriptions, completed application forms, documented references, interviews, criminal background checks, and documentation of each step.

☐ A lawsuit for negligent hiring is based on the theory that the employer is liable for the actions of an employee who was unfit or who created an unreasonable risk of harm. Negligent hiring is an accusation against an employer for being negligent in the hiring or selection process. The alleged harm or injuries sustained by a participant were the direct result of actions taken by an unqualified staff member. This definition also extends to volunteers. Parents have many expectations for the selection of staff and volunteers that may have access to their children.

☐ Job descriptions for each position should include the essential functions of the job (refer to Worksheet P-27: Serving Persons With Disabilities and www.ada.gov for ADA requirements), any special knowledge or skills required, the level of responsibility required, and the line of accountability and supervision. Each position has a different set of issues to consider, but special considerations should be given for those staff members working directly with children. The application includes a signed release for a background check.

☐ Each new applicant for a paid or volunteer position should complete a personnel application form. Applications or personnel files should be updated as a part of the evaluation process.

Employers should not ask about any of the following, because to not hire a candidate because of any one of them is discriminatory:

- Race
- Color
- Sex
- Religion
- National origin
- Birthplace
- Age
- Disability
- Marital/family status

Age discrimination protects individuals who are 40 years of age or older from employment discrimination based on age. Asking if the applicant is at least 16, or over 18, is acceptable to meet the minimum age requirements in positions directly supervising children.

❑ A personal interview should be conducted with each applicant (either face-to-face or by phone). Although some applicants may not be working directly with children, if the organization serves youth, those applicants may have access to records or information on children. Appendix 23 has a list of sample questions to ask staff members who may be working directly with children and a list of questions that should be avoided in the hiring process.

❑ Reference checks on all prospective staff members and volunteers should be conducted and documented prior to assuming job responsibilities. References can be in the form of a letter, a completed reference form, or documentation of a personal telephone discussion. Verification includes checking work history for "gaps" and to see if an applicant has been employed as claimed.

❑ Criminal background check of adults who could have access to children or their personal information should be included in the screening process. Screening should be done upon entry as a staff member or volunteer and after any break in service. In addition to the more extensive criminal background check, the U.S Department of Justice National Sex Offender Public Registry provides a check of sexual offenders in the national data base as a free service at www.nsopr.gov.

❑ Procedures should be in place for decisions regarding a "hit" on a criminal background check. What types of "hits" would be a disqualifying offense? For example, felonies or misdemeanors classified as an offense against a person, against public order (e.g., prostitution, obscenity, child pornography), violation of a law for possession or distribution of a controlled substance, etc., could be samples of "hits" that disqualify a person from a position working directly with children. Does the decision vary with the job and or the conviction? Does a time limitation exist on some types of "hits"? Records obtained should be kept in restricted files. The Nonprofit Risk Management Center has additional information on criminal background checks and a list of state criminal history record repositories (www.nonprofitrisk.org).

❑ Voluntary disclosure statements are signed statements attesting to the nonconviction of crimes against children. These statements may be used for staff members and volunteers such as parents helping with a small group where they are supervised by another adult, those under 18, or international staff for whom no available record exists. Parent or short-term supervised volunteers should sign a Confirmation of Volunteer Status and Agreements to confirm that they are participating as volunteers. This statement may be added to the application form.

❑ A driving record should be obtained from those persons who regularly transport children. Work with the organization's insurance agent to obtain records and design a policy regarding what kinds of violations, such as driving under the influence (D.U.I.), speeding, reckless operation, etc., will prohibit someone from transporting participants in the program.

❑ The application and screening process should be reviewed by a legal or human resources professional at least every three years. Once appointed to a position, all staff or volunteers working directly with children should have photographs attached to their personnel records for identification at a later time if needed.

PROGRAM WORKSHEET P-55

Staff Selection and Training for Emergencies

Rationale

It is important to select staff members who have demonstrated an ability to handle emergency situations. It is also important to provide training in recognizing and handling emergency situations. Emergency procedures also help staff members know what is expected in a crisis and how to deal with a situation in a calm, rational way.

Plan

1.	What questions are routinely asked during the interviewing process to attest to a staff member's ability to handle or react in case of emergency?
2.	What information or certifications are required to verify training in handling emergencies?
3.	What training in first-aid and emergency procedures is provided to staff?
	What written first-aid and emergency procedures are supplied to staff members?
	How and when?
	How and when are first-aid and emergency situations reviewed and rehearsed?
4.	What physical warning signs are staff members instructed to look for in participants or other staff members?

Guidelines and Information to Help Complete the Plan

❏ The interviewing process might include such questions as, "Have you ever been in an emergency?" If yes, "How did you react?" "What experience have you had in handling emergencies with children?"

❏ As a part of the application process, ask for copies of certificates showing courses completed, such as water safety instruction, first aid, etc.

❏ Staff members should receive written procedures on their responsibilities for healthcare and emergencies. In addition to emergency procedures and first-aid training, include observation games in staff training. Such training should help staff members readily recognize a potential hazard or emergency situation. Observation games might include identification of missing safety equipment or first-aid kits in a program area, signs of hypothermia, or a person's actions that should alert someone to a potentially dangerous situation.

❑ First-aid and emergency procedures should be reviewed and rehearsed periodically, as well as before any trip. Warning signs indicating a physical condition that might lead to an emergency include signs of fatigue, depression, anger, excessive heat or cold, etc.

PROGRAM WORKSHEET P-56

Employment Practices

Rationale

The organization is responsible for keeping informed of state and federal laws and the reporting and recordkeeping requirements. In some states, summer camps may be exempt from federal minimum-wage requirements if they are considered seasonal. Note: This plan should be consistent with the organization's personnel policies and Worksheet O-29: Employment Practices. This worksheet also includes information on dismissal of paid and volunteer staff.

Plan

1. List positions by title		
Exempt:	Non-exempt:	

2. For a summer camp or religious or nonprofit educational conference center to be exempt from federal minimum-wage requirements, it must be considered seasonal. It may be considered seasonal if:		
It is in operation for fewer than seven months each year.		
The average receipts for any six months of the previous year do not exceed one-third of the average receipts for the other six months of the year.		
	What is the income per month?	Check lowest six months
January		
February		
March		
April		
May		
June		
July		
August		
September		
October		
November		
December		
Formula		Answer
A. Total income for lowest six months		

B.	Divide A by 6	
C.	Total of greatest six months of income	
D.	Divide C by 6	
E.	Divide D by 3	
F.	Is B less than E?	

3. In addition, the operation must be open to the general public and not just agency membership. Does the organization allow anyone of appropriate age and qualifications to register?

4.	Are timesheets required for non-exempt employees?	If not, why not?
	Any timesheets required for exempt employees are because:	
	Timesheets are kept by:	

5. Person responsible for OSHA records, including maintaining the log, summary, and record of each reportable occupational injury and/or illness:

Location where OSHA records are kept:

6.	Labor Law Posters are posted at the following worksites:	Person responsible for ensuring that posters are continually displayed:

7. Procedures for handling concerns/complaints about wages, benefits, hours and working conditions are:

8. The organization has personnel policies that include:

Employment Policies/Practices	Date Last Reviewed
Employment at will	
Equal employment opportunity	
Problem-solving process	
Hiring	
Employment of relatives	
Employment categories	
Introductory period	
Change in status	
Position descriptions	
Americans With Disabilities Act	
Performance appraisal process	
Safety	
Personnel files	
Employee Conduct and Business Practices	Date Last Reviewed
Harassment	
Consensual relationships	
Attendance and punctuality	
Professional appearance	

	Internal investigation/search	
	Conflicts of interest	
	Ethics	
	Technologies—computers/Internet	
	Outside work	
	Use of illegal drugs/abuse of alcohol	
	Personal finances	
	Corrective action	
	Separation	
	Pay Practices	Date Last Reviewed
	Time records	
	Pay periods and paydays	
	Overtime	
	Leave Benefits	Date Last Reviewed
	Holidays	
	Vacation	
	Sick leave or personal leave	
	Medical leaves of absence	
	Funeral leave	
	Military leave	
	Jury duty leave	
	Benefit Information	Date Last Reviewed
	ERISA Rights	
	Brief summary of group insurance	
	Health continuation	
	Coverage—COBRA	
	HIPAA	
	Receipt of Personnel Policies Acknowledgement	Date Last Reviewed
9.	The organization has policies for dismal of volunteers	Date Last Reviewed

Guidelines and Information to Help Complete the Plan

❑ The major federal employment laws currently affecting long-term care employees include (refer to Appendix 22):

- Title VII of Civil Rights Act of 1964
- Age Discrimination in Employment Act (ADEA)

- Section 1981 of the Civil Rights Act of 1966
- Civil Rights Act of 1991
- National Labor Relations Act
- Fair Labor Standards Act
- Occupational Safety and Health Act
- Americans with Disabilities Act (ADA)
- Family and Medical Leave Act of 1993
- Veterans Protection/Preference Laws Veterans Protection/Preference Laws
- Pregnancy Discrimination Act of 1978
- Immigration Reform and Control Act of 1986
- Equal Pay Act

❑ The Fair Labor Standards Act addresses wage and hour requirements for minimum wage as well as overtime for exempt and non-exempt employees. Employment records relating to wages, hours (work time schedules), sex, occupation, condition of employment, etc., must be kept for two years. General employee information must be kept for three years. The Fair Labor Standards Act provides exemptions for summer camps or religious or nonprofit educational conference centers if they meet one of the following requirements, in addition to being open to the general public:

- Does not operate more than seven months during any calendar year
- The average receipts during any six months of the previous year do not exceed one-third of the average receipts for the other six months of the year

  This plan provides the formula for this seasonal exemption and details how to determine if a camp is considered seasonal. Some states do not recognize this federal exemption for summer camps (refer to www.dol.gov).

❑ No statute of limitations exists for fraud. Severe financial ramifications may arise out of classifying a person incorrectly, including exempt vs. non-exempt and employee vs. independent contractor.

❑ In most cases, a caretaker or site manager and kitchen staff are considered non-exempt employees and qualify for minimum wage and overtime. An employee may receive a salary based on the work hours expected per week. Overtime must be documented and paid for any hours over 40 in a week. Because the time needed in the summer is greater in many cases, it may be more economical to hire a seasonal assistant to handle the longer hours. Another option is for the organization to pay the individual a flat rate per work week. Even though the work days and hours may vary per week during the year, the employer must meet the minimum-wage and overtime requirements for hours in a week. Housing and food benefits may not be considered a part of the salary, and overtime must be paid at "time-and-a-half" of the hourly salary.

❑ OSHA requires that employers with more than 10 full- or part-time employees at any one time in a calendar year must keep injury and illness records on paid staff. They should be kept at the workplace for at least five years after the year to which they relate (refer to OSHA's recordkeeping requirements at www.osha.gov).

❑ In addition to the OSHA requirements, recordkeeping requirements are associated with the aforementioned laws (refer to Worksheet O-21: Record Retention and Destruction). Additional state requirements may also be in place.

❑ The National Labor Relations Act gives employees the right to unionize, or the right of collective bargaining for wages, working conditions, and benefits. Although unions are not common in 501(c)(3) organizations, this law also addresses an employer's retaliation against two or more employees complaining about wages, hours, or working conditions.

❑ At-will employment is a doctrine that defines an employment relationship in which either party can terminate the relationship with no liability if no contract exists governing the employment relationship. According to this legal doctrine, any hiring is presumed to be "at will"; that is, the employer is free to discharge individuals "for good cause, or bad cause, or no cause at all," and the employee is equally free to quit, strike, or otherwise cease work.

❑ No statute of limitations exists for fraud. Severe financial ramifications may arise out of classifying a person incorrectly, including exempt vs. non-exempt and employee vs. independent contractor.

❑ In many states, an employee handbook with personnel policies and practices is viewed as a legal contract. The organization must be careful about selecting words and phrases that can be misinterpreted or allow no flexibility, such as permanent; will, should, and shall; probationary period; fair; is cause for termination; and shall be terminated.

❑ Persons being paid an hourly wage cannot also be "volunteers" doing the same work for additional hours, though they may volunteer in a different area. The organization should have volunteer policies and procedures that include dismissal of volunteers (refer to Appendix 30).

> *Sample policy: Volunteers may be asked to give up their volunteer roles for failure to comply with the policies and procedures of the organization. Volunteers may wish to discuss the reasons for dismissal with their supervisor. Prior to*

dismissal, the supervisor and the executive director must agree to dismiss the volunteer. Grounds for dismissal may include, but are not limited to, failure to perform assigned duties, failure to follow organization policies and procedures, failure to meet minimum standards of performance, abuse of staff or others, alcohol or drug abuse while volunteering, theft of organization property, misconduct, or subordination.

PROGRAM WORKSHEET P-57

Staff Training

Rationale

Staff selection, training, and supervision are key components to providing a quality, safe experience for youth. Appropriate training at all levels is the responsibility of the corporate entity. Responsibility for content, implementation, and documentation is usually delegated to the administration.

Plan

1.	The board has approved a budget for staff training based on a need for basic and ongoing staff development that includes:
	Training for administrators
	Training for supervisors
	Training for specialists
	Training for direct leadership
	Training for support staff
2.	Training topics for all staff:
	Purpose, needs, and outcomes desired for participant development
	General characteristics of program organization, structure, and activities offered, competencies required, and program operating procedures
	Nature of participant groups served
	Recognition, prevention, and reporting of child abuse (child to child or adult to child) during or outside the program
	Safety regulations and emergency procedures and staff role
	Behavior management and camper-supervision techniques for providing a physically and emotionally safe environment
	Clear expectations for staff performance and conduct, and effectively relating to participants and other staff members
	General procedures for operation
3.	Training records are:

Completed by:	Title:
Labeled and stored in:	
Training records include:	

	Outline and objectives
	Roster of training participants
	Dates of training
	Number of hours and participant attendance
	Instructor(s)
	Any statements of verification of training
	Procedures for providing training for late hires and persons who missed part of the training
	Provisions for in-service training

Guidelines and Information to Help Complete the Plan

❑ Certification and documentation of training specific to each activity requiring specialized knowledge and/or skills are covered on Worksheet P-61: Activities Requiring Staff Members With Specialized Training or Certification. In addition to the specialized skills, volunteer and paid staff should receive training the general training for all staff.

❑ All staff members should receive training in:

- Safety regulations, injury prevention, and emergency procedures, including:
  - √ How to identify hazards and enforce safety regulations
  - √ Reporting incidents and accidents
  - √ Recognition, prevention, and reporting responsibilities in possible child-abuse situations (physical, emotional, sexual, and verbal)
  - √ How to deal with intruders
  - √ Search and rescue procedures
  - √ Supervision when intermingled with the public
  - √ Emergency communication plans and procedures
  - √ Transportation procedures

- General practices for participant/staff relationships, including:
  - √ A supervision plan
  - √ Effectively relating to participants
  - √ Behavior-management policies
  - √ Appropriate and inappropriate staff/participant and staff/staff behaviors, including any form of harassment or bullying
  - √ Supervision techniques

- General procedures, including:
  - Maintenance routines and reporting problems
  - Monitoring equipment
  - First-aid and healthcare procedures
  - Handling flammable or poisonous materials
  - Handling and using power tools (program, kitchen, maintenance)
  - Food preparation and storage procedures
  - Use of technological and program equipment

❑ Training rosters serve as verification that training did take place and that the specific training topics were covered.

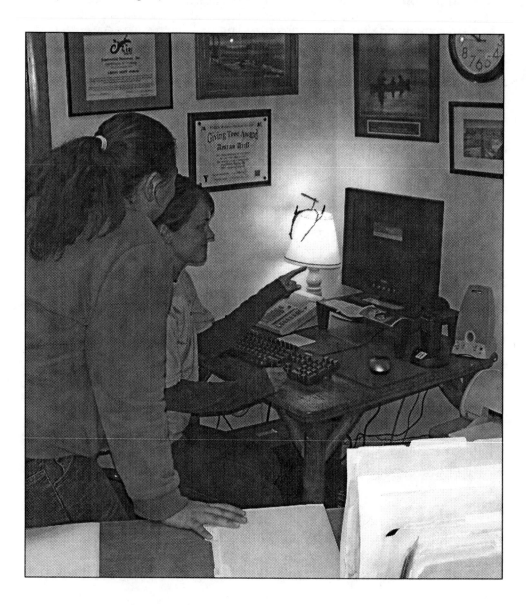

PROGRAM WORKSHEET P-58

Supervision of Staff

Rationale

The responsibility for supervision of staff, especially those who work directly with children, includes observation of the relationships among children and the staff member during both planned activity times and the more informal individual or group living times.

Plan

1. List the positions that supervise staff members who work directly with children or identify where that list can be found.	
Supervisors	People They Supervise
Have staff members been provided a chart showing this information?	
2. What is the pattern for circulation as it relates to the various positions listed?	
3. What problems in supervision might occur?	
4. Where are the guidelines for acceptable and unacceptable staff behaviors that the supervisors have been instructed to look for?	
5. Guidelines and training in supervision and performance for supervisors includes:	
How to monitor the performance of the staff members they supervise	
How to identify, model, reinforce, and correct staff members' appropriate and inappropriate behaviors	
6. How and when do opportunities for staff observation, feedback, conferences, and/or evaluations take place?	

Guidelines and Information to Help Complete the Plan

❏ In most cases, it is difficult for any one person to supervise more than eight staff members at a time.

❏ Training for supervisors should include an understanding of the job expectations and the plan for supervision. Clear guidelines must be established for identifying and addressing both the appropriate and inappropriate staff behaviors (refer to Appendix 28).

❏ The plan should include a pattern for circulation or observation that includes different times of the day and different activities, including free times and times when children might be bathing, changing clothes, or alone with a staff member. Staff and participants should respect each other's privacy, but sometimes children may have to undress with others present. The supervision plan should include staff members working in pairs.

❏ Observation of staff members should include how the children are responding to them. Are they happy, responsive, and comfortable in their relationship? Do the children's actions or words alert the supervisor to possible problems? A child (or multiple children) might show a change in behavior around some staff members. A child might cry or exhibit unusual shyness, show fear, anger, or depression, or otherwise exhibit an unusual behavior.

❏ Staff conferences and/or evaluations should happen frequently and cover job performance and relationships—both with children and other staff members—and also help them develop a plan for improvement.

PROGRAM WORKSHEET P-59

Harassment—Sexual and Other

Rationale

All employees and volunteers have the right to work in an environment free of all forms of discrimination, including harassment. Sexual or other types of harassment including inappropriate actions that are based on race, creed, color, gender, age, disability, religion, or national origin and interfere with work performance or create an intimidating, hostile, or offensive work environment. Note: This plan should be consistent with the organization's personnel policies on Worksheet O-30: Harassment—Sexual and Other.

Plan

1.	The policy that prohibits sexual harassment and other types of harassment is:
	How are staff/volunteers informed of the policy?
2.	The consequences of such harassment is:
	Who is responsible for deciding on the consequences?
3.	The complaint procedures are:
	Who is responsible for investigating the complaint?
	Where are complaints of sexual harassment retained?
4.	Who is responsible for determining and taking appropriate corrective action?

Guidelines and Information to Help Complete the Plan

❑ The policy should include the employee's right to work in an environment free from harassment and state that the organization will not tolerate sexual or other types of harassment of its employees or volunteers in any form. Abuse of the dignity of anyone through ethnic, racist, or sexist slurs or through other derogatory or objectionable conduct is offensive employee behavior and will lead to corrective action. Harassment or bullying of participants is considered in Worksheet P-53: Conduct of Participants and Staff Members.

❑ The policy should also forbid a supervisor from threatening an employee with suggestions that submission to, or rejection of, sexual advances will in any way influence any personnel decision regarding employment, evaluation, wages, advancement, assigned duties, shifts, or any other condition of employment.

❑ Sexual harassment includes such actions as repeated offensive sexual flirtation, advances, propositions, continual or repeated abuse of a sexual nature, graphic verbal commentary about an individual's body, sexually degrading words to describe an individual, and the display in the workplace of sexually suggestive objects or pictures. Sexual favoritism in the workplace that adversely affects the employment opportunities of third parties may take the form of implicit "quid pro quo" harassment and/or "hostile work environment" harassment.

❑ The procedures for making/dealing with a complaint should include the serious nature of such a charge and state that such a charge will be treated with the strictest confidence and should be reported, not shared with coworkers. Procedures should include the following steps: .

- The employee/volunteer should clearly express displeasure to the harasser.

- The employee/volunteer should report the situation to his or her supervisor unless the supervisor is the harasser, in which case the report should be made to that person's supervisor or a member of the administrative staff.

- A designated director, or in the case of the executive director, a member of the personnel committee will investigate the complaint. The employee should not suffer retaliation for filing a complaint. The records should not be entered into the employee's file, but be retained in a separate confidential file.

- When the investigation confirms the allegations, appropriate corrective action will be taken.

PROGRAM WORKSHEET P-60

Preventing Child Abuse

Rationale

The prevention of child abuse is of great concern to organizations, families, and society in general. A comprehensive plan includes the staff-selection process; education of staff, volunteers, and youth; reporting procedures; and the establishment of other obstacles to abuse. Refer to Worksheet P-54: Screening of Staff Members and Volunteers for the selection process. Worksheet O-10: Report of Alleged Child Abuse includes information on the steps to take if a report is made.

Plan

1.	Staff training includes:
	Information on the four types of abuse—neglect, emotional, sexual, and physical
	Information on the signs of childhood stress and signs of abuse
	Information on child abuse procedures, including groups being supervised by two adults or being within sound or sight of a second adult
	Clear expectations about adult–child contact
	Procedures to protect adults from unfounded allegations of abuse
	Dealing with disclosure of abuse and reporting requirements
	Techniques for preventing child-to-child abuse
2.	Staff members sign a statement indicating:
	They have received and read appropriate policies/procedures and they have received training.
	They have read and agreed to a code of conduct.
	They understand reporting procedures.
	They understand that contacting participants outside of the program is not appropriate.
3.	When and how do participants receive information/training on how to avoid abuse and what to do in case of threatened or actual abuse?
4.	Program guidelines or policies to provide an emotionally and physically safe environment include:
	Participants know how to get help with problems.
	Participants are under the supervision of a staff member at all times.
	"Hazing" of children is not permitted.
	Bullying is not tolerated.
	Excessive tickling, teasing, wrestling, personal jokes, etc., is not appropriate.

5.	Other procedures to reduce the risk of, or opportunity for, abuse in facility design or in situations when an adult needs to be alone with a child:
6.	What is the procedure for staff members to report suspicion or disclosure of abuse:
	Involving someone outside the program?
	By an adult within the program?
	By another youth in the program?
7.	What are the reporting requirements in the state?
8.	What is a reportable incident?
9.	What is the timeframe for reporting?
10.	Who should a disclosure be reported to on the staff?

Guidelines and Information to Help Complete the Plan

❏ Staff training includes information about not being alone with a single child and should be an ongoing, interactive process that includes information and opportunities for role play and discussions on items listed in this worksheet.

❏ To establish obstacles to abuse, organization procedures/policies should include such topics as:

- Always having two adults on any program site

- Designing programs for groups and avoiding any one-to-one activities

- Encouraging open, comfortable, informal discussions and not encouraging "secrets"

- Providing facilities and group-living activities with a respect for privacy, but not so private that a child screaming for help could not be heard.

- Contacting participants outside of the program (before or after) without permission of the organization is not appropriate. This policy includes email, phone, mail, and in-person contact. Organized events (reunions, etc.) or contacts (birthday cards, promotional postcards written during the program and saved to mail later, etc.), should be handled by the administration and should not include personal address or contact information on the participant or the staff member. Refer to Worksheet P-52: Participant Supervision Plan for policies on supervision.

❏ It is the responsibility of the program administrator and a mandated reporter to know the reporting laws in the state and to whom a report should be made before a program begins—generally, it is a Department of Human or Social Services or the Child Protection Division. The Child Welfare Information Gateway provides information on reporting child abuse and phone numbers of reporting agencies by state (www.childwelfare.gov).

❑ The administrator should also know if a timeframe exists and what behaviors are reportable. It is helpful to get to know the child-protection authorities before the program has an incident. Invite them to help train the staff or provide training resources. Find out what support services they provide or recommend if a report made.

❑ Staff members should know the procedures for reporting and documenting alleged abuse both within and outside the program. Disclosure procedures should be consistent with state and local community standards and reports should be addressed in an expedient and confidential manner. In some states the requirements state that the person to whom the information was disclosed must directly report to the authorities. In other states, that person may report to his employer and the employer may call on his behalf to initiate the investigation. Worksheet O-10: Report of Alleged Child Abuse explains the steps to take when a report is received.

❑ Child-to-child abuse has increased over the past five years and often starts at a young age with bullying or excessive teasing. Sometimes it is planned off-site on the Internet before the program begins or during the course of programs from which children leave at the end of the day. Children should know when and how to get help. Research shows a link between bullying and child-to-child sexual abuse. Refer to Worksheet P-53: Conduct of Participants and Staff Members and include techniques for handling children that threaten or participate in sexual or physical bullying. Social services can generally help if the abuser is a minor.

❑ Facility designs should be reviewed to prevent opportunities for children to be in rooms or areas where they could not be seen or heard by others. For example, single bathroom doors should have vents installed. Procedures should be established for another adult to be present or notification given to the person in charge when a single child has cause to be alone in a room with an adult (e.g., a nurse needs to examine a child in private).

❑ Appendix 17 includes a Sample of Recommended Program Policies for Child Abuse Prevention for Camp Fire USA Programs.

PROGRAM WORKSHEET P-61

Activities Requiring Staff Members With Specialized Training or Certification

Rationale

Staff members with a certification or a verified set of predetermined knowledge of specialized activities and the rules related to them will lessen confusion and ensure the safety of all participants.

Plan

Check Activities Offered	List Risks	Completed Specialized Activity Sheet (Refer to Appendix 18)	By Whom?
Archery			
Riflery			
Overnights			
All-day hikes			
Adventure/challenge			
Gymnastics			
Motorized vehicle			
Bicycling			
Swimming			
Boating			
Waterskiing			
Canoeing			
Sailing			
Horseback riding			
Outdoor living Skills			
Crafts requiring heat			
Sledding			
Skateboarding			
Other:			

Guidelines and Information to Help Complete the Plan

❑ Specialized activities may include those listed on the worksheet and others such as exploring caves, trip camping, some craft activities, using tools, etc. The board should be familiar with what activities are being offered that require persons with specialized training or certification.

❑ Specialized activities should be done in an area with controlled access to equipment and signs warning that the area is off-limits unless participants are supervised by a qualified leader.

❑ Duplicate and complete a participation sheet for each activity requiring specialized certification or training (refer to Appendix 18). Include a system to inform staff members, guests, and family members of rules regarding supervised or unsupervised participation in activities. Appendix 19 is used for activities that do not require certification or specialized training.

❑ Determine prerequisites, equipment checks, orientation and training needs, supervision skills, staff-to-camper participation ratios, emergency procedures, diversion activities, and whether any circumstances exist in which a person may participate in a specialized activity alone. The safety orientation should include a checklist that is reviewed and signed by a staff member.

PROGRAM WORKSHEET P-62

Weather and/or Environmental Health Effects on the Program

Rationale

Changes in weather and environmental conditions could necessitate changes in food service and/or physical activity to prevent an illness or accident from occurring.

Plan

1.	What effect do high temperatures have on participants and staff members?
	When temperature goes above:
	Normal activities are changed by:
	Menu is changed by:
	Warning signs or physical conditions to look for in participants/personnel:
	Action to be taken when such conditions are noted:
2.	What effect do low temperatures have?
	When temperature goes below:
	Normal activities are changed by:
	Menu is changed by:
	Warning signs or physical conditions to look for in participants/personnel:
	Actions to be taken when such conditions are noted:
3.	What effect, if any, do these other weather or environmental conditions have on the program?
	Extreme dampness:
	Extreme dryness:
	High pollen index/count:
	Ozone alert:
	Other:
4.	Changes in normal activities, menus, and physical conditions to watch for:

Guidelines and Information to Help Complete the Plan

❑ Staff members should be trained to identify physical conditions of participants and personnel caused by extreme weather conditions. These conditions might include heat exhaustion, sunstroke, hypothermia, frostbite, dehydration, and difficulty breathing.

❑ Staff members should also receive training in how to alter schedules, activities, and foods for varying weather conditions.

PROGRAM WORKSHEET P-63

Participants in Off-Site Programs or Excursions

Rationale

To avoid confusion and to provide for the safety of participants and staff members, procedures for off-site programming should be established and clearly understood by all parties.

Plan

1. Itinerary and roster of participants for all off-site trips is provided to:	
List by Name	Or Position
By program leader:	When:
2. Who is responsible for securing permission to use other sites for the organization's programs?	
3. What experience and/or training is required of the leader?	
4. What are the eligibility requirements for participation?	
5. What is the staff–participant ratio required?	
6. What safety regulations are participants and staff instructed to abide by?	
7. What safety procedures are participants required to follow when intermingling with the public?	
How are participants confined by these procedures?	
8. What emergency procedures are participants required to follow when visiting another site or facility?	
How are they informed of these procedures?	
9. How is permission obtained for medical services en route to, or at, another site?	
10. How and when is the physical condition of staff members and participants ascertained before departure and upon return?	
11. How are parents informed that participants are going to another site?	

Guidelines and Information to Help Complete the Plan

❑ The itinerary for an off-site trip should include departure and return times and destination routes taken. Safety procedures should include locations and responsibilities of staff while on the trip, what to do if separated from the group or approached by a stranger, and any precautions regarding the use of public transportation or of other public or privately owned facilities. Contact should be made in advance with the operator of the other site to establish whose emergency procedures to use and to whom participants and staff are responsible.

❑ If using contract services, such as contracted horseback riding at a nearby stable, it is suggested that safety procedures be written into the contract, along with the expected number of qualified instructors, safety of equipment, and insurance coverage requirements. Staff members accompanying participants should have written procedures specifying any supervisory roles and responsibilities.

Appendix

Glossary of Legal Terms

Acquittal: A release, absolution, or discharge of an obligation or liability. In criminal law, the finding of not guilty.

Ad litem: A person who is appointed to bring suit or defend a suit for someone who lacks the legal capacity.

Attractive nuisance: Negligence for leaving a piece of equipment or other condition on the property that would be both attractive and dangerous to curious children. These items have included tractors, unguarded swimming pools, open pits, and abandoned refrigerators. Liability could be placed on the people owning or controlling the premises, even when the child was a trespasser who sneaked onto the property.

Assumption of risk: A doctrine under which a person may not recover for an injury received when he has voluntarily exposed himself to a known danger.

Burden of proof: In the law of evidence, the necessity or duty of affirmatively proving a fact or facts in dispute on an issue raised between the parties in a lawsuit. In a criminal case, the prosecution must prove each element of the crime "beyond a reasonable doubt" to establish the defendant's guilt. In a civil case, it is the responsibility of a plaintiff in a lawsuit to provide evidence supporting the claim against a defendant.

Civil: Relating to private rights and remedies sought by civil actions, as contrasted with criminal proceedings.

Class action: A lawsuit brought by one or more persons on behalf of a larger group.

Complaint: The legal document that usually begins a civil lawsuit. It states the facts and identifies the action the court is asked to take or the formal written charge that a person has committed a criminal offense.

Contributory fault: A method of apportioning an award for damages depending on what percent the jury determines is the fault of the injured party.

Damages: Money awarded by a court to a person injured by the unlawful act or negligence of another person.

Discovery period: The time allowed the insured after the termination of a policy to discover a loss that occurred during the period covered.

Doctrine of respondent superior: The corporate entity being accountable for the actions of employees (or volunteers) if they are acting within the scope of their responsibility and authority.

Doctrine of in loco parentis (in place of the parent): The corporate entity or an individual assumes the rights, duties, and responsibilities of the parents in regard to conduct and discipline of the child.

Exculpatory: Clauses that purport to waive the right of an injured party to recover damages due to negligence.

Expert witness: A person who is recognized as a professional or specialist who appears in court to explain and testify about matters related to his expertise.

Indemnification: Hold-harmless clauses or provisions shift the responsibility for payment of damages to someone else by contract.

Indictment: A written accusation of a crime that has been submitted to the grand jury to determine if sufficient reason exists for believing that a crime has been committed and that the accused committed it. If probable cause is discovered, the person will be indicted and arraigned.

Inherent risks: Risks that are such an integral part of an activity that they cannot be removed without changing the basic nature of the activity.

Intentional tort: Wrong perpetrated by one who intends to break the law.

Liable: Legally responsible.

Loss ratio: A percentage figure arrived at by dividing the dollar amount of the claims paid by the premium collected.

Negligence: Careless conduct that produces foreseeable results, causing injury or property loss.

Nonfeasance: Nonperformance of an act that should be performed; failure to perform a required duty or total neglect of duty.

Probable cause: A reasonable belief that a crime has or is being committed; the basis for all lawful searches, seizures, and arrests.

Proximate cause: The last negligent act that contributes to an injury. A person generally is liable only if an injury was proximately caused by his action or by his failure to act when he had a duty to act.

Punitive damages: Money award given to punish the defendant or wrongdoer.

Reasonable doubt: An accused person is entitled to acquittal if, in the minds of the jury, his or her guilt has not been proved beyond a "reasonable doubt"; the state of mind of jurors in which they cannot say they feel an abiding conviction as to the truth of the charge.

Reasonable and prudent person: A phrase used to denote a hypothetical person who exercises qualities of attention, knowledge, intelligence, and judgment that society requires of its members for the protection of their own interest and the interests of others. Thus, the test of negligence is based on either a failure to do something that a reasonable and prudent (wise) person, guided by considerations that ordinarily regulate conduct, would do, or on the doing of something that a reasonable and prudent person would not do.

Risk-financing techniques: Methods to retain the loss and determine how to finance it or transfer the cost to another party or all the ways of generating funds to pay for losses that risk-control techniques do not entirely prevent.

Risk-control techniques: Methods to reduce, eliminate, or minimize the risk of loss.

Slander: Spoken defamation that tends to injure a person's reputation.

Standard of care: "The way it ought to be done." The degree of care or prudence practitioners of the same specialty would utilize under similar conditions. The standard of care may be established by common practice, statute, or specialty boards or organizations.

Tort: A private or civil wrong or injury for which the court provides a remedy through an action for damages.

Waiver: A clause that asks a person to intentionally give up a right.

APPENDIX 2

Policy Manual Checklist

The following is a list of suggested policies and related worksheets

Check all that have been completed			
Policies		Worksheet(s)	Date revised
Administration			
	Mailing list	O-21, O-26, Appendix 10, 26	
	Media releases	O-1, O-9, P-1	
	Owned or rented/leased vehicles	O-23, P-50	
	Policy manual	O-21, Appendix 2	
	Record management and retention policy	O-21, P-38	
	Releasing personal information	O-9, O-21, O14 , O-26 P 32, P 38, P45	
	Reporting of accidents/incidences	O-35, P-43 Appendix 6	
	Serving alcohol	O-24	
	Storage and handling of hazardous materials	O-15, P-29	
	Use of organizational property/equipment	O-23, P-23 P 50	
Board			
	Authority of board	O-11	
	Conflict-of-interest policy	O-11, O-12, O-22, Appendix 5	
	Removal of board members	O-11	
Financial			
	Audit by an independent accountant	O-22	
	Authority to commit funds/sign checks	O-22, P-41	
	Business interruption	O-13, P-21	
	Cash receipts and disbursements	O-22, P-41	
	Competitive bids	O-22	
	Fixed assets and inventory	O-22	
	Fundraising	O-24, O-26	
	Gifts	Appendix 9	
	Internal controls	O-22	
	Insurance	O-19 P 34	
	Investment	O-22	
	Line of credit	O-22	

Policies	Worksheet(s)	Date revised
Method of accounting	O-22	
Monthly financial statements	O-22	
Petty cash	P-41	
Product sales	O-24, O 33	
Purchase orders	O-22	
Refunds	O-22, O-27, P-37, P-41, P-40	
Reimbursements	O-22, P-41	
Restricted contributions	O-24	
Unrestricted contributions	O-24	
Write-off of accounts received	O-22	
Healthcare		
Dispensing medications	P-33	
Scope and limits of healthcare	P-31	
Human Relations		
Business use of privately owned vehicles	O-23, , P-50	
Discrimination in hiring	O-29	
Disqualification of applicants/volunteers /employees	O-29, P-54, P56	
Drug, alcohol, smoking policies	P-53	
Harassment—sexual or other types (bullying)	O-30, P-52, P-53, P-59	
Personnel policies	O-28, O-29, O-32, P-52, P-53, P-54, P 55 P-56, P59	
Security	O-10, O-25, P8	
Screening, criminal background checks	O-29,O-28, P-38, P-54, P-55	
Technological equipment usage policy	O-19, O-26, P-53, Appendix 26,27	
Youth Program Services		
Bullying	P-52, P53	
Child abuse prevention and reporting	P-52, P53P-60	
Drugs and alcohol	P-53	
Incident report	O-35, P-43	
Inclusion and reasonable accommodations, nondiscrimination	O-17, P-27	
Parent notification	P-9, P48	
Participant conduct, discipline, and dismissal; corporal punishment	P-49, P-52, P-53, P-57, Appendix	
Participant supervision	P-52	

	Policies	Worksheet(s)	Date revised
	Personal property	P-53	
	Privacy policy	O-21, O-24, O-26, Appendix	
	Program consistent with purpose	O-24	
	Safety policy	O-4, O-11, O-13, O-14, O15,O16, O-26, O27, P-4, P-6, P-21, P-22, P28	
	Transporting participants and staff members	P-30	
	Dismissal of volunteers	P–56, Appendix 4, 30	
	Weapons	P-49	

APPENDIX 3

American Camp Association Standards and Risk-Management Worksheet Cross Reference

About the American Camp Association

The American Camp Association (ACA) is a community of camp professionals dedicated to ensuring the high quality of camp programs, a greater public understanding of and support for the value of the camp experience, and an increase in the number of children, youth, and adults of all social, cultural, and economic groups who participate in the camp experience. Established in 1910, ACA operates as a private, nonprofit educational organization with members in all 50 states and several foreign countries. Its members represent a diverse constituency of camp owners and directors, executives, educators, clergy, businesses, consultants, camp and organization staff members, volunteers, students, retirees, and other individuals associated with the operation of camps for children and adults.

The services provided by ACA include educational programs and conferences, accreditation services, networking, monitoring of legislation at the federal and state levels, *Camping Magazine*, public relations efforts, and an on-line bookstore providing educational resources related to camping, conferencing, and outdoor education. ACA also serves as a consultant and advisor to many state and federal agencies in the field of camping and to colleges and universities in the fields of outdoor education and recreation.

The programs of the Association are administered through numerous local sections. Members belong to the national organization and to a local section responsible for delivering services, including the accreditation programs. Section and national officers are elected by the membership and serve without pay. The organization is supported primarily by the dues and contributions of its members. Other support comes from conference fees, the sale of publications, project grants, and fees for services.

The ACA community of camps promote active participation, caring relationships, and focus on the emotional, social, spiritual, and physical growth of an individual. Camps vary in their purpose and desired outcomes, but each encourages risk taking, valuing the resources of the natural world, healthy lifestyles, and learning through a variety of fun and life-changing experiences.

Because of our diverse membership and exceptional programs, children and adults have the opportunity to learn powerful lessons in community, character building, skill development, and healthy living. As a leading authority in child development, the ACA works to preserve, promote, and improve the camp experience.

Worksheet	Organizational Crisis Management	ACA Standard(s)
O-1	Who is in Charge Where?	
O-2	Emergency Phone Numbers	See program worksheet
O-3	Agency Emergency Contacts	
O-4	Emergency Procedures for Hazards and/or Disasters—Office	OM-8
O-5	Emergency Procedures for Office Evacuation and Fires	
O-6	Utilities—Office	SF-5, SF-6
O-7	First Aid/CPR and Exposure to Bloodborne Pathogens—Office	SF-17, see program worksheet
O-8	Death of a Participant, Volunteer, Staff Member, or Family Member	OM-1
O-9	Emergency Media Plan	
O-10	Report of Alleged Child Abuse	
Worksheet	**Organizational Management**	**ACA Standard(s)**
O-11	Legal Liabilities o f Trustees/Directors	OM-1
O-12	Legal Counsel	SF-7, SF-8, SF-11, SF-19
O-13	Office/Site Hazards	SF-2
O-14	Office Operations, Maintenance, and Fire Prevention and Safety	
O-15	Storage And Handling of Hazardous, Flammable, or Poisonous Materials	OM-1
O-16	Food Handling and Foodborne Illness	OM-1, OM-9
O-17	Serving Persons With Disabilities	OM-9
O-18	Insurance Coverage	OM-9
O-19	Reevaluating Insurance	
O-20	Insurance Safety Audit for Organization-Owned Sites	OM-1
O-21	Record Retention and Destruction	
O-22	Operational Financial Risks	OM-1
O-23	Business Use of Vehicles and Driver Authorization and Responsibility	OM-1
O-24	Fundraising and Special Events	
O-25	Security	OM-1
O-26	Technological Usage and Record Security	
O-27	Contracts for Services	OM-1, OM-18, OM-19
O-28	Screening of Staff And Volunteers	
O-29	Employment Practices	HR-8
O-30	Harassment—Sexual and Other	
O-31	Complaints	
O-32	Supervision of Staff	
O-33	Product Tampering	

Worksheet	Organizational Management	ACA Standard(s)
O-34	Intellectual Property, Copyrights, and Royalties	
O-35	Incident Report	
O-36	Risk-Reduction Analyses	OM-3
Worksheet	Program Crisis Management	ACA Standard(s)
P-1	Who is in Charge Where?	
P-2	Emergency Phone Numbers	SF-3, HW-1, HW-3
P-3	Agency Emergency Contacts	
P-4	Emergency Procedures for Hazards and/or Disasters	OM-7, OM-8
P-5	Utilities	SF-5, SF-6
P-6	Firefighting and Other Emergency Equipment and Procedures	SF-12
P-7	Emergency Communication	OM-1, OM-15
P-8	Security	OM-6, OM-17
P-9	Parent Contact	HW-19
P-10	Missing Persons	OM-8, OM-14
P-11	Diversion Activities	
P-12	Site Evacuation	SF-1, OM-7
P-13	Participant and Staff Whereabouts	OM-8
P-14	Emergency On-Site Transportation	TR-1
P-15	Transportation Emergencies	TR-3, TR-4, TR-5, TR-6, TR-7, TR-8, TR-9, TR-10, TR-11, TR-14–18
P-16	First Aid	HW-1, HW-13, HW-17, HW-23, HW-24, HW-25
P-17	Exposure to Bloodborne Pathogens	SF-17
P-18	Insect- and Rodent-Transmitted Diseases	OM-1, HW-13
P-19	Youth Suicide and Self Mutilation	
P-20	Death of a Participant, Volunteer, Staff Member, or Family Member	OM-1
Worksheet	Program Management	ACA Standard(s)
P-21	Program Site Hazard Identification—Natural and Man-Made	SF-2, SF-9, SF-16, OM-1
P-22	Site Operations And Maintenance	OM-1, SF-7, SF-8, SF-9, SF-10, SF-11, SF-19, SF-21
P-23	Property Use and Liability	OM-18, OM-19
P-24	Safe Water Supply	SF-4, SF-17, SF-18
P-25	Notification of Operation	SF-3
P-26	Fire Prevention and Safety	SF-1, SF-12, SF-13, SF-14, SF-15, SF-16
P-27	Serving Persons With Disabilities	OM-1, HW-15

Worksheet	Program Management	ACA Standard(s)
P-28	Food Handling and Foodborne Illness	OM-1, SF-19, SF-20, SF-22, SF-23, SF-24, 2F-25, SF-26, SF-27
P-29	Storage and Handling of Hazardous, Flammable, or Poisonous Materials	SF-2
P-30	Transporting Participants and Staff Members	TR-6, TR-7, TR-8, TR-9, TR-10, TR-11, TR-12, TR-13, TR-14, TR-15, TR-16, TR-17, TR-18
P-31	Health Services and Supervision	HW-11, HW-3, HW-12, HW-15, HW-16, HW-17, HW-18
P-32	Health Screening and Records	HW-2, HW-5, HW-6, HW-8, HW-10, HW-19, HW-21
P-33	Personal Medications	HW-3, HW-12, HW-16, HW-20
P-34	Insurance Safety Audit for Organization-Owned Sites	
P-35	Federal, State, and Local Laws, Ordinances, Codes, and Regulations	
P-36	Interstate and International Laws	
P-37	Waivers, Permissions, and Agreements for Participation	HW-7, PD-11
P-38	Program Record Retention and Destruction	HW-3, HW-22
P-39	Intellectual Property Infringements, Copyrights, and Royalties	
P-40	Contracts for Services	OM-1, OM-18, OM-19
P-41	Operational Financial Risks	OM-1
P-42	Participant Risk-Reduction Analyses	OM-3, OM-4, OM-13
P-43	Incident Report	TR-7, OM-13
P-44	Emergency Drills	
P-45	Participant Information, Registration, Check-In, and Check-Out	OM-1, OM-1, HW-5
P-46	Drop-In Programs	
P-47	Guests on the Site	
P-48	Parent Notification of Changes	HW-19
P-49	Weapons and Firearms	OM-1, OM-2, OM-10
P-50	Business Use of Vehicles and Driver Authorization and Responsibility	TR-12, OM-1
P-51	Complaints	
P-52	Participant Supervision Plan	OM-8, OM-16, HR-9, HR-14, HR-15, HR-16, HR-17
P-53	Conduct of Participants and Staff Members	HR-15, HR-16, OM-1, OM-8, OM-10, OM-11

Worksheet	Program Management	ACA Standard(s)
P-54	Screening of Staff Members and Volunteers	PD-14, PD-15, PD-17, HR-4a, HR-18, HR-19, HR-20
P-55	Staff Selection and Training for Emergencies	OM-12, HW-13
P-56	Employment Practices	HR-3, HR-8, HR-10, HR-21
P-57	Staff Training	HR-7, HR-12, HR-13, PD-16, OM-12, OM-16
P-58	Supervision of Staff	PD-14, PD-15, PD-17, HR-18, HR-19, HR-20
P-59	Harassment—Sexual And Other	HR-8
P-60	Preventing Child Abuse	HR-11, HR-15
P-61	Activities Requiring Staff Members With Specialized Training or Certification	PD-19
P-62	Weather and/or Environmental Health Effects on the Program	OM-1
P-63	Participants in Off-Site Field Trips or Excursions	PD-1

APPENDIX 4

Sample Legal Compliance Checklist for 501(c)(3) Nonprofits

Excerpt from *Non-Profit Legal Toolkit*, a publication of Texas C-Bar. Used with permission. Based in part on materials prepared by the National Economic Development and Law Center in Oakland, CA.

The following checklist is distributed for informational purposes only and should not be construed as legal services to any organization or individual. The checklist should be used as a starting point for a nonprofit to evaluate whether it is following Texas and federal reporting requirements and laws. Some of the items listed are not mandated by law but are sound business practices that an organization should follow to help ensure that it avoids problems. Numerous other laws and reporting requirements exist that a nonprofit may have to comply with that are not included in this checklist.

Monitoring by the Board

❑ The corporation provides each director and officer with a copy of the organization's articles of incorporation and bylaws.

❑ The corporation assigns the responsibility for meeting all filing and reporting requirements to appropriate directors and staff.

❑ The board or a board committee regularly determines that all filing and reporting requirements have been met in a timely manner, or that appropriate and timely corrective action has been taken.

Personnel/Employment

❑ The corporation has applied for and been assigned a federal identification number by the Internal Revenue Service (IRS).

❑ The corporation complies with the reporting requirements of their state.

❑ The corporation withholds federal income taxes and federal social security and Medicare taxes from taxable wages paid to employees, pays the employer share of taxes, and deposits all such funds in a timely manner and with the appropriate IRS forms.

❑ The corporation maintains personnel records for at least four years.

❑ The corporation obtains a completed IRS Form I-9 and Form W-4 from all new employees.

❑ The corporation furnishes each employee with a completed IRS Form W-2 by January 31 for the previous calendar year.

❑ The corporation files quarterly wage reports (IRS Form 941) with the IRS.

❑ The corporation posts or provides to its employees the required employment notices, including notices and posters required by the state, EEOC, OSHA, and U.S. Department of Labor.

❑ The corporation complies with wage and hours laws, workplace safety laws, and nondiscrimination laws (including Title VII and the Americans with Disabilities Act).

❑ The corporation complies with its employee benefit plan requirements.

❑ The corporation has adopted an updated personnel policy manual and complies with the personnel policies and procedures contained in the manual.

❑ The corporation complies with the IRS rules governing the status of independent contractors, prepares proper documentation of all independent contractor agreements, and reports compensation to independent contractors on IRS Form 1099 MISC.

❑ The corporation provides to each employee from whom the organization did not withhold any income tax a notice about the Earned Income Tax Credit, by providing the employee with IRS Notice 797.

Federal Tax and Financial Filings and Reports

❑ The corporation files annual tax information returns (IRS Form 990 or 990-EZ). If the organization has unrelated business income, it files IRS Form 990-T.

❑ The corporation obtains an annual financial audit from an independent auditor and, if required by federal funding sources, the organization obtains an A-133 audit.

❑ The corporation engages legal counsel to conduct an annual review of its past year's operations and coming year's proposed operations to identify any conflicts and inconsistencies with the information previously provided to the IRS, and for an opinion on whether the corporation is or will be engaged in unrelated business activity.

❑ The corporation complies with IRS disclosure, substantiation, and reporting requirements for charitable contributions received.

❑ The corporation observes the IRS prohibition on political campaign activities.

❑ For corporations within the IRS advance ruling period, the organization conducts an annual review to determine its compliance with public charity status requirements and obtains a final ruling on its public charity status from the IRS in a timely manner.

❑ The corporation observes the limitations on lobbying activities and maintains appropriate records to document its lobbying expenditures and activities.

❑ If the corporation has an employee benefit plan, the organization makes annual benefit plan filings (IRS Form 5500) as required.

Other Filings and Reports

❑ The corporation has applied for and maintains the appropriate property tax exemptions with the county assessor.

❑ The corporation has obtained a nonprofit mailing permit to use special bulk postal rates.

Liability Protection

❑ The corporation understands the policy limits of insurance policies, including: the events covered, exclusions, amount of coverage, deductibles, whether policies are "occurrence" or "claims made" policies, and any gaps in coverage.

❑ The corporation maintains appropriate commercial general liability insurance, with reasonable exclusions and limitations, with coverage for the acts and omissions of the organization and its employees and volunteers in the amount of at least $500,000 for each person, $1,000,000 for each single occurrence for death or bodily injury, and $100,000 for each single occurrence for injury to, or the destruction of, property.

❑ The corporation maintains appropriate bonding for those persons who handle its funds, with reasonable limitations and exclusions.

❑ The corporation maintains, as applicable, errors and omissions or other professional liability insurance, with reasonable exclusions and limitations.

❑ The corporation maintains appropriate Directors and Officers liability insurance, with reasonable exclusions and limitations, or annually reviews the affordability of such insurance.

❑ The corporation maintains appropriate property and automobile insurance, with reasonable limitations and exclusions.

❑ The corporation maintains appropriate workers' compensation insurance, with reasonable limitations and exclusions.

❏ The corporation maintains appropriate employment practices liability coverage, with reasonable limitations and exclusions.

❏ The corporation has copies of executed waivers of liability for volunteers and clients.

❏ The corporation has adopted policies and procedures to modify risks and monitors their implementation.

❏ The corporation promptly advises insurance companies of facts that could give rise to claims in accordance with notice provisions of the policies.

Operations

❏ The corporation has selected a bank after comparing and negotiating rates and fees.

❏ The corporation has authorized at least two persons as check signers.

❏ The corporation appropriately invests its assets that are held for investment.

❏ The corporation maintains an up-to-date copy of its articles of incorporation, bylaws, 501(c)(3) tax exemption application and determination letter, and franchise tax exemption letter from the state and keeps a copy at its principal office.

❏ The corporation has obtained a sales tax exemption from the state.

❏ The corporation has obtained other federal, state, or local licenses as required for its activities.

❏ The corporation prepares and maintains for at least three years adequate and correct books and records of accounts, including records relating to all income and expenditures, and prepares or approves an annual report of financial activity.

❏ The corporation, unless it falls under a state statutory exception, makes all of its financial records available to members of the public for inspection.

❏ The corporation prepares and maintains minutes of board, committee, and member meetings for a minimum of three calendar years following the end of the fiscal year.

❏ The corporation maintains copies of notices of board and member meetings, written waivers of notice, consents to votes taken without a meeting, and approvals of all minutes.

❏ The corporation maintains copies of written director and officer resignations, proxies, and similar documents.

❑ The corporation maintains an alphabetized list of members (if any), with name, address, and class of membership.

❑ The corporation makes available for public inspection a copy of its federal tax exemption application, IRS tax exemption determination letter, and IRS Forms 990 from the previous three years, and provides a copy on request.

❑ The corporation complies with its bylaws, including the provisions on the terms of directors, election of officers, quorums, and obtaining approval for certain actions. The corporation holds all meetings it is required to hold and provides proper notice of meetings.

❑ The corporation has at least three directors, and has two different directors serving as president and secretary.

Transactions

❑ The corporation maintains a procurement policy to ensure that purchases are at a fair market value or are otherwise favorable to the organization and, if applicable, the corporation complies with federal procurement standards.

❑ The corporation maintains a financial system that requires receipt of written invoices prior to payment for any services or goods.

❑ The corporation conducts appropriate investigations to ascertain that loans, leases, and other transactions are at fair market value or are otherwise favorable to the corporation.

❑ The corporation prepares appropriate documentation in support of all transactions with directors, officers, or other insiders, and to demonstrate the reasonableness of all compensation.

❑ The corporation has adopted a conflict-of-interest policy for transactions and meets all requirements for approval of transactions involving a conflict of interest, including transactions with organizations under its control.

❑ The corporation engages legal counsel to review proposed contracts and agreements, corporate obligations to perform acts that might jeopardize its tax exempt status, and whether appropriate safeguards are in place to assure that corporate funds granted to other organizations are being used for tax exempt purposes.

❑ The corporation receives the benefits of, and meets its obligations under, all leases, loans, contracts, partnerships, joint ventures, and similar agreements.

IRS Sample Conflict-of-Interest Policy

[Insert the organization's name]

A. Article I

Purpose

The purpose of the conflict–of-interest policy is to protect the organization's interest when it is contemplating entering into a transaction or arrangement that might benefit the private interest of an officer or director of the organization.

B. Article II

Definitions

1. Interested Person: Any director, principal officer, or member of a committee with board-delegated powers who has a direct or indirect financial interest, as defined in Article II, Section 2.

2. Financial Interest: A person has a financial interest if he has, directly or indirectly, through business, investment, or family:

> a. An ownership or investment interest in any entity with which the organization has a transaction or arrangement, or
>
> b. A compensation arrangement with the organization or with any entity or individual with which the organization has a transaction or arrangement, or
>
> c. A potential ownership or investment interest in, or compensation arrangement with, any entity or individual with which the organization is negotiating a transaction or arrangement.

Compensation includes direct and indirect remuneration, as well as gifts or favors that are substantial in nature. A financial interest is not necessarily a conflict of interest. Under Article III, Section 2, a person who has a financial interest may have a conflict of interest only if the appropriate board or committee decides that a conflict of interest exists.

C. Article III

Procedures

1. Duty to Disclose: In connection with any actual or possible conflicts of interest, an interested person must disclose the existence of his financial interest and must be given the opportunity to disclose all

material facts to the directors and members of committees with board-delegated powers considering the proposed transaction or arrangement.

2. Determining Whether a Conflict of Interest Exists: After disclosure of the financial interest and all material facts, and after any discussion with the interested person, he shall leave the board or committee meeting while the determination of a conflict of interest is discussed and voted upon. The remaining board or committee members shall decide if a conflict of interest exists.

3. Procedures for Addressing the Conflict of Interest: When it has been determined under Section 2 that a conflict of interest exists, the board or committee will then evaluate the particular transaction or arrangement.

a. An interested person may make a presentation at the board or committee meeting, but after such presentation, he shall leave the meeting during the discussion of, and the vote on, the transaction or arrangement that results in the conflict of interest.

b. The chairperson of the board or committee shall, if appropriate, appoint a disinterested person or committee to investigate alternatives to the proposed transaction or arrangement.

c. After exercising due diligence, the board or committee shall determine whether the organization can obtain a more advantageous transaction or arrangement with reasonable efforts from a person or entity that would not give rise to a conflict of interest.

d. If a more advantageous transaction or arrangement is not reasonably attainable under circumstances that would not give rise to a conflict of interest, the board or committee shall determine by a majority vote of the disinterested directors whether the transaction or arrangement is in the organization's best interest and for its own benefit and whether the transaction is fair and reasonable to the organization and shall make its decision as to whether to enter into the transaction or arrangement in conformity with such determination.

4. Violations of the Conflict-of-Interest Policy

a. If the board or committee has reasonable cause to believe that a member has failed to disclose actual or possible conflicts of interest, it shall inform the member of the basis for such belief and afford the member an opportunity to explain the alleged failure to disclose.

b. If, after hearing the response of the member and making such further investigation as may be warranted in the circumstance, the board or committee determines that the member has in fact failed to disclose an actual or possible conflict of interest, it shall take appropriate disciplinary and corrective action.

D. Article IV

Records of Proceedings

The minutes of the board and all committees with board-delegated powers shall contain:

1. The names of the persons who disclosed or otherwise were found to have a financial interest in connection with an actual or possible conflict of interest, the nature of the financial interest, any action taken to determine whether a conflict of interest was present, and the board's or committee's decision as to whether a conflict of interest in fact existed

2. The names of the persons who were present for discussions and votes relating to the transaction or arrangement, the content of the discussion, including any alternatives to the proposed transaction or arrangement, and a record of any votes taken in connection therewith

E. Article V

Compensation Committee

A voting member of the board or a voting member of any committee whose jurisdiction includes compensation matters and who receives compensation, directly or indirectly, from the organization for services is precluded from voting on matters pertaining to that member's compensation.

F. Article VI

Annual Statements

Each director, principal officer, and member of a committee with board-delegated powers shall annually sign a statement that affirms that such person:

1. Has received a copy of the conflicts of interest policy

2. Has read and understands the policy

3. Has agreed to comply with the policy

4. Understands that the organization is a charitable organization and that to maintain its federal tax exemption, it must engage primarily in activities that accomplish one or more of its tax-exempt purposes.

In addition, each director, principal officer, and member of a committee with board-designed powers shall list his business affiliations, including memberships on boards of other nonprofit institutions, and shall also disclose any business relationships that members of his family have or are seeking with the organization. He shall also update the statement as appropriate during the year.

G. Article VII

Periodic Reviews

To ensure that the organization operates in a manner consistent with its charitable purposes and that it does not engage in activities that could jeopardize its status as an organization exempt from federal income tax, periodic reviews shall be conducted. The periodic reviews shall at a minimum include the following subjects:

1. Whether compensation arrangements and benefits are reasonable and are the result of arm's length bargaining.

2. Whether any partnership and joint venture arrangements, and arrangements with management service organizations, conform to written policies, are properly recorded, reflect reasonable payments for goods and services, further the organization's charitable purposes, and do not result in inurement or impermissible private benefit.

In conducting these periodic reviews, the organization may, but need not, use outside advisors. If outside experts are used, their use shall not relieve the board of its responsibility for ensuring that periodic reviews are conducted.

APPENDIX 5A

Conflicts-of-Interest Disclosure Statement

[Insert the organization's name]

I, as a director, officer, or member of a committee with board-designated powers, affirm that:

- I have received a copy of the organization's Conflict-of-Interest Policy
- I have read and understood the Policy
- I agree to comply with the Policy
- I understand that the organization is a charitable organization, and that to maintain its federal tax exemption, it must engage primarily in activities that accomplish one or more of its tax-exempt purposes.

My business affiliations, including employment and memberships on any boards of directors of for-profit and nonprofit organizations, are as follows:

To the best of my knowledge, none of my family members has or is seeking any business relationship with the organization that could present a conflict of interest, except as noted below:

I agree to update this form as appropriate.

_____

Signature

_____

Name Printed

_____

Date

APPENDIX 6

Sample Accident/Incident Report

Date:

Program/event:

Does this report contain sensitive information?   Yes   No

Complet a report for each person involved:

Last Name			First Name		Middle Name/Initial	
Age	Sex	Role or Status at Event (check one):	Staff	Youth Participant	Volunteer	Other (specify)
Parent/Guardian (if minor)					Phone #	
Address						
Date of Accident/ Incident	Time of Day	Type of Accident/ Incident:	Behavioral	Accident	Illness	Other: (specify)
Name(s) adults on the scene:						
Name of adult(s) rendering aid:						
On-site health services used:						
Doctor or outside medical services used:						
Parent Signed Authorization used:						
Were emergency or law-enforcement services called?						
On-Site Notification and Witnesses						

Notified	Position	Name	Time	Who contacted this person?
	Program Supervisor			
	Program Director/Administrator			
	Health supervisor			
	Other staff members or volunteers			

Witness's Name	Phone
Address	

Witness's Name	Phone
Address	

Others:

Off-Site Notification (see procedures for agency notification)						
Check all that apply:	Titles	Notified	Name	Date	Time	Who contacted this person?
	Executive Director					
	Board President /Board Member					
	Parent or Guardian					
	Emergency Contact					
	Legal Council					
	OSHA (when required)					
	Spokesperson					
	Other:					
	Insurance Company					

Notification	Accident Insurance	Date	Worker's Compensation	Date
Claim forms completed by:				
Forms given to:				

Description of Incident: Describe in detail, but give only known facts; use additional pages if needed.

1. Sequence of activity (e.g., at the end of the activity, at meal time, at the beginning of the swimming lesson, during leisure time). What had proceeded the incident in terms of types of activities?

2. Location (e.g., where did the incident occur in the activity space in relation to instructor/supervisor and other participants?) A diagram is frequently helpful.

3. Exactly what was the person involved doing and how did the incident occur?
What was going on? Who was involved?

4. Procedure followed in rendering aid (e.g., what help was secured, if any).

5. It may be helpful to note the response of the involved person. Is he calm,
crying, mad, out of control, dazed? Was he supportive of what was being done
in responding to the accident/incident?

6. Disposition of case (e.g., Was the person sent home? Was he hospitalized?
Did he return? Were law enforcement officers called?)

Follow-up required:

Person(s) completing all or part of this report:

Name	Position	Signature	Date

Person(s) completing the disposition or follow-up portion of this report:

Name	Position	Signature	Date

APPENDIX 6A

Accident/Incident Report Instructions

The purpose of the accident/incident report is to document what has happened during an accident or incident. This information is needed for a variety of reasons.

- To encourage individuals to think through these various steps during an accident/incident

- To inform a supervisor of accidents/incidents and how they were handled

- As documentation that proper procedures were followed during an accident/incident

- To document everything that occurred before, during, and after an accident/incident.

- To develop information to help the organization prevent similar accidents/incidents in the future

- To document an illness that requires a participant be sent to a doctor or hospital

An *accident* is an unforeseen, unintended event that results in harm or injury to a person or to property.

An *incident* is an emergency or crisis that is often related to the behavior of people and may or may not be intentional or harm another person or property. Incidents include actions such as kidnapping, missing persons, harassment, intrusion, fighting, child abuse, theft, and drug or alcohol abuse.

An *emergency* involves danger and immediate potential of serious personal harm or property loss. When the danger is eliminated, the emergency is over. Once an emergency is over and the element of danger or the potential for additional harm or loss has subsided, the situation may still require crisis management.

A *crisis* is an unstable situation or crucial time or state of affairs that has reached a critical phase. A crisis may contain elements of danger or a dangerous condition but, until immediate potential of serious personal harm or property loss exists, it is not an emergency.

1. What accidents/incidents need to be reported?

Look at the purposes of this report. If an accident or incident would benefit from one of the purposes listed, then complete an accident/incident report.

2. When do I need to do what with the report?

The report should be completed as soon as possible. In many cases, some distinct advantages exist for having the form during the accident/incident and following the contact procedures and noting the times on this form as you are notifying the people listed. In any case, the report should be completed within 24 hours of the accident/incident. Once you have completed the report, give the report to a supervisor. It is the responsibility of the supervisor to decide the disposition of the report.

3. Who completes the report?

Much of the report can be completed by the on-site supervisor (e.g., leader, camp director, program director, event chair). It is imperative that the person most directly involved with the accident/incident write the page that describes in detail the accident/incident. A program administrator (i.e., a paid staff person) can finish the form, especially any follow-up that needs to occur. In any case, the program administrator needs to review the information on the form with the person most directly involved with the accident/incident.

4. What's the difference between adults and witnesses on the scene?

"Adults on the scene" should be the responsible adults (not the name of the person involved, even if that person was the supervisor and/or an adult) who supervised the program/event or who gave first aid or other assistance. "Other Witnesses on the Scene" might be other adults who gave assistance and/or adults or youth who saw what happened. It is okay to attach a page with additional names and addresses.

5. How detailed do I need to be in the attached description?

The level of detail needed would depend on the severity of the accident/incident. Always remember that more information is better (especially if potential exists for a lawsuit down the line). But remember, incident reports can be subpoenaed for legal evidence, so information should relate only to the facts, not what should or could have been done or any statement placing blame on any party. Be sure that the person who writes the detailed description signs and prints his name and gives his position or title on the detailed description.

6. What if the incident or information is sensitive or confidential?

If the information is confidential (e.g., in the case of child abuse: the victim, the accuser, and the accused perpetrator), this report might have "John Doe" as the name of the person involved. The actual who, what, when, where, why, and how are to be written in the detailed description, which is to be attached to the report form. Circle yes next to "Sensitive Information" at the top of the report, place the report in an envelope marked confidential, and give it to your supervisor or the Executive Director. This procedure ensures that the information is documented, yet confidential.

APPENDIX 7

Sample Waiver and/or Release Forms

(These forms are only samples and should be reviewed by the organization's legal counsel for consistency with state law.)

Parent/Legal Guardian Permission Form

I have read the _____ program information provided and understand the nature of the activities and the health and safety measures. I give permission for my child to attend and participate in activities on and off the program site.

I understand and agree to cooperate with all regulations and procedures, and I waive any claims against _____ [the organization], except for claims arising from gross negligence or willful acts of the organization or its agents that may arise from participation in the activities of the organization.

I understand that reasonable measures will be taken to safeguard the health and safety of all participants and that I will be notified as soon as possible in case of any emergency affecting my child (or ward). In the event that I cannot be reached in an emergency, I hereby give permission to the physician selected by the director to secure and administer whatever emergency medical or surgical treatment is necessary. I accept responsibility for the cost of such medical treatments.

I consent to the taking and use of any slides, photographs, or videotaping during the program, whether for advertising, promotion, or publicity purposes by _____ [the organization] and waive all claims for any compensation for such use or for damage.

Parent or Guardian's Signature
_____ Date _____

(*If medical personnel are available on the program site, the following sentence may be added prior to paragraph 3.*)

I hereby give permission to the medical personnel selected by the director to provide routine healthcare and to release any records necessary for insurance purposes.

Photo Release Form

I consent to the taking and use of any slides, photographs, or videotaping of myself and/or my child during the program for advertising, promotion, publicity, or any other lawful purposes by _____ [the organization] now or in the future, whether that use is known to me or unknown. I waive any right to inspect or approve the photographs or electronic matter and waive any right to royalties or other compensation arising from, or related to the use of, the photographs.

Parent or Guardian's Signature
_____ Date _____

APPENDIX 7A

Consent Form for a Trip Away From the Regular Program Site

[Insert the organization's name, address, and contact number]

Date: _____

Dear Parent/Guardian:

Our program is planning to go on a trip to: _____

Date of Trip _____ Time of Departure _____

Place of Departure _____

Time of Return _____ Place of Return _____

Cost of Trip _____ Food _____ Misc. _____

Each participant should bring: _____

The adults accompanying the group are: _____

_____

The drivers are: _____

If there is any undue delay in getting home, I will get in touch with:

Name_____ Phone_____

The section at the bottom of this form must be signed and returned to me before your child goes on the trip. If there is any health condition that should be watched for while on the trip, please include a statement detailing the situation.

Leader's Signature _____ Phone _____

I am familiar with the proposed destination, _____,
the mode of transportation, the leadership accompanying the club, that all

drivers are licensed and at least 21 years old, and other circumstances of this activity. I certify that my child is in good health and can participate in all of the normal activities of the program. (State any exceptions below or on the back). I understand that reasonable measures will be taken to safeguard the health and safety of the participants and that I will be notified as soon as possible in case of an emergency. However, in the event of sickness or accident, I will not hold the program leaders or _____ [the organization] responsible. In case of sickness or accident, I authorize the calling of a doctor and/or the providing of other necessary medical services at my expense.

Child's Name _____

Parent or Legal Guardian's Signature _____

Phone _____ Address _____ Date _____

Person Other Than the Parent (for emergency use): _____

Phone _____ Address _____Relationship _____

APPENDIX 7B

Acknowledgment of Disclosure of Risk and Permission to Participate in an Organization Activity

Note: Parent or Guardian must execute a separate form for each child participating in an organization activity.

1. I certify that I am the parent and/or legal guardian of _____ [name of child] and am legally authorized to sign this document on my child's behalf.

2. I hereby authorize my child to participate in _____ [type of trip or nature of activity] sponsored by the _____ [organization name] and that will occur on _____ [date], and continue through _____ [date; complete if the activity requires more than a single day].

3. I acknowledge the risks associated with participation in this activity/program as explained in the brochure.

4. The following is a list, complete to the best of my knowledge, of my child's permanent and/or temporary disabilities as of this date, including allergies, that I believe may require special attention, auxiliary aids or services, or that may require removal of physical or communications barriers: _____

_____

5. The following are the auxiliary aids, services, and special attention that my child requires to engage in this activity, as well as the physical and/or communications barriers that I believe need to be removed for my child to participate in this activity:

_____

_____

6. I hereby represent and confirm that, to the best of my knowledge, my child suffers from no permanent and/or temporary physical or mental disability that requires any special attention, auxiliary aids or services, and/or removal of barriers except those set forth in paragraphs 4 and 5.

7. I acknowledge that I have carefully read this document, that I know and understand its content, and that I sign this document as parent or legal guardian of _____ [child's name] by my own free act.

8. I acknowledge that all information contained in this document is true and correct and that _____ [organization] and its

representatives have the right to rely upon the accuracy of this information. I also acknowledge that _____ [organization] has the right to reject my child from participation in this event if I fail or refuse to provide and acknowledge, by my signature, the accuracy of the information requested herein.

Signature of Parent or Legal Guardian _____

Date: _____

APPENDIX 7C

Sample Hold-Harmless Clauses

Sample Hold-Harmless Clause for Contract Work

_____ [name of contractor] agrees to indemnify and hold harmless the _____ [organization], its agents, employees, or any other person against loss or expense, including attorneys fees, by reason of the liability imposed by law upon the organization, except in cases of the organization's sole negligence, for damage because of bodily injury, including death at any time resulting therefrom, sustained by any person or persons, or on account of damage to property arising out of or in consequence of this agreement, whether such injuries to persons or damage to property are due or claim to be due to any passive negligence of the organization, its employees or agents, or any other person.

It is further understood and agreed that the contractor shall at the option of the _____ [organization] defend the _____ [organization] with appropriate counsel and shall further bear all costs and expenses, including the expense of counsel, in the defense of any suit arising hereunder.

Sample 1: Hold-Harmless Clause for Rental or Leasing of a Facility or Equipment

Lessee agrees to defend, indemnify, and hold harmless the leaser, and all of the officers, agents, and employees from and against any harm and/or claim made by a third party arising out of or in any way connected with lessee's actions and/or failure to act in respect to use of the facility or equipment, provided, however, that this agreement shall not extend to liabilities incurred from any negligent acts or omissions on the part of leaser and its officers, agents or employees.

Sample 2: Hold-Harmless Clause for Rental or Leasing of a Facility or Equipment

_____ agrees to indemnify and hold harmless _____, its officers, agents, and employees from and against every expense, including attorney's fees, liability, or payment by reason of any damages or injury to person (including death) or property (including loss of use or theft thereof) arising out of or in connection with the program, including use of occupancy of _____ property, facilities or equipment, provided that such damages or injury are caused in whole or in part by _____ its officer, agents, employees, or participants.

APPENDIX 7D

Sample Volunteer Release and Waiver of Liability

Please read carefully. This is a legal document that affects your legal rights.

This Release and Waiver of Liability executed on this _____ day of
_____, 20_____ by _____ (the
"Volunteer"), in favor of _____ [organization], a nonprofit corporation, their
directors, officers, employees, members of the boards of directors, and agents.

The Volunteer desires to work as a volunteer for _____ [organization]
and engage in the activities related to being a volunteer. The Volunteer
understands that the activities may include constructing and rehabilitating
structures or maintaining the grounds at its office, camp, or other program site,
working in the office, or assisting with youth program or community events.

**The volunteer hereby freely, voluntarily, and without duress executes
this release under the following terms:**

1. Release and Waiver. Volunteer does hereby release and forever discharge
and hold harmless _____ [organization] and its successors and assigns
from any and all liability, claims, and demands of whatever kind of nature,
either in law or in equity, which arise or may hereafter arise from volunteer's
activities with _____ [organization].

    Volunteer understands that this release discharges _____
[organization] from any liability claims that the Volunteer may have against
_____ [organization] with respect to any bodily injury, personal injury,
illness, death, or property damage that may result from Volunteer's activities
with _____ [organization], whether caused by the negligence of
_____ [organization] or its officers, directors, employees, members of
the board of directors, or otherwise. Volunteer also understands that
_____ [organization] does not assume any responsibility for or
obligation to provide financial assistance or other assistance, including but not
limited to medical, health, or disability insurance in the event of injury or illness.

2. Medical Treatment. Volunteer does hereby release and forever discharge
_____ [organization] from any claim whatsoever that arises or may
hereafter arise on account of any first aid, treatment, or service rendered in
connection with the Volunteer's activities with _____ [organization].

3. Assumption of the Risk. The Volunteer understands that the activities may
include work that may be hazardous to the volunteer, including, but not limited

to, construction, loading and unloading, and transportation to and from the work sites.

Volunteer hereby expressly and specifically assumes the risk of injury or harm in the activities and releases _____ [organization] from all liability for injury, illness, death, or property damage resulting from the activities.

4. Insurance. The Volunteer understands that, except as otherwise agreed to by _____ [organization], in writing, _____ [organization] does not carry or maintain health, medical, or disability insurance coverage for any volunteer.

Each Volunteer is expected and encouraged to obtain his or her own medical or health insurance coverage.

5. Photographic Release. Volunteer does hereby grant and convey into _____ [organization] all rights, titles, and interests in any and all photographic images and video or audio recordings made by _____ [organization], or on _____ [organization's] behalf, during Volunteer's activities with _____ [organization], including but not limited to, any royalties, proceeds, or other benefits derived from such photographs or recordings.

6. Other. Volunteer expressly agrees that this release is intended to be as broad and inclusive as permitted by the laws of the State of _____, and that this release shall be governed by and interpreted in accordance with the laws of the State of _____. Volunteer agrees that in the event that any clause or provision of this release shall be held to be invalid by any court of competent jurisdiction, the invalidity of such clause or provision shall not otherwise affect the remaining provisions of this release, which shall continue to be enforceable.

IN WITNESS WHEREOF, Volunteer has executed this Release as of the day and year first above written.

Witness: _____

       Volunteer: _____

       Address: _____

       _____

       Phone: _____(Home)

       _____(Other)

       Date: _____

APPENDIX 7E

Sample Volunteer Release and Waiver of Liability for Minors

Please read carefully. This is a legal document that affects your legal rights.

This Release and Waiver of Liability, (the "Release"), executed on this _____ day of _____, 20_____ by _____ (the "Volunteer"), in favor of _____, a nonprofit corporation, their directors, officers, employees, members of the boards of directors, and agents.

The volunteer desires to work as a volunteer for _____ [organization] and engage in the activities related to being a volunteer. The volunteer understands that the activities may include constructing and rehabilitating structures or maintaining the grounds at its office, camp, or other program site; working in the office; or assisting with youth program or community events.

The volunteer hereby freely, voluntarily, and without duress executes this release under the following terms:

1. Release and Waiver. Volunteer does hereby release and forever discharge and hold harmless _____ [organization] and its successors and assigns from any and all liability, claims, and demands of whatever kind of nature, either in law or in equity, which arise or may hereafter arise from Volunteer's activities with _____ [organization].

Volunteer understands that this release discharges _____ [organization] from any liability claims that Volunteer may have against _____ [organization] with respect to any bodily injury, personal injury, illness, death, or property damage that may result from Volunteer's activities with _____ [organization], whether caused by the negligence of _____ [organization] or its officers, directors, employees, members of the board of directors, or otherwise. Volunteer also understands that _____ [organization] does not assume any responsibility for or obligation to provide financial assistance or other assistance, including but not limited to medical, health, or disability insurance in the event of injury or illness.

2. Medical Treatment. Volunteer does hereby release and forever discharge _____ [organization] from any claim whatsoever that arises or may hereafter arise on account of any first aid, treatment, or service rendered in connection with the volunteer's activities with _____ [organization].

3. Assumption of the Risk. The volunteer understands that the activities may include work that may be hazardous to the volunteer, including, but not limited to, construction, loading and unloading, and transportation to and from the work sites.

Volunteer hereby expressly and specifically assumes the risk of injury or harm in the activities and releases _____ [organization] from all liability for injury, illness, death, or property damage resulting from the activities.

4. Insurance. Volunteer understands that, except as otherwise agreed to by _____ [organization], in writing, _____ [organization] does not carry or maintain health, medical, or disability insurance coverage for any Volunteer.

Each Volunteer is expected and encouraged to obtain his or her own medical or health insurance coverage.

5. Photographic Release. Volunteer does hereby grant and convey into _____ [organization] all rights, titles, and interests in any and all photographic images and video or audio recordings made by _____ [organization], or on _____ [organization's] behalf, during the volunteer's activities with _____ [organization], including but not limited to, any royalties, proceeds, or other benefits derived from such photographs or recordings.

6. Other. Volunteer expressly agrees that this Release is intended to be as broad and inclusive as permitted by the laws of the State of _____, and that this release shall be governed by and interpreted in accordance with the laws of the State of _____. Volunteer agrees that in the event that any clause or provision of this release shall be held to be invalid by any court of competent jurisdiction, the invalidity of such clause or provision shall not otherwise affect the remaining provisions of this release, which shall continue to be enforceable.

IN WITNESS WHEREOF, Volunteer has executed this release as of the day and year first above written.

Witness: _____

Volunteer: _____

Parent or Guardian: _____

Address: _____

_____

Phone: _____(Home)

_____(Other)

Date: _____

APPENDIX 8

Sample Code of Ethics

Camp Fire USA National Headquarters—Code of Ethics

I. Introduction

Camp Fire USA National Headquarters (hereinafter "Camp Fire USA" or "Camp Fire") is a national youth and family development organization accountable to its chartered councils and licensed community partners, the government and the general public. It must consistently earn the trust of its various constituents and the public every day—trust that can only be garnered by adhering to the highest ethical standards for the nonprofit sector. Camp Fire aspires to no less.

Adhering to relevant laws and regulations is the minimum standard of expected behavior for a government-sanctioned nonprofit organization. Camp Fire USA aspires not just to obey the law; we aspire to embrace the spirit of the law. We shall go beyond legal requirements to ensure that our actions are consistent with our mission and how we describe ourselves to others. Transparency, openness, and responsiveness to public concerns are integral to our practices.

Camp Fire USA embraces this Code of Ethics.

II. Mission and Values

Camp Fire USA embraces and lives up to its mission: "Camp Fire USA builds caring, confident youth and future leaders."

Camp Fire USA embraces and holds fast to its core values:

- We believe that children and youth are our most precious resources.

- We believe in an approach to youth development that builds assets and empowers individuals.

- We believe that the best youth development occurs in small groups where children and youth are actively involved in creating their own learning.

- We are committed to coeducation, providing opportunities for boys, girls, and families to develop together.

- We provide caring, trained mentors to work with children and youth.

- We are inclusive, welcoming children, youth, and adults regardless of race, religion, socioeconomic status, disability, sexual orientation, or other aspect of diversity.

- We believe in the power of nature to awaken a child's senses, curiosity, and desire to learn.

- We foster leadership, engaging children and youth to give service and make decisions in a democratic society.

- We provide safe, fun, and nurturing environments for children and youth.

- We enrich parents' and other adults' lives by expanding their skills and encouraging them to share their talents and build relationships with children and youth.

- We respond to community needs with our programs and expertise.

- We advocate on behalf of children, youth, and families.

III. Specific Provisions of the Code of Ethics

A. Personal and Professional Integrity

All staff members and trustees of the organization act with honesty, integrity, and openness in all their dealings as representatives of the organization. The organization promotes a working environment that values respect, fairness, and integrity.

Employees may share grievances and perceived improprieties through appropriate management channels and to the National Board President if they believe concerns are not being adequately addressed.

B. Mission

The organization's mission, "Camp Fire USA builds caring, confident youth and future leaders," has been adopted by Camp Fire's National Board of Trustees. All Camp Fire programs support this mission, and all who work for, or on behalf of, the organization understand and are loyal to the mission. The mission is responsive to the various constituencies of Camp Fire and is of value to society at large.

C. Governance

The organization has an active and voluntary governing body, a National Board of Trustees, that is responsible for setting the mission and strategic direction of the organization and for oversight of the finances and policies of the organization. The governing body, working on its own or in concert with a governance committee or other resources:

- Ensures that its trustees have the requisite skills and experience to carry out their duties and that all members understand and fulfill their governance duties, acting for the benefit of the organization and its public purpose

- Is responsible for the hiring, termination, and regular review of the performance of the chief executive officer, and ensures that the compensation of the chief executive officer is reasonable and appropriate
- Ensures that the chief executive officer and appropriate staff provide the governing body with timely and comprehensive information so that the governing body can effectively carry out its duties
- Ensures that the organization conducts all transactions and dealings with integrity and honesty
- Ensures that the organization promotes working relationships with trustees, staff, councils, and other constituencies that are based on mutual respect, fairness, and openness
- Ensures that the organization is fair and inclusive in its hiring and promotion policies and practices
- Ensures that policies of the organization are in writing, clearly articulated, and officially adopted
- Ensures that the resources of the organization are responsibly and prudently managed
- Ensures that the organization has the capacity to carry out its programs effectively

D. Legal Compliance

Camp Fire USA is knowledgeable of, and complies with, all laws, regulations, and applicable international conventions.

E. Responsible Stewardship

Camp Fire USA manages its funds responsibly and prudently. This policy includes the following considerations:

- It spends the majority of its annual budget on programs and services in pursuance of its mission.
- It spends the necessary amount on administrative expenses to ensure effective accounting systems, internal controls, competent staff, and other expenditures critical to professional management.
- It compensates staff, and any others who may receive compensation, reasonably and appropriately.
- It strives to accumulate the reserve funds necessary to ensure perpetuity and achievement of strategic goals.
- It has a written investment policy that is reviewed annually by the National Board of Trustees.

- It ensures that all spending practices and policies are fair, reasonable, and appropriate to fulfill the mission of Camp Fire USA.

- All financial reports are factually accurate and complete in all material respects.

- The financial statements and control systems are audited annually by a qualified external auditor selected by an audit committee, which has been appointed by the National Board of Trustees.

F. Conflicts of Interest

Camp Fire USA, its staff, and trustees place the mission and integrity of the organization above their own interests in the course of their efforts on behalf of Camp Fire. To ensure that no conflicts of interest or appearances thereof occur, staff members shall, on an annual basis, and trustees shall, as they are elected, sign a statement providing that they:

- Will not place their personal or professional interests in conflict with the interests of Camp Fire USA

- Will not benefit personally or financially from any dealing with Camp Fire USA

- Will avoid any impropriety or appearance of impropriety in the performance of their duties on behalf of Camp Fire USA

- If trustee, will immediately notify the National Board President of any potential conflict and, if staff, will immediately notify the national chief executive officer or chief financial officer of any potential conflict

- Will not request or accept personal payments, favors, or gifts of substantial value from current or potential vendors

- Will not participate in activities that are competitive with the interests of Camp Fire USA

- Will declare any personal, business, or professional involvements or conflicts of interest with the interests of Camp Fire USA and recuse themselves from all votes and/or affected activities after such disclosure

- Will abide by this Code of Ethics

G. Openness and Disclosure

Camp Fire USA is responsive, in a timely manner, to reasonable requests for information. All information about Camp Fire fully and honestly reflects the policies and practices of the organization. Basic information about the organization, such as the Form 990 and audited financial statements, is available to the public. All financial, organizational, and program reports will be complete and accurate in all material respects.

H. Program and Services Accountability

Camp Fire USA regularly reviews the effectiveness of programs and services and has mechanisms to incorporate lessons learned into future programs and services. Camp Fire is committed to improving programs, services, and organizational effectiveness and develops mechanisms to promote learning from its activities and in the youth and family development field. Camp Fire is responsive to changes in the field and is responsive to the needs of its constituencies.

I. Inclusiveness and Diversity

Camp Fire USA embraces diversity and inclusiveness among its staff, trustees, and among its various constituencies. It acts consistent with its core value on inclusiveness. Camp Fire takes meaningful steps to promote inclusiveness in its hiring, retention, promotion, board recruitment, and constituencies served.

J. Fundraising

Camp Fire USA is truthful in soliciting funds from public sources, private institutions, businesses, and individuals. Camp Fire respects the privacy concerns of donors and does not share donor contact information outside the organization. It expends funds consistent with donor intent and discloses important and relevant information to potential donors.

In raising funds, Camp Fire USA respects the rights of donors, as follows:

- To be informed of the mission of the organization and how resources will be used effectively and for their intended purposes
- To be informed of the identity of those serving on the organization's governing board and to expect the board to exercise prudent judgment in its stewardship responsibilities
- To have access to the organization's most recent financial reports
- To be assured their gifts will be used for the purposes for which they were given
- To receive appropriate acknowledgement and recognition
- To be assured that information about their donations is handled with respect and with confidentiality to the extent provided by the law
- To expect that all relationships with individuals representing organizations of interest to the donor will be professional in nature
- To be informed of whether those seeking donations are volunteers or employees of the organization
- To feel free to ask questions when making a donation and to receive prompt, truthful and forthright answers

IV. Amendments

Camp Fire USA's National Board of Trustees shall review the Code of Ethics on an annual basis and may amend it from time to time.

V. Formal Inaugural Acceptance

Camp Fire USA's National Board of Trustees hereby adopts this Code of Ethics effective March 1, 2005.

Affirmation of Code of Ethics of Camp Fire USA

As an employee of volunteer for Camp Fire USA, I hereby express my understanding of, and commitment to, the Code of Ethics of Camp Fire USA.

I further affirm that I have no current or anticipated conflicts with the Code and that, should such a potential conflict arise, I shall disclose it as set forth in the Code.

_____

(Signature)

APPENDIX 9

Sample Gift-Giving Policy—Camp Fire USA

A. Mission Statement

Camp Fire USA builds caring, confident youth and future leaders.

B. Fundraising Principles

The guiding principle underlying all Camp Fire USA fundraising programs and campaigns is to strengthen and protect the good will and stewardship of the organization. Internal and external constituencies include:

- Children, youth, and families
- Board of directors, staff, and volunteers
- Alumni, donors, friends, and community partners
- Local, state, and national civic leaders

By functioning in this way, all fundraising efforts will ensure the growth and perpetuity of the Camp Fire program and the outcomes produced for children, youth, and families.

We favor giving decisions that both satisfy the philanthropic intent of the donor and meet the short- and long-term goals of Camp Fire USA. We need to demonstrate our belief in the philanthropic tradition and the essentials of relationship fundraising throughout the planning, cultivation, solicitation, and recognition phases of all fundraising programs and campaigns.

C. Purpose and Intent of the Policy

The purpose of all fundraising programs and campaigns is to encourage and solicit unrestricted and restricted gifts and grants in support of the mission of Camp Fire USA.

This policy is established to assure fair and equal treatment of all donors and to enable the organization to protect its tax exempt status. It addresses the solicitation, acceptance, receipt, management, use, and disposition of gifts to ensure accountability to our constituents and any federal or state agency having jurisdiction.

Oversight and implementation of this policy is the responsibility of the Chief Executive Officer and the Director of Development. Issues not readily resolved by these individuals will be referred to the Board of Directors or appropriate committee for resolution.

D. Definitions

Annual fund: All unrestricted and restricted gifts given in a fiscal year that are used for current operations

Capital campaign: Efforts to raise substantial funds (not designated for current operations) for new buildings and equipment, renovations of existing facilities, and/or endowment funds

Capital gift: A gift supporting physical plant additions, such as new buildings or renovations of existing buildings, and specific capital equipment

Constituency: In fundraising, a category of donors and prospects, such as corporations, foundations, organizations, and individuals (board, alumni, parents, friends, civic leaders, etc.)

Cultivation: The process of developing the interest of a prospective donor through education, communication, involvement, and a presentation of needs/funding priorities to result in a gift to Camp Fire USA

Designated gift: A gift with a preferred general use specified by the donor. The specific use is determined by the board or Chief Executive Officer. While it is intended that the organization will respect the preference of the donor to the extent it fulfills Camp Fire's purpose, such a designation is not binding upon the organization.

Donor recognition: The policy and practice of recognizing gifts through immediate acknowledgment by letter, card, personalized note, personalized expressions of appreciation directly to donors, published lists of contributors, tangible items of recognition that may indicate gift level, gift clubs, or involvement opportunities, to name a few

Endowment: A gift given to provide income through earnings from a protected fund. Based on the conditions of the original gift, use of the income can be either donor or National Board designated.

Unrestricted endowment gift: Earnings are designated by the board within the guidelines established by the board.

Field of interest endowment gift: Earnings are designated for use within a specific category. Categories are determined by the board and include, but are not limited to, scholarships, program support, facilities maintenance, technical assistance, and staff development and training. Specific use within the category is determined by the board through the budget-approval process.

Restricted endowment gift: Earnings are used as designated by the donor or the donor's designee, and may be used only for that specific purpose.

Gift-in-kind: A gift of equipment, supplies, professional services, contract services, etc.

Planned gift: A gift made through a bequest, contract, or trust. It may provide income or some other benefit to the donor (or another person) during his or her lifetime.

Proposal: A written request for a gift or grant that usually includes an introduction, the background of the submitting organization, a problem statement and/or needs assessment, a project/program description with objectives, a plan of action, evaluation procedures, and budget.

Restricted gift: A gift donated for a purpose agreed upon by the donor and Camp Fire USA

Unrestricted gift: A gift that is to be used in the best interest of the organization. The board directs the use of these gifts through the approval of the budget.

E. Ethical Standards

Camp Fire USA's gift policy fosters the highest standards of behavior, ensuring that all fundraising activities are conducted in accordance with the Association of Fundraising Professionals' *Code of Ethical Principles* and the *Standards of Professional Practice* of the Association of Fundraising Professionals and the National Committee on Planned Giving.

Camp Fire USA and those authorized to solicit gifts will comply with these codes and practices and use qualified tax/estate planning counsel where appropriate. Applicable standards of practice include, but are not limited to, the following:

- The Director of Development or his or her designee will represent himself or herself only as a development professional, and not as a legal, financial, or tax advisor. It is recommended that the donor have any "statement of intent" related to gift planning arrangements reviewed by his or her own financial or legal counsel. When appropriate, the following statement shall be included in written materials: "This document provides information about charitable gifts and gift planning opportunities. Before making a gift, we recommend that you consult your own legal, financial, or tax advisor."

- In all matters involving a donor or prospect, the donor's objectives shall be given consideration, and no agreement, charitable trust, or other commitment shall be urged upon a donor at the expense of his or her best interest, even if this practice results in a smaller gift or no gift to the organization.

- A donor's request for anonymity will always be honored. The only exception is if Camp Fire USA is required by law to make the information available.

Camp Fire USA will only accept gifts that are consistent with the advancement of its mission. The board is responsible for assuring that sufficient revenue is generated to carry out plans and programs resulting from board action. Further, it is expected that all board members will support and actively promote the organization's fundraising efforts.

Authority: No individual or ancillary group may solicit funds in the name of, or on behalf of, Camp Fire USA unless expressly authorized to do so by the board or the Chief Executive Officer. Solicitation activities must be consistent with the organization's strategic plan and be approved by the Chief Executive Officer or the Director of Development.

Gift acceptance: The Chief Executive Officer and the Director of Development may receive any gift on behalf of Camp Fire USA, subject to the following:

Authority to Raise Funds and Accept Gifts:

- The Chief Executive Officer or the Director of Development may accept any unrestricted gift of intangible property. An unrestricted gift greater than $50,000 will be reported to the executive committee of the board, with a use recommendation from the Chief Executive Officer.

- The Chief Executive Officer or the Director of Development may accept a restricted gift of intangible property of $50,000 or less. The executive committee of the board must approve the acceptance of a restricted gift of intangible property greater than $50,000. An exception may be made for a preapproved project, such as those identified in a capital campaign or specific elements of the strategic plan.

- Any gift of real estate and tangible personal property will be reviewed on a case-by-case basis and must be approved by the executive committee or other designated committee of the board.

- The acceptance of non-publicly traded securities will be at the discretion of the Executive Committee or other designated committee of the board.

- In all cases, gifts accepted and received must be consistent with Camp Fire USA's mission and stated core values.

F. Form of Gift and Confirmation of Value

A gift to Camp Fire USA may be offered in any of the following forms: cash/securities; wills and trusts; qualified retirement plans; life insurance; gift annuities; charitable lead trusts; charitable remainder unitrusts and annuity trusts; gifts of real estate; and tangible personal property. The board may decline to accept any gift if it is determined that:

- The gift is not in the best interest of the organization or the donor

- The gift requires a financial commitment from the organization that exposes Camp Fire USA to risk or embarrassment of any kind. Any gift to Camp Fire USA becomes the property of the organization.

Gift value: In general, an employee of Camp Fire USA may not provide any donor with an appraisal or confirmation of the value of a gift, other than a gift of cash, a check, or securities that are publicly traded.

G. Recognition and Stewardship

Annual campaign: A gift that either is restricted or designated for the current budget will be credited toward the donor's total giving for the annual campaign. Any other gift will be recognized in another category(ies).

Gift club or society: Listing in a gift club or giving society is based on total giving.

- The value of an anonymous donor gift will not be included in a gift club or gift society listing unless otherwise approved by the donor.

- A donor will receive "soft" credit on his or her account for any matching gift; however, a donor will receive credit for his or her personal gift alone for the purpose of a gift club or gift society listing.

Matching gift: A gift from an employer that matches a gift by its employee will be recognized under a separate category.

Named facilities and endowments: Any naming opportunity requires the approval of the National Board or its designee prior to acceptance of the gift. A donor must give:

- 50% of the total cost of the facility or improvement in order to name the facility or improvement

- A minimum of $250,000 to create and name a restricted endowment

- An amount sufficient to generate annual earnings equal to 50% of the estimated average annual maintenance cost to create and name an endowment for maintenance of new, renovated, or remodeled facilities or equipment

- A minimum contribution of $75,000 to create and name a field of interest or unrestricted endowment

Stewardship of endowments: Each donor of a named endowment will be provided annually with a report that includes the following:

- Established or book value of the original gift
- New gifts to the endowment during the past fiscal year
- Earnings attributed to the fund for the past fiscal year
- Market value of the fund
- Proceeds distributed for the past fiscal year

In addition, the donor of a named or restricted endowment will be provided with details on the specific use of the funds in accordance with the gift agreement. The donor of a named, designated, or unrestricted endowment will be provided with a summary of how the funds from the designated category were utilized without identifying the specific use of the funds from the endowment.

A summary report on the total endowment fund, its growth, and its use will be provided in the annual honor roll.

H. Retention of "Outside" Fundraising Counsel

Fundraising counsel retained by Camp Fire USA will be paid a fixed fee and not a percentage of funds raised.

APPENDIX 10

Sample Records Management, Retention, and Destruction Policy

Overview

This document will serve as the official records management, retention, and destruction policy of this organization. The timetable found in Appendix 10a applies to the official copy of the legal information/records. If the information/record is stored on an electronic medium, then that copy shall be the official copy unless a statute or regulation specifies otherwise.

Recordkeeping requirements fall under several federal laws and regulations, ranging from the Code of Federal Regulations to the Internal Revenue Service to the Americans with Disabilities Act. The general requirement is that all records must be kept as long as the contents may become material in the administration of any law or regulation.

All records shall be stored in boxes that are clearly labeled with the following information: department/division, box number, contents, and destroy date. The labels will be color coded by area as follows and inserted into a plastic sleeve affixed to the box.

Storage of Records

- Accounting/Finance—green
- Merchandise Services—pink
- Human Resources—blue
- Program Services—peach
- Field Services—lavender
- Development—tan
- Marketing and Communications—goldenrod
- Office of CEO—white

It is the role of each division director to decide which records will be kept in permanent storage. All boxes labeled as "permanent" will be moved to the warehouse location. If an employee needs to gain access to the boxes at the warehouse, he will need authorization from the division director and make arrangements with the warehouse manager in advance. The security of personal information is considered in all access and storage decisions.

All records with personal information are to be shredded to protect staff and participant privacy. Personnel, financial, and legal records that need to be destroyed are to be shredded.

Administration of the Policy

This policy will be administered by the Chief Financial Officer.

Effective Date—This policy is effective _____.

Distribution—All employees of _____.

APPENDIX 10A

Sample Record-Retention Timetable

Accounting and Finance	Retention Period
Accounts Payable:	
Paid Vendor Invoices and Other Supporting Documentation	7 years
Reports: Posting Registers, Month-End Journal, Month-End Aging, and Unbilled (unmatched) Receipts Inventory	7 years
Accounts Receivable:	
Reports: Posting Registers, Preclosing Aging, Month-End Aging	7 years
Month-End Accounts Receivable Statements	7 years
Invoices to Customers and Members (numeric file)	7 years
Adjustments (filed in customer files)	7 years
Bank:	
Cancelled Checks	7 years
Bank Statements and Reconciliations	7 years
Lockbox, Cash Receipts, Duplicate Deposit Slips	7 years
Mortgage Loans and Settlement Sheets	Permanent
Fixed Assets Information:	
Gross Book Value, Acquisition Date, Depreciation Taken, Net Book Value, Tag Number, etc.	Permanent
Depreciation Records	7 years
Disposed Assets Information	7 years
Property Deeds	Permanent
General Ledger:	
Fiscal Year-End General Ledger Details and Trial Balance	Permanent
General Ledger Journal Entries	7 years
Chart of Accounts	7 years
IRS Form 990	Permanent
Annual Audit/Audited Financial Statements/Work Papers	Permanent
Inventory:	
Inventory Reports: Posting Registers/Month-End On-Hand by Location	7 years
Inventory Receiving Records (including in-house printing receipts)	2 years
Physical Inventory Counts and Related Cost Records	7 years
Inventory Adjustments: Transfer Issues and Cost Adjustments	7 years

Accounting and Finance	Retention Period
Other:	
Grant Information	As required by contract/ funder
Annual Budgets (also kept permanently in board minutes)	Permanent
Financial Statements, Internal, Interim (not audited)	7 years
Contribution Documentation	6 years
Agreements, Purchase Orders (numeric and vendor files), and Contracts Leases	7 years after termination/ expiration of license or termination of contract
Software Licenses	6 years after use of software ends, or termination/ expiration of license
Personal Property/Sales and Use Tax	7 years
Expense Analysis Schedules	7 years
Federal, State and Local Tax Exemption Application and Related Correspondence	Permanent
Petty Cash Receipts	7 years
Other Federal Forms	7 years
Payroll	Retention Period
Payroll Registers and Reports (including earnings, tax withholding and other deductions)	Permanent
W-4s, I-9s, etc.	6 years
Tax Filings: Federal, State, Local (941, W-2s, W-3s, 1099s, Unemployment)	Permanent
Employee Information Files	7 years
Tax Deposits	6 years
Direct Deposit Records	3 years after an employee leaves the organization
Garnishments/Levies	3 years
Canceled and Voided Payroll Checks	6 years
Timesheets	7 years
Payroll Records and Summaries by Pay Period (including 303s)	7 years
Human Resources	**Retention Period**
Employment Records/Employee Personnel Files	Permanent
Medical/Health Records	Permanent

Human Resources	Retention Period
Employment contracts or similar documentation, pay history and related information, and payroll election for benefits including: Pension, Health Coverage, Other Benefits	6 years after termination
Employment Application/Resumes (by position)	7 years
Employment Notices	1 year
Job Descriptions	2 years
Training Manuals/Records	Permanent
Benefits Records, Plan Documentation, and Related Modifications	Permanent
Worker's Compensation Files	10 years
Request for Disability	1 year
Whistleblower Files	7 years
Insurance Policies (expired)	Permanent
Insurance Records, Current Accident Reports, Receipts, and Claims	Permanent
Pension Records Paid to Employees or Beneficiaries (after final payment)	Permanent
Settled Insurance Claims	3 years
Investigation Documents and Reports	4 years
Retirement and Pension Records	Permanent
Garnishments/Levies	3 years
General Information	**Retention Period**
Correspondence (general)	7 years
Correspondence (legal and important only)	Permanent
Polices	Permanent
Procedure Manuals	Permanent
Organization Charts	Permanent
Travel Information	3 years
Contracts and Leases (still in effect)	Permanent
Contracts and Leases (expired)	7 years
Record-Retention Policies	Permanent
Insurance\Risk Management	**Retention Period**
Risk-Management Plan	Permanent
Medical Records	Minors 3 beyond age of majority. Also refer to OSHA regarding medical logs for staff members.
Incident Reports	Permanent
Insurance Records: Accident Reports, Fire-Inspection Reports, Insurance Policies, and Safety Records	6 years

Insurance\Risk Management	Retention Period
Insurance Claims/Correspondence	5 years
Insurance Certificates/Binders	2 years
Insurance Liability Information	10 years
Insurance Policies (building and miscellaneous)	7 years
Communications	**Retention Period**
Publications	Permanent
Press Releases	Permanent
Special Project Files: Annual Meeting Marketing/Communications Materials, etc	50 years
Miscellaneous Events Files	2 years
Media Relations Publications: Spokesperson Statements, Interviews, etc.	50 years
Annual Report	Permanent
Marketing and Advertising	**Retention Period**
Product Development	10 years
Market Research	1 year
Graphics/Drawings/Artwork	10 years
Advertising	10 years
Sales Reports	6 years
Items not Listed	10 years
Corporate Information	**Retention Period**
Board of Trustees Rosters/Trustees Meeting Notices/Minutes of Board Meetings (annual budgets also kept in accounting files)	Permanent
Articles of Incorporation, Corporate Bylaws, Amendments Thereto, Corporate Documents	Permanent
Committee Minutes, Reports, and Presentations	Permanent
Election Records	Permanent
Corporate History	Permanent
Strategic Plan Documents	Length of Plan
Patents, Copyrights, Trademarks, Service Marks, etc.	Permanent
Litigation: Pleadings, Subpoenas, Court Files	5 years from date of final disposition
Nonlitigation: Advice/Counseling, Subject/Research Files	5 years, with a review
Business Licenses	Permanent
Correspondence: General, Members, and Constituents	6 years
Correspondence: Legal	Permanent
Mortgage Loans and Settlement Sheets	Permanent

Corporate Information	Retention Period
Major Agreements: Acquisitions, Divestitures, Mergers, etc., Requiring Board Approval	20 years
Program Services	Retention Period
Correspondence	3 years
Participant Registration, Permissions, Waivers, Photo Releases, etc.	Adults: 6 years
Minors: 3 years after age of majority	
Training Schedule, Attendance Records	Permanent
Program Promotional Materials, Forms	Permanent
Reports: Annual Reports, Participation Reports, Insurance Reports	Permanent
Reports: Fundraising Reports, Staff Actions, Board Reports	5 years
HR Information Reports, Paid Staff Lists, Volunteer Lists	Permanent
Program Business Plans, Budgets, Fundraising Forms, Financial Information	7 years
Petty cash vouchers	3 years
Development	Retention Period
Alumni Records:	Permanent
Biographical Records	Permanent
Cash and Noncash Gift Records	4 years
Bequests and Estate Information	Permanent
Gift Records:	
Biographical Records	4 years after donor is deceased
Cash and Noncash Gift Records	4 years
Grants:	
Grant Records only one proposal, final report, and substantive correspondence permanently	After 7 years, retain
Grant Applications; Denied	7 years
Memorial Gifts	Permanent
Pledges	7 years after date of last entry

APPENDIX 11

Sample Vehicle-Inspection Form

Drivers that use vehicles that regularly transport youth or adults should complete the following checklist. The frequency of the checks will depend on local codes or organization policy.

Motor Vehicle Inspection Checklist by Driver

Vehicle and Type:	Driver:		License Plate #:
	Owned By:		

Date	Inspection of:	Check if Safe	Repair Needed to Travel	Initials of Driver
	Tire Pressure:			
	Lights: Headlights Tail lights Turn signals Back-up lights Emergency flashers			
	Windshield Wipers Fluid			
	Horn			
	Brakes			
	Fluid Levels			
	Other:			

Date	Safety Equipment	Check if Available	Papers	Check if Available
	Tire jack		Vehicle registration or rental agreement	
	Reflectors		Emergency procedures	
	First-aid kit		Insurance card or papers	
	Flashlight		Insurance claim forms	
	Container of fresh water		Incident report forms	
	Fire extinguisher		Motion-sickness bag	

Date	Safety Equipment	Check if Available	Papers	Check if Available
	Jumper cables		Permission forms	
	Cell phone or money for call		Emergency contact numbers	
	Disposable camera			
	Blanket			
	Chains (as appropriate)			

APPENDIX 12

Sample Behavior-Management Policy

The organization's staff and volunteers all want to have positive interactions with the children with whom they work, but often fall short of those expectations. Effective behavior management begins with the program philosophy, is influenced by the environment, and is carried out within agreeable limits and boundaries.

Discipline is a dynamic process of child guidance. The long-term goal is to encourage the development of self-control.

As part of a program that can have a major influence on a child's development, the organization's staff and volunteers have a responsibility to help children learn to be self-directed and in control of their behavior. To help accomplish this goal, a written policy about behavior management has been developed.

The organization's philosophy of behavior management is consistent with the mission and core values of the organization. To promote this philosophy, the program has been carefully planned to foster positive behavior in school-age care programming.

To accomplish this goal:

- Children are involved in rule-setting and help determine the consequences for misbehavior.

- The site and activities are set up to promote positive interaction among children.

- Staff members encourage children to learn how to solve problems and settle differences among themselves.

All disciplinary efforts are based on these practices. When a child's behavior creates a risk for the emotional or physical health and safety of another child or the staff, the following procedures shall be followed:

- The child is separated from the problem activity or situation.

- A staff member listens to the child and discusses the consequences of further misbehavior.

- Repeated misbehavior will be handled by a telephone conversation or conference with the parent.

- The parent, child, and staff member agree to a plan that will improve behavior or the child will face the possibility of termination from the program.

The development of behavior-management policies should include more than consequences for misbehavior. To be effective, a variety of strategies should be employed.

Preventive strategies will keep conflict and stress to a minimum. Examples of preventive strategies include:

- The environment is conducive to positive interaction.
- Adults model appropriate behavior and use their authority wisely.
- Staff members develop caring relationships with youth.
- Program activities are flexible in response to the changing interests of children.
- Activities are age-appropriate and relevant to the needs, interests, values, and capabilities of youth.
- Emotional expression is encouraged.

Interactive strategies will provide youth and adults with the opportunity to constructively cope with stress and conflict. Examples of interactive strategies include:

- Limits for behavior are fair, reasonable, and understood by youth.
- Youth understand the natural and logical consequences of exceeding limits.
- Adults help youth appropriately express negative feelings.
- Problem-solving and conflict-resolution opportunities are included in the program. The democratic process of decision-making is used.
- Adults find opportunities to help youth see themselves as kind, cooperative people who are capable of solving problems and resolving conflict.
- Praise and encouragement recognize actual effort and accomplishment (rather than "good character").
- Adults redirect aimless or inappropriate behavior into more constructive activities.

Crisis strategies will be necessary when youth and/or adults face occasional loss of control. Examples of control strategies include:

- When adults lose control, they practice emergency coping techniques such as leaving the situation, deep breathing, etc.
- When youth lose control, staff members handle them in accordance with the program's policy.
- At no time shall corporal punishment or any other humiliating or frightening discipline techniques be used as a means of controlling behavior.

APPENDIX 13

Sample Camp Discipline Code

Mission Statement

The organization aspires to be a growing and increasingly effective co-ed youth agency, providing programs that develop personal life skills, social responsibility, health, and leadership, and that respond to the needs of youth in a changing society.

The goals of the Camp Discipline Code are:

- To ensure the safety and well-being of all campers
- To ensure that all youth benefit from the outdoor learning experience
- To ensure that every camper has the opportunity to complete programs available and suitable to his age and experience level
- To enable all youth to manage their social behavior
- To create a framework for cooperative effort between campers and staff

Campers will be responsible for:

- Their adult and peer relations
- Their compliance with camp procedures and practices

The camp staff will be responsible for:

- Creating and implementing a program of outdoor education and recreation that maximizes the opportunity for campers to achieve success
- Working cooperatively with campers to facilitate their success in outdoor education and recreation
- Ensuring that camp rules are frequently reviewed with, and clearly understood by, youth.
- Demonstrating consistency and reliability in implementing the behavior-expectation code and discipline code
- Respecting and protecting the rights of all youth at camp

The behavior-expectation code states that campers will:

- Follow the safety rules of camp
- Cooperate with other campers and staff. Respect the rights and properties of others

- Listen and follow instructions
- Participate in all activities with their cabin group

The camp staff will provide leadership, guidance, and assistance to all youth in meeting their behavior expectations. Campers who choose to behave in a socially appropriate manner will maximize the benefits they receive from the camping experience. The camp staff recognizes that, for some youth, the prospect of time away from home can be threatening and frightening. The staff will be sensitive to each child's needs; will work with each child individually to alleviate fears and concerns; will structure programs and activities to meet the abilities and needs of each child; and will exercise patience and sensitivity toward campers' behavior.

The staff understands that children may misbehave and that the majority of those misbehaviors will be minor or inconsequential. Sometimes a child's misbehavior may be serious enough to warrant adult intervention. The following are some examples of serious misbehavior at camp.

Social misbehavior:

- Swearing
- Refusing to follow instructions, directions, or safety rules
- Bullying other campers
- Harassing other campers by teasing, name-calling, or playing with their possessions

Group misbehavior:

- Refusing to follow instructions, directions, or safety rules
- Disrupting the program process
- Refusing to participate in program activities
- Harassing other campers during program activities by pushing, shoving, swearing, and intimidating

APPENDIX 14

Sample Code of Conduct—California 4-H

California 4-H Youth Development Program (4-HYDP)—University of California Cooperative Extension

The following guidelines are designed to make everyone's experience at 4-H events satisfying to all attending. Therefore, all participants, members, volunteers, and 4-H YDP staff shall adhere to the core values of the University of California 4-H Youth Development Program, and respect the individual rights, safety, and property of others.

While attending all 4-H meetings, projects, programs, and events, the following rules apply:

1. Everyone is expected to attend all planned sessions, workshops, field trips, and meetings of the event, and be appropriately dressed. Chaperones and project volunteers are responsible for ensuring that members participate in all aspects of the planned program activities.

2. The possession and use of alcoholic beverages, tobacco products, and drugs (other than prescription medication) is prohibited.

3. Setting off fire alarms or tampering with fire extinguishing equipment or other emergency equipment is prohibited.

4. Gambling and betting by adults and youth representing 4-H is prohibited.

5. Obscene and discriminatory language, roughhousing, and insubordination will not be tolerated at any time.

6. Youth members and volunteers will demonstrate respect for one another at all times.

7. Display of overly affectionate attention between participants is prohibited.

While attending overnight events, the following rules also apply:

1. All participants must be in their assigned area at curfew and comply with the quiet hours and lights out.

2. No member or volunteer may leave the grounds unless permission is secured from the adult in charge. 4-H members must be accompanied by an adult.

3. Only 4-H participants may be in dormitory areas. No one will be in the sleeping areas of members of the opposite gender. Lounges may be used for working committees and social activities.

4. Youth must comply with other rules of the event.

Penalties for Infractions

Infractions of the 4-H Code of Conduct must be promptly reported by anyone observing them to the adult in charge of the delegation/project and to the person in charge of the event and who will bear final responsibility for disciplinary action. The parent/guardian and the County 4-H Office will be notified of action taken. Penalties may include any or all of the following:

- Sending the participant home
- Barring the participant from future 4-H events
- Assessing the participant the cost of damages and repairs for damage or destruction of property
- Releasing the participant to the nearest law enforcement agency and/or the proper authorities
- Termination of 4-H membership

I have read the Code of Conduct and agree to abide by its rules. I understand that infraction of this Code will result in any or all of the penalties listed above.

County: _____

Signature of Member: _____ Date: _____

Signature of Parent/Guardian: _____ Date: _____

APPENDIX 15

Sample Code of Conduct—
Camp Fire USA (for Teens)

Note: To avoid a double standard, this document was written for teens and adults to sign themselves. It may need to be revised for appropriateness for youth under 11 years old.

Camp Fire USA's mission is to build caring, confident youth and future leaders. Camp Fire USA achieves this mission by having a set of core values and a program philosophy that provide guidance to establishing a positive environment for youth development and family-strengthening experiences.

Age-appropriate programs are designed with intentional outcomes and activities that provide a progression of sequenced learning to help youth have life-enhancing experiences to develop assets that are essential to their future. Youth and adults work in partnership in a small group structure to plan and evaluate what they do; individuals build confidence and leadership skills and are recognized for their accomplishments.

In such an environment, youth find a safe, fun, and inclusive place with caring adults, where they form lasting relationships, develop a sense of belonging, and make a contribution to the lives of their families and their communities.

As a youth participant or adult in a Camp Fire USA program, I agree to conduct myself in a manner that will be a credit to Camp Fire USA, partner organizations, my community, and me.

I will:

- Participate with the group as expected and comply with program schedule
- Abide by all rules and regulations issued by Camp Fire USA, the program administration, and the owners/managers of the facilities where the program is being held
- Demonstrate cooperation with, and respect for, staff, volunteers, and other participants
- Show respect for the rights, privacy, and property of others
- Not use, possess, or be under the influence of any illegal substances (tobacco products, alcohol, or drugs, etc.)
- Take responsibility for my personal property

- Be thoughtful of my actions and understand that "horseplay" and pranks may cause physical or emotional injury

- Not humiliate, ridicule, threaten, or degrade others

- Allow any bags or pockets to be searched if program administration requests to do so

- Not possess or use fireworks, firearms, or weapons of any kind or other items that could cause injury or damage to persons or property

- Not be present in the sleeping facilities of a member of the opposite sex unless either an adult is also present or five or more participants are present in the room, two of which are the same sex (3-2 rule)

- Dress appropriately for the program I am participating in and not bring or wear offensive, obscene, suggestive, or immodest clothing

- Not use abusive, vulgar, foul, offensive, or sexually inappropriate language

- Not engage in uninvited physical contact or intimate sexual activity with other youth, staff members, or guests, including romantic displays, kissing, or fondling. Possession of sexually explicit materials is prohibited.

I understand that:

- Any violation of state or federal laws will be treated as such and the proper authorities notified

- All youth participants and adults share equally the responsibility for their actions when violations of the Code of Conduct are witnessed. Those who decide to be present when a violation occurs shall, by their own choice, be considered a participant in the violation.

I have read and agree to abide by this Code of Conduct and I will be responsible for all consequences of my behavior. I also understand I may be sent home for violations at my own or my parent's expense.

Signature _____ Youth_____ Adult _____

Address_____ Phone _____

City _____State _____ Zip _____

Council

Council address

Council phone number

Program administrator's name

APPENDIX 16

Sample Dismissal Clauses/Policies

Sample for the Registration Form

I, _____, as legal guardian of _____, authorize my child to participate in camp programs. I understand that to provide a safe and cooperative group experience, a child may be dismissed from the program for reasons including behavior, illness/injury, or homesickness.

Parents are encouraged to contact the _____ office for more information about the program itself or about visiting the program.

In the Parent Packet

In the event that it is deemed necessary for my child to be dismissed from the program, I understand that I or a designated emergency contact am responsible for transportation of my child upon notification of dismissal. Failure to comply may result in notification and involvement of child protection or other legal authorities.

The organization reserves the right to refuse re-admittance based upon previous dismissal due to behavior.

Sample Program Discipline and Dismissal Policy

_____ [organization] is interested in the welfare of all children. Participants in the program are expected to follow the rules of the program and obey the direction of the staff. A child's failure or inability to follow rules or obey direction may cause a serious discipline problem. A serious disciplinary problem may also occur when a child hampers the smooth flow of the program by requiring constant one-on-one attention, inflicts physical or emotional harm on other children, abuses staff members, or is otherwise unable to conform to the rules and guidelines of the program.

If a child becomes a serious discipline problem, the staff will notify the parents of the situation and discuss a solution. If improvement does not occur, or a solution cannot be determined, the staff may recommend that a child be dismissed from the program. The staff members will discuss the situation with their supervisor and decide who will discuss the dismissal procedure with the parents and proceed with the dismissal. Acceptance into the program is conditioned on the above policy and _____ [organization] has the right to dismiss a child from the program.

APPENDIX 16A

Sample Camp Dismissal Policy

A participant may be dismissed from the program due to disruptive behavior, illness, or homesickness.

Children are entitled to a pleasant and harmonious environment during the _____ [organization] program. The program cannot serve children who display chronically or severely disruptive behavior. Chronically disruptive behavior is defined as verbal or physical activity that may include, but is not limited to, behavior that:

- Requires constant attention from the staff
- Inflicts physical or emotional harm on children or staff members
- Displays destructive behavior
- Continually ignores or disobeys program safety rules
- Includes use or possession of illegal drugs, weapons, or explosives

Reasonable efforts will be made to assist children in adjusting to the program setting. If the child cannot adjust to the program setting and behave appropriately, then the child may be dismissed. Dismissal due to illness/injury will be at the discretion of the program director and the healthcare staff. This policy may include, but is not limited to, contagious diseases and extended illnesses.

Dismissal due to homesickness will be at the discretion of the program director in consultation with the parent.

Procedures for Dismissal

Prior to establishing procedures, legal and other sources should be consulted for compliance with Americans with Disabilities Act concerns.

- Document the situation and actions taken and write an incident report
- Notify the specified parent or contact person.
- Explain the situation and the current status of the child to the contact person, so he knows what the child will be doing while waiting to go home. For example, is he still in his group or in severe situations, has he been separated from his group.
- Make and agree upon arrangements for removal from the program, including the time, who will pick up the child, and the mode of transportation.

- Obtain the signature of specified parent or contact person at the time of release from the camp.

- Share the program's expectations with the parents if the child desires to return to the program the following year. Notify the executive director of the actions taken per organization guidelines.

- Provide procedures in Spanish (or appropriate languages) when necessary

APPENDIX 17

Sample Recommended Program Policies for Child Abuse Prevention (or Child Protection) in Camp Fire USA Programs

Camp Fire USA is committed to providing positive youth-development opportunities for children and youth and therefore recommends the following information, administrative policies, and guidelines be adopted by the council board and distributed to volunteer and paid staff.

Physical abuse includes deliberate acts of violence that injure or even kill a child. Unexplained bruises, broken bones, or burn marks on a child may be signs of physical abuse.

Emotional abuse commonly includes repeated verbal abuse of a child in the form of shouting, threats, and degrading or humiliating criticism. Other types of emotional abuse include confinement, such as shutting a child in a dark closet, and social isolation, such as denying a child friends.

Sexual abuse includes, but is not limited to, any contact or interaction between a child and an adult when the child is being used for the sexual stimulation of the adult or of a third person. The behavior may or may not involve touching. Sexual behavior between a child and an adult is always considered forced, whether or not the child has consented.

Neglect/maltreatment is failure to provide for a child's physical and emotional needs, such as food, shelter, clothing, and supervision.

Even the appearance of wrong or a false allegation can cause irreparable damage to the reputation of the accused staff member, the program, and Camp Fire USA.

Administrative Policies

The following are administrative policies to help protect program participants from abuse and volunteer and program staff from false accusations.

1. The screening process for program volunteers and paid staff includes a completed application, reference checks, criminal background check, voluntary disclosure statement, and personal interview. Volunteers such as parents or instructional specialists assisting a volunteer or paid staff member with events or short-term programs may not be required to have a background check, but may be asked to sign a voluntary disclosure statement, and if driving, have an appropriate license and a clean driving record.

2. Criminal background checks should be compiled to include a five-year history. Background checks or voluntary disclosure statements that disclose a conviction will be reviewed for appropriateness for the job. Persons with convictions for child abuse or other crimes against children, drug offenses, or violent crimes against people or animals should not work with children or have access to children's records.

3. Staff will receive training and written guidelines for:

- The disciplining of children

- Adult/child contact

- General program operation policies for abuse prevention by staff or other participants

- Protecting themselves from false accusations of abuse

- Information on potential issues that may require intervention or referral, including identifying symptoms of child abuse and handling participant disclosures

4. The plan for supervision of volunteer and paid staff working directly with children includes on-site program visits by supervising staff without notice.

5. Procedures for child-abuse complaints are made known to all staff responsible for the management of Camp Fire USA programs or the supervision of participants.

6. In the event of an accusation of child abuse, the staff member in charge will take prompt and immediate action as follows:

- At the first report of probable cause to believe that a child-abuse incident has occurred, the staff member receiving the report will notify the staff member in charge, the executive director, or a designate. However, if the executive director is not immediately available, the staff member cannot in any way deter the reporting of child abuse by mandated reporters.

- Report any alleged abuse that takes place at a program site or any allegation of abuse prior to a child's arrival at a program site. (Most states mandate each child-care provider to report information they have learned in their professional role regarding suspected child abuse. In most states, mandated reporters are granted immunity from prosecution.)

- The staff member will make the report in accordance with relevant state or local child-abuse reporting requirements and will cooperate to the extent of the law with any legal authority involved.

- In the event that the reported incident(s) involves a program volunteer or employed staff, the executive director or his or her designee will, without exception, suspend the volunteer or staff person from the program. The parents or legal guardian of the child(ren) involved in the alleged incident will be promptly notified in accordance with the directions of the relevant state or local agency.

- Whether the incident or alleged offense takes place on or off the program site, it will be considered job-related (because of the youth-involved nature of the program).

- Reinstatement of the employed staff person will occur only after all allegations have been cleared to the satisfaction of the director. All staff and volunteers must be sensitive to the need for confidentiality in the handling of this information and, therefore, should only discuss the incident with the executive director or his or her designee.

- The executive director should also notify Camp Fire USA national headquarters, the board president, and the organization's insurance agent.

7. Personal information is maintained in a way that protects the privacy of participants and staff, including guidelines for who has access to what information, how the information is secured, and the disposal of the information.

Guidelines for the Discipline of Children

Camp Fire USA's staff training advocates positive guidance and discipline with an emphasis on positive reinforcement, redirection, prevention, and intervention. At no time will discipline include depriving a minor of sleep, food, or restroom privileges; placing a minor alone without supervision; or subjecting a child to ridicule, shame, threat, sexual harassment, corporal punishment (striking, biting, kicking, squeezing), washing out the mouth, use of abusive or derogatory language, or excessive physical exercise or restraint.

Guidelines for Adult/Child Contact

Camp Fire USA encourages appropriate touch as an important part of helping a child grow into a loving, caring adult. However, Camp Fire USA also recognizes a person's need for personal space, and prohibits inappropriate touch or other means of sexually exploiting children. The following are guidelines for adult/child contact for volunteer and paid staff:

- Staff should limit the touching of a child to the hand, shoulder, or upper back and never touch a child in a place on a the body that is normally covered by a bathing suit, unless for a clear medical necessity, and then only with supervision from another adult.

- Staff should not touch a child against his or her will or when it causes discomfort, whether expressed verbally or nonverbally (unless in the case of clear and present danger to the child).

- Given the physical size and strength of staff members, discretion and restraint should be used in all physical contact activities with minors. Excess tickling, wrestling, or teasing of a child is inappropriate.

- Staff members will under no circumstances share a bed or sleeping bag with a minor.

- Staff members will not give back rubs unless another adult is present, and then only with clothes on.

- Staff members should not show favoritism, encourage crushes or romantic fantasies, or discuss their own personal sexual behavior.

- Staff members are not to maintain personal relations with individual participants, in-person or by phone, mail, or email outside of the program context or job responsibilities, or after the program has ended.

- Staff members provide parents with information on the parameters of the program, including location, a calendar of official Camp Fire USA meetings and events, permission for participation, and information about reporting concerns to the council.

General Program Operation Guidelines for Abuse Prevention by Staff or Other Participants

1. Camp Fire USA staff design and monitor emotionally and physically safe program environments, interactions, and activities for youth and intervene when safety demands it. The following are general guidelines to reduce the vulnerability of children to abuse:

- Participants know where and how to get help with any problem they are having with other participants or the adults working with them.

- Participants are under the supervision of a staff member at all times. Provisions are made for appropriate coverage by another "on-duty" staff member when their staff member has time off.

- "Hazing" of children by participants or staff is not permitted.

- Provisions are made for individual privacy (doors, curtains, etc.) for showering, toileting, and changing clothes, or double-coverage of children by adults will be in place during changing times.

- Younger children should be encouraged to change their own clothes as much as possible.

- Children are never to be alone with a staff member in his or her quarters. When a one-on-one meeting is necessary, it should take place within view of other staff members or participants.

- Tickling or teasing a child to the point where that child is overstimulated or uncomfortable is unacceptable.

- Pillow fights, wrestling matches, personal jokes, and similar spontaneous activities between children should be limited and carefully supervised.

2. One of Camp Fire USA's core values is to provide safe, fun, and nurturing environments for children and youth and thus recognizes that the quality of the program experience deteriorates in direct proportion to the extent of unreasonable risks to which a participant is subjected. Children, youth, and their parents must have confidence that safety measures have been taken to minimize risk and that the experience will be a safe one.

3. Additional information on child abuse, including symptoms of abuse, is available from the following resources:

- http://www.acf.hhs.gov/program/cb/

- www.kidsafe-caps.org

- http://www.acf.hhs.gov/programs/cb/systems/index.htm#ncands

Sample Program Operational Plan for Activities Requiring Staff Members With Specialized Training or Certification

1. Activity _____ # _____

2. Authoritative source for plan _____

3. Outcomes (sample outcomes from Camp Fire USA)

Check if Completed	Outcome	Action to Achieve Outcome	Indicators
	Greater self-awareness and positive values		
	Increased social skills and sense of belonging		
	Increased knowledge of and appreciation for the natural environment		
	Increased sense of competency and empowerment (include progression, challenge, success, decision-making)		

4. Location/boundaries/controlled access

5. Eligibility requirements for participants (age, height, experience, competency, demonstration, etc.)

6. Staff qualifications, certification, and/or skill verification

7. Camper/staff supervision ratio and minimum number of staff members to operate the activity

8. Equipment needed, including protective equipment

9. Equipment maintenance procedures and responsibility, access policies, etc.

10. Any actions needed to minimize environmental impact

11. Safety orientation (when required and by whom; safety rules attached or on the back)

APPENDIX 19

Sample Program Operational Plan for Activities Not Requiring Staff Members With Specialized Training or Certification

1. Activity _____# _____

2. Outcomes (sample outcomes from Camp Fire USA)

Check if Completed	Outcome	Action to Achieve Outcome	Indicators
	Greater self-awareness and positive values		
	Increased social skills and sense of belonging		
	Increased knowledge of and appreciation for the natural environment		
	Increased sense of competency and empowerment (include progression, challenge, success, decision-making)		

3. Location/boundaries/controlled access

4. Eligibility requirements for participants (age, height, experience, competency demonstration, etc.)

5. Staff qualifications and/or skill verification

6. Camper/staff supervision ratio and minimum number of staff to operate the activity

7. Equipment/materials needed

8. Any actions need to minimize environmental impact.

9. Safety orientation (if required and by whom; attach any safety rules on the back)

APPENDIX 20

Sample Form for Dealing With Complaints

Name of person taking complaint:		

Position:	Date and time:	
Complaint made in person	By email	
By phone	Other:	

Name of person making the complaint:		

Parent	Vendor	Program leader
Youth	Program administrator	Other:

Home phone number:	Cell phone number:
Business phone number:	

Nature of complaint:		

Behavior complaint	Child-abuse complaint	Program complaint.
Supervision complaint	Product complaint	Personnel complaint

Complaint:		

Date:	Time:	Location:

1. Persons involved and roles:	

2. Problem:	

3. Notify or discuss with:	Date and time:

4. Follow-up required/promised:	

APPENDIX 21

Employment Tax Requirements

(Source: IRS website: www.irs.gov)

This article discusses the basic requirements for a tax-exempt organization's compliance with employment tax and wage reporting compliance.

- Determine employer identification number requirements, complete and submit EIN Request (Form SS-4).

Tax-exempt organizations must use their EIN if required to file employment tax returns or give tax statements to employees or annuitants. (Note: The tax-exempt organization should have only one EIN. Once the organization receives an EIN, the organization will use it from one year to the next.)

- Determine employee status and verify work eligibility by filing Form I-9, Employment Eligibility Verification.

All U.S. employers, including tax-exempt organizations who hire workers, must verify the employment and identity of all employees hired to work in the United States. Both the tax-exempt organization and the employee must complete the U.S. Citizenship and Immigration Services (USCIS) Form I-9, *Employment Eligibility Verification.*

Employers must maintain completed Forms I-9 in their files for three years after the date of hire or one year after the date employment ends, whichever is later. The form can be obtained from the USCIS offices, by calling 1-800-829-3676 or by visiting the USCIS website. EOs may contact the USCIS at 1-800-375-5283 for more information about employers' responsibilities.

- Request Form W-4, the employee withholding form, and verify employee ID information (SSN).

To know how much federal income tax to withhold from an employee's wages, the tax-exempt organization should have a Form W-4, *Employee's Withholding Allowance Certificate*, on file for each employee. The amount to be withheld is determined by the employee's gross wages and the information submitted by the employee on Form W-4.

The information on Form W-4 includes:

√ employee's marital status;

√ number of withholding allowances claimed;

√ employee's request to have additional tax withheld; or

√ employee's claim to exemption from withholding.

The tax-exempt organization should ask each new employee to provide a signed Form W-4 by his or her first day of work. This certificate is effective with the first wage payment and lasts until the employee files a new certificate.

If an employee does not provide the organization with a Form W-4, the organization should withhold tax as if the employee were a single person who has claimed no withholding allowances. If not enough tax is withheld and the employee has not provided a Form W-4 or has claimed an exemption from withholding, the employee may be subject to penalties. An employee who claims exemption from withholding must renew his or her status by filing a new Form W-4 with the employer by February 15 of each year.

Note: Student status does not automatically exempt the employee from income tax withholding.

Generally, Forms W-4 should be retained for the tax-exempt organization's records. Note, however, that in some circumstances the organization must send copies to the IRS.

For more information on withholding, see Publication 505, *Tax Withholding and Estimated Tax.*

A tax-exempt organization can help its employees determine whether they are having the right amount of income tax withheld by ordering and distributing copies of Publication 919, *How Do I Adjust My Tax Withholding?*

- An employee should use Form W-5, *Earned Income Credit Advance Payment Certificate* if he or she expects to be eligible to receive advance payments.

The EIC is a tax credit for certain workers whose earned income is below a certain level. Because it is a "credit," the EIC is subtracted from the amount of tax. Even workers who are not required to file a tax return because their wages are below the minimum income-level requirements to file may be able to receive the credit. They must file a tax return in order to receive the credit, however.

The tax-exempt organization can use the advance EIC tables in Publication 15 to figure the correct amount of advance EIC payment. For deposit purposes, advance payments reduce withheld income taxes and employee and employer social security and Medicare taxes, thereby reducing the tax-exempt organization's total tax liability.

For more information, see Chapter 10, Advance Earned Income Credit (EIC) Payment, in Publication 15.

Note: In 2004, an employee's advance EIC payments are limited to a total of $1,563, although the credit may be more. An employee must claim any additional amount of EIC on his or her tax return.

- The tax-exempt organization must notify each employee from whom the organization did not withhold any income tax about the EIC.

The organization will meet the notification requirements by giving the employee either Notice 797, *Possible Refund on Your Federal Income Tax Returns Because of the Earned Income Credit* (EIC); the tax-exempt organization's own written statement if it has the exact wording of Notice 797; or the official Form W-2, *Wage and Tax Statement*, which contains a statement on the back of Copy C. Exception: The tax-exempt organization does not need to notify those employees who claimed exemption from withholding on Form W-4.

- Calculate and deduct employees' income tax, social security, and Medicare amounts.

- Make required deposits of taxes withheld plus any related employer taxes according to the instructions in Circular E (Publication 15).

- File Form 941 quarterly, and Form 940 annually (if required) and furnish a copy of Form W-2, Wage and Tax Statement, to each employee who received wages during the year.

Form W-2 must show total wages and other compensation paid (even if not subject to withholding); total wages subject to social security and Medicare taxes; allocated tips (if any); amounts deducted for income, social security and Medicare taxes; and the total advance EIC payment. In all cases, the tax-exempt organization must give each of its employees Form W-2 by January 31 following the end of the calendar year covered. Forms W-2 provided to employees must be legible; Forms W-2 that are not computer-generated are sometimes illegible.

The employee may request Form W-2 earlier, and employees often do so when employment ends before the close of the year. The tax-exempt organization must give the employee a Form W-2 within 30 days of the employee's request or within 30 days of the final wage payment, whichever is later.

The tax-exempt organization should keep any undeliverable employee copies of Form W-2 (Copies B and C) as part of its records for four years.

√ The tax-exempt organization must file Form W-3, Transmittal of Wage and Tax Statements, to transmit Copy A of Forms W-2 to the Social Security Administration by the last day of February after the calendar year for which the Forms W-2 are prepared. (If the organization files electronically, it may file by March 31.) The Social Security Administration will process these forms and provide the IRS with the income tax data that it needs from those forms. The mailing address for the forms is on Form W-3.

Note: The totals on Form W-3 should equal the total of all Forms 941 the tax-exempt organization filed for the year.

The tax-exempt organization must use the same name and taxpayer identification number when completing all transmittal documents (Forms W-3), even if the organization files transmittals from more than one location.

The tax-exempt organization must use the same name on transmittals and information returns that were used on the income tax return or other returns filed under the same taxpayer identification number.

- File Form 945, *Annual Return of Withheld Federal Income Tax*, to report income tax withheld from non-payroll payments, such as pensions, IRAs, gambling winnings, and backup withholding.

- File Form 1096, *Annual Summary and Transmittal of U.S. Information Returns*, to transmit Copy A of Forms 1099, 1098, 5498, and W-2G to the IRS.

The tax-exempt organization must file Form 1096 with each type of return by February 28. If the tax-exempt organization files electronically, the organization may file by March 31.

- File required information returns, such as Form 1099-MISC.

A tax-exempt organization does not withhold income tax or social security and Medicare taxes from, or pay social security and Medicare taxes or federal unemployment tax on amounts it pays to an independent contractor ("non-employee"). Generally, if the organization pays at least $600 during the year to a non-employee for services (including parts and materials) performed in the course of the organization's business, it must furnish a Form 1099-MISC, *Miscellaneous Income*, to that person by January 31 of the following year.

The tax-exempt organization will need the social security number or EIN of an independent contractor to complete Form 1099-MISC. If the independent contractor is a sole proprietor, the SSN is preferred. The organization should always ask the independent contractor to complete Form W-9, *Request for Taxpayer Identification Number and Certification*, before beginning work.

If the tax-exempt organization does not obtain an SSN or EIN before the organization pays the contractor, the organization must withhold income tax from the payment, generally referred to as backup withholding. Backup withholding rules require that 28% of the payment be withheld, and reported on Form 945, *Annual Return of Withheld Federal Income Tax*.

Note: Do not report payments to corporations on Form 1099-MISC unless reporting payments for medical, health or legal services. Refer to the General Instructions for Forms 1099, 1098, 5498 and W2G for more information on 1099 reporting and withholding requirements.

- File Form 8027, *Employer's Annual Information Return of Tip Income* to report tip income and allocated tips.

This generally applies to tax-exempt organizations who have service employees, such as wait staff at a country club exempt under Code section 501(c)(7).

APPENDIX 22

Federal Employment Laws and Regulations

Federal Employment Law	Enforcement Agency
Title VII (Civil Rights Act of 1964) prohibits discrimination on the basis of sex, race, religion, color, or national origin. Also prohibits retaliation for filing a charge, testifying, etc. Civil Rights Act of 1991 expands remedies under Title VII and makes suits easier for plaintiffs alleging discrimination. Pregnancy Discrimination Act of 1978 prohibits sex discrimination on basis of pregnancy, childbirth, or related medical conditions	Equal Employment Opportunity Commission (EEOC)
Age Discrimination in Employment Act (ADEA) prohibits discrimination on the basis of age (40 and over).	EEOC
National Child Protection Act of 1993 establishes a central computerized database of child-abuse crime information. States are required to report arrests, convictions, and final dispositions of child-abuse offenders.	States are encouraged, but not required, to pass laws requiring childcare providers to obtain background checks on paid staff and volunteers.
Fair Labor Standards Act regulates payment of wages and overtime requirements, exempt/non exempt classifications, etc.	Secretary of Labor
Occupational Safety and Health Act requires employers to provide workplaces free from recognized hazards to employees and requires employers to comply with occupational safety and health standards issued by the Occupational Safety & Health Administration (OSHA). Requires employers to have programs for hazardous materials; locking out/tagging out machinery; and protecting employees from bloodborne diseases.	OSHA
Americans with Disabilities Act increases access to public accommodations for disabled persons and prohibits discrimination in employment on the basis of disability.	Department of Justice (Access) EEOC (Employment)
Family and Medical Leave Act of 1993 provides employees with 12 weeks of unpaid leave for maternity, adoption, personal, and family illness.	Secretary of Labor
Veterans protection/preference laws require employers to grant leave to employees for military service and return employees to work after military service.	U.S. Attorney General
Whistleblower Laws make it illegal for employers to retaliate against employees who report violations of the law to the proper authorities, participate in legal proceedings, or refuse to break the law.	Secretary of Labor

APPENDIX 23

Sample Interview Questions and Questions to Avoid

These sample questions are for applicants who would be working directly with children:

1. Tell me about any experience you have working directly with children.

2. What did you like the best/least about those positions?

3. What do you think are the key issues facing youth today?

4. What experience do you have in addressing these issues?

5. What did you like/dislike about your supervisor?

6. How would you describe yourself?

7. How would a friend describe you?

8. In your experiences with youth, what kinds of problems or issues have you had to deal with?

9. Why do you want to work with children?

10. What age group or gender do you prefer to work with?

11. Given the following situation (design several typical scenarios), what would you do?

Some Questions to Avoid in an Interview

Other than the direct questions that are illegal to ask (refer to Worksheets O-28 and P-54: Screening of Staff Members and Volunteers), it is best to avoid questions addressing the following issues:

1. In many states, you cannot ask the age of the applicant unless the job requires a minimum age because the applicant will be caring for children. You may ask what schools the applicant attended and how many years he attended or what degrees he was awarded.

2. The name of applicant's church, synagogue, mosque, pastor, minister, or rabbi, etc.

3. If the applicant is married or how many children he has

4. How long the applicant has lived at his current address or if he owns or rents the home. You may ask if he has recently moved from another state.

5. Any information about personal finances

6. If he has ever been arrested (being arrested does not necessarily result in a conviction). Questions related to conviction other than a minor traffic offense are permitted in some states if the possible crimes are limited to those that are pertinent to the duties being applied for.

7. Clubs or political parties he belongs to, or how he spends his spare time

8. Whether he can speak or write another language, unless doing so is a bona fide job requirement

9. Whether he uses lawful drug or alcohol products, smokes, takes any prescription drugs, or is undergoing any treatment for addiction disorders or substance abuse

10. If the applicant is good at handling stressful situations or if he has ever demonstrated any physical response to stressful working conditions

11. If he is an American citizen or any question related to national origin or race. Assume every applicant does have work authorization and require proof after the decision to hire has been made.

APPENDIX 24

Sample Form for Staff and Volunteer Training Report

Training:	Date:
Person completing the form:	Title:

Subject(s):	
Outline and objectives of training content attached	

Instructor(s) signature:

Number of hours:	Total number of participants:

Signatures of participants who received training (list or attach signed roster):

List participants that missed portions of the training:	Date(s) and method of informing participants of material covered:

APPENDIX 25

Sample Sexual Harassment Policy

Definition

To provide a work environment that respects the rights of employees, any form of sexual harassment must not be tolerated. Sexual harassment includes:

- Unwelcome sexual advances
- Requests for sexual favors
- Verbal or physical conduct of a sexual nature that has the purpose or effect of interfering unreasonably with an individual's work performance or creating an intimidating, hostile, or offensive work environment

Organization Policy

All employees have a right to work in an environment free of discrimination, which encompasses freedom from sexual harassment. The organization prohibits sexual harassment of its employees in any form.

Such conduct may result in disciplinary action up to and including dismissal. Specifically, no supervisor shall threaten or insinuate either explicitly or implicitly that any employee's submission to, or rejection of, sexual advances will in any way influence any personnel decision regarding that employee's employment, evaluation, wages, advancement, assigned duties, shifts, or any other condition of employment.

Other sexually harassing conduct in the workplace, whether physical or verbal, committed by supervisors or nonsupervisory personnel is also prohibited. This definition includes repeated offensive sexual flirtation, advances, propositions, continual or repeated abuse of a sexual nature, graphic verbal commentary about an individual's body, sexually degrading words to describe an individual, and the display in the workplace of sexually suggestive objects or pictures.

Complaint Procedure

Employees should keep in mind that a charge of sexual harassment is very serious. Any situation that possibly involves such a charge should be treated with the strictest confidentiality and should not be discussed with coworkers. Rather, employees who believe they are the victims of sexual harassment on the job shall follow the grievance procedures listed below.

The (organization) provides the opportunity for a staff member to request a formal review of involuntary termination or personnel action that has resulted in disagreement as follows:

1. The staff member should discuss the situation with her or his immediate supervisor.

2. Within the staff, the Executive Director is the final resource in an attempt to appeal a termination or resolve a disagreement. If the situation cannot be resolved, the staff member may request, in writing, a review by the Board or Personnel Committee with the full knowledge of the Executive Director.

3. The Board or Personnel Committee will review the situation and make recommendations to the Executive Director.

Step I: If the employee is being harassed by someone other than his or her supervisor, that employee should express displeasure clearly to the harasser. This first step is vital. It is important that the employee making the complaint be certain that he or she is not misinterpreting the words or actions of another employee.

Step 2: The employee must report the situation to his or her supervisor. Should the harasser be the employee's own supervisor, the employee should report the situation directly to a member of the Management Team, who will contact appropriate agency representatives.

Step 3: The organization will investigate the employee's complaint. The employee will not suffer retaliation for filing a complaint. Complaints of sexual harassment are not entered into employees' personnel files. They are retained separately in confidential files. Where the investigation confirms the allegations, appropriate corrective action will be taken.

Safety of Employees

The organization will take every precaution for the safety of its employees. Employees are required by law to exercise safety precautions and to report any unsafe conditions. All accidents must be reported immediately to the supervisor. The provisions, conditions, and reporting of requirements to the Department of Labor and Industry and the Occupational Safety Health Act will be adhered to in cases of accidents to employees while they are at work.

APPENDIX 26

Sample Technology/Equipment Security and Usage Policy

Introduction

This policy may be modified or replaced as circumstances change and/or as assessments of risks and benefits develop. This policy is designed to address staff and volunteer usage of technology associated with day-to-day business. It is provided to all staff and volunteers upon acceptance to serve in official organization roles.

All of the organization's telephone and electronic communications systems/equipment, computers, and other business equipment [including telephones, voice mail, electronic or computer mail (e-mail), Internet access, facsimile (fax) machines, and similar devices] are the sole property of the organization. Any information that is received from, sent to, transmitted by, or stored in the systems/equipment is also the property of the organization.

The above-mentioned communication devices should be used primarily for business. Occasional personal use of these communication devices may be acceptable only on an employee's own time (e.g., lunch hour, before or after work hours) or at other times as approved by the executive director, provided that it in no way interferes with the employee's job performance and other work-related expectations, nor with organization usage. However, no employee, youth, or volunteer may at any time conduct a business or engage in unlawful, illegal, unethical, discriminatory, disruptive, threatening, or offensive activities or practices that may discredit the organization.

The organization also maintains distinct ownership and control of all council websites, intranets, and extranets. The council and the national organization explicitly control usage of the organization logo and all national and council images.

Computers

The computer hardware provided to you is owned by organization and is provided for organizational business. The organization purchases and licenses the use of various computer software for business purposes and does not own the copyright to this software or its related documentation. Unless authorized by the software developer, the organization does not have the right to reproduce such software for use on more than one computer. Employees may only use software stored on their organization desktop computers or the local area network according to the manufacturer software licensing agreement. The organization prohibits the illegal duplication of software and its related documentation. Failure to observe manufacturer copyright or license agreements may result in disciplinary action from the organization or legal action by the copyright owner.

It is imperative that an employee not disable his or her computer's virus scan and that he or she perform virus scan updates as instructed by the network administrator. To protect the organization's equipment, employees should not bring software from home or any other source for use at the office without prior approval from the executive director and/or the network administrator.

Employees are prohibited from using the organization computer system to create and send any messages, images, or files that are unlawful, illegal, unethical, discriminatory, offensive, or disruptive. This policy includes, but is not limited to, any messages that contain sexual implications, racial slurs, gender-specific comments, or other messages that offensively address someone's age, sexual orientation, religious or political beliefs, national origin, disability, or other classes protected by applicable law.

Internet

The organization may provide employees with Internet access to facilitate the operations of the organization. In general, employees and volunteers should use the Internet for business purposes only. The Internet should not be used while at the organization in a manner that is unlawful, illegal, unethical, discriminatory, disruptive, threatening, or offensive to others, or in ways that may be harmful to workplace morale.

Employees or volunteers using the Internet may not transmit copyrighted materials belonging to entities other than the organization. One copy of copyrighted material may be downloaded for your own personal use in research (in the case of staff). Users are not permitted to copy, transfer, rename, add, or delete information or programs belonging to other users unless given express permission to do so by the owner. Failure to observe copyright or license agreements may result in disciplinary action from the organization or legal action from the copyright owner.

The organization prohibits the use of subscription-based services (Internet sites requiring subscriptions before access) without prior executive director approval.

Chats and newsgroups are public forums where it is prohibited to reveal proprietary or confidential information about the organization, its employees, board members, or donor base. Employees who release protected information via a newsgroup or chat—whether or not the release is intentional—may be subject to disciplinary action.

Listserves may be established to serve the needs of the council at the discretion of the executive director. Prior to their establishment, procedures should be identified that:

1. Control membership of the discussion group

2. Ensure discussion participants are over the age of majority

3. Ensure that discussion does not occur concerning identifiable program participants

4. Identify at least two organization staff members as being responsible for monitoring the activities of the list

It is the responsibility of the assigned staff members to notify all users about any created discussion group and the procedures and policies that regulate its use.

The organization has software and systems in place that can monitor and record all Internet usage as needed (if applicable). These security systems are capable of recording each Internet site visit, chat, newsgroup, or e-mail message, as well as each file transfer into and out of internal networks for every user. The organization reserves the right to review Internet activity and analyze usage patterns to ensure that Internet resources are devoted to maintaining the highest levels of productivity. The organization further reserves the right to inspect any and all files stored in any directory on the network or workstation to ensure compliance with organization policies and procedures.

The proliferation of social networking websites (e.g., MySpace, Facebook) provides members and others with additional opportunities to gain information. For these reasons, all employees must be cognizant of the impression they create about themselves and the organization when they create and/or participate in these kinds of websites.

The organization has an appropriate interest in ensuring that all individuals associated with it, including its members, are assured appropriate confidentiality and treated with respect and professionalism at all times. The organization also has an interest in ensuring that anything that is in the public domain about the organization is in the best interests of the organization and reflects positively on the organization. Accordingly, the following standards should be adhered to by all employees in connection with the use of the Internet and other electronic communications media:

1. If an employee creates or maintains a website or blog about himself (e.g., MySpace, Facebook), he must exercise the highest degree of good judgment regarding the material placed on that site or blog. For example, such individuals should ask themselves the following question: "What would a prospective or current employee/participant/parent think about me and/or the organization if he accessed this site or blog?" If the answer is that the individual might perceive something negative, then the material that may create a negative impression about the individual or organization should not be placed on the site or blog.

2. If an individual participates in a blog or other site, he may not identify himself as associated with the organization, either explicitly or implicitly, unless authorized in writing by the organization.

3. Content placed on the Internet or transmitted via other media may not be potentially or actually defamatory, abusive, threatening, harassing, invasive of privacy, or injurious to any member or any other employee.

Organization Official Product Sales

From time to time, a member within a council may use the Internet to publicly market and sell a product. Because the Internet does not recognize organization jurisdictions, it is possible for jurisdictional disputes over the sale of a product to occur. Where possible, the organization should avoid using the Internet to officially sell products and should counsel any member who is found using the Internet in this manner.

Official Organization Websites

If the organization maintains an official website, any picture, drawing, rendering, or other image requires the expressed written approval of all adults and at least one parent or guardian of any youth under the age of 18 to be posted on the site. Specifically, if information is collected or disseminated, such as e-mail addresses, birth dates, addresses, genders, or any other personal information from youth and children under the age of 13, it must meet the requirements of the Children's Online Privacy Protection Act (COPPA). These requirements include:

1. Obtaining verifiable parental consent before collecting, using, or disclosing information from a child (under the age of 13)

2. Having and posting a privacy notice on the home page of the website and at each location where personal information of a child is being collected

3. Understanding the responsibility to protect children's privacy and safety

Additionally, the organization's websites will refrain from identifying pictured children or adults and will utilize password protection to access areas where personal matters may be discussed. Also, the organization will refrain from revealing the identity of persons participating in chat rooms or online discussions and from using photographs of individuals without their knowledge or consent.

Internet Privacy Policy Statement

The organization has an Internet Privacy Policy Statement available on the organization's website for anything that utilizes the web in securing personal information from users and participants. This policy covers treatment of personally identifiable information that may be collected when a user is on the organization website.

Volunteer-Managed Websites and Listserves

Any privately managed, non-organization websites or listserves purporting to serve as volunteer, leader, parent, or youth communication services shall comply with organizational graphic standards. Additionally, these sites require the approval of the executive director or board of directors and shall comply with all requests and/or requirements from the local and/or national organization. Under no circumstances will images, pictures, and personal information such as phone numbers or addresses of any youth or child under the age of majority be maintained on any privately managed website or listserve. See state statutes for further information.

Any privately managed non-organization website or listserve must contain the following certification prominently displayed on the site's splash page or e-mail listserve:

> This website [or listserve] has been approved by the organization and is expressly designed to aid in the communication by and among volunteer leaders, parents, the organization members, and youth associated with the council. This site complies with all Children's Online Privacy Protection Act guidelines and meets the organization's graphic and content standards.

> Although this site is not an official organization website, it exists to supplement and encourage organization participation. No "links" to other websites are allowed without the expressed approval of organizational authorities.

> No registered user of this site may engage in unlawful, illegal, unethical, discriminatory, disruptive, threatening, or offensive activity or practice. If any member or user is found violating local or national Internet policies, the offending user or member will be removed from active organization membership or participation.

Telephone

The organization provides employees with telephone and voicemail access (if applicable) to facilitate the operations of the organization. In general, employees should use the telephone for business purposes only. The telephone should not be used while at the organization in a manner that is unethical, discriminatory, disruptive, threatening, or offensive to others, or in ways that may be harmful to workplace morale. This policy includes, but is not limited to, unlawful or offensive conversations or voicemail messages that contain sexual implications, racial slurs, gender-specific comments, or other messages that offensively address someone's age, sexual orientation, religious or political beliefs, national origin, disability, or other classes protected by applicable law. The executive director or administrator of human resources (if applicable) reviews the monthly long- distance phone bills for any unusual activity. Long-distance charges for calls of a personal nature will be paid by the employees who made the calls.

Facsimiles (Faxes)

The organization provides employees with facsimile (fax) machine access to facilitate the operations of the organization. In general, employees and volunteers should use the fax machine for business purposes only. The fax machine should not be used while at the organization in a manner that is unethical, discriminatory, disruptive, threatening, or offensive to others, or in ways that may be harmful to workplace morale. This policy includes, but is not limited to, items faxed by employees that are unlawful or offensive in content or that contain sexual implications, racial slurs, gender-specific comments, or other messages that offensively address someone's age, sexual orientation, religious or political beliefs, national origin, disability, or other classes protected by applicable law. This policy also includes facsimiles of proprietary, confidential, or unauthorized copyrighted information (of this organization or other organizations).

Summary

Abuse of the above-stated office equipment or software through excessive personal use or use in violation of the law and/or organization policy or practice will result in disciplinary action, up to and including termination of employment, termination of volunteer responsibilities, and/or revocation of membership. The organization reserves the right, at its discretion, to access and monitor any use of, or storage in, the organization's computer, Internet, telephone, or fax systems, including any information electronically stored or transmitted on these systems, without the knowledge or consent of employees, volunteers, or users.

APPENDIX 26A

Sample Acknowledgment and Release—Technology/Equipment Security, Usage, and Privacy Policy

The attached is the organization's policy on Technology/Equipment Security and Usage in the workplace, as well as a Privacy Policy. As an agent of the organization, I understand that I must comply with this policy as a condition of working or volunteering at the organization. I further agree that if I witness any abuse of the organization's Computer, Internet, Telephone, and Fax Usage Policy, I will report such incidents immediately to a member of management for investigation.

I, _____, acknowledge that I have been given a copy of the organization's Technology/Equipment Security and Usage Policy and the Privacy Policy and that these policies have been reviewed with me. I have been provided with an opportunity to ask questions and fully understand my rights and responsibilities as a full-time, part-time, or temporary employee, volunteer, or member of the organization.

I acknowledge that I am subject to, and must comply with, a number of state and federal laws involving the confidential handling of personal information regarding both customers/clients of the organization and other employees or volunteers. These laws may include but not be limited to FACTA, HIPAA, The Economic Espionage Act, The Privacy Act, Gramm/Leach/Billey, Identity Theft Laws (where applicable), Trade Secrets Protections, and Implied Contract Breach.

I acknowledge that I must maintain the confidentially of all documents, credit cards, and personal information of any type and that such information may only be used for their intended business purpose. Any other use of said information is strictly prohibited and is cause for immediate dismissal. Additionally, should any misuse of information be made by me, I understand that I am fully accountable both civilly and criminally.

I further agree to follow the rules and abide by these policies.

_____   _____

Signature   Date

_____   _____

Human Resources   Date

APPENDIX 27

Sample Internet Privacy Policy Statement

_____ [organization] takes your privacy seriously. Please read the following to learn more about our privacy policy.

A. What This Privacy Policy Covers

This privacy policy covers the organization's treatment of personally identifiable information that the organization collects when you are on any portion of the organization's website, and when you use organization services.

B. Information Collection and Use

The organization collects personally identifiable information when you register online; when you use or purchase certain organization products or services; or if you make a charitable donation to the organization online.

The organization may use this information for general purposes: to customize the content you see; to register you for services, to fulfill your requests for certain products; and to contact you about special activities, new services, or products and fundraising.

C. Information Sharing and Disclosure

The organization will not sell or rent your personally identifiable information to anyone. The organization will only send personally identifiable information about you to other companies or people when:

1. A need exists to share your information to provide the product or service you have requested

2. A need exists to send the information to companies who work on behalf of the organization to provide a product or service to you (Unless we tell you differently, these companies do not have any right to use the personally identifiable information we provide to them beyond what is necessary to assist us.)

3. A need exists to respond to subpoenas, court orders, or legal processes

4. The organization finds that your action on their website violates the organization's Terms of Service or any of the usage guidelines for specific products or services

D. Your Ability to Edit and Delete Your Account Information and Preferences

The organization gives you the ability to edit your information and preferences at any time, including whether or not you want the organization to contact you about special programs and services. You may request deletion of your website account by sending an email to _____ [organization's email address].

E. Security

Your account information is password-protected for your privacy and security. In certain areas, the organization uses industry-standard SSL-encryption to protect data transmissions.

F. Changes to This Privacy Policy

The organization may amend this policy from time to time. If any substantial changes are made to the way your personal information is used, you will be notified.

G. Questions or Suggestions

If you have questions or suggestions about this website or this privacy policy, please e-mail _____ [organization's email address].

APPENDIX 28

Sample Guidelines for Direct Program Leader Behavior

The organization expects certain behavior on the part of program leaders. This behavior protects the children and protects leaders from unfounded allegations of child abuse.

- Two responsible persons are present at all program sites, as well as on field and camping trips. At least one adult should be within eyesight or hearing of participants at all times.

- When taking a coeducational group camping, both male and female adults should be present.

- Adults may not take participants out for one-on-one activities.

- While adults must respect the privacy of participants, they should be within hearing distance when they are changing clothes, showering, or using the toilet. Adults should protect their own privacy also.

- Parents should always be welcome to visit a program.

- Leaders must restrict contact on the program site to people who have a relationship to the program. One-on-one contact between children and other adults at the site is not tolerated.

APPENDIX 29

Sample Form for Documentation of Staff Performance

Identification of acceptable and unacceptable or inappropriate behaviors and/or relationships among staff members is a part of a supervisor's job.

Name:	Period of Observation:
Name of Supervisor:	
To help staff members improve their performance, rate the observed traits on a scale of 1 (needs improvement) to 10 (excellent)	
1. Positive role model	1 2 3 4 5 6 7 8 9 10
2. Follows safety rules	1 2 3 4 5 6 7 8 9 10
3. Enforces safety rules	1 2 3 4 5 6 7 8 9 10
4. Punctuality	1 2 3 4 5 6 7 8 9 10
5. Team player	1 2 3 4 5 6 7 8 9 10
6. Follows direction	1 2 3 4 5 6 7 8 9 10
7. Positive attitude	1 2 3 4 5 6 7 8 9 10
8. Relationships with children	1 2 3 4 5 6 7 8 9 10
9. Self-motivated	1 2 3 4 5 6 7 8 9 10
10. Judgment	1 2 3 4 5 6 7 8 9 10
11. Problem-solving	1 2 3 4 5 6 7 8 9 10
12.	1 2 3 4 5 6 7 8 9 10
13.	1 2 3 4 5 6 7 8 9 10
14.	1 2 3 4 5 6 7 8 9 10
Comments on above observations:	
Consequences of any inappropriate behavior:	

Recommendations or suggestions for future action from the supervisor or staff member:	
Follow-up required and by when:	
Signature of Staff Member:	Date:
Signature of Supervisor:	Date:

APPENDIX 30

Sample Guidelines for Volunteer Dismissal

Options When Volunteer Performance is Below Expectations

When volunteer performance is substandard, or the service is no longer benefiting the organization, it may be necessary to take corrective action. Some options to consider:

- Retraining
- Transferring the volunteer to a new position
- Dismissing the individual from the volunteer program

Guidelines for Dismissing Volunteers

- It's advisable to only dismiss volunteers when other techniques have been unsuccessful or when the volunteer's behavior is severe in nature. If you have to dismiss a volunteer, document the volunteer's behaviors that have led to the dismissal and document any attempts that were made to resolve the situation prior to the decision to dismiss the volunteer.

- Make sure that you can adequately explain the reason(s) why the volunteer is being dismissed. Refer to your organization's policies and standards of behavior for volunteers.

- Possible steps to consider when dismissing a volunteer are to meet with him to discuss the situation and follow up the dismissal with a letter that specifically explains the volunteer's dismissal from his responsibilities and duties with the organization. Any written communication should be specific and explain the circumstances thoroughly.

Instances exist when the dismissal of a volunteer is necessary to maintain the credibility and reputation of the organization and the volunteer program. Volunteers should be informed from the beginning of their service that they may be terminated at any time, with or without cause. It is important to go over the organization's volunteer policies and procedures with volunteers. It is also vital to discuss unsafe or inappropriate conduct and all grounds of dismissal with volunteers before they begin their service with the organization.

	Yes	No
1. Prior to Making a Decision		
Do you have the volunteer's signed application, Code of Conduct, and Disclosure Statement?		
Have you allowed the volunteer to share his or her side of the story?		
Have you tried or considered other options for dealing with the volunteer?		
2. Making the Decision		
Did the volunteer have prior knowledge of the issue?		
Is the dismissal your last resort or is the behavior severe enough to warrant a dismissal?		
Is the decision consistent with other volunteer dismissals?		
Have you reviewed your organization's policies and procedures related to volunteer issues?		
Are you handling the situation at an appropriate pace?		
3. Documentation		
Have you clearly documented the situation?		
Does the documentation include the facts, as you believe them to be true?		
Does the documentation describe specific behaviors or actions that are inappropriate?		
Does the documentation include previous meetings with the volunteer that relate to the current issue?		
Does the documentation support a specific violation of your organization's Code of Conduct, Disclosure Statement, or Volunteer Policies and Procedures?		
4. Communicating the Decision		
Have you arranged for a private location to meet with the volunteer?		
Have you determined who should know about the dismissal?		
Have you discussed the issue, as appropriate, with other staff, volunteers, or participants?		
Does a prepared statement need to be developed?		
Have you prepared a letter to the volunteer that clearly states his or her dismissal as a volunteer?		

Sample of Universal Blood and Body Fluid Precautions

"Universal precautions" constitutes an approach to infection control that treats all human blood and certain human body fluids as if they were known to be infectious for HIV, Hepatitis B, and other bloodborne pathogens. Since blood can carry all types of infectious diseases even when a person does not feel or look ill, knowledge of, and training in, universal precautions is essential for anyone that might come into contact with blood or other body fluids. The Centers for Disease Control and Prevention (CDC) has recommended the following guidelines to prevent cross contamination from bloodborne pathogens:

1. All healthcare workers should use appropriate barrier precautions to prevent skin and mucous-membrane exposure when contact with blood or body fluid of any person is anticipated.

2. Gloves should be worn for touching blood and body fluids, mucous membranes, or non-intact skin of all persons, and for handling items or surfaces soiled with blood or body fluids. Gloves should be removed properly—pulling inside out—and changed after contact with each person. Place gloves in a bag with waste.

3. Surfaces soiled with blood or body fluids should be flooded with bleach solution, alcohol, or a dry sanitary absorbent agent. Gloves should always be worn to clean surfaces soiled with blood, but are not usually needed to handle urine-soaked bedding, unless blood is obvious. Disposable towels and tissues or other contaminated materials should be disposed of in a plastic lined container. Biohazard bags should be used for dressings or materials used to soak up blood or other infectious waste.

4. Hands and other skin surfaces should be washed immediately and thoroughly if contaminated with blood or other body fluids. Hands should be washed immediately after gloves are removed.

5. Masks and protective eye wear, gowns, or aprons should be worn during procedures that are likely to generate droplets or splashes of blood or other body fluids.

6. Needles should not be recapped, purposely bent or broken by hand, removed from disposable syringes, or otherwise manipulated by hand. After use, disposable syringes and needles, scalpel blades, and other sharp items should be placed in puncture-resistant containers for disposal. The containers should be located as close as practical to the use area.

7. Although saliva has not been implicated in HIV/AIDS transmission, mouthpieces, resuscitation bags, or other ventilation devices should be

available for use in areas in which the need for resuscitation is predictable.

8. Healthcare workers who have draining lesions or weeping dermatitis should refrain from all direct care and from handling equipment until the condition resolves.

APPENDIX 31A

Sample Statement of Informed Consent and Verification of Training

_____ [organization] will give instruction and provide equipment to each staff member in universal precautions according to recommendations from the Centers for Disease Control and Prevention. The documentation of such instruction will be retained in staff records.

I understand that as an employee, I might be exposed to infectious diseases such as the HIV virus that causes AIDS (Acquired Immunodeficiency Syndrome) by direct contact with blood and other body fluids. I agree to follow universal precautions while I am employed at _____ [organization]. I understand that these procedures protect me and others from infectious and/or communicable diseases.

I received this training in universal precautions on _____ [date].

Signed _____

Trainer _____Title _____Date _____

APPENDIX 31B

Sample Office Exposure Control Plan

This information is provided to employees in partial compliance with OSHA's Bloodborne Pathogen Standard. It is the intent to educate people about issues related to exposure to body fluids, to use management techniques and equipment to minimize exposure risks for employees, and to monitor individuals' use of these techniques. It is recognized that universal precautions is an effective control measure. This document describes the application and monitoring of potential sources of risk, the steps taken to protect employees, and the actions taken if blood or body-fluid exposure occurs.

- Job classifications that, by virtue of job description, incur the risk of exposure to blood and other body fluids: (usually no one in the office environment.)

- Job classifications that, by virtue of job description, provide first-aid care as an ancillary task rather than a primary task: office employees instructed to respond in emergency situations to the level of their training per State Good Samaritan regulations

- Other office employees, volunteers, or visitors to the office are not expected to provide first aid, but rather refer people in need of healthcare to emergency medical services (EMS) or private physicians.

Office employees and regular office volunteers are oriented to the potential for exposure. A record of who received the education and its content is kept for three years. This orientation includes:

A. *Identification of risk areas:* Contact with bloodborne pathogens (e.g., hepatitis, HIV), contact with airborne pathogens (e.g., common cold, TB), contact with surface-borne pathogens (e.g., staph infections)

B. *Education about the nature of the risk:* Method of transmission, virulence of pathogens, resistance factors related to potential hosts, symptoms, and information sources that provide clues to potential risk areas

C. *Work practices designed to minimize exposure:*

    1. Availability of personal protective equipment (PPE)—gloves, antimicrobial soap, CPR masks

    2. Double-bagging via plastic bags and disposal procedure for hazardous waste

    3. Use of universal precautions by staff

    4. Education for office employees and volunteers

5. Hepatitis B vaccination recommended—employees and volunteers to contact their private physicians

6. Resource personnel to answer questions—employees' private physicians and/or State Department of Health

D. *Behavior expected from employees to minimize risk:*

1. Use of PPE

a. Gloves are used when in contact with body fluids or providing skin treatment (e.g., applying medication to poison ivy, washing a rash)

b. CPR mask is used to provide CPR/artificial respiration

2. Minimum 15-second hand washing with antimicrobial soap after:

a. Removing gloves,

b. Contact with potential risk

c. Unprotected contact with any body fluid

3. Minimum 60-second hand washing with antimicrobial soap after blood splash

4. Participation in education about disease control

5. Immediate reporting of suspected exposure (e.g., needle stick) to a supervisor

6. Performing job tasks in a manner that minimizes/eliminates exposure potential

7. Evaluation of compliance with the exposure control plan as part of the personnel management system

Office Staff

While the potential for exposure to bloodborne pathogens is minimal for staff, it does exist. The staff is expected to respond to emergencies at the level of their training while initiating the emergency response system. Since emergency response occurs within minutes, the potential for exposure is limited and most likely confined to initiating CPR/artificial respiration and slowing severe bleeding.

In keeping with accepted practices, an appointed (trained) staff member educates staff during orientation about appropriate response practices:

1. Staff members are instructed to use a CPR mask for CPR and artificial respiration; masks are kept in designated place in the office, with the first-aid kit.

2. Staff members are instructed to use gloves when the potential for contact with blood or blood-tinged fluids exist. Gloves are in all first-aid kits. Staff members who want to carry a pair on their person may obtain them from the office supply.

3. Staff members are instructed to respond in emergency situations to the level of their training per State Good Samaritan regulations.

4. Staff members are instructed to immediately initiate the emergency response system.

5. Staff members participate in a discussion of "emergencies" to establish defining attributes of their response.

6. Staff members are educated to approach care of minor injuries from a coaching perspective and specifically directed to refer injured people to their personal healthcare provider if self-care is inappropriate or inadequate.

APPENDIX 31C

Sample Camp Exposure Control Plan

This information is provided to camp employees in partial compliance with OSHA's Bloodborne Pathogen Standard. It is the intent of the camp to educate people about issues related to exposure to body fluids, to use management techniques and equipment to minimize exposure risks for employees, and to monitor individuals' use of these techniques. The camp program recognizes universal precautions as an effective control measure. This document describes the application and monitoring of potential sources of risk in the camp program, the steps taken by the camp to protect employees, and the actions taken by the camp if blood or body-fluid exposure occurs.

- Job classifications that, by virtue of job description, incur the risk of exposure to blood and other body fluids: healthcare director, camp nurses, student nurses

- Job classifications that, by virtue of job description, provide first-aid care as an ancillary task rather than a primary task: Counselors and camp staff

- All other job classifications are not expected to provide first aid, but rather refer people in need of healthcare to the healthcare director.

The healthcare director and camp nurses (i.e., the camp healthcare team) can reasonably expect to come in contact with blood and other body fluids. The potential for exposure to transmitted diseases is greatest for these staff members. Consequently, the program follows the following practices.

Members of the camp health care team are oriented to the potential for exposure by the camp's healthcare director. A record of who received the education and its content is kept for three years. This orientation includes:

A. *Identification of risk areas:* Contact with bloodborne pathogens (e.g., hepatitis, HIV), contact with airborne pathogens (e.g., common cold, TB), contact with surface-borne pathogens (e.g., staph infections)

B. *Education about the nature of the risk:* Method of transmission, virulence of pathogens, resistance factors related to potential hosts, symptoms, and information sources that provide clues to potential risk areas

C. *Work practices designed to minimize exposure:*

   1. Availability of personal protective equipment (PPE)—gloves, CPR masks, antimicrobial soap

2. Double-bagging via red bags and disposal procedure for hazardous waste

3. Screening individuals who come to the program

4. Requiring participants to provide health information

5. Use of universal precautions by staff

6. Education for people working in risk areas: healthcare team members, lifeguards, housekeeping, kitchen staff

7. Hepatitis B vaccination recommended for nurses

8. Sharps container provided with biohazard labels affixed

9. Resource personnel to answer questions: healthcare director, supervising physician, and State Department of Health

D. *Behavior expected from employees to minimize risk:*

1. Use of PPE

a. Gloves are used when in contact with body fluids or providing skin treatment (e.g., applying medication to poison ivy, washing a rash).

b. CPR masks are used to provide CPR/artificial respiration.

2. Minimum 15-second hand washing with antimicrobial soap after:

a. Removing gloves

b. Contact with potential risk

c. Unprotected contact with any body fluid

3. Minimum 60-second hand washing with antimicrobial soap after blood splash

4. Sharps disposed of properly: No recapping of needles; all sharps (lancets, needles) placed in sharps container immediately after use; full sharps container given to _____ [designated person] for disposal through a local hospital

5. Participation in education about disease control

6. Immediate reporting of suspected exposure (e.g., needle stick) to a supervisor and the healthcare director.

7. Performing job tasks in a manner that minimizes/eliminates exposure potential

8. Evaluation of compliance with the camp exposure control plan as part of the camp personnel management system

Camp Counseling Staff

While the potential for exposure to bloodborne pathogens is minimal for general counseling staff, it does exist. The camp healthcare plan vests authority in general staff to respond to emergencies at the level of their training while initiating the camp emergency response system. Since camp emergency response occurs within minutes, the potential for exposure is limited and most likely confined to initiating CPR/artificial respiration and slowing severe bleeding.

In keeping with accepted practices, the camp's healthcare director educates camp staff during precamp training about appropriate response practices:

1. Staff members are instructed to use a CPR mask for CPR and artificial respiration; masks are kept at the pool, waterfront, in first-aid kits, and in vehicles and the health center.

2. Staff members are instructed to use gloves when the potential for contact with blood or blood-tinged fluids exists. Gloves are in all first-aid kits. Staff members who want to carry a pair on their person may obtain them from the health center.

3. Staff members are instructed to respond in emergency situations to the level of their training per State Good Samaritan regulations.

4. Staff members are instructed to immediately initiate the camp emergency response system.

5. Staff members participate in a discussion of "emergencies" to establish defining attributes of their responses.

6. Staff members are educated to approach care of minor injuries from a coaching perspective and specifically directed to refer injured people to the camp healthcare team if selfcare is inappropriate or impossible.

APPENDIX 31D

Hepatitis B Vaccination Statement

[In response to the OSHA Bloodborne Pathogens rule (1992), which requires that employers provide access to the Hepatitis B vaccine to "all occupationally exposed" employees, this form has been used by some ACA camps. This form may be a piece of the camp's OSHA-required Exposure Control Plan or from a local OSHA regulating agency.]

I understand that due to my occupational exposure to blood or other potentially infectious materials, I may be at risk of acquiring the hepatitis B virus (HBV) infection. I have been given information on the hepatitis B vaccine, including information on its efficacy, safety, method of administration, and the benefits of being vaccinated, and understand that the vaccine and vaccination will be offered free of charge.

❑ **Option 1**

_____ [name of employee] has completed the following inoculations using:

❑ Recombivax-HB

❑ Enerix-B vaccine

Inoculation 1: Date _____ Given at _____

Inoculation 2: Date _____ Given at _____

Inoculation 3: Date _____ Given at _____

or

❑ See attached medical form for additional information

❑ **Option 2**

I have been given the opportunity to be vaccinated with the Hepatitis B vaccine at no charge to myself. I decline the vaccination at this time. I understand that by declining this vaccine, I continue to be at risk of acquiring hepatitis B, a serious disease. If, in the future, I continue to have occupational exposure to blood or other potentially infectious materials and I want to be vaccinated with the hepatitis B vaccine, I can receive the vaccination series at no charge to me.

Please check either Option 1 or Option 2 above, and then sign and date below:

Employee name (please print): _____

Employee signature: _____

Date: _____

APPENDIX 31E

Sample Postexposure Timeline for Camp

Camp employees who have a blood exposure incident are eligible for follow-up treatment. Follow-up is initiated by the employee who must immediately (within 15 minutes) notify the camp nurse when a blood exposure incident occurs. The following plan is initiated. Records of the incident are maintained for the duration of employment plus 30 years by the camp director and according to OSHA requirements (i.e., separate from personnel records). Camp administration debriefs each incident in an effort to identify ways to improve the camp's exposure risk.

Timeline	Employee's Actions	Camp Nurse's Actions	Camp Director's Actions
Within 24 hours	Exposure incident occurs Report incident to the camp nurse within 15 minutes Begin prophylactic treatment Complete the worker's compensation form and incident report with the camp director	Notify camp director Begin 15-second scrub of area with bacteriostatic soap, followed by application of disinfectant Contact supervising doctor and refer the individual for assessment Begin psycho-social support process	Determine the source of contamination and initiate a request to have the source screened for infectious diseases Notify insurance Create an incident report file with supporting documentation Contact a mental health professional for the employee Complete the worker's compensation form and incident report form with the employee
Within next 48 hours	Continue medical follow-up per doctor orders Begin counseling support	Monitor individual adjustment to the situation Answer questions as needed Provide needed cares	Follow testing of the source individual as warranted Consult with a mental health professional to arrange postcamp therapy as needed

Timeline	Employee's Actions	Camp Nurse's Actions	Camp Director's Actions
Beyond first three days	Continue postexposure prophylaxis as directed by the doctor Participate in a review of the incident	Participate in a review of the incident	Maintain contact with the employee to follow the incident Lead a review of the incident Review the incident and adapt camp practices as needed to manage the risk and to minimize the chance for a repeat of the situation Maintain records for the duration of employment, plus 30 years.

APPENDIX 31F

Confidential Exposure Incident Report

Should any staff member have a blood exposure incident, an Exposure Incident Report Form must be completed as soon as possible.

Date
Completed: _____   Employee
Name: _____

Date of
Exposure: _____ SS #: _____ DOB: _____

Time of   AM   Home   Business
Exposure: _____ PM   Phone: (____)_____   Phone: (____)_____

Vaccination   Job
Status:_____   Title: _____

Location of incident (be specific): _____

Describe what happened: _____

_____

_____

What task was the employee performing when the exposure occurred?

_____

Was the employee wearing PPE?   ❑ No ❑ Yes   Type: _____

Did the PPE fail?   ❑ No ❑ Yes   If yes, in what way: _____

To what body fluid(s) was the employee exposed? _____

On what part of the employee's body did this fluid fall? _____

Estimate the size of the area covered by the fluid (consider taking a photo)

_____

For how long was the fluid in contact with the employee's body? _____

Did a foreign body (needle, nail, dental wire, machine part, etc.) penetrate the employee's body?   ❑ No ❑ Yes

If yes, what was the object and where did it penetrate? _____

Was any fluid injected into the employee's body?   ❑ No ❑ Yes

If yes, what fluid and how much? _____

Did the employee receive medical attention?   ❑ No ❑ Yes

If yes, where? _____ When? _____ By whom? _____

Name, address & phone of the source individual(s) _____

_____

_____

Other pertinent information: _____

_____

Signature of Person Completing this Report: _____

Print Name of Person Completing This Report _____

APPENDIX 32

Sample Form—
Risk Analysis Health Summary Report

This summary is for the health supervisor or program supervisor to use with a volunteer or paid staff member to keep a running total of incidents by nature of injury or illness, by age, and by classification. Keep track of injuries and illnesses during the program by using slash marks to indicate in the nature of injury or illness, the profile of the individual involved, and the classification of the injury or illness reported.

Volunteer/Staff Reporting:	Position:
Program:	Dates/Session Covered:

Nature of Injury	**Total**
Fracture/dislocation	
Laceration	
Sprain	
Dental	
Poison ivy/oak	
Contusion/abrasions	
Stings/bites	
Puncture wound	
Foreign bodies	
Other:	
Nature of Illness	**Total**
Sore throat/tonsils	
Respiratory	
Allergy/rash	
Stomachaches/viruses	
Ear infection	
Eye infection	
Urinary tract infection	
Other:	

Youth/Adult Profile	Total
Youth K to 3rd grade	
Youth 4th to 6th grade	
Youth 7th to 12th grade	
Volunteer	
Paid staff member	
Classification	**Total**
Less serious injury	
Serious injury	
Less serious illness	
Serious illness	
Less serious behavior	
Serious behavior	

Comment on any situation on activity during this period that seemed to be associated with the above injuries/illnesses.

Index

About Camp Fire USA

Camp Fire USA is one of the nation's leading not-for-profit youth development organizations, currently serving nearly 750,000 children and youth annually. Camp Fire USA, with national headquarters in Kansas City, MO, provides inclusive, coeducational programs in hundreds of communities across the United States. Founded in 1910 as the first nonsectarian, interracial organization for girls in the United States, Camp Fire USA is open to youth and adults regardless of race, religion, socioeconomic status, disability, sexual orientation, or other aspect of diversity. Camp Fire USA serves youth from birth to age 21, helping boys and girls learn—and play—side by side in comfortable, informal settings.

Camp Fire USA's mission is to build caring, confident youth and future leaders. As a socially responsible youth development agency, Camp Fire USA takes pride in its long-standing commitment to providing quality programs and services that develop the personal resilience, intellectual curiosity, and social values that today's youth need.

Camp Fire USA's outcome-based programs include youth leadership, self-reliance, after-school groups, camping and environmental education, and child care. Camp Fire USA's programs are designed and implemented to build life skills, teach environmental stewardship, and foster positive intercultural relationships.

For more information, contact the national headquarters at:

Camp Fire USA
1100 Walnut Street
Kansas City, MO 64106
816-285-2010
info@campfireusa.org

About the Author

Connie Coutellier is an international trainer, consultant, and author. She is a national field executive for Camp Fire USA and a past national president and director of professional development for the American Camp Association. A list of the books she has written includes *Camp Is for the Camper, Day Camp From Day One, Management of Risks and Emergencies,* and *The Outdoor Book.* She has more than 15 years of experience as a day and resident camp director in four camps in the USA and one in Malaysia, and over 30 years of experience in youth development and outdoor program administration training and development. She has written online training courses, assisted in the writing of the *ACA Outdoor Living Skills* books, and served as a consultant for both the development of the *ACA's Basic Camp Management* book and the curriculum for the ACA and the International Camping Fellowship camp director courses.

"Accidents will happen, but good risk-management planning will prevent, reduce or control the loss."